INFORMATION AND ORGANIZATION

Information and Organization

*A New Perspective on the Theory of
the Firm*

MARK CASSON

OXFORD
UNIVERSITY PRESS

This book has been printed digitally and produced in a standard specification
in order to ensure its continuing availability

OXFORD
UNIVERSITY PRESS

Great Clarendon Street, Oxford OX2 6DP

Oxford University Press is a department of the University of Oxford.
It furthers the University's objective of excellence in research, scholarship,
and education by publishing worldwide in

Oxford New York

Auckland Bangkok Buenos Aires Cape Town Chennai
Dar es Salaam Delhi Hong Kong Istanbul Karachi Kolkata
Kuala Lumpur Madrid Melbourne Mexico City Mumbai Nairobi
São Paulo Shanghai Taipei Tokyo Toronto

Oxford is a registered trade mark of Oxford University Press
in the UK and in certain other countries

Published in the United States
by Oxford University Press Inc., New York

© Mark Casson 1997

The moral rights of the author have been asserted

Database right Oxford University Press (maker)

Reprinted 2004

ISBN 0-19-829780-7

.

Preface and Acknowledgements

This book offers a vision of the economy as a system of structured information flow. The structuring is effected by institutions, and in particular, by firms, which specialize in processing the information needed to allocate resources properly. Firms are the institutional embodiment of the visions of individual entrepreneurs who believe that they have found a better way of allocating resources. Entrepreneurial vision is only a partial vision, however, in the sense that it does not encompass the entire economy, but only a subset of it. Free market economies encourage the exploitation of such partial visions because they encourage intermediation—it is by intermediating between potential buyers and potential sellers that entrepreneurial visions are realized. A legal framework of private property, coupled with entrepreneurial ambition and curiosity, and a moral framework to control the incidence of cheating, allows very sophisticated structures of information processing to emerge. These structures control an elaborate division of labour in the material dimension, whilst themselves exploiting the division of labour in the dimension of information and control. Each firm is a small component of the overall structure of information flow. Markets provide a switching mechanism by which different components can be connected up to each other. This is a highly flexible system which allows the overall structure to evolve as circumstances change. The appropriate changes are identified by entrepreneurs who create new firms to be slotted into the existing structure, and thereby incrementally change the structure itself.

This vision has evolved over the last fifteen years during which I have been researching a variety of topics connected with the theory of the firm—entrepreneurship, business culture, multinational enterprise, joint ventures, and the like. In each of these areas it is necessary to modify the orthodox theory of the firm in some way in order to make it work properly. I have gradually realized that the various modifications required all have one thing in common, and that is they give the use of information by the firm a more central role. Information already plays an important role in agency theory and in transaction cost theory, which are generally recognized as important building blocks in the theory of the firm. But the emphasis in these theories is in the adversarial use of information rather than the use of information for creative purposes. One person exploits an asymmetry of information with the idea of benefiting themselves at the expense of other people. Other people then collect information about them in order to punish them for the harm they do; it is hoped that the threat of punishment will be an effective deterrent. In this approach the emphasis is on people collecting information about other people rather than on people collecting information about the environment in which they operate. This account of the role of information within the firm is misleading because it is seriously incomplete. This book aims to remove the distortion inherent in this vision by emphasizing once again, as many other economists have done before, that the primary role of information within the firm is to support decision-taking, and in particular to implement ideas for coordinating the use of resources in a better way.

The book is written for a general audience. It should be accessible to scholars and graduate students in management studies (especially organizational behaviour and marketing), business and economic history, and industrial economics. It is written in plain jargon-free English as far as possible. At the same time, the book represents a specialist contribution to the theory of the firm. The arguments, though informal, are intended to be rigorous, and difficult points are confronted rather than evaded. Many of the arguments verbalize mathematical reasoning based upon formal models which have been published elsewhere. Specialist readers are invited to follow up the appropriate references.

The avenue of research opening up as a result of this book is long and wide. It is impossible to answer all of the questions which naturally present themselves within a single volume. It is my intention to write a sequel which will analyse in more detail the communication and storage of information, and explore the connection between information, organization, and culture.

I am grateful to many people for discussions on the topic of this book—in particular to my colleagues at the University of Reading and my Ph.D. students there. Indeed, one of these students, Ivana Paniccia, is a co-author of Chapter 7, whilst another, Nigel Wadeson, made an important contribution to Chapter 6.

I am particularly grateful to Ann Carlos and Simon Ville for authoritative advice on the chartered trading companies, which are discussed in Chapter 9, and to Jean François Hennart for some stimulating discussions about the free-standing companies which are discussed in Chapter 8. Special thanks are also due to Howard Cox, who collaborated with me on Chapter 4, and to Eric Jones, who offered valuable insights on the historical significance of information costs, as discussed in Chapter 10.

A preliminary version of Chapter 1 was presented to the Colloquium in Honour of George Richardson held at St John's College, Oxford, in January 1995. I am grateful to the organizers, Brian Loasby and Nicolai Foss, for their encouragement, and to George Richardson and other members of the workshop for their comments. A previous version of Chapter 3 appeared in *Management International Review* earlier this year. Some of the material in Chapter 4 will appear in *The Formation of Inter-organizational Networks*, to be published by Oxford University Press. I am grateful to the editor, Mark Ebers, and to his anonymous referees, for forcing me to clarify my ideas on the subject of this chapter. Chapter 8 is based upon my remarks as discussant at the Special Session on Free-standing Companies held at the International Economic History Congress in Milan 1994. With the kindly advice of Mira Wilkins, Hans Schröter and Will Hausman, these have been worked up into a chapter of a forthcoming book on *Free-standing Companies in the World Economy, 1830–1995*, which will also be published by Oxford University Press.

Other academics who have kindly offered comments and criticism, or facilitated seminar and conference presentations connected with the book, include Georges Blanc, James Foreman-Peck, Michael Kitson, Ram Mudambi, Neil Kay, Martin Ricketts, and Keetie Sluyterman. As noted above, my colleagues at Reading have been very supportive of my research—especially John Cantwell, Tony Corley, Andrew Godley, Peter Hart, Geoff Jones, Jim Pemberton, Alan Roberts, and Animesh Shrivastava.

It is well known that anonymous publisher's readers can be a source of extremely forthright comments, but fortunately, in the present case, their comments have been most constructive and helpful too. No one, though, can quite match the brutal frankness of my good friend Peter Buckley, who is always available to put me straight on any number of points. My wife Janet and daughter Catherine have pointed out that despite all the final revisions, the book is certain to contain a number of mistakes which have not been discovered yet.

New information technology figures quite prominently in several chapters of this book, but I have to confess that I have still not really mastered it. I must therefore thank Lauraine Newcombe for providing secretarial assistance at a time when she was under considerable pressure on another job, and Jill Turner who, assisted by Melanie Waller, typed the manuscript with the same speed and accuracy that she has provided to my previous books. Finally, I would like to express my thanks to Oxford University Press—and in particular to Andrew Schuller—who patiently awaited the arrival of the typescript for over a year and only once expressed the mildest cynicism about my excuses. I am grateful to them all.

Contents

Figures

Tables

PART I

BASIC PRINCIPLES

1

Information Cost
and Economic Organization

1.1. Introduction

It is only recently that information has begun to receive the attention from economists that it really deserves. Many insights—theoretical and practical, contemporary and historical—will be derived from the economics of information once the relevant theory becomes better developed. This book explains the wider significance of some elementary aspects of the economics of information. It offers a vision of the economy as an information system, to counterbalance the more conventional view of the economy as a system of material flow. The focus is on the handling of data relating to goods and services rather than on the handling of goods themselves.

This vision is inspired by the work of Hayek (1937), Richardson (1960) and Marschak (1974). Although each of these writers has a different emphasis, they all perceive economic institutions as mechanisms for allocating decision-making responsibilities and for structuring information flow. In this context firms and markets are simply alternative institutional means of achieving the same objective, as explained by Coase (1937).

On this view, the structure of institutions existing at any given time can be interpreted as a rational response to the social need to economize on information costs. As information costs change, so too does the institutional structure of the economy. In particular, as technological progress drives down communication costs over longer distances, so institutions adapt by increasing the geographical scope of their activities. This institutional evolution, in its turn, supports a higher level of economic development.

The role of information in the coordination of economic activities was first emphasized by Hayek (1937), who explained how the market system motivates entrepreneurs to search out information for their private use. This information is then communicated to other people indirectly in the form of price quotations. In this way everyone becomes aware of the relative scarcities of different products. Each individual who scans price information therefore receives sufficient guidance to make decisions which are in harmony with those of other people.

Richardson (1960) too emphasized the importance of information to the coordination process. He was concerned with the general issue of how a complex economic system is coordinated, and in particular with the coordination of individual investment plans in related activities. He showed how informal structures of inter-firm collaboration may emerge to fill the gaps in knowledge that would otherwise distort the decisions of firms.

The contributions of Hayek and Richardson are significant because in the Walrasian model of general competitive equilibrium favoured by mainstream neo-classical economists all the handling of information is effected costlessly by an altruistic auctioneer. For example, in the contrived extension of general equilibrium theory offered by Debreu (1959), new markets are invented to address each new coordination problem that arises. The auctioneer harmonizes individual plans over space, over time, and over every conceivable state of the world as well.

For some purposes the fiction of the auctioneer is fairly innocuous—and, indeed, quite helpful in simplifying otherwise intractable analytical problems—but in analysing information the assumption of an auctioneer is a pernicious one. Because the auctioneer performs for free the functions that entrepreneurs perform for real, it leaves no room for entrepreneurs in the modelling of markets. In general, it leaves no room for analysing the way that real people collect and use information.

Although information is crucial to coordination, coordination is not the only role of information in the economy. Coordination harmonizes different decisions but, quite apart from this, information can improve the quality of individual decisions too. Thus two individuals who are ignorant of a new technology may coordinate their use of the old technology quite successfully, but they would be even better off if they informed themselves of the new technology and coordinated their use of that instead.

It was not until Marschak (1974) that a systematic account of the role of information in the economy was provided. Marschak approached information from a decision theory perspective. This is very useful, because 'economic man' is basically 'man the decision-maker'. Thus a full analysis of the role of economic information must consider the impact of information on decisions of every kind. This perspective emphasizes that information is an asset (Machlup, 1962). Better information leads to better decisions, on account of both better individual judgement and better coordination of different individual decisions. Better decisions lead, in turn, to better use of resources, and hence to higher social welfare.

1.2. Re-drawing the wheel of wealth

The vision of the economy as an information system is in sharp contrast to the materialistic vision of the economy found in standard economic textbooks. A typical textbook summarizes the economy in terms of a wheel of wealth, in which households supply factors of production to firms, who use them to produce goods which households themselves consume (see e.g.

Parkin and King, 1995, p. 13). Markets coordinate the flows of factors from households to firms and the flows of products from firms to households. These market relationships are often summarized in terms of mere accounting identities, equating household expenditures to firms' revenues, and household factor incomes to the sum of firms' costs and profits. Admittedly these *ex post* valuations are effected at prices determined *ex ante* by market forces, but then these market forces are interpreted simply in terms of known demands and supplies. The information flows required to discover and then to reconcile the demands and supplies are ignored. So as long as the known demands and supplies vary with price in an appropriate way, it is said, an equilibrium set of prices will prevail.

An equilibrium is guaranteed if demand curves slope down and supply curves slope up. This generates a problem in modelling the product market, because technological economies of scale imply that the supply curve may slope down instead. One answer is to postulate the existence of a fixed factor—usually called entrepreneurship—which limits both the number and size of firms in an industry. Given this fixed factor, a theory of the representative firm can be developed. The behaviour of this firm, when aggregated up, generates a supply curve of the requisite type. This has created the neoclassical firm—a firm in which the only strategic decision is how to adjust inputs and outputs to changes in factor and product prices.

This account is a travesty of the way that the economy actually works. By ignoring the informational problems of the market system, it confronts the firm with an idealized environment far removed from the actual conditions faced in the real world. It equates the firm with a producer, ignoring the fact that many firms are actually responsible for the organization of the market process itself. Firms create markets by innovating new products. They engage in arbitrage and speculation, integrating markets over space and time. Retailers and wholesalers hold inventories which help to buffer fluctuations in supply and demand. Advertising agencies help to disseminate information on product quality. Banks handle specialized information on the debts that are created when payments cannot be fully synchronized with the delivery of products. A simple way of summarizing these points is to say that firms are specialized intermediators. In a very general sense firms intermediate between households as factor owners and households as consumers.

The materialistic view of the economy suggests that the essence of intermediation is production. It is the need to combine different factor inputs in given proportions, and in quantities sufficient to exploit economies of scale, that calls for intermediation by the firm. The information-based view of the economy suggests that the essence of intermediation is the organization of trade instead. This type of intermediation is effected by market-making firms. Trade requires people to make contact with each other, to communicate their wants, and explain what they offer in return, to negotiate a price and to monitor the fulfilment of their contracts. The costs of these activities can be reduced through intermediation. Intermediation is thus a value-adding activity; indeed, it is one of the most important sources of added value in the entire economy.

Firms typically take the initiative in simplifying trade for the benefit of households. For example, firms fix stable and uniform prices for their products to reduce negotiation costs. They invest in a reputation for integrity which allows their customers to trust them even where the legal enforcement of contracts may be relatively weak.

A simple example of market-making is illustrated in Fig. 1.1. Part (a) illustrates the traditional 'wheel of wealth', while part (b) introduces intermediation in the product market. Material flows are identified by a double line. Units which generate or transform material flows are indicated by boxes. The purely materialistic picture of the economy at the top of the figure represents firms exclusively as transformers of physical factor inputs

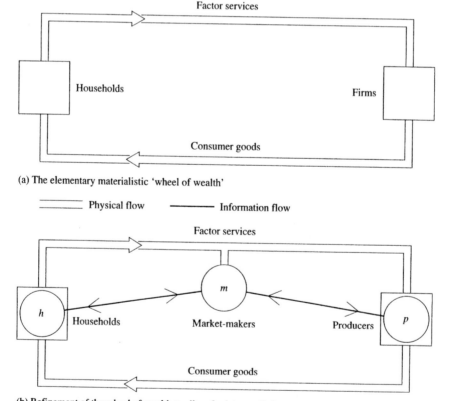

(a) The elementary materialistic 'wheel of wealth'

(b) Refinement of the wheel of wealth to allow for intermediation

FIG. 1.1. *Re-drawing the wheel of wealth*

into physical consumer goods. Households use up these goods in consumption to generate energy for labour, or they abstain from consumption and recycle the goods in the form of capital.

The second part of the Fig. 1.1 introduces information flow. Information flows are indicated by a single line. It is these information flows which coordinate the flow of consumer products: they ensure that the mix of products generated corresponds to household preferences. Information flows take place between individual minds, and to highlight this fact individual minds are illustrated by circles, to distinguish them from the squares which represent the units that handle physical flows. Where an individual acts as both a physical consumer and as a decision-maker, or as both a manual worker and a decision-maker, they are represented as a circle inside a square.

Information flows, as shown in Fig. 1.1, are intermediated by the market-maker. The individual market-maker is indicated by m, to distinguish him from the individual householder, indicated by h, and the individual producer, indicated by p. It is through intermediation that the market-maker m coordinates decisions made by h and p. The coordination involves two-way flows of information, as indicated by the double arrows in the figure. Thus while material flows usually go in one direction only, information flow is a two-way affair.

Intermediation incurs costs because of the handling of information involved. This handling is effected by people employed for the purpose. There is, therefore, a flow of factor services into intermediation. There is no physical output, though: the output of intermediation consists purely of the decisions about prices and quantities that the intermediator makes.

Market-making itself may be decomposed into separate activities. The division of labour between price and output fixing on the one hand and retail distribution on the other is an important case in point. Price and output can be fixed at headquarters on the basis of information about supply and demand, as suggested in Fig. 1.1. It is not necessary for the headquarters to physically handle the product. Retailing, on the other hand, is usually about finding a convenient location at which to display and store the product in order to service customers on demand. Retailing of this kind definitely requires handling the product (though the retailing of specialist services may not—see below). Retailing is usually replicated at different locations whereas headquarters activities are not.

The role of retailing is illustrated in Fig. 1.2. Part (a) highlights the fact that the retailer d physically handles the product (as indicated by the square surrounding the circle) whereas the market-making headquarters m does not. The retailer intermediates between the producer and the consumer so far as material flow is concerned. He also intermediates between the market-maker and the household so far as information flow is concerned; for example, he conveys information about the product's specification and

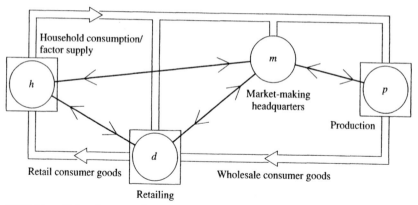

(a) Division of labour between price-output decision-making and retail distribution

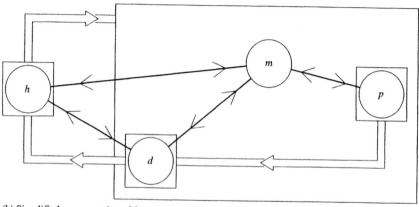

(b) Simplified representation of factor flows

FIG. 1.2. *Schematic illustration of intermediation*

quality by displaying the product on his shelves. The retailer does not intermediate all the information flow between the market-maker and the household, however; thus the market-maker may advertise the product directly to households through the media, and also fix a recommended retail price.

The market-maker intermediates between the retailer and the producer. Although the producer may arrange to ship the product direct to the retailer, the overall quantity available for distribution may be fixed by the market-maker. The producer will invoice the market-maker at the price contracted for supply, whilst the market-maker will invoice the retailer at the discounted recommended retail price. Thus the goods pass effectively in and out of the market-maker's ownership *en route* from producer to retailer. The significance of this is considered in more detail below.

The gap between the discounted retail price and the production price provides the market-maker with a margin out of which he can cover his information costs. These costs stem from his employment of managerial and clerical workers, as indicated by the flow of factor services into market-making identified in Fig. 1.2. Likewise the discount on the recommended retail price provides the retailer with a margin from which to cover his own labour costs. Unlike the pure market-maker, the retailer employs manual as well as clerical staff because he is involved in handling the product too. The input of factor services into retailing is also indicated in Fig. 1.2.

The representation of factor flows in part (a) of Fig. 1.2 is a complicating factor. In developing more sophisticated diagrams this complication becomes such a nuisance that it needs to be dispensed with if possible. Part (b) of Fig. 1.2 introduces a notational convention which resolves this problem. All the activities that employ factor inputs are included in a single large box, shown centred slightly to the right in Fig. 1.2, and the factors are depicted flowing into the box as a whole rather than into the separate activities as before. This convention is used in all subsequent diagrams to handle not only factor flows but other kinds of flow as well.

Intermediation can occur not only between producers and households, but between one producer and another. Different producers may take responsibility for different stages of production. Between each stage of production there is typically a market, and so there is an opportunity for a market-making firm to reduce information costs. In some cases, however, adjacent stages of production may be integrated under common ownership, in which case intermediation becomes internal to the firm. The management of the integrated operations may then be interpreted as the intermediation of an internal market.

Intermediation can also be effected between other intermediators. Thus in international trade specialized import and export merchants in each country may be coordinated by the activities of an international merchant house. The merchant house buys from the export merchant and re-sells to the import merchant. The traded commodity passes through the hands of three separate intermediators before it completes its journey from the producer to the consumer. Each of these intermediators brings distinctive information to bear on the organization of the product flow.

1.3. Comparative statics and homeostasis

One reason why information flow is often ignored in conventional economics is that change is usually perceived as a once-and-for-all rather than a continuing occurrence. This is exemplified by the importance of comparative static analysis in economics. A once-and-for-all change in the environment which alters relative scarcities calls for a once-and-for-all reallocation of resources. This change is associated with a once-and-for-all change in relative prices which incidentally alters the distribution of income too. The combination of price and income effects adjusts the economy to a new equilibrium. Each individual makes the relevant substitutions, guided by the changes in prices. These prices contain all the information that individuals need to make adjustments that will harmonize with those of others. Because they are equilibrium prices no unfortunate surprises can occur. No costs are involved in handling information because the relevant prices are costlessly provided by the Walrasian auctioneer.

Once information costs are introduced, of course, this simple story falls apart. Adjustment becomes costly, trade may take place at disequilibrium prices, and surprises can definitely occur. Information costs introduce numerous complications. It is possible to unravel many of these complications, however, by recognizing that in practice change is a more or less continuous process. When change is continuous then institutions will emerge to channel information routinely in an appropriate way. The process of change becomes embedded in institutionalized procedures. By understanding these procedures it is possible to analyse change in a systematic way.

The workings of institutions can be understood by recognizing that the control of information costs is itself an economic problem. By making judgements about the volatility of the environment, and the magnitude of information costs, institutions can be designed in an efficient way. They can trade off the value of the services they produce against the costs of the information they require. Their organizational structures can be designed to maximize value net of information cost (Casson, 1995b, p. 76). Even if no institution is actually designed in this way, competition between alternative institutional forms will tend to select for efficient design in the long run. Even the market system itself can be analysed as an institution from this perspective. Indeed, an analysis of this kind lies at the heart of the Austrian critique of state socialism, which is widely believed, in the light of recent events in Eastern Europe, to have demonstrated its long-run predictive power. When information relevant to the direction of change is widely distributed amongst the population, it is claimed, the market system provides people with the best incentive to synthesize this information in an effective way (Hayek, 1937).

There are three main types of volatility in the environment with which organizations must cope. None of these is handled satisfactorily by conventional economics. The first is long-run structural change of the kind described by Schumpeter (1934, 1939). Most formal economic models take economic structure as given, and therefore ignore change of this type. Changes of this kind are typically of large amplitude and low frequency: they do not occur often, but when they do their effects are widespread. In the context of intermediation, the emergence of a new market-making opportunity is an example of this kind. Such a change may initiate the formation of a new firm which pioneers a new market, or even a new industry.

The second type of volatility is associated with fluctuations in demand and supply within an established market. Changes in demand and supply are of lower amplitude but higher frequency than the structural changes described above. It is this kind of volatility that the ordinary procedures for setting price and output are designed to address, as indicated above. These procedures are examined in detail in Section 1.6 below.

The third type of volatility is the main focus of attention here. Like the first type of volatility, it is largely ignored in conventional economics, though it is extensively discussed in operational research. It is caused by shocks of low amplitude but very high frequency. It is associated with breakdowns and interruptions of supply that disrupt the equilibrium flow. Coordination calls for the equilibrium to be restored as soon as possible. Restoration of equilibrium typically requires the supply of remedial services. During the lag which occurs before the remedy is complete, temporary substitutions may have to be made. Unlike the substitutions required by the first type of volatility, these are not of a permanent nature. They are often particularly costly to make, moreover. For this reason spare capacity or a precautionary inventory is often held to make the substitution easier. By making these substitutions easier it is less important to have early warning of the disruptions, which means that information costs are reduced.

Consider, for example, a pure production firm. This is constantly threatened by disruption due to the breakdown of machinery, delivery of faulty batches of raw materials, absenteeism due to worker illness, and so on. All of these stochastic factors can undermine the continuity of production on which economical operation depends. The necessary response of monitoring reliability, requisitioning repairs and getting workers to 'cover' for each other requires an intensive flow of information. The organization of the firm must be designed to provide early warning of problems, to diagnose faults and arrange replacements as quickly as possible.

Similar observations can be made about the impact of stochastic factors on household behaviour. Although members of households like variety in their consumption, they prefer to achieve variety by consuming the same desired mixture of goods each period, rather than by erratic fluctuations in which a different good dominates consumption in each successive period. Households therefore value continuity in the flow of goods that they normally consume, just as firms value continuity of material flow through the production process. If something happens to disrupt this continuity then it must be put right immediately. This creates an intermittent demand for remedial goods and services—goods, often of a specialized nature, which are required urgently to rectify a problem situation. Examples of intermittent demands include medicines to treat illnesses and plumbing services for household repairs. By contrast, the best examples of continuous household demands relate to the fulfilment of basic needs—food for energy, transport to work, and so on.

Another way of putting this is to say that both household and firm need to maintain homeostasis in a stochastic environment. Homeostasis creates a continuous demand for certain basic inputs—food for the household, raw materials for the firm—and an intermittent demand for remedial goods and services (Casson, 1990, pp. 60–4).

Homeostasis is a requirement for the market-making firm as well. In one sense, of course, the market-making firm thrives on helping households and producer firms to procure their intermittent needs as easily as possible. Most households and producer firms can quickly learn how best to satisfy their recurrent needs, but they will have less experience of meeting their intermittent needs and will therefore have a greater need in this context for the services of a market-making firm. But in order for the market-making firm to help households and producer firms to satisfy their intermittent needs, the market-making firm must regularly update its knowledge of the major sources of intermittent demand and the best sources from which remedial services can be procured. This continuous updating needs to be maintained in a homeostatic equilibrium of its own. Illnesses amongst key staff, and breakdowns in office equipment such as fax machines and photocopiers, threaten homeostasis in the processing of information by the market-making firm. The market-making firm is therefore itself a source of intermittent demand—which other market-making firms may then seek to satisfy. Thus a business services sector develops to supply temporary staff at short notice—for example to repair office machinery and to offer bureau services for faxing and photocopying which can be used whilst repairs are being carried out.

The implications of this discussion are summarized in Fig. 1.3. Two types of good are distinguished: the regular good (indexed 1), whose continuous flow is the hallmark of a conventional equilibrium, and the occasional good (indexed 2), which is required for maintaining homeostasis in the system. (A relevant analogy in the marketing literature is between convenience goods and speciality goods, though the correspondence between the two sets of concepts is by no means complete; see Baker, 1991.) Because the effects of individual stochastic factors tend to average out, on account of their statistical independence, it is possible to visualize a conventional equilibrium in which a steady quantity of occasional goods is produced and consumed alongside the regular goods. It is important to emphasize, however, that this equilibrium only exists when demands and supplies are aggregated to the industry level. At the individual level there remains a continual threat of temporary imbalance between the supply and demand for occasional goods because of the heterogeneous nature of the highly specialized goods that constitute this sector.

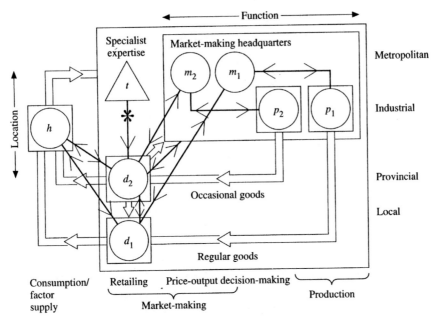

FIG. 1.3. *Intermediation of markets in regular goods and occasional goods*

The industry-level equilibrium is illustrated by the two parallel flows shown in Fig. 1.3. As noted above, occasional goods are required by producers as well as by households; this is illustrated in Fig. 1.3 by the flow of goods from the retailer of occasional goods, d_2, to the producers and market-makers (and to the retailer of regular goods, d_1).

Figure 1.3 highlights the fact that there are two types of retailing rather than just one, and that one is much more information-intensive than the other. The retailing of occasional services, d_2, often requires sophisticated diagnosis of the customer's problem. Where regular services are concerned, however, the customer is already well acquainted with how to solve his problem—all the retailer d_1 needs to do is to provide conveniently situated premises where the relevant product is stocked. When the customer is a regular consumer he does not need advice on where to find the retail outlet, either. Moreover his credit worthiness will be well-known to the retailer. By contrast, retailers of occasional goods will have to tell their customers where to find them, and will have to investigate their customers' status carefully before they extend any credit to them. There are thus several different aspects of the retailing of occasional goods that make it a peculiarly information-intensive activity.

As already noted, the provision of occasional retail services often requires considerable diagnostic expertise. In some cases the retailer may have to refer the customer to a technical specialist—a doctor, lawyer, architect, etc.—who will advise on which particular type of remedy should be supplied. To keep such specialists fully occupied, they will have to deal with referrals from retailers in many different locations. The supply of specialist expertise is indicated in Fig. 1.3 by a single line with an asterisk along it. The single line is used to indicate that the flow involves information rather than a material good, while the asterisk is used to distinguish this flow of information from the flows of information used for coordination purposes, which appear elsewhere in the figure.

The specialist is indicated by a triangle to indicate that he is a source of information (or a memory-bank) rather than just a processor of it. To facilitate access by occasional clients, the specialist will tend to be located in a major metropolitan area—an area which has become a metropolis because of its role as a personal transport and communications hub. The same factor—ease of communication—also explains why the market-maker's headquarters will also tend to be located in the metropolis.

Production, by contrast, will tend to be located in industrial areas, often near estuary ports (for convenience in handling freight and in disposing of waste products). There will be some agglomeration of production in order to exploit economies of scale in infrastructure, but probably not so much as in the location of the information-based activities described above.

Retailing of regular goods will tend to be the most widely dispersed of all the activities. This is because regular goods are often perishable and bulky. Customers therefore need to make frequent trips to collect them and this requires their retail premises to be close to where the customer lives or works (Henderson, 1988). This is less important for occasional goods. It is necessary for retailers of occasional goods to have a fairly wide catchment area in order to keep their premises fully utilised. Thus while the retailing of regular customers may be quite local, the retailing of occasional goods will be concentrated in regional centres such as provincial towns and cities.

These links between function and location are illustrated by the horizontal and vertical axes shown in Fig. 1.3. The horizontal axis shows that market-makers and retailers do indeed 'intermediate' between the producers on the right-hand side of the figure and the consumers on the left. The vertical axis indicates that the main forms of intermediation—market-making and retailing—do, however, have divergent locational implications, with market-making tending to agglomerate in the metropolis and retailing being dispersed around the provinces as well. Within retailing there is a further distinction between markets for regular and occasional goods, with the handling of regular goods being much more dispersed than the handling of occasional goods, particularly when the role of technical specialists in the retailing of occasional goods is taken into account.

1.4. Ownership of the product

So far intermediation has been discussed just from the standpoint of material flow and information flow. This has served to make the point that the pattern of intermediation can differ in these respects. The obvious distinction is that retailers intermediate in both material flow and information flow while pure market-makers intermediate only in information flow. This is part of the more general phenomenon that intermediation tends to be more crucial in information flow than in material flow.

The analysis so far has, admittedly, been rather crude. Thus in discussing material flow, nothing has been said about the role of common carriers, notably ships and railways, in transporting freight. Neither has the role of wholesale warehouses as a buffer between producers and retailers been considered at all. But conversely, the wide range of consultancy services, library facilities and news media that intermediate information flow have been ignored as well. Introducing these factors would refine the discussion considerably, but would not alter the main conclusions.

There is, however, another qualitatively different aspect of intermediation which merits attention at this stage. This concerns intermediation in the ownership of the product. As the material resources flow around the wheel of wealth, their ownership changes. In a free enterprise market economy ownership may change many times. Households sell labour services to firms. Manual services supplied to producers may be converted into product under subcontracting arrangements set up on the initiative of market-making firms. The product may then be sold on to retailers who in turn re-sell it to consumers. There are also sales internal to the corporate sector. Thus the retailers of occasional goods sell business services to other firms, as indicated above. Where multi-stage production is involved, firms at each stage may purchase intermediate products and sell them on to the next stage after reprocessing.

At the other extreme to this is the completely socialized economy in which all market-making is undertaken by a single enterprise, namely the state. The state procures labour from households and directs it to state-owned firms. Throughout their transformation from manual labour to consumer product, goods remain the property of the state.

A crucial feature of the preceding account of the free market economy is that the market-making firm will normally intermediate in the ownership of the product even though it does not physically handle the product itself. If it is asked why the market-making firm does this, then the simple answer is that the firm is supplying information to the market even though it does not handle the product itself. This suggests that the provision of information is crucial to the ownership issue. But why should this be the case?

The basic answer is that ownership of resources is the principal route by which people extract rents from information. This is because information is very difficult to sell in its own right. The reasons for this are considered in detail elsewhere (see, for example, Casson, 1982, pp. 201–8, and section 2.9 below). Because of the problems of selling it, information must be exploited in some other way. Since the economic value of information used for coordination purposes derives ultimately from the benefits of improved decision-making, the natural way to exploit it is by acquiring the power to take the relevant decisions instead. Decision-making power is normally conferred by ownership, and so ownership becomes the instrument for exploiting information.

The market-maker therefore acquires ownership as a means of exploiting the information in his possession. He extracts rents from this information by buying and then reselling the product. In this way he covers his costs of collecting information out of the profits on trade. In the same way, the retailer acquires ownership from the market-maker in order to exploit his own more local knowledge of the market in an effective way. The information exploited by the producer is of a more technological kind. He exploits this information by buying labour from his workers and converting it into product that he owns. The workers forgo any natural right to the product that they might claim in return for their wage.

Another way of looking at the ownership issue is to say that by acquiring ownership of resources the possessor of information insures potential users of the information against the consequences of its being false. This in turn creates a strong incentive for the possessor of the information to make every effort to ensure that it is correct. It motivates the owner to assure the quality of information, in other words (Casson, 1987, p. 14). The producer insures other people against the possibility that his technology may not work because any failure in technology will be reflected in a shortfall in the output of the product he owns. His workers, in particular, are insured because they get paid whatever their productivity turns out to be. The retailer insures the households against the possibility that they may not want the product when they see it by keeping any unsold stock in his own hands. The market-maker insures the producers against the possibility that retailers will not wish to stock the product by placing firm orders at a given price. He also insures the retailers against the possibility that supplies may be disrupted through an increase in production costs by accepting firm orders from retailers at a given price.

The structure of ownership implied by this pattern of insurance is illustrated in Fig. 1.4. For simplicity Fig. 1.4 confines itself to just the regular goods (type 1). The dashed and dotted lines divide the figure into different domains of ownership; four different owners participate in the wheel of wealth, as indicated at the bottom of the figure. It can be seen that corresponding to each individual mind that is processing information there is a stage of the circular flow at which ownership is claimed. This stage corresponds to the stage at which the benefits of correct information of a certain

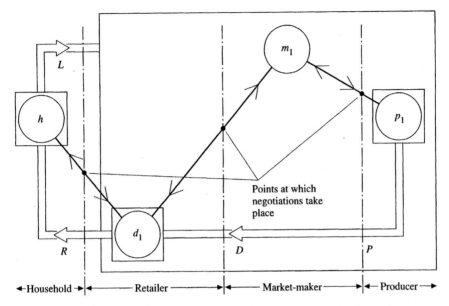

FIG. 1.4. *Ownership structure in a 'dis-integrated' wheel of wealth*

type are most strongly felt and, conversely, the stage at which the costs of misinformation of this type are most directly borne.

Where a boundary between two ownership domains intersects the product flow, a market exists in which buyers and sellers trade at arm's length. There are four such markets in the figure: a labour market, L, where households sell labour to the business sector (i.e. to producers, retailers, and market-makers as a whole), a wholesale procurement market, P, where market-makers buy in bulk from producers, a wholesale distribution market, D, where market-makers resell in smaller consignments to distributors, and finally the retail market, R, where retailers sell in even smaller quantities to the households. In each market there is a corresponding price: the wage rate, the factory-gate price, the wholesale price and the retail price respectively. It is through negotiations over these prices that the owners indirectly share their information with each other and so coordinate the flow as a whole. The households share their information on consumption preferences with retailers, and on their work preferences with their employers; the retailers share their information with their household customers and with their market-making suppliers, and so on. As negotiations in different markets proceed in parallel, each owner can share with others not only what he has discovered for himself, but what he has learnt from his negotiations with other parties. The information exchanged in one market is therefore linked to the information exchanged in the others. In this way the economic system as a whole is coordinated by information flow through the market system.

The structure illustrated in Fig. 1.4 is one of complete vertical disintegration, in the sense that there is separate ownership at every stage. In the context of this figure, the case for vertical integration hinges on the nature of the information that is exploited at each stage. The role of the market-maker is crucial in this respect. The market-maker synthesizes information concerning both of the adjacent stages—retailing and production. The quality of this synthesis depends crucially on the quality of information that he uses. If he has doubts about the quality of this information, then extending his ownership to adjacent stages may provide the reassurance that he needs.

He may be concerned, for example, that producers and retailers are bluffing about the conditions that they face. The producers may be exaggerating their costs of production, and the retailers understating their market prospects. This is particularly likely where the producers believe that they have monopoly power and the retailers believe that they have monopsony power. Under these circumstances, a monopolist or monopsonist knows that the true conditions are known to him alone and cannot be revealed by the behaviour of a competitor. There are two aspects of this that may give cause for concern.

The first is that through their bluffing the producers are obtaining a higher price, and the retailers a lower price, than they deserve. The answer is for the market-maker to break the monopoly or monopsony power by investing in his own production and retail facilities. This not only stimulates competition by increasing capacity at these stages, but also provides the market-maker with his own sources of information which he can use to 'benchmark' the claims of others.

In some cases, however, it may be costly to break up a monopoly or monopsony at an adjacent stage. Economies of scale, for example, may deter the replication of retail premises and production facilities. Another consideration is that the established firms may enjoy goodwill with their customers or suppliers. In such cases merger or acquisition can provide a viable alternative. The simple redistribution of profit from adjacent stages cannot be the motivation for integration in this case, however, for the monopoly or monopsony earnings of the incumbent firms will be capitalized in their acquisition price. The motivation is rather that bluffing not only redistributes profit but distorts the coordination of output too. For example, when each party is dishonestly claiming adverse conditions, output may be set at a level below that which would maximize the joint profits of all the parties involved. With integration into a single enterprise, prices no longer redistribute profits, and a strategic advantage to bluffing no longer exists. Information does not have to be encoded in offer prices any more; it can be supplied directly as factual information to the headquarters of the firm.

Headquarters can therefore effect an accurate synthesis of information and restore output to its optimal level.

It is not only the negotiation process that gives cause for concern over the quality of information, however. Once a deal has been struck, and a contract made, there remains the question of whether it will be properly fulfilled. This is a question about the quality of the promises made, and the need to check up on whether they were genuine or not. Defaulting on the quantity delivered, or on payment for it, is not usually difficult to detect, but default on quality is another matter. Faults in complex high-technology products are not normally evident on casual inspection—it is only when the goods are used that the faults become apparent, when the consequences to the user can be very severe. The same point applies to many of the specialized occasional services referred to earlier.

Reputation is an important safeguard where quality assurance is concerned. This is particularly true of producers in a high-technology industry. The number of such producers may be quite small, however, obliging the market-maker to search more widely for suitable sources of supply. There is also the risk that reputable producers may collude, disguising a cartel price as a quality premium for their product. Industry associations and professional associations can provide a respectable social front for such activity. The desire to access a low-cost high-quality source of supply may persuade the market-maker to integrate back into production himself. This is a particularly attractive option when new technology was an important factor in the innovation of the product in the first place.

The quality control argument does not apply with the same force in retailing, though examples of backward integration by retailers can certainly be found. Most market-makers invest quite heavily in branding their products in order to provide the kind of reputation for them that the retailer requires. The market-maker's reputation derives in turn from its success in controlling quality in production—which is the point at which backward integration normally comes into the picture.

There are, therefore, two distinct types of argument relating to the integration of the firm. Relative to the contractual phase, one is an *ex ante* argument relating to the negotiation of the contract under conditions of imperfect competition; this is analogous, in many ways, to Williamson's (1985) asset-specificity factor. The second is an *ex post* argument related to quality control; this argument figures most prominently in international business applications of the theory of the firm (especially Casson, 1987, pp. 84–7). The gist of the argument, in both cases, is that some of the information supplied in a market-making synthesis may not be true. Integrating ownership changes the incentive structure under which the supply of information takes place (Richardson, 1972). It neutralizes strategies designed to redistribute profit (in one way or another) between the participants and so eliminates distortion. This in turn improves the quality of the output decision and maximizes the overall profit generated within the wheel of wealth.

1.5. The information content of the employment relation

It was noted in the previous section that by acquiring ownership of relevant resources an owner can insure potential users of his information against the risk that the information may be wrong. This insurance is effected by his assuming responsibility for the consequences himself. How effective this insurance is depends, though, on the way that property rights are defined. In practice the owner is unlikely to be the only person affected by the way that a resource is used. The consequences may be quite serious for anyone else who is affected too.

Ideally, a unit of ownership should be defined in such a way that no one except the owner is affected (adversely or otherwise) by the owner's exercise of his rights—there should be no 'externalities', in other words. In practice units of ownership do not always fulfil this condition. This is because, in order to make their enforcement easier, the rights of ownership are often made coterminous with the *de facto* rights conferred by possession of a resource. This means that in practice the owner acquires a very general set of rights encompassing nearly all possible uses of the resource. This is in spite of the fact that the exercise of these rights in certain ways could have significant effects on other people. The standard example is that when a producer transforms a good in a particular way he may pollute the environment of a neighbouring household.

Ideally, uses which generate external effects such as this should be singled out, and the rights to deploy a resource in such ways assigned separately. To guarantee that the use of the resource leaves no one worse off than in the *status quo*, it is appropriate to assign these rights to those who will be adversely affected by the particular use concerned. If the distribution of the benefits and losses does not matter, however, then the important thing is simply that the rights are properly defined and capable of being bought and sold. Indeed, in a world of no information costs, and no concern for distributional implications, it would not matter whether the rights were initially assigned to the owner or to those who were harmed, since those who were harmed could just as easily acquire the rights from the owner to stop him doing something as he could acquire the rights from them to enable him to do it instead (Coase, 1960).

If this principle were widely used in practice, then in the limiting case where every possible use of the resource affects other people, the right to each use would be traded separately. The exploitation of information through ownership would be effected not by purchasing a general right to a resource and then controlling its use but by purchasing the relevant specific right and using the resource just in the way that this right permits (Casson, 1982, p. 47).

In practice a sub-division of rights along these lines does not often occur because of the magnitude of the information costs involved. Externalities are tolerated because the administrative costs of correcting them are believed to exceed the efficiency losses that are incurred.

This analysis has a particular bearing on the employment contract. When a worker agrees to accept orders from his employer he is liable to be asked to do some things that he does not particularly like. Although he has, in one sense, sold his labour, he still retains an interest in how it is used. The question then arises as to whether this is fair, and whether a worker would rationally alienate his rights in this way. It is frequently argued that there is a serious problem here, and that the straightforward sale of labour to the firm indicated in the wheel of wealth diagram disguises exploitation by the employer.

In principle the problem could be addressed by workers selling a series of specific rights to firms instead of a comprehensive general right. Employer and employee would negotiate over the price for each particular task (Coase, 1937). A worker would negotiate separately for the sale of each permission to assign him to a task that he did not particularly like. Thus the initial sale of labour to the employer would merely transfer to the employer the general right of sole access to the product of the worker's labour. This would be of little value without parallel agreements relating to the nature of the tasks to which worker could be assigned.

It is obvious, though, that the information costs of such an arrangement would be very high. The more specific the worker's skills, and the more specialized the nature of the work, the greater will be the problem of bilateral monopoly power and the more complicated the bluffing strategies will become. To economize on information costs the worker may well agree to accept the authority of the employer within certain limits, relying on his own judgement as to the frequency with which unpleasant tasks will have to be performed (Casson, 1982, p. 196). Provided that a share of the savings in information costs accrues to the worker, there is nothing particularly unfair about this result.

It might be argued, though, that the worker cannot correctly estimate the relevant frequency. This is untrue, however. As indicated in the following section, firms which minimize information costs will follow managerial decision rules which prescribe, amongst other things, which tasks workers must perform under which particular sets of circumstances. A worker who knows the rules simply has to estimate the frequency with which the relevant conditions will occur. This is a judgement about the environment in which the firm operates; if one person's judgement is no better than anyone else's then the worker is not systematically disadvantaged by this process.

It is quite likely, of course, that the firm will in fact have privileged information about its environment. The firm may withhold this information if it believes that it will adversely affect the worker's evaluation of his job. The firm may also be secretive about its managerial procedures if it believes that knowledge of these would have a similar effect. All this amounts to in practice, though, is that there is an element of asymmetric information, and that the possessor of the privileged information—namely the firm—is withholding it for strategic purposes. It is no different, in principle, from the situation confronting the consumer of any good whose quality is difficult to discern. A judgement simply has to be taken about the integrity of the other party. Anyone who deals with a party who lacks reputation in this respect must be prepared to pay the cost of being cheated. The worker dealing with the firm as employer is in no different position, in principle, to the consumer dealing with the firm as supplier; both must recognize the strategic implications of asymmetric information, and adjust their own behaviour accordingly.

It is information costs, therefore, which ultimately explain why employment contracts do not specify in advance the tasks which workers will perform. Further support for this view comes from considering ways in which the impact of these information costs can be reduced. One approach is for employees with similar preferences for different types of work to club together and negotiate collectively over the pricing of individual tasks. This is, in fact, the principle that underlies a good deal of industrial collective bargaining. Although it is fashionable to interpret union behaviour in terms of a labour cartel, the micro-structure of industrial bargaining is difficult to explain purely in terms of the discriminatory exercise of union monopoly power. The tasks which warrant additional pay are not just those for which the employer's derived demand is least elastic, but those which workers find most unpleasant too. Some particularly demeaning tasks are proscribed altogether; in other words the union, acting on behalf of its members, withholds certain specific permissions from the employer, along the lines described above. The degree of specificity is often quite high—as reflected in the detail contained in the union rule book. The fact that labour contracts are more specific in unionized industries, where the costs of information are shared between employees, than in non-unionized industries, where they are not, thus provides considerable support for the importance of information costs in the specification of the labour contract.

1.6. Information costs and the product market

The influence of information costs on the specificity of contracts applies to the product market too. Market-making firms make markets in general rather than specific rights. If all products were highly specific then the information costs incurred by the market-makers would be very great. In each market a large margin between buying price and selling price would be required to cover these costs and this margin might be so great as to eliminate the market altogether.

The general thrust of market-making is to reduce information costs, and one way of doing this is to reduce the number of specific goods that are traded by replacing a set of specific goods with a general purpose good. The typical general-purpose good is a multi-component good with some kind of switching mechanism (Casson, 1982, pp. 189–93). Its versatility derives from the possibility of activating different combinations of components for different tasks (a 'music centre' is a good case in point). A single market in a versatile good substitutes for a multiplicity of markets in more specific goods. The market in the versatile good itself will still exhibit high information costs, because all the different uses of the good have to be explained to the purchasers of it. Since one market replaces several, however, overall information costs in the economy are reduced. Customers prefer the versatile good because it reduces their own costs of searching for specialized goods. The versatile good may also be relatively cheap; since it has a larger market than the specialized goods it replaces, it is more likely to benefit from economies of mass production.

Customers who possess versatile goods get to exercise more 'control' over their possessions because they can use the switching mechanism to make the good perform different tasks. They may even value their ability to 'play' with the good in this way for the emotional satisfaction it provides. Decisions which were previously made in the context of purchases of specialized goods are now made in the context of the utilization of a versatile good. Just as the employer, in the previous case, acquired control over labour in order to reduce information costs, so the employee, in his capacity as consumer, can acquire control as well, and for the same reason. The main difference is simply that the employer acquires control over another human being whilst the consumer acquires control over household machinery instead. The motor car is the classic example of a versatile multi-component good which gives its owner emotional satisfaction from the exercise of control.

Having said this, it is always open to firms to create new markets for specific rights and specific products as well. Specific rights, for example, are very common in travel and tourism, where people purchase the right to occupy a particular seat on a particular flight or a particular hotel room for a particular night. Time-sharing is an example where a general right of ownership is temporally subdivided to create more specific rights. The principal constraint on the number of new specific markets that develop is that many of the costs of market-making are fixed costs independent of the volume of trade. If specific markets proliferate too much then the volume of trade in each market will tend to shrink to the point where individual markets can no longer cover their fixed costs. In this way competitive entry and exit controls the diversity of specific markets that exist in the economy as a whole.

The historical trend in market-making innovation seems to be a rising one for both versatile and specific goods: there are more versatile goods to economize on information costs, yet more specific goods being traded too. The explanation seems to be that technical ingenuity is increasing at the same time that information costs are falling (Casson, 1994a). Indeed, the fall in information costs is partly driven by advances in telecommunications which stem from technical ingenuity. The fall in information costs explains why it is economic to trade a wider variety of specific goods, whilst technical ingenuity explains why, despite these falling costs, it is still economic to invest in new ways of economizing on those costs that still remain. There are other factors too, of course. Rising incomes tend to enlarge the demand for specialized goods relative to standardized goods, thereby increasing the information-content of transactions. Thus even if information costs are falling in costs per unit of information, they are actually increasing in terms of cost per unit value of trade. If this interpretation is correct, then it seems likely the rising trend in both types of innovation is likely to continue for some time yet.

1.7. The organization of market-making

If the processing of the information required to coordinate the economy is concentrated in the hands of specialist market-making firms, as the preceding discussion suggests, then it is clearly important that this information is processed within these firms as efficiently as possible. It was noted in Section 1.3 that the volatility of the economic environment exposes market-making firms to continuous shocks. Some of these shocks are transmitted through demand and others through supply. Because the shocks are unpredictable, it does not make sense for a firm to draw up a fixed plan for all future prices and production levels at the outset. It is better for the firm to defer decisions on each period's price and output plan to the beginning of the period concerned so that these decisions can be taken in the light of the latest information on market conditions. However, in so far as the shocks experienced are of a transitory nature, and the pattern of volatility is the same from period to period, the firm can establish routine procedures for handling the information and deciding the plan. These procedures are equivalent to a contingent plan in which the firm decides in advance, not what it will do, but how it will respond to whatever circumstances it discovers are prevailing at the time. There are many alternative procedures to choose from and it is important that the firm selects the appropriate one.

A key issue concerning these procedures relates to the amount of information that the firm decides to collect. It is possible for the firm to have too little information on some aspects of the situation, with a consequent risk of mistaken decisions, and too much information on others, so that its managers are swamped with information that is irrelevant to their needs. When information is costly to collect, there is a trade-off between the cost of collection on the one hand, and the quality of decision-making on the other. Collecting too little information leaves too much uncertainty unresolved, while collecting too much simply wastes scarce managerial resources.

One way of economizing on information is to choose an appropriate level of aggregation at which to analyse the problem. Should the firm collect information on individual consumers and individual producers for example, in order to generate a detailed picture of the market, or should it simply form estimates of aggregate market trends? The answer depends largely on the nature of the stochastic forces driving fluctuations in demand and supply. If there is a systematic factor, such as fashion, which impacts on all consumers, then a knowledge of this systematic factor may be sufficient to predict changes in demand. The larger is the systematic component, and the smaller the individual-specific component, in each consumer's demand, the more likely it is that a knowledge of the systematic component will suffice. Moreover, given the statistical independence of the individual-specific components, the more consumers there are, the more likely it is that fluctuations caused by individual-specific components will cancel one another out at the aggregate level.

The cost of information is also a relevant consideration, of course. Knowledge of individual preferences is often difficult for the market-maker to obtain because of the intermediation of the retailer. It is doubtful if the market-maker would want this information anyway, though. The information is highly subjective and has to be collected from many different people. By contrast systematic information, such as fashion trends, can often be detected at the retail level by noting the characteristics of the goods to which consumers are switching their demand. It can also be assessed at very low cost from media sources. Thus information on systematic factors is very much cheaper for the 'market-maker to obtain. Since the market-maker orders in bulk from the producers, information on systematic factors may be quite sufficient for his purposes. Only the retailer, who deals in smaller quantities with many more people, requires specific information.

Similar considerations apply to the supply side of the market. The number of producers is normally very much smaller than the number of consumers, and individual-specific factors, such as the vintage of the producer's capital equipment, and the skills of his workforce, are more important too. The smaller number of participants also means that there is no additional intermediator who filters information like a retailer does. The volatility of individual-specific components is therefore likely to be greater than before, and the cost of information on them somewhat lower. Thus although systematic factors remain important, collecting information on individual-specific factors is now important too. This means that the level to which information is disaggregated when it is collected will normally be greater on the production side than on the consumption side of the firm.

How will the collection of all this information be organized? Will the job be given to a single person, or will it be shared out between different people? There is a limit to how much information one person can process, and this limit may be quite low when the information concerned is diverse (Marschak and Radner, 1972). This certainly applies to the market-making firm, where the range of factors impacting on demand and supply is very wide. If different people become involved, will they be encouraged to specialize in collecting particular types of information?

This raises the general issue of the managerial division of labour within the firm (Carter, 1995). Increasing the subdivision of managerial tasks allows people to specialize more intensively according to their personal comparative advantage. They handle just that kind of information to which they are most suited. Comparative advantage is here interpreted not just in the static sense of being good at their job to begin with, but in the dynamic sense of being able to learn it quickly and exploit economies of habit-formation in the long run.

Specialization can become excessive, however. Information often arises quite naturally as a byproduct of doing something else. For example, systematic information on demand may be obtained by a marketing executive as a byproduct of liaison with retailers. Similarly, systematic information on supply may be obtained by a production executive as a byproduct of negotiating with subcontractors. In such cases the division of labour in information processing may be driven largely by the nature of the division of labour in the implementation of the price and output plan. In fact, of course, the interaction is two-way, with the division of labour in implementation being determined with its implications for information-handling very much in mind.

A still more significant constraint on the managerial division of labour is the cost of communication involved. If one person collects all the relevant information and takes the decision themselves then no communication costs are incurred, except in their announcement of the decision to those responsible for its implementation. If different people specialize in collecting different items, however, then considerable communication may be involved in effecting a synthesis. Steps can, of course, be taken to reduce communication costs; for example, by establishing a common language and common culture within the firm. Such standardization reduces the marginal cost of communication, though against this must be set the fixed costs of creating the standards in the first place.

Communication costs impose a tax on an inter-personal division of labour in the synthesis of information. The higher are internal communication costs, the lower the degree of specialization will be. Communication costs affect the way that the synthesis is structured too. Some information is particularly costly to communicate because it is 'tacit' information which cannot be properly understood unless the context is clear. If the context is unclear then a lot of effort must be made to explain it. It is therefore advantageous, when synthesizing information, to specialize decision-making on the person who collects the most tacit information since this affords the greatest savings in communication costs.

Within any organization the most tacit information is likely to come directly from external sources and to concern unique or unfamiliar events. Internal sources are more likely to generate explicit information about recurrent and familiar events. The information generated by functional specialists such as the marketing executive and the production executive is therefore more likely to be explicit than the information generated by the person responsible for monitoring unexpected changes in the environment as a whole. This suggests that an efficient synthesis of information involves functional specialists reporting information to a synthesizer who handles the external relations of the firm.

The synthesizer is also the decision-maker because it is more efficient for him to encode his synthesis in the form of a decision than to simply share his synthesis with the functional specialists in the firm and leave them to take decisions for themselves in the light of what they have been told. A decision about price and output is relatively explicit, whereas the synthesis is likely to be tacit because of the external information that enters into it. The synthesizer therefore does not brief the functional specialists on the situation as he sees it, but simply tells the functional specialists what they are to do. This authority relation reduces communication costs. It creates a hierarchical structure in which the executives report information to a superior who hands down orders based on a synthesis, which incorporates his own tacit information on the environment of the firm (Casson, 1995b, pp. 73–5).

1.8. Sequential synthesis and the distribution of power within the firm

Another important principle in the economy of information is that overall information costs are reduced, on average, when information is collected sequentially (Casson, 1994d, p. 65). There is no point in collecting additional information once sufficient information has been collected that a decision can be made. Whether a decision can be made at a given point depends, however, on what the information that has already been collected turns out to be. Information on certain aspects of a situation may be more likely to generate a decisive result at an early stage than information on some other aspect of the situation. It pays, in general, to investigate a potentially decisive aspect of a situation first. For if the information turns out as expected then the decision-making process can be terminated before all the information that might otherwise have had to be collected has been obtained. It therefore pays, in general, not to commit to the collection of a given set of information in advance. The only commitment should be to a procedure which collects information in a particular order. This procedure contains a rule which determines whether the search for information should stop at each particular stage.

An efficient organization will select the optimal sequential procedure. This procedure will normally involve collecting information on the most volatile aspect of the environment first, and proceed through other aspects, in order of diminishing volatility, until a point is reached where no further investigation is ever likely to be warranted. How soon this point is reached depends upon the general level of information costs. The higher the level of information costs, the sooner the search is likely to terminate because of the greater incentive to economize on the amount of information used.

The acquisition of additional information generally affords diminishing marginal returns because the errors that are averted by the use of the additional information become smaller as more information is collected. The biggest errors tend to be eliminated at the outset. Enlarging the synthesis of information generates more and more fine-tuning, and the gains from fine-tuning eventually diminish to the point where the collection of further information is no longer worth the cost.

The sequence in which information is collected has an important influence on the distribution of power within the firm. Suppose, for example, that the firm has decided that the optimal approach to planning is simply to synthesize information on a systematic component of demand with information on a systematic component of supply. For the reasons explained above, information on demand is collected by a marketing executive and information on supply by a production executive. If demand is very volatile whilst supply is not then it may pay to investigate demand before investigating supply. If demand conditions are extreme, it may be evident what the firms need to do, in terms of price and output, without reference to supply. It is only if demand conditions turn out to be moderate rather than extreme that supply conditions will influence the plan. In such a case it clearly pays to investigate demand conditions first. The decision to investigate supply conditions is deferred until demand conditions are known. In this case considerable power resides with the marketing executive. He is always consulted, whereas the production executive may not be consulted at all. What is crucial, though, is that the marketing executive effectively determines, by the information he supplies, whether his production colleague is consulted or not. Under these conditions the firm may be said to be 'marketing-led'.

The converse is also possible, of course. If supply conditions are more volatile than demand conditions then the production executive may be consulted first, and the firm becomes 'production-led'. There are two reasons for believing, though, that in practice most firms will be marketing-led rather than production-led. The first is the considerable impact of fashion, and other social factors generally, on consumer demand. Secondly, there is the impact of the business cycle, and in particular the fluctuations in aggregate income characteristic of sticky-price economies. These income changes seem, like social changes, to have a differentially large impact on the demand side of the economy, at least in the short run. Unlike social changes, though, they affect aggregate consumption rather than the mix of products consumed. Production-led firms do exist, of course, but they are mainly confined to a few industries—agriculture, for example, where weather conditions are important, and mature manufacturing industries in which opportunities arise to relocate to new cheap-labour locations.

In some cases the difference in volatility between demand and supply may be so great that it is known in advance that only the most volatile factor is worth investigating at all. Such a view can also emerge when the cost of investigating the less volatile factor is very high. The result is an autocratic organization: a single source of information is deemed the only relevant one, and the autocrat is the person who has access to this information source. The autocrat consults no one because he believes that what they could find out could not possibly change his decision, or could change it only at an unacceptable cost.

Autocratic organization is often dismissed as inefficient, but from an information cost perspective it is quite appropriate in certain situations. The question is whether these circumstances commonly prevail or not. The answer is that they do—for example, in the retailing of regular products. Retailing is so strongly marketing-led that for many purposes supply volatility can be ignored altogether. Anticipating fashion, and gauging the probable impact of advertising and special promotions, is the key success—particularly when the product is perishable and needs to be sold within a short time. This calls for a single source of expertise and suggests that the key decision—on what to order for stock—should be taken by a single person within the firm. This may well explain the apparent predominance of autocratically-managed small firms in the retail sector.

1.9. Diagnosis and search

It is not just the process of synthesis that is sequential. Analysis is a sequential process too. Analysis is important because information is usually generated in a symptomatic form. Economic fundamentals such as individual preferences and the state of technological know-how cannot be directly observed. It is the symptoms of these hidden fundamentals that constitute the data with which the market-maker must work. Thus if a retailer reports that a lot of customers, having inspected a branded product, decide not to buy it, this may suggest that customers are looking for something new, or that they prefer a rival product, available elsewhere, instead.

This example also shows that symptoms can be ambiguous. They sometimes support more than one interpretation. There may be a suspicion that the 'signal' contains a lot of noise, or that the effects of different hidden factors are getting mixed up. In this case additional information may help to clarify the matter. But what additional information is required and in what order should it be collected?

Medical diagnosis provides a relevant metaphor. The initial symptom is that the patient feels ill, but they don't know why. The general practitioner considers the most volatile factors in the environment and carries out a low-cost test for the most common cause. If the patient's temperature is high then he diagnoses influenza because that is the most probable explanation. Only if the illness does not clear up is additional expenditure on information incurred. Further symptoms are elicited, and the patient may eventually be referred to a specialist for help. The specialist uses high-cost information to detect extremely rare conditions. In very unfortunate cases the cost of additional information may become prohibitive, and the patient cannot be offered further treatment because no adequate diagnosis is available.

Whenever breakdowns of any kind occur, diagnostic problems are raised. Managerial efficiency requires that the market-making firm can deal quickly and effectively with commonly occurring problems in its own administrative activities. A typical response is to hold stocks of replacement parts in a convenient location (toner cartridges for a photocopier, for example, may be held in the stationery store), and to employ a versatile administrative assistant who can provide temporary cover for colleagues who are ill.

Sequential procedures have another, more strategic implication for the market-making firm. Consumers and workers use sequential procedures too: consumers search sequentially in choosing which brand of product to buy, and workers use search sequentially when finding a job (Lippman and McCall, 1976). Insight into other people's search procedures can be a competitive advantage for the firm. Consider, for example, the marketing of an occasional good—a luxury consumer durable, say. To minimize his search costs the consumer will search in a sequence which he believes will produce a decision as soon as possible. If he believes that the market is highly competitive then he will find little advantage in shopping around for the best price. He correctly assumes the retailers in the same locality will match each other's prices. His strategy is therefore to begin his search with the product that seems to be closest in specification to his own particular needs. If a match is obtained at the outset then a purchase will be made right away. Under these conditions it is advantageous for a market-maker to persuade consumers to investigate his product first. The lower down the sequence he is, the more likely the customer is to buy something else without investigating his product at all.

Rivalry between market-makers then becomes rivalry for priority in the customer's search. Unique characteristics with widespread appeal become the basis of advertised claims, since these are most likely to generate the desired response—namely an early visit to the appropriate retailer. Once the customer has arrived, the retailer can point out other desirable characteristics of the product, and then close the deal on the basis that a better price cannot be found anywhere else.

1.10. Retailing

The preceding discussion may have given the impression that retailing, though important, is very much a poor relation of market-making, especially where branded products are concerned. Since many economists ignore retailing altogether, the present approach may presumably be welcomed as an attempt to redress this imbalance. Nevertheless there are certainly strategic aspects to retailing about which nothing has so far been said.

The tendency for retail premises to agglomerate at major transport hubs is sometimes cited as an example of 'spontaneous order' within the market system. Agglomeration benefits customers because it facilitates price and quality comparisons, and enables a variety of goods to be obtained on a single indivisible trip. It is not usually the product of zoning by planners, but rather of the strategic incentives faced by individual firms. Any firm that locates away from the hub faces major creditibility problems because it appears to have isolated itself from competition, and therefore cannot deter its local clientele from going to the hub in the belief that they can get a better price there. Once the 'first mover' has chosen a prime location at a node of the transport network, therefore, there is a strong incentive for all other entrants to follow him there.

Further strategic aspects arise at the hub itself, however. Sequential search by customers, as described above, has a spatial dimension to it because a lot of 'window shopping' is done on foot. The competitive struggle for priority in the search agenda therefore affects the location of retail premises within a town. Being nearest to the car park, for example, may be a key advantage of a retail site. This in turn means that the planners who control the flow of traffic and pedestrians in the centre of the town have enormous influence over the value of retail sites. Attempts to capture these rents explain the considerable influence on local government exercised by entrepreneurs in the retail property sector.

Another important feature of retailers is that they handle much of the individual-specific information that the pure market-maker ignores. The market-maker may well decide that he is only interested in fashions and other systematic factors in demand. There comes a point, however, where the individual customer has to express his demand by placing an order for the product. The skills of the retailer come to the fore in ensuring that this order can be placed with a minimum of information cost. The reduction of costs is a major feature of the retailing of regular goods. By setting a take-it-or-leave it price for each product the retailer can eliminate negotiation costs. By displaying the product on the shelves, and signposting the store clearly, he obviates the need for the customer to explain what he wants. By insisting on payment by cash rather than credit, the retailer avoids having to find out who the customer is.

These information economies incur some risks, however. By quoting fixed prices the retailer neutralizes one of the mechanisms for rationing out scarce stock. To control the risk of a stock-out, it is necessary to hold a larger inventory. The greater the commitment to price stability, the greater the inventory that must be held. In this way the retailer trades off the cost of storage against the savings in information costs that price stability affords.

Specialist retailers face a rather different set of problems. They must offer a highly customized service, in which the skill lies not in suppressing communication but making it as effective as possible. Training sales staff in social skills is important here. Because of the non-standard nature of the products, holding inventory is of less importance than careful customization and rapid supply response. Effective communication with producers, and a reliable delivery system, are important elements here. Because customized products tend to be more expensive, granting credit to the customer may be more important too. Thus the specialist retailer needs to know more not only about the customer's requirements but about his credit-worthiness as well.

Where breakdowns create a state of crisis for customer, remedial services are often supplied under an insurance contract. Such contracts often require the customer to pay for regular preventative maintenance. In some cases the customer is tied in to the original supplier of a product through an extended warranty contract. The provision of services through insurance contracts underlines the information-intensive nature of the retailing of specialist goods.

Retailers providing solutions to sensitive or hazardous problems may find themselves subject to regulation. Pharmacists, for example, cannot sell certain products except on prescription. This illustrates one of the points made earlier (Section 1.5) about the nature of ownership: while the retailer may own the product, he cannot sell it to whomever he likes. His ownership is incomplete in the sense that there is a special right concerning the sale of the product which can only be exercised with the permission of someone else.

Regulation over retailers can also be exercised by market-makers—for example, through resale price maintenance, territorial restrictions on sales, and other vertical restraints. This reinforces the earlier point about the limited scope of the retailer's ownership rights. It also illustrates the point made at the start, about the preeminance of the market-maker. It is almost unheard of for retailers to control the activities of market-makers, but quite common for market-makers to control the activities of retailers. The market-maker often assumes overall responsibility for the management of the distribution channel, because ultimately it is the market-maker who specializes in taking the strategic decisions. The force of these decisions does not always depend on the exercise of conventional ownership rights, for these rights often pass on to retailers as the product moves down the distribution channel. Strategy is implemented through specific rights instead—rights which are reserved to the market-maker in the contract of sale. These rights are reserved because it is the market-maker and not the retailer who effects the strategic synthesis of information. It is the market-maker who ultimately controls price and regulates retail competition in order to appropriate the full reward to his wide-ranging synthesis of information.

1.11. Summary and conclusions

This chapter has sought to demonstrate the central role of information in economic organization. It has shown how the costs of collecting information and communicating it influence the structure of institutions. The influence reflects important trade-offs involving information costs. These trade-offs are very general—they apply to both markets and firms, and to the relations between firms and markets as well.

It is a mistake to think of the economy in purely material terms, as many economists unfortunately still do. Richardson, Hayek and Marschak were amongst the first to demonstrate the advantages of thinking of the economy as an information system instead. In the modern service-oriented economy the information sector is extremely large—often larger than the manufacturing sector, indeed. The importance of information needs to be reflected in the metaphors that economists use, and the symbolic ways in which they summarize the economic system.

The division of labour in the modern economy is driven not by the advance of the division of labour in manufacturing, although this still continues apace, but by the shifting division of labour between manual and mental work. Market-making is an important example of purely mental work. It allows specialists to relieve consumers and workers of much of the responsibility for coordination. Mental work is important in retailing too, but there it is combined with manual work as well.

The division of labour also applies within mental work. There is a trade-off, however, between increasing specialization in mental work, and the greater costs of communication involved. This trade-off is a key influence on organizational structure, both at the level of the economy as a whole, and within the individual firm.

Access to information has important implications for the ownership of resources. People who specialize in handling different types of information also specialize in owning particular types of resource. As a result, different people may own a product at different stages of its production and distribution. They coordinate the flow by communicating with each other through negotiations. Where there are problems in ensuring the quality of the information conveyed in this way, ownership at adjacent stages may be consolidated. Information on different stages is then synthesized not through negotiation but through a hierarchy. The synthesis is normally effected by a sequential procedure, and it is this procedure which determines whether the firm is marketing-led or production-led, and whether it is consultative or autocratic. The sequential principle has other implications too, which illuminate the strategies of both market-making and retail firms.

2

The Process of Coordination

2.1. Introduction

Although coordination is a concept that is absolutely central to economics, the issues it raises are often treated as if they were mere technical issues whose resolution is of interest to specialists alone. Most economists believe that the core issues in their subject are fully understood. Progress in economics, they feel, involves simply adding to the edifice of an impressive building whose foundations are well established and known to be secure. There is a good deal of truth in this view, but it should not be an excuse for complacency. There remain issues connected with coordination which are certainly important and are by no means fully resolved.

These issues surface from time to time, but tend to be quickly forgotten again. This happened with Hayek's (1937) discussion of the role of knowledge in coordinating trade, and with Richardson's (1960) analysis of the informal mechanisms of coordination that are used in industry. The main reason why these issues are so often evaded is that they are genuinely difficult to discuss. They are certainly difficult to formalize, because no single specific model can do justice to them. To explain why the economy as a whole is the way it is, it is necessary to examine the difficulties involved in organizing the economy in alternative ways. These counter-factual scenarios are difficult to visualize intuitively because nothing like them is normally seen in practice. This makes the analysis difficult to follow. Notwithstanding this, it is important to keep debate on these fundamental issues alive. To contribute to this debate is the primary purpose of this chapter.

The chapter emphasizes that the information requirements of coordination are very considerable. Because so many different items of information are required for coordination it takes only a modest level of information cost per unit to make the overall cost of coordination very high indeed. Economic efficiency does not require that coordination should be perfect, however. The information costs of coordination must be traded off against the benefits in order to optimize the degree of coordination. The institutional arrangements which, in practice, govern coordination in a market economy can only be properly understood as a response to a trade-off of this kind.

The information requirements of coordination can be sharply reduced by carrying out coordination as a sequential and localized process rather than as a simultaneous economy-wide process. They can also be reduced by using a specialized medium of exchange, backed up by a banking system. The medium of exchange replaces complex multilateral arrangements with a series of bilateral ones. Inventories are a useful way of reducing information requirements as well (see Chapter 1). Each of these information economies is examined in this chapter.

When all of these economies are exploited simultaneously, coordination can, in fact, appear as a relatively uncoordinated process. The coordination that does occur is so subtle that it sometimes requires considerable insight to discern it. In this connection it is important to distinguish between a lack of coordination which is a rational response to information costs, and a lack of coordination caused by inefficient social or legal arrangements. The fact that capitalist market economies often appear uncoordinated does not mean that they are, in fact, inefficient, because they may be rationally conserving information costs. But equally, any given coordination failure cannot necessarily be explained away in these terms. Capitalist market economies may indeed be inefficient because their performance depends crucially on the social and legal institutions through which they operate. Any weakness in this institutional framework can seriously impair their efficiency.

Consider, for example, the issue of innovation. The lack of coordination in a market economy is particularly evident in the field of innovation. Innovations are effectively large coordination projects that accomplish something new. But except in centrally planned economies, innovations are not normally effected on an economy-wide basis. Each innovation is partial and localized. Innovations in different but related sectors of the economy are not coordinated before they are made. Because of the very large gains that are afforded by the coordination of innovations in related sectors—for example, steel, engineering and motor vehicles—it is difficult to rationalize the apparent lack of coordination in capitalist economies in terms of information costs. The explanation seems to be that the difficulties of synthesizing information are aggravated by deliberate secrecy. When legal rights over patents and know-how are difficult to enforce, secrecy substitutes for the law as an appropriation mechanism. By using secrecy to exclude imitators, innovators incidentally damage coordination with other innovators as well. Such coordination failure can induce serious losses which inhibit the growth of the economy.

The principle of coordination applies not only to material goods and services but to the handling of information flows as well. An efficient economy achieves a given degree of coordination of material goods and services at minimum information cost. To minimize information costs, coordination of information flows is in turn required. There are, for example, different routes by which information can be communicated between any two people; the coordination of information flow implies that each communication is effected by the cheapest route. For the reasons already given in the context of material flow, the coordination of information flow does not have to be perfect, though. The degree of coordination must simply be at the level appropriate in the light of the relevant costs. The appropriation problems that influence the coordination of innovations, influence the coordination of information flows too. They can result in too many people competing to discover one kind of information and too few people attempting to discover another, as explained in detail below.

These remarks imply that coordination must be regarded as a process, in which one small step leads on to another, rather than as an activity in which there is a single giant leap to the fully-coordinated economy. The sequence of steps is not fully optimized as it is within a formal organization where decision-making has been reduced to routine. It does have a logic to it, however, even if that logic is sometimes difficult to discern. The existence of this logic implies that the institutional arrangements governing coordination are able to adapt—albeit slowly—to changing conditions. Thus as transport and communication costs have fallen, and opportunities for multilateral trade have increased, so money and banking institutions have evolved to support the more sophisticated pattern of trade that these changes allow. The apparently uncoordinated nature of coordination does not therefore mean that coordination defies analysis, but rather the analysis of changes in methods of coordination require a thorough appreciation of the wide-ranging implications of information costs.

2.2. The concept of coordination

Coordination may be defined as an improvement in the allocation of resources. The idea that coordination improves the allocation of resources implies that the allocation of resources cannot have been optimal to begin with. One reason why many economists find it difficult to understand coordination properly is that they cannot accept that anything like this could be wrong at the outset. They are trained to believe in the Walrasian myth that in a market economy the allocation of resources is naturally ideal.

The main reason why the initial allocation of resources is not ideal is that to identify the ideal allocation of resources requires information, and information is costly to collect. An integral part of the coordination process is to collect this information and put it to use, as explained above.

The concept of coordination is unambiguous so far as a single individual is concerned, but not for society as a whole. Coordination for a single individual is a reallocation of resources that makes them better off. But in a social context, what one person considers better another may consider worse. Economists typically invoke the criterion of Pareto-improvement to address this problem. Coordination occurs when someone is made better off without anyone else being made worse off. Implementing coordination with this criterion in mind means that arranging for the beneficiaries to compensate the losers is an integral part of the coordination process.

When all resources are in private ownership, the payment of compensation is assured by the requirement that coordination be a voluntary process. Anyone whose resources are needed as part of a coordination plan can withhold those resources until they are satisfied that they will be better off. Unless they are fully compensated, therefore, the coordination plan cannot proceed (Menger, 1871).

It is worth noting, in passing, that the concept of Pareto-improvement is often invoked in the context of planning by the state. Here, however, the compensation paid is usually of a purely hypothetical nature. The decision criterion is to proceed with the plan if the winners could in principle compensate the losers, even though the compensation may not actually be paid (Kaldor, 1939; Little, 1957). The administrative principles underlying this approach are very different from those which apply when compensation is actually paid, however. As indicated below, the payment of compensation generates market-like arrangements which involve negotiations over the amount of compensation and the evolution of money as a specialized means of payment. These features tend to be missing when the planning of coordination is effected entirely by the state.

The concept of coordination appears in a number of different contexts in economics. These contexts are so diverse that it is not always evident that the issues they raise are essentially the same. A simple example of coordination is the repair of a breakdown in machinery, or the utilization of a previously idle resource. Most examples of coordination are more complicated than this, however. The classic example of coordination, and the main focus of this chapter, is the creation of trade. Trade permits hitherto self-sufficient individuals to exploit economies of specialization in production and to allocate goods between them on the basis of their individual tastes.

Coordination can be expressed in terms of either problems or opportunities. Problems and opportunities are basically the same coordination issue looked at from different perspectives. The 'problem view' takes the ideal situation (or at least a better situation) as the norm, and asks why this situation has not been achieved. It may be, for example, that this better situation prevailed before and that the situation has now lapsed into something worse. The potential still exists to restore the original situation, and indeed the solution of the problem is usually to do exactly this. An 'opportunity view', on the other hand, takes the existing situation as the norm and notes that it is possible to do better. The answer is to exploit the opportunity whilst it is available. Given the tendency for people to use the previous situation as their norm, a problem normally arises from a worsening of their situation, and an opportunity from a potential improvement in it.

In the context of trade, for example, the transition from self-sufficiency to interdependence exemplifies the taking of an opportunity. This opportunity is very common because it stems from a downward historical trend in transport and communication costs (see Chapter 10). On the other hand correcting a trade distortion to restore a free-trade equilibrium represents the solution of a problem. Such problems arise because politicians often create impediments to trade as an indirect method of redistributing income. Both cases raise similar issues because self-sufficiency is simply an extreme case of the distortion of trade. It is just that the perception of the problem is different, stemming from the use of different norms. The norms are different because in the first case the situation is steadily improving whilst in the second case it has suddenly become worse.

Problems and opportunities are essentially subjective, in that they arise from changes in the environment as perceived by the people concerned (Casson, 1990, p. 48). The perceived environment may change either because the actual environment has changed, and this has been correctly perceived, or because the perception has changed even though the environment has not.

Consider the case of an actual change in the environment first. Any realistic discussion of coordination must recognize that the environment is in a constant state of flux. Changes are continually occurring, and adjustments are continuously required in order to sustain an equilibrium. Many changes occur quite regularly and it is therefore plausible to set up organizations to respond to these changes in a routine way (see Chapter 1). Other changes are of a more occasional nature. They may occur only once in a lifetime—indeed, it may be uncertain whether they will ever occur at all. It is difficult to respond to changes of this kind without improvisation. It remains an open question, however, as to whether it is possible to co-ordinate the taking of improvised decisions in a systematic way (see below).

Perceptions of the environment may change even when the environment does not. This is because new information on the current state of the environment is continually becoming available. This is particularly important when the information relates to permanent features of the environment. Permanent information does not obsolesce in the way that transitory information does. It is worthwhile memorizing because it is just as useful tomorrow as it is today. Memory enables individuals to learn, and it allows society to transmit knowledge from one generation to another. The accumulation of a stock of permanent information creates a progressive dynamic in the economy. This explains why so much coordination is seen in the positive light of opportunities for innovation rather than in the more negative light of arresting a process of decline.

2.3. The network structure of communication in a market system

In an ideal world, such as that of Walrasian theory, coordination is an economy-wide process. One of the great insights of Walrasian theory is that in an economic system everything depends upon everything else. Every good is potentially a substitute or a complement for any other good so far as consumers are concerned, and the same is true so far as producers are concerned as well. A shock to the economic system is therefore like a pebble dropping in a pond—the waves spread out in all directions at once. Unlike the pebble, however, the wave created by a shock to the Walrasian system spreads instantaneously, causing immediate adjustments throughout the system. There are no obstacles to the spread of the waves—the surface of the pond is perfectly smooth and free of all obstructions.

In the Walrasian world everyone is connected to everyone else through the Walrasian auctioneer. Information flow is costless and complete. The opposite of the Walrasian world is one in which no one is in touch with anyone else at all. Real world economies lie somewhere between these two extremes. The most natural information linkages are between geographical neighbours. It is easy for neighbours to make contact through chance encounters, and to communicate face to face. It is also especially advantageous for people who specialize in producing one type of good to establish communication with those of their neighbours who specialize in producing other goods of which they have the greatest need. In the absence of intermediation, therefore, the strongest information links are likely to be between pairs of neighbours who specialize in producing something that their other neighbour requires.

Consider, for example, a simple barter economy in which two goods are produced. The structure of the economy is illustrated in Fig. 2.1. The top part of the figure illustrates the potential material flows involved. It focuses on just one of the two goods; the flow of this good is illustrated by double lines, just as in Chapter 1. The economy comprises five households. Each household is represented by a square. The household production units A and B supply the good to the household consumption units, X, Y and Z. The consumers pay in kind with reverse consignments of the other good.

In principle, each consumer can obtain supplies from either producer, and conversely each producer can supply any of the consumers. This is illustrated by the six possible trade linkages shown in Fig. 2.1. It is assumed, however, that information costs restrict the amount of coordination that can be achieved. Without communication between the individual households, trade cannot proceed.

The communication of information is illustrated in the bottom part of the figure. Communication is effected between individuals. The individual head of each household is represented by a circle. The position of the circle indicates the household unit to which the individual corresponds. Commu-

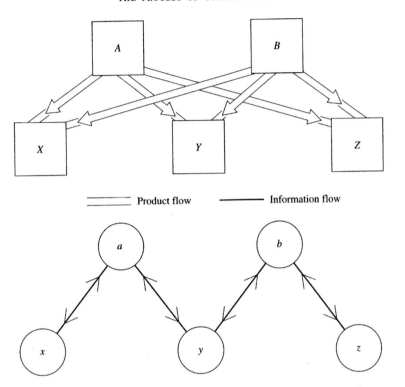

Fig. 2.1. *A simple division of labour coordinated by communication between neighbours*

nication between a pair of individuals is represented by a single line, as in Chapter 1.

In a world of no communication, the heads of households are all isolated from each other. There are therefore no lines between the circles. Because there is no communication, no trade can take place. None of the linkages portrayed in the top part of the figure can be activated until communication has been established.

If communication is established between neighbours then the pattern shown in Fig. 2.1 emerges. Communication is a two-way process, as indicated by the way that arrows point in both directions along each line. With only neighbours linked, individual x, the head of household X, is in touch only with individual a, the head of household A. Likewise, z, the head of household Z, is in touch only with b, the head of household B. However, a is in touch with both x and y (the head of household Y), b is in touch with both y and z, and y is in touch with both a and b. This means that four of the six linkages can be activated. A can supply product to either X or Y, and B can supply product to either Y or Z. Two of the linkages cannot function, however: A cannot supply Z, and B cannot supply X.

Matters can be improved by intermediation. Intermediation is a systematic way of increasing the number of linkages from the level associated with neighbourly contact (Leibenstein, 1978). Intermediation can be effected by either central planning or decentralized initiatives. The problem with central planning is that the optimization of a network of communication is a difficult task—particularly when the network exists to support trade. It requires a comprehensive knowledge of who will want to trade with whom which it is almost impossible for one person to acquire. There are so many issues on which judgement can differ that a more pluralistic approach is normally appropriate. This decentralizes decisions about intermediation to a number of different individuals.

Each of these individuals is likely to have only a partial perception of the network requirements. Their initiatives are therefore likely to be organized on a localized basis. Thus, returning to the example, an intermediator m_1 may spot an opportunity to establish communication between b and x, thereby activating the trade link between B and X. Similarly, an intermediator m_2 may spot an opportunity to establish communication between a and z, thereby activating the trade link between A and Z.

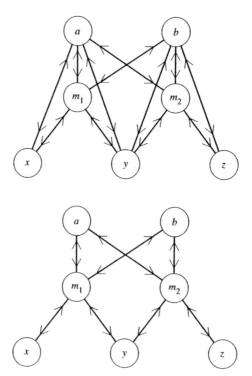

FIG. 2.2. *Local intermediation with and without direct links between neighbours*

The situation is illustrated in the top part of Fig. 2.2. Besides creating new linkages, each intermediator also offers new alternatives to existing linkages. Thus intermediator m_1 can offer alternative channels of communication between a and x, a and y, and b and y, while intermediator m_2 can offer alternative channels of communication between b and y, b and z, and a and y.

Maintaining open channels of communication incurs fixed costs—remembering the address of the other party, for example—and so some rationalization of communication channels is likely to occur. If the intermediators have lower information costs than the ordinary households—and in particular lower memory costs—then it may be advantageous for the households to divert all their communications through the intermediators. This generates the sparser network of communication shown in the bottom part of Fig. 2.2. The intermediator m_1 now enjoys a degree of monopoly power over consumer x, but on the other hand x can access both producer a and producer b through a single communication with m_1, and has no need to keep his direct channel with a open any more. Similarly the intermediator m_2 enjoys a degree of monopoly power over consumer z, but z can access both a and b through m_2 and has no need to maintain his own channel direct to b any more.

Even with the elimination of direct communication, however, there is still some duplication of linkages. Thus a and y are linked *via* both m_1 and m_2, as are b and y. This brings the local intermediators into competition with each other in serving the needs of a, b, and y. Competition between m_1 and m_2 could be controlled by a cartel of some kind. But while this would prevent the dissipation of revenues, it would do little to reduce costs. Costs could be reduced by eliminating one of the links to y, but apart from the difficulty of deciding who was to sever their link, the savings produced could be relatively small.

The obvious way to reduce the costs of the network is to rationalize the entire structure by eliminating the duplication of effort by m_1 and m_2. This not only reduces the number of channels that need to be kept open, but saves the fixed costs of one of the communications hubs as well. The resulting structure is illustrated in Fig. 2.3. All communication now takes place through a single intermediator m_0. It represents the classic 'star' configuration associated with the intermediation of a network using a single hub.

Given the obvious advantages of the star configuration, it may be asked why private intermediators do not begin with this configuration at the outset. Part of the answer has been given already: there is no one intermediator who is in touch with all potential traders at the outset. The true size of the market is not fully known. The other part of the answer is that the value of the market—in terms of the gains from trade accruing to the producers and their customers—is not known either. Experiments in

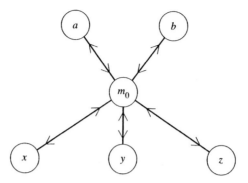

FIG. 2.3. *Coordination by a single economy-wide intermediator*

market-making are required to estimate these gains, and these experiments are best conducted on a local basis to minimize the costs that will be lost if the experiment fails.

It is tempting to identify the scenario of complete rationalization with the regime of a Walrasian auctioneer. This is misleading, however, because the Walrasian auctioneer is far more efficient than any real world intermediator can ever be. It is not merely that the Walrasian auctioneer faces no information costs, and so can afford to offer his services for free. It is also that he is sufficiently altruistic to forgo the potential monopoly profits afforded by his unique situation and to actually supply his services for free. In practice the household producers and consumers will fear a monopolistic intermediator's selfish exploitation of his market power. When a monopoly develops, therefore, they will tend to be sympathetic to any outsider who enters the market in order to break this monopoly power. Although the fixed costs of intermediation create a potential barrier to entry, therefore, a monopoly of intermediation may prove difficult to sustain in practice.

2.4. Spatial aspects of intermediation

The gains to intermediation are greatest when the people who have most to benefit from trade are a long distance away from each other. This means that they cannot make contact naturally through neighbourly interactions, and so require a specialist to make contact on their behalf. People living in different countries with different climates, for example, may derive enormous benefit from agricultural trade. The setting up of such trade requires a deliberate investment in information though, which a specialist merchant entrepreneur may have to undertake on their behalf.

Distance can, of course, be an obstacle to trade as well as to communication, because it increases transport costs. The gains to intermediation tend to be greatest when the impact of distance on transport is much less than its impact on communication. In this respect it is important to note that maritime transport is usually cheaper than land or air transport where bulk cargoes are concerned. On the other hand, because it tends to be slow and time-consuming, it is not so advantageous for purposes of communication. Maritime transport is thus a good example of a case where distance is a greater obstacle to communication than it is to trade. Maritime transport of agricultural products, for example, is pre-eminent as an arena in which intermediation is valuable. It is surely no accident that historically so much merchant enterprise has begun in this way.

Agricultural products tend to be fairly homogeneous (apart from obvious differences which can be handled by grading according to superficial characteristics such as size, ripeness, bruising and so on). This means that consumers do not typically need much help in determining which particular variety of the product is the right one for them. Neither do producers need much advice on which particular variety they should produce. By contrast, specialist services of the kind described in Chapter 1 are much more heterogeneous, and vary according to characteristics which cannot be superficially assessed. Professional services, such as medicine, law and accountancy, are a case in point. The more heterogeneous the product, the more difficult it is to match the demand and the supply in an appropriate way.

Matching is an important aspect of intermediation, and it is one that affords a potential source of economies of scale. With a given degree of heterogeneity, the larger is the number of buyers and sellers, the greater is the probability that everyone will achieve exactly the match they desire. The economy of scale is generated by a positive externality effect. Each additional buyer or seller who arrives at the market place not only stands to make a useful match for themselves, but also increases the probability that their opposite numbers in the market can make the match they most desire. A monopolistic intermediator who controls a market of this kind can appropriate these externalities for himself by setting a wider margin between his buying and selling price.

Even apparently homogeneous products can reveal heterogeneity of this kind. The time dimension is an important example of this. Where products are perishable, the timing of their consumption is crucial, and where people wish to buy immediately before they consume then the timing of delivery is crucial too. The demand for food to be eaten out is a case in point. If each seller supplies a small consignment of given size, and each buyer takes away a small consignment, then an increasing number of buyers and sellers raises the probability that each buyer can buy just as soon as he wants and each seller can sell immediately on arrival at the market.

When the product can be stored, the widening of the market helps to reduce inventory charges. Random fluctuations in arrivals are more likely to cancel out, so that less inventory is required, per unit volume of trade, to smooth out differences in the arrival rates.

Increasing returns to matching are not necessarily internal to the inter-mediating firm, however. They are internal mainly to the market location, as explained in Chapter 1. Whether they are internal to a firm depends upon whether some firm can control access to the key location or not. In effect, this means controlling access to neighbouring sites within 'shopping dis-tance' of his own. The distance between centres is important too (Krugman, 1991). The greater the external benefits of accurate and speedy matching, the greater is the tendency to agglomeration, and the greater the distance between rival centres tends to be. This increases the market power of individual centres, since a higher proportion of people who use a given centre are at an intra-marginal location, much closer to the centre they use than to the ones they do not. Any firm that enjoys a monopoly at such a location is likely to have considerable market power.

2.5. Adjustment costs

A dense network of communication, though costly to maintain, provides an economy with considerable flexibility in responding to shocks. It is because the economy is continually disrupted by shocks that communication is required on a continuous basis. When everyone is connected to everyone else by a reasonably short path, then everyone can share in the process of adjustment to every shock. When the cost of adjustment borne by a single individual accelerates as the size of the shock increases, it is advantageous to spread the burden of adjustment. By widening the field of adjustment, the individual burdens are very significantly reduced.

There is, however, a fixed cost of adjustment which stems partly from the cost of receiving the message and partly from the set up cost of any change. Because these costs are independent of the size of the change, small adjust-ments may not be worth making at all. This sets a limit on how far the burden of adjustment should be spread. As the number of people required to adjust to any shock increases, so the total fixed costs increase until the savings in variable costs are outweighed. At this point no further people should be involved in the adjustment process.

The lower the fixed costs of adjustment, the greater the number of people it is advantageous to involve. The more people that are involved in adjust-ing to any given shock, the more advantageous is a dense network of communication channels between them. Thus when the fixed costs of ad-justment are high, the advantages of intermediation in creating communica-tion networks tend to be low. As the fixed costs of adjustment fall, so the advantages of intermediation increase.

The same point applies to the frequency with which disturbances occur.

In any economy where shocks are frequent, and the fixed costs of adjustment are relatively low, investing in communication channels is well worthwhile because the channels of communication can be regularly used. Where shocks are only occasional, however, investment in communications infrastructure is less worthwhile. Intermediation designed to increase the density of the network is less likely to be profitable in this case, for there are fewer situations where the coordination of individual adjustments is required.

The size of the shock is important too. The larger the shock, the greater are the gains to dissipating its impact, relative to the costs of involving other people. An economy subject to very large shocks thus has a strong incentive to invest in dense networks of communication. The obvious example is an economy at war—the importance of supporting people who are in dangerous situations is so great that very dense networks are required to mobilize everyone's efforts. This normally helps to engender a high level of social cohesion.

Delay is another important factor to take into account. The disruptive effect of a shock is normally minimized by a rapid response. Although rapid adjustments are normally more costly than slow ones, speed is often desirable because on balance the benefit outweighs the cost. Every link in a communications network is a potential source of delay. Thus where speed of adjustment is at a premium, maintaining direct links with neighbours may well be worthwhile. In the limit, of course, it would be possible to maintain direct links with everyone, but this will normally be prohibitively costly. A suitable compromise is to invest in intermediation as a method of shortening the average number of linkages involved in communicating with distant people.

Intermediation may itself involve several stages, information being passed on from one communications hub to another until almost everyone has had an opportunity to share in the adjustment to the shock. Even though several stages may be involved, the number of stages will, on average, be significantly less than if purely local channels linking chains of neighbours were used to disseminate the information instead.

Figure 2.4 illustrates the process of adjusting to a single shock. The shock is assumed to be external to the system, and to be localized in its impact. It is represented by a black spot. The propagation of information about the shock is represented by a solid arrow. It is assumed that the shock initially impinges on household Y and is initially recognized by individual y. A storm may have damaged part of Y's house, for example, and additional resources are required to repair the damage. It is assumed to begin with that only local linkages are in place. If the fixed costs of adjustment are very high then individual y will bear the entire burden of adjustment himself. It may be so expensive, for example, for producers a and b to consign additional supplies to the site that y decides to finance repairs by reducing his own consumption

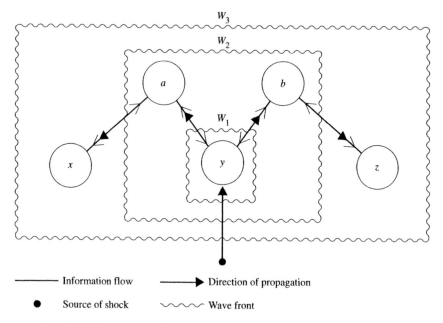

Information flow   Direction of propagation

Source of shock   Wave front

Fig. 2.4. *Propagation of a localized shock, showing how the distance of propagation varies according to the size of the fixed adjustment costs*

instead. As the fixed cost of adjusting consignments falls, however, it becomes worthwhile to requisition additional supplies from a and b. As costs fall even further, a and b may decide to compensate for their increased supplies to y by reducing their supplies to x and z respectively. Since the marginal contribution to adjustment effected by involving x and z is smaller than that effected by involving a and b, however, it is only after a significant fall in adjustment costs that this extension of the process will be worthwhile.

The propagation of the shocks is illustrated in Fig. 2.4 by the path of the solid arrows. The shock is transmitted in the first step from y to a and b, and in two independent second steps, from a to x and from b to z. As the shock is transmitted over a wider field, so its force dissipates. The distance it travels is governed by the size of the shock relative to the fixed adjustment costs. When adjustment costs are high it may never spread beyond the wavefront W_1. As adjustment costs fall, it spreads further to W_2, embracing producers a and b as well as the consumer y. Finally, for low adjustment costs the wave front W_3 is attained, which encompasses the whole of the economy.

Intermediation speeds up the propagation of shocks and widens their field of influence by providing a shorter route to more distant parts of the system. Consider, for example, the effect of a shock impinging on consumer *x*. When adjustment costs are low, the efficient response will be economy-wide, and this includes, for example, a compensating change in consumption by individual *z*. In the absence of intermediation, the wave front will spread out from *x* via *a*, *y*, and *b*, to reach *z* after four separate steps. When each step takes time, and delay is costly, the response by *z* may be relatively ineffectual. However, with two localized intermediators supplementing the local linkages, as illustrated in the top part of Fig. 2.2, the number of steps is reduced to three, and response is thereby speeded up.

With a single economy-wide intermediator, the number of steps is reduced further to only two. As Fig. 2.5 shows, the intermediator m_0 establishes two-step links between *x* and *b*, and between *x* and *z*, which did not exist before. Although the shock is partly propagated through the producer *a*, the producer *b* no longer participates in the propagation process; *b* simply absorbs the shock at the end of the second step. This shows that the larger is the hub, in terms of its number of connections, the greater is its role in propagating and expediting shocks.

2.6. Complementarities

Substitution effects lie at the core of the adjustment process described above. When one individual increases their demand for a good in response to a shock, others reduce their demands in response. In the absence of

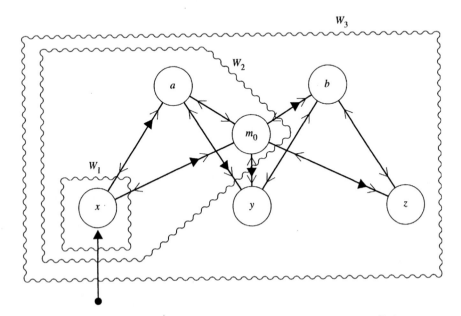

FIG. 2.5. *Faster propagation of a shock resulting from intermediation*

intermediation, the substitution signals are transmitted in a sequence of short steps, whereas when an intermediator is present, the signals are broadcast by the intermediator, once he has received the message, in a single step. Intermediation thus widens the range over which substitutions can be quickly made.

Despite its importance, though, there is more than just substitution involved in the process of adjustment. Complementarities are involved as well. In the previous model, for example, production by households a and b is complementary to consumption by households x, y, and z, and vice versa. The producers have no demand unless the consumers purchase, and the consumers have no supplies unless the producers are willing to sell. Producer–consumer complementarity is thus a key element in the adjustment process. When a consumer increases demand it is not only other consumers who adjust, by reducing their consumption, but the producers too. The producers increase their output to meet the demand, but because they do not normally adjust production fully, they pass on some of the shock by reducing supplies to other consumers as well. Conversely, when a producer reduces his supplies it is not only other producers who adjust, by increasing output, but consumers as well. It is because consumers do not reduce their demand by the full amount of the reduction in supplies that the burden of adjustment falls partly on the other producers too.

The industrial system involves many complementarities. Under a sophisticated division of labour, many products are generated by multi-stage production processes in which the levels of output at the different stages have to be maintained in fixed proportion to one another. Such a system is illustrated in Fig. 2.6. Five stages of production are shown, beginning with the upstream activity in the top row of the figure and ending with the downstream activity in the bottom row. There are five plants at the upstream stage, the downstream stage and the middle stage, and four plants at the other two stages. Each of these plants is controlled by a different manager. Managers a–e control the five upstream plants, managers f–j control the four plants at the next stage, and so on, down to the managers v–z who control the downstream stage. Although in principle any plant at one stage can supply any other plant at an adjacent stage, the costs of communication, it is assumed, restrict direct communication to neighbouring plants. Thus the downstream producer x, say, can only obtain supplies from producers s and t because they are the only people he can make contact with. Applying this principle to every plant creates the lattice of linkages shown in Fig. 2.6.

If there is a shock to the system, such as a sudden increase in demand by producer x, as shown in Fig. 2.6, then the shock propagates from x back through the successive stages of production until after five steps the upstream producers a–e are finally reached. The five steps involved are illustrated by the wave fronts W_1–W_5. The shape of the wave fronts shows quite

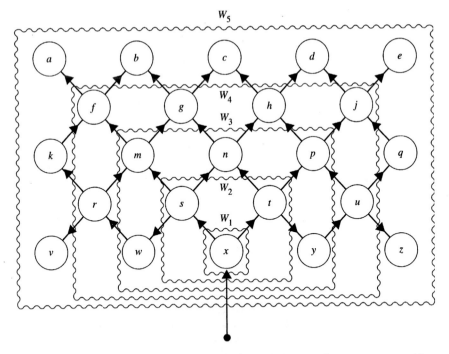

FIG. 2.6. *Propagation of shocks through a multi-stage production process with neighbourhood communication*

Note: In the interests of simplicity the arrows indicating two-way flows of information have been omitted from the figure and only the solid arrows indicating the propagation of shocks are shown.

vividly how substitution effects spread adjustment horizontally across producers at the same stage of production, whilst the complementarities spread the adjustments vertically through producers at adjacent stages of production. There is, however, no particular significance to the upward thrust of the adjustment illustrated in Fig. 2.6. If the disturbance had occurred at the upstream stage instead, then the adjustments would have moved downward, whilst if they had occurred at the middle stage, then they would have moved both upward and downward until both the upstream and downstream stages were reached.

Other patterns of complementarity are possible, of course. Some industries, notably the motor industry, have a component-assembly structure, in which the intermediate stages generate sub-assemblies out of which the final product is made. In other industries, such as oil-refining, metal-refining and food processing, byproducts are generated in fixed proportions—there is joint production, in other words. If, in addition, there are economies of scale, then there may be no substitution possibilities at any given stage

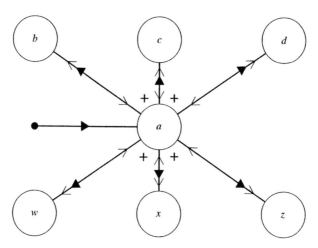

Fig. 2.7. *Impact of a shock on a production system with pure complementarity*

because efficiency dictates that there should be only one plant at each stage. This can lead to pure complementarity effects.

An example of this kind is illustrated in Fig. 2.7. An assembly process controlled by manager a is supplied with three different components, produced under the respective control of managers b, c, and d. Assembly generates a principal product utilized by manager x and two byproducts, comprising waste materials from the assembly plant, which are used by managers w and z. Each activity takes place in its own dedicated plant. The complementarities are illustrated in Fig. 2.7 by the plus signs placed between the flows of information relating to the complementary products. If a shock occurs to this system, then it will spread out very widely. Complementarities transmit shocks directly from one product market to another. The more complementarities that are involved, the wider the spread of the effects.

The most sensitive area of this industrial system is the assembly process. Figure 2.7 shows that a shock to this part of the system (caused, for example, by a breakdown in the assembly line) has immediate repercussions for all the other activities in the system. While a shock to any other part of the system will also spread to the rest of the system, because the system is so tightly-coupled, it will do so only with a lag.

2.7. Flexible response in a tightly-coupled system

Given the rigidities created by complementarities, it is natural to consider how an economic system can benefit from a sophisticated division of labour, and from economies of scale, whilst maintaining a suitable degree of flexibility. The obvious approach is to forgo some of the technological econ-omies by using more small-scale multi-purpose production units instead of just a few large-scale specialized ones. There are more subtle approaches too, however.

One is to accommodate short-term fluctuations in demand and supply by holding inventory, as discussed in Section 2.4 above. Given the localized nature of many shocks, spill-overs can often be contained by holding a precautionary stock of inventory. Inventory may have to be held in any case, to match up different batch sizes at adjacent stages of production; in this case the precautionary motive simply increases the average stock that is held. So far as long-term fluctuations are concerned, idle capacity may be created by investing in plants of exceptionally large size. This allows in-creases in demand to be accommodated without bottlenecks emerging within the system.

The amount of precautionary inventory that needs to be held depends on the amount of information that is collected in order to coordinate the economy. If a large amount of information is collected through continuous monitoring of the environment, then a rapid response can be made to any change in the situation. This means that only a small adjustment may be required to a typical shock. It also means that plans can be made immedi-ately to replenish inventory by increasing production. Thus only a small amount of inventory may need to be held when a large amount of infor-mation is collected. Conversely, when the environment is monitored only intermittently, the response to shocks will tend to be sluggish and the magnitude of the adjustment required correspondingly great. When com-bined with a slow response in production, this means that a larger inventory is required. There is, therefore, a trade-off between information costs and inventory costs—a trade-off mediated by speed of response. High informa-tion costs economize on inventory costs by accelerating the response to shocks. Conversely, large inventories economize on information costs at the expense of a slower response.

The contribution of inventory is maximized by holding it in the most appropriate location. This is normally at a transport hub. Holding inventory at a hub allows it to be rushed to the widest range of destinations in the shortest possible time. It also allows inventory to be replenished promptly from as wide a range of alternative sources as possible.

The management of inventory is best effected by an intermediator. The intermediator is based at a communications hub to minimize overall infor-mation costs. This communications hub may coincide with the transport hub, though it is often some distance away: because management is more labour-intensive and less space-intensive than warehousing, it benefits from a different structure of local costs. Where management and warehousing are separated to take advantage of cost differentials, there must, of course, be a good communication link between them. In some cases the inventory is concentrated in the hands of a high-level intermediator such as a whole-saler, whilst in other cases it tends to be dispersed into the hands of local intermediators such as retailers (as discussed in Chapter 1).

When the product is perishable, or highly customized, inventory may be difficult to hold. In this case, the needs of flexibility can sometimes be met by increasing the density of information flow. One possibility is to establish direct communication between people at the same stage of production. 'Horizontal' information flow of this kind speeds up the process of substitution. An example is given in Fig. 2.8. Each plant manager is in touch not only with the managers of neighbouring plants at adjacent stages, but with the managers of neighbouring plants at his own stage of production too. This allows neighbours to help each other out directly without waiting for signals to reach them via producers at an adjacent stage. It is a slightly unusual form of cooperation in that it involves collaboration between people who are normally rivals to one another. Those who believe that competition increases the efficiency of coordination often deplore such horizontal communication because they believe that it encourages collusion instead.

Figure 2.8 shows that when the initial shock is experienced by manager x he turns not only to s and t for additional inputs but to his rivals w and y as well. They assist either by transferring product of their own to x, or by

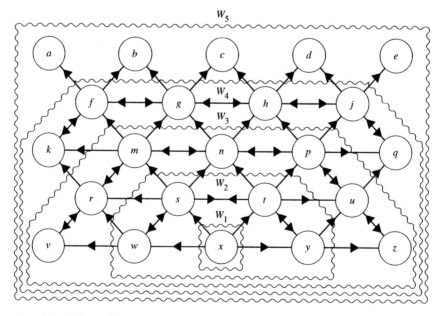

FIG. 2.8. *Effects of horizontal communication on the propagation of shocks in an industrial system*

spontaneously reducing their own demands on s and t without waiting for s and t to ration them. The effects of this increase in the density of communication are indicated by the modified shapes of the wave fronts W_2–W_5. The waves now spread out more rapidly in the horizontal direction. Another refinement is that the shock propagates in a two-way fashion along the orbits around x.

A particularly useful form of collaboration is between intermediators themselves. When there are several local intermediators in the same market, the establishment of communication between them can help each of them to economize on inventory, since any one of them who comes under local pressure can turn to the others for help. The same result could, of course, be achieved by a high-level intermediator, but in many cases there are too few ordinary intermediators to merit intermediation between intermediators along these lines. Links between intermediators are common in a number of sectors—the inter-bank wholesale market in the financial sector, and dealer networks in the motor trade are cases in point. Such networks have not received as much attention from economists as they deserve.

There are other ways of increasing the density of communication. An obvious strategy is to increase the size of the neighbourhood within which direct communication takes place. When each individual uses a wider range of contacts than before, people can reach each other, on average, in a shorter number of steps. Each individual plays a greater role in intermediating within his circle of acquaintances since this circle is much larger than before. Widening the circle of local acquaintances has the same sort of effect as local intermediation, but the effect is achieved without having full-time specialists in this role. This form of extended social networking is relatively uncommon in the West, but is more usual in Japan.

2.8. The information intensity of coordination

Material changes in the environment are not the only kind of shock that can affect the economic system. As noted in Section 2.2, changes in perceptions can disturb the economy too. Suppose a change occurs which initially goes unrecognized. If the change is for the worse, and the situation goes uncorrected, then symptoms of 'ill health' in the economy will begin to appear. Diagnosis of these symptoms may then lead to recognition of the change. In the light of this, corrective action may be taken and the situation returned to normal.

If the change affords an opportunity rather than a problem, however, then the symptoms may be more difficult to recognize. This is particularly true where opportunities for trade are concerned. One reason why intermediators are normally required to establish trade is that the opportunities are so difficult to recognize. The difficulty lies principally in the wide range of information that needs to be synthesized, and its highly subjective nature. Even in bilateral barter, the information requirements are relatively high. Discovering and exploiting an opportunity for multilateral trade is even more of a challenge.

Consider, for example, two individuals, a and b, initially locked by mutual ignorance into a no-trade situation of mutual self-sufficiency. Individual a is good at producing commodity 1 but prefers to consume commodity 2. Individual b represents the converse of this: he is good at producing commodity 2 but likes consuming commodity 1. It would be advantageous for individual a to produce commodity 1 for individual b to consume, and for individual b to reciprocate by producing commodity 2 for individual a to consume. In the absence of intermediation, however, individual b produces commodity 2 for his own consumption because he does not know how to find a market for commodity 1. He is self-sufficient in commodity 2, whilst individual a is self-sufficient in commodity 1.

A necessary condition for Pareto-efficiency is that marginal rates of substitution are equalized. For any pair of commodities, the marginal rate of substitution in consumption must be the same for both parties. The marginal rates of substitution in production must be equal too, for otherwise gains from mutual specialization in production are being lost. Finally, the marginal rate of substitution in consumption for each individual should equal their marginal rate of substitution in production. If this condition is not satisfied then they will gain by producing and consuming more of one good and less of another. (These conditions vary slightly if the quantity of some commodity can be changed only in discrete units, or if it is not produced or consumed at all.)

These conditions are not satisfied under the initial state of self-sufficiency. To equalize the marginal rates of substitution trade must occur: individual a must specialize in producing commodity 1 for export to individual b, while individual b must specialize in producing commodity 2 for export to individual a.

Coordination through trade consists, as this example shows, of a set of *interrelated substitutions*. Each substitution is governed by a marginal rate. It is differences between these marginal rates that afford opportunities for coordination. It follows that identification of a coordination opportunity requires information about these marginal rates. It is not information about a single marginal rate that is important, because the condition for efficiency is not that the marginal rate attains a particular value, but that it should be equal to other marginal rates. To test for equality at least two different marginal rates need to be known. A synthesis of information about marginal rates is therefore required to identify a coordination opportunity (Richardson, 1960).

In this example, four different marginal rates of substitution have to be known in order to obtain a full picture of the situation. This is only a relatively simple case, however. As the number of individuals multiplies, the number of relevant marginal rates increases *pro rata*. As the number of commodities increases the number of marginal rates increases even faster because of the many different pairwise permutations that become possible. Despite the economies of specialization, therefore, the demands of synthesis become very severe.

Consider, for example, a three-person three-commodity economy. It is a natural generalization of the two-person two-commodity economy discussed above. Each individual again specializes in producing a particular kind of good. Individual *a* specializes in commodity 1 and individual *b* in commodity 2, just as before, while the new individual, *c*, specializes in producing the new commodity, 3. The natural outcome of such specialization is the pattern of trade illustrated on the left-hand side of Fig. 2.9. Individual *a* exports 1 to *b* in return for 2, and exports 1 to *c* in return for 3. In general, each individual exports to the other two and receives a different import from them in return. To highlight the multilateral nature of trade, however, it is useful to focus on the simpler case shown on the right of Fig. 2.9. Here each individual likes only two of the three commodities: the commodity he produces and one other. Individual *a* likes commodity 3 but not commodity 2, *b* likes 1 but not 3, and *c* likes 2 but not 1. Coordination then requires the simple pattern of multilateral trade shown on the right-hand side of Fig. 2.9. Individual *a* exports 1 to *b*, *b* exports 2 to *c*, and *c* exports 3 to 1. Each individual pays the other with exports provided by a third party.

In this three-person three-commodity economy there are eighteen different marginal rates of substitution. Each of the three individuals has six different rates, three concerned with consumption and three with production. The three rates relate to substitutions between commodities 1 and 2, 2 and 3, and 3 and 1. Initially there is no communication between the indi-

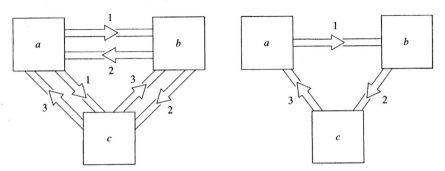

FIG. 2.9. *Derivation of a simplified structure of multilateral trade*

Note: The numbers adjacent to the arrows indicate the commodity which is being exported.

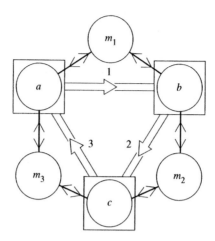

FIG. 2.10. *Complementary intermediation establishes multilateral trade*

viduals, as Fig. 2.9 shows. Achieving a full synthesis of information has become a formidable task.

The most obvious way of simplifying the problem is to break down the cycle of trade into a number of different stages and to allow each stage to be carried out independently of the others. This allows different intermediators to specialize in different aspects of what for any one of them would be a formidable task. To see how this could work, suppose that there are three intermediators involved in the creation of trade. Each intermediator knows only the marginal rates of substitution for the individuals with whom he deals.

The situation is illustrated in Fig. 2.10. Intermediator m_1 realizes that individual a's marginal rate of substitution in production between commodities 1 and 3 is different from individual b's marginal rate of substitution between them in consumption. He arranges for individual a to specialize in producing commodity 1 instead of commodity 3 on the understanding that the commodity 3 he would have produced will be made available by individual b in return for exports of commodity 1. This plan is incomplete, however, in the sense that there is no guarantee that individual b can get hold of the requisite amount of commodity 3. The plan does not specify that individual b should produce it himself, nor does it specify where else it might have come from.

The second intermediator, m_2, knows that individual b's marginal rate of substitution in production between commodities 1 and 2 is different from individual c's marginal rate of substitution between them in consumption. He arranges for individual b to specialize in producing commodity 2 instead of commodity 1 on the understanding that the commodity that he would have produced is made available by individual c in return for exports of commodity 2. This plan is also incomplete because it does not specify how individual c is going to get hold of commodity 1.

The third (and final) intermediator, m_3, knows that individual c's marginal rate of substitution in production between commodity 2 and commodity 3 is different from individual a's corresponding marginal rate of substitution in consumption. He arranges for individual c to specialize in producing commodity 3 instead of commodity 2 on the understanding that individual a will make available the commodity 2 forgone in return for exports of commodity 3. This plan too is incomplete because it does not specify where individual a's supplies of commodity 2 are coming from.

Each of these partial plans complements the others: if all three plans are implemented simultaneously then they reproduce the integrated plan. Individual a exports commodity 1 to individual b; individual b exports commodity 2 to individual c; while individual c exports commodity 3 to individual a. Each individual specializes in the production of an export good in which he has a comparative advantage, and consumes imports of the good which he most prefers.

The incompleteness of the plan leaves an unresolved administrative problem about the way that exporters are paid. Although individual a is importing good 3 from individual c, it is actually individual b who has promised to make delivery of good 3 (in return for his supplies of good 1). Similarly, although individual b is importing good 1 from individual a, it is actually individual c who has promised to deliver good 1 (in return for his supplies of good 2). Finally, although individual c is importing good 2 from individual b, it is actually individual a who has promised to deliver good 2 (in return for his supplies of good 3).

The difficulty stems from the fact that the compensation principle has been implemented through bilateral barter. Implementation is bilateral because the original integrated plan of multilateral trade has been disintegrated to reduce the demands for information synthesis. The administrative requirement for the final integration of the separate plans is that the interlocking obligations must be sorted out. There are various ways in which this can be done.

The most cumbersome solution is for each individual to buy up the goods that he needs to settle his debts. Thus individual a buys commodity 2 from individual b in order to pass it on to individual c. Individual b buys commodity 3 from individual c in order to pass it on to individual a. Finally, individual c buys commodity 1 from individual a in order to pass it on to individual b. In order to pay for his delivery of commodity 2, individual a must offer something else in return. Whatever it is he offers, individual b can use it to pay for his delivery of commodity 3, and individual c can then use it to pay for his delivery of commodity 1. So this commodity finishes up again with individual a. Trade has therefore been completed by a two-stage barter procedure, in which the first stage gets people to produce the right goods and the second stage gets the right people to consume them.

The obvious disadvantage of this arrangement is that goods are no longer directly exported to the people who require them. They are exported to the people from whom imports are received, who then pass them on to other people. A much simpler alternative involves the use of inventories. Each individual holds an inventory of the good in which payment is made. These inventories are never used up but are simply circulated amongst the people involved. The use of inventories to settle payments separates the settlement of payments from the export of goods, and so restores the simplicity of the previous pattern of trade.

The simplest arrangement of this type is one in which each individual begins by holding an inventory of a good that he neither produces nor likes to consume. Individual a holds an inventory of commodity 2 which he uses to pay individual c for his imports of commodity 3. Individual b holds an inventory of commodity 3 which he uses to pay individual a for his imports of commodity 1; and individual c holds an inventory of commodity 1 which he uses to pay individual b for his imports of commodity 2. Settlement is effected simply by moving the inventory around. The goods that are eventually consumed get transported only once, instead of twice, because it is the inventory that gets transported the second time instead. If goods deteriorate in transport then it will be the inventory goods, which are never consumed, that deteriorate, rather than the export goods, which are consumed. Payment by inventory therefore improves the quality of consumer goods.

Payment by inventory is of far greater significance than this, however, because it leads directly to the concept of money as a specialized medium of exchange. Because the inventory is never consumed, there is flexibility over the form that the inventory can take. Economies of standardization can be achieved by replacing the different types of inventory with just a single type. For analytical convenience this type will be labelled commodity 4. All agreements then stipulate that payment will be made in terms of commodity 4. Thus individual a pays individual c for supplies of commodity 3 by offering commodity 4 in return, and the other individuals follow a similar approach.

Standardization of the means of payment offers a number of advantages (Goodhart, 1975). To begin with, the settlement system reproduces itself in a convenient manner. When the settlement process has been completed, the distribution of the inventory is the same as it was before. When different commodities are held by different individuals this is not the case. Each commodity cycles round between different individuals and returns to its original holder only after three periods. Three different payment arrangements are therefore required, each corresponding to a particular configuration of inventory-holding with which the period may begin. When commodity 4 is used it is only the different units of commodity 4 that are in different places at the end of the process: the quantity held by each individual is the same. Provided commodity 4 is homogeneous, therefore, the initial distribution and the final distribution are effectively the same. The same set of payment arrangements can therefore be made in each successive period.

A further consequence of homogeneity is that the inventory can be readily stored in a central place such as a bank. There is no need to actually move the inventory around. It is sufficient to relabel the ownership of the inventory while it remains in the central store. From a purely physical point of view, heterogeneous inventory can also be centrally stored, of course, but much greater trust is required of the owners in this case. Each individual may fear that their account is being debited with the better units and credited with the worse units unless they can personally supervise the settlement process at the bank.

Central storage is only effective, however, when communication costs are low. Standardization is the key here; it permits a single specialized means of payment to be chosen with the requirements of both transport and communication specifically in mind. These requirements identify the familiar functional requirements of money: durability, portability, divisibility, and so on.

Standardization makes it unnecessary to specify in detail the means of payment. Furthermore, since all transactions involve the same means of payment, this means of payment becomes the natural unit of account. It is therefore natural to express all marginal rates of substitution in terms of substitution between every other good on the one hand and the unit of account on the other. The marginal rate of substitution in consumption, when expressed in units of account, becomes the demand price, while the marginal rate of substitution in production, when expressed in units of account, becomes cost or, equivalently, supply price. The efficiency criterion equating the marginal rate of substitution in consumption to the marginal rate of substitution in production thus becomes the condition that demand price and supply price should be equal.

Expressing all marginal rates of substitution in terms of the same good provides a parsimonious way of summarizing information on marginal rates of substitution in general. The marginal rate of substitution between any two goods can be calculated as the ratio of their respective marginal rates of substitution against the unit of account. This means, in effect, that the crucial information required for intermediation consists of the demand prices and the supply prices described above. If the demand price for a commodity exceeds its supply price then an opportunity for coordination exists. In particular, if one person's demand price exceeds another person's supply price then there is an opportunity for them to trade. Conversely, if the prices are equal then coordination is not required.

2.9. The appropriation of rents through negotiation

The intermediators do for real the job that would otherwise have to be done by the hypothetical Walrasian auctioneer. The Walrasian auctioneer incurs no information costs, and behaves in an altruistic manner, as noted in Section 2.3 above. By contrast the intermediators incur real costs and are not motivated purely by altruism. They need rents of some sort to cover their costs of collecting information.

They could be rewarded for their services out of tax revenues collected by the state. It is generally agreed, however, that the state would find it difficult to judge the quality of the information they supply. The effort involved in assessing every item of information submitted for payment would be phenomenal, unless just a few items of great significance were involved, as discussed below. It would seem more appropriate for the intermediator to sell the information directly to the traders who will benefit from its use.

The problem here is that an intermediator does not own the information in the sense of possessing an exclusive legal right to its use. In selling the information to the users he cannot tell them about the product in advance of the sale, for they can then remember what he told them and avoid paying him for the information. But, on the other hand, if they do not know what the information is that is on offer then they will be reluctant to buy it. It may be something they already know, which is therefore valueless to them. It may be something completely wrong, made up specially to sell as a bogus product, or it may simply be the result of incompetent investigation. The intermediator cannot offer evidence to reassure the traders because that would give the information away. This is, essentially, a problem of quality control created by the lack of property rights in information. The seller of the information resorts to secrecy in order to protect his interests and the buyer cannot therefore evaluate the product. A standard response where ordinary commodities is concerned is for the seller to offer a sample to the buyer, but this is unsatisfactory in this context because information is a satiation good—the buyer only needs a single unit and so supplying a sample destroys the demand.

Under these circumstances the natural response is for the intermediator to integrate forward into the exploitation of the information. He intervenes in the trading process by negotiating with the seller to buy the product, and simultaneously negotiating with the buyer to sell the product. By keeping the buyer and seller apart through separate negotiations he is able to appropriate a margin between the buying price and the selling price. This margin is equivalent to the tax he could levy on the trade if he had a regular property right to the information.

It is worth noting that in this strategy secrecy has a dual role. It is important in excluding other people from the use of the information, as noted above, but it is also crucial in sustaining the intermediator's bargaining power. By the time the intermediator negotiates with the buyer and the seller his cost of collecting information about the trading opportunity is a sunk cost. If both the buyer and the seller recognize this then the intermediator is in a weak position. This applies whether he is seeking to buy and resell the product, or whether he is seeking to license the use of his information to the buyer and seller together.

The intermediator has two main factors in his favour as he attempts to extract rents for himself through the negotiation process. The first is that he knows all the relevant marginal rates of substitution, as reflected in the demand price and the supply price, whereas the buyer and seller know only the marginal rates of substitution that pertain to themselves. The seller does not know for how much the intermediator can resell the product, nor does the buyer know how much the intermediator can purchase it for. It is therefore easier for the intermediator to bluff the traders than the other way round.

The second factor is that the intermediator can build a reputation more easily than the traders can. If the intermediator specializes in collecting and synthesizing information then he is involved in trade on a regular basis. He therefore has a record that he can point to which underpins the claims he makes about his negotiation strategy. It is therefore more economic for an intermediator to invest in a hard-line no-compromise reputation, at the risk of losing a few trades, than it is for an ordinary trader to do so.

The intervention of the intermediator in the process of trade alters the structure of information flow. The intermediators as well as the ordinary transactors now communicate with the bank, since they too must make payments for the goods in which they trade. The situation is illustrated schematically in Fig. 2.11. The bank z is at the centre of the network of traders a, b, c who trade indirectly with each other through the intermediators m_1, m_2, and m_3. Individual a exports goods to individual b through the intermediator m_1. In return, m_1 pays individual a, his supplier, by crediting his account with z. Intermediator m_1's account is in turn credited by individual b with the payment for the goods m_1 has resold to him. The cycle is completed when individual a uses his account to pay intermediator m_3 for goods produced by individual c.

2.10. Competitive threats and the coordination plan

There is another factor that an intermediator can turn to his advantage in his negotiations with traders, although it requires additional investment in information if it is to work. The intermediator can build flexibility into his coordination plan. His plan may involve two different buyers and two different sellers, for example. The buyers and sellers can then be played off

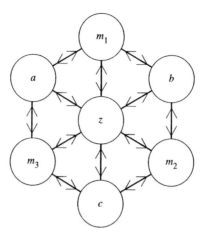

FIG. 2.11. *'Hub and spoke' communication network created by the use of a banking system to support intermediated trade*

against each other in the negotiation process. Each seller is informed that there is an alternative source of supply that will be used if he takes too hard a line, and each buyer is told that there is an alternative source of demand. The buyers have to be kept apart from each other, of course, as do the sellers, to avoid collusion—just as the single buyer and the single seller had to be kept apart to begin with to avoid the intermediator being cut out altogether.

Pursuing this approach systematically is liable to increase information costs quite significantly, however, particularly as the intermediator has to get in touch with people increasingly far from his own locality. This suggests a rather different tactic: namely to collect information on systematic factors that impact on traders as a whole, and to rely on statistical averages to match up supply and demand. Instead of building separate linkages between individual traders, the intermediator builds a whole family of possible linkages in one step. Instead of collecting a large amount of detailed information, he collects a small amount of information at a higher level of aggregation. He creates trade by advertising his intention to buy and sell, inviting prospective traders to approach him, instead of approaching them individually himself. Rather than researching their individual marginal rates of substitution he uses the threat of competition to persuade the traders to reveal what their true marginal rates of substitution are. He cannot force a fully accurate revelation of information in this way. All he can normally do is to quote a uniform buying price and a uniform selling price, and announce that he is indifferent from whom he buys or to whom he sells at these prices. Each buyer and seller therefore knows that he faces competition from other buyers and sellers at the relevant quoted price.

Buyers and sellers are therefore induced to tell the truth about how their own valuation compares to the price. They do not reveal their exact valuation, but by placing their order (or refusing to do so) they reveal important detailed information which it could have been expensive to collect directly.

There are, of course, numerous refinements of this approach. Discriminatory prices may be charged if categories of people with different elasticities of demand can be readily distinguished. Inventory can be held to accommodate the short run mismatches between demand and supply which tend to be amplified when prices are fixed in advance. The important thing though, is that the intermediator has a strategic incentive to extend the scope of his coordination plan in such a way that he can negotiate with the owners of relevant resources in a competitive environment. The particular way in which rents have to be extracted from information in a private enterprise economy biases intermediators to develop coordination plans that can be implemented under competitive conditions in this way.

2.11. The financing of coordination

The picture of the intermediator that emerges from the preceding discussion is of someone who acts as a nexus of contracts. He constructs a set of multilateral arrangements by negotiating separate bilateral contracts with other parties. In this respect the intermediator resembles the market-making firm. He also resembles 'the firm as a nexus of treaties', as described by Aoki and Williamson (1991). Many firms are indeed simply intermediators cloaked in a corporate legal identity. It is not surprising to discover that the logic of the coordination process leads the intermediator to resemble the firm in other ways as well.

One of the similarities is in the need for finance. The need for finance is often explained in terms of the need to purchase capital equipment. This reflects a characteristic emphasis in economics on the firm as a production unit (see Chapter 1). Quite apart from the fact that capital equipment can be rented or leased rather than purchased outright, this ignores a more fundamental reason why firms need finance. This is because intermediation is normally a sequential process. It is not just that different intermediators intervene in sequence, but that each intermediator acts sequentially too. The firm needs to buy before it can resell, for example, and this creates a demand for working capital. Intermediation does not have to be a sequential process—it is possible, in principle, for all contracts to be completed simultaneously, and for each contract to be conditioned on the successful completion of all the others. This would impose great inconvenience on the people with whom the intermediator was dealing, however. It could also lead to delays which would allow other intermediators to discover similar information and set up a rival coordination plan.

If the intermediator had enormous reputation then he could create his own capital for himself. His own promise to pay would be just as good as a payment itself. In this case the intermediator could defer settling with his suppliers until his revenue had been obtained. Without this reputation, however, he must pay promptly in cash—or at least in a paper currency issued by someone more reputable than himself. If his personal fortune is large then no problem is involved. Otherwise the intermediator must seek external sources of finance.

The danger here lies with the appropriation of the value of his information. Financial backers will need reassurance over the way the funds are to be used. In the absence of suitable collateral, such as land and buildings, they will need to know about the coordination plan. Once he has shared his information with his prospective backers, however, the intermediator faces a potential rival who has both the information and the funds, while he still has only the information itself. Financial backers therefore need a reputation for integrity—they must keep other people's coordination plans confidential, and refrain from entering into intermediation of the same kind themselves. Otherwise intermediators will be afraid to approach them for funds. Banks who finance intermediation must therefore maintain a reputation as 'honest brokers'.

Even if the bank, or other financial backer, approves of the coordination plan, things can still go wrong because the plan cannot be completely specified at the outset. Scope for judgement will still remain in the implementation of the plan, and the bank may lose confidence in the intermediator if mistakes are made. Loans may therefore be advanced only on a short-term basis, giving the bank effective power to bring in a receiver to run the firm if it wants, through the simple strategy of not renewing the loan. Any financial backer can insist on non-executive representation on the board, possibly with the power to out-vote the intermediator (if the intermediator is a minority owner) or to dismiss him if he is also an employee. External finance always has its price in terms of managerial independence; investing a personal fortune, and growing the firm through re-investment of profit, is the only real guarantee of autonomy for the intermediator.

2.12. Visionary innovation

The emphasis throughout this chapter has been on the tension between the economy-wide nature of coordination that exists in theory, and the limited and localized synthesis of information that underpins coordination in practice. It has been shown how the need to economize on information costs leads to a single integrated coordination plan being replaced by a set of localized coordination plans, some of which will overlap and some of which will not. The boundary of each plan's implementation is set by the increasing costs of synthesizing information from a wider area. Even with specialized synthesis the costs will increase as the field of coordination expands. Furthermore, a local plan may itself emerge as a retrospective rationalization of apparently uncoordinated acts: thus a single trade promoted by an intermediator may throw individual inventories out of equilibrium and so encourage other intermediators to complete the remaining sequence of trades that is required.

Given the myopic nature of such intermediation, the only thing that can sometimes be said in the intermediators' favour is that they are less myopic than the traders themselves, who know practically nothing about their environment except what they learn through the intermediators' offers. It is possible, though, that from time to time heroic individuals in the Schumpeterian mould emerge (Schumpeter, 1934). These intermediators may have a vision which transcends the confines of a single locality or even a single market. Such a visionary may have plans to introduce a new technology which, by combining inputs in different proportions, simultaneously impacts upon an entire set of markets. He may plan to open up a new shipping route, or railway line, along which all sorts of traffic can be carried. This will simultaneously integrate regional markets for a whole range of different commodities. As a final example, he may create a new utility industry, or dramatically expand capacity in an existing one, thereby creating new substitution possibilities in a range of industries or, at very least increasing the flexibility of the economy by augmenting spare capacity in an existing industry. Visions of this kind can not only change the industrial structure of the economy but also alter the parameters which govern the nature of the coordination process itself.

Entrepreneurial vision of this kind is likely to be formulated at a fairly high degree of aggregation and to be based on the synthesis of permanent rather than transitory information (see Chapter 3). Because it is wide-ranging, it is very likely that the implementation of one vision of this kind will impact significantly on the implementation of another vision of the same kind carried out at about the same time. In contrast to purely local plans, the gains from optimizing the interactions between two visionary plans are likely to be large compared to the additional information costs involved.

This suggests that the coordination of large-scale innovations should be organized in some suitable way. When organization is mentioned there is a tendency to think immediately of the firm. A straightforward application of this idea suggests that potential innovators would become employees of a single very large firm. The top management of this firm would then decide which innovations should proceed and which should not on the basis of the complementarities and the substitution possibilities between them. The danger with this approach is that is discourages the innovators from putting forward their ideas because their ideas become the property of the firm, and the only reward for the innovator is additional salary or promotion, offered at the employer's discretion. In any case, most firms are designed to handle routine forms of coordination rather than to assess unique and imaginative proposals submitted on an intermittent basis. Unless the concept of the firm is radically altered, therefore, it is quite likely that top management will lack the skills to judge the plans correctly (Buckley and Casson, 1992).

There are more flexible ways in which this objective could be achieved, however. One of them is to vest all authority to proceed with large-scale plans with the state, but leave the risks and rewards to accrue to the entrepreneur. Special licences or charters may be required, as was common two or three centuries ago (see Chapter 9). The objections to this are well-known, however. Most of them hinge at some point on an alleged lack of entrepreneurial vision amongst the employees of a state bureaucracy. Whether this problem is endemic, or simply a consequence of the recruit-ment practices of state institutions and the cultural attitudes that underpin them, is debatable, however.

Another possibility is to throw the responsibility for coordination upon industrial banks or institutional investors whose decisions over loans and the underwriting of share issues are crucial to the viability of visionary projects. One approach is to mandate different banks to oversee the launch of visionary projects in particular sectors of the economy—chemicals, heavy engineering, transport infrastructure, and so on—provided, of course, that they liaise over projects whose effects spill over into one another's areas. One of the difficulties here is that the banks' own judgements may be clouded by conflicts and ambiguities in their responsibilities to their clients, their shareholders and the state.

A third possibility, and perhaps the most attractive one, is to persuade the visionary entrepreneurs to share their ideas with each other. The prob-lem here arises from the use of secrecy as an exclusion device. Each entre-preneur's idea is of potential value to the others. If he is to share his idea with them then he needs to be able to trust them not to poach it, or to exploit it in competition with himself. Unlike 'honest brokers' such as banks, other entrepreneurs may not have given any undertaking to refrain from poaching of this kind.

Under these circumstances a great deal depends upon the culture of the entrepreneurial elite. If the entrepreneurs feel that they belong to the same family—either literally, because of common ancestry, or metaphorically, because of common schooling or common religion—then they may be willing to trust each other. Each entrepreneur trusts the others not to steal his ideas, and the others can therefore trust that entrepreneur to tell the truth. The entrepreneurs appropriate rents by maintaining secrecy, not at the individual level, but as a group (see Chapter 4).

The advantages of this arrangement are greater the wider the boundaries of the group are drawn. A group that spans all major industrial sectors, and includes government and the major banks, is likely to be most effective. There is, however, the risk that the group merely develops into a cartel. Apart from the consequences for the distribution of income, inefficiencies are likely to arise from the exclusion of potentially promising new entrepreneurs. The wider the group, the more power it has to exclude new entrepreneurs by refusing them supplies of key inputs, and denying them finance, etc. Given the need to trust new recruits it is quite appropriate that they should be carefully screened, but inappropriate that they should be denied entry on grounds other than competence and trust. The problem can be overstated, however. If the aim of the group is to exploit interdependencies between complementary innovations, and not merely to inhibit the wasteful duplication of substitute innovations, then it is in everyone's interests to welcome entrepreneurs with new ideas into the group.

A common culture of the kind that underpins high trust tends to improve the clarity of communication too. Culture standardizes the assumptions people make about the environment, and therefore helps them to construe the messages they receive from other people correctly. Culture therefore reduces information costs not only by making messages more honest and reliable, but by making them more readily understood as well. An economy with an effective culture will therefore face lower information costs and so find it easier to coordinate its innovations. The innovation process will not be so localized and sequential as it can be when information costs are high.

This does not mean that when culture is weak there will be no attempt at coordination at all. Individual entrepreneurs will still conjecture what other entrepreneurs are likely to do, and they may even invest in collecting information to improve the accuracy of these conjectures. No entrepreneur, however, will be really sure what conjectures other people are making about them. Moreover, in the absence of any definite information, there will be a tendency for entrepreneurs to assume that no other entrepreneur will be making a complementary innovation, and therefore to perceive the principal strategic issue as one of deterring imitation instead. This encourages pre-emptive innovations, which are premature in the sense that they would have been more successful if the entrepreneur had waited for complementary innovations to become ready as well. Coordination will therefore be less complete than if each entrepreneur had systematically informed the others of what he planned to do.

2.13. The supply of information

It has been clearly established by now that coordination may be a relatively uncoordinated process. This is true of the coordination of material flow through multilateral trade. It is even more true of the coordination of innovations, because costs of communication are exacerbated by secrecy. It can now be shown that it is even true of the supply of information itself. Whatever the source of information, its supply needs to be coordinated, and so the question of the optimal degree of coordination arises in this context too.

It was shown in Chapter 1 that the supply of information for routine coordination tasks is organized by market-making firms. But what about the non-routine information required for innovation? How is the supply of that coordinated? Is there a larger kind of organization at the national or international level which coordinates the search for information? In general, there is not. Undiscovered information is unappropriated territory. In a free society anyone can search for it wherever they like. It is possible to go further, and assert that undiscovered information often lies in uncharted territory—uncharted in the sense that there are no reference points, or grid lines, to divide up the territory where the discoveries may lie. The various branches of new knowledge cannot be defined in advance with sufficient accuracy to allow highly specific areas of investigation to be 'staked out'. Even if it were thought politically acceptable to parcel out territory for particular investigators to monopolize, it would not usually be possible to define the boundaries with sufficient accuracy to enforce territorial rights effectively. There are already enough difficulties over the circumvention of patents, which relate to ideas that have already been discovered, to alert society to the difficulty of extending the same principle to undiscovered knowledge too.

The uncharted territory is so wide that it is difficult for investigators to find out who else is searching in it. To find out about others they must belong to a professional association or amateur leisure interest group through which they can meet other people who are likely to be doing the same sort of thing.

Furthermore, there is no guarantee that if the number of people already in the field is known that this number will converge to a social optimum. Because the right to investigate is freely available, the expected reward of the marginal investigator is equal to the average reward for the investigators as a whole—provided all investigators are of equal ability, of course. This creates an 'externality' problem. Any new investigator who enters a territory damages the interests of those already in it by reducing the odds that they will find any given item of information first. Part of the entrant's expected gain is therefore a loss incurred by other people that he does not have to compensate them for (Casson, 1994a).

It is reasonable to suppose that the principle of diminishing marginal returns applies to prospecting for information just as it does to other activities. In a given state of knowledge there is only a certain number of further discoveries that can be made in a given time, and as the number of searchers increases the probability that one of them discovers something that the others would not have discovered becomes increasingly slight. With diminishing marginal returns to prospecting, the average rate of return always exceeds the marginal rate of return, and so the number of searchers will tend to be excessive when it is governed by the average rate.

There is a complication, however, which arises from the possibility that the private gains from discovery could be dissipated altogether if two or more people make the same discovery at the same time. If they agree to collude then they can share the rewards between them, but if they cannot agree on this then competition may break out between them instead. Since the costs of discovery are essentially sunk costs, competition will drive down the rents they obtain from their discovery to zero. In this case private reward will be significantly less than social reward. This means that if the risk of competitive exploitation of a simultaneous discovery is great, the average private return to search may fall so far below the average social return that it is actually less than the marginal social return. In this case the numbers of searchers, far from being excessive, will actually be too low.

2.14. Conclusion

This chapter has examined selected aspects of the coordination process and their implications for information costs. It has shown that the coordination process itself is a great deal less 'coordinated' than the Walrasian model suggests. Coordination is not effected by a single economy-wide plan of trade drawn up by a Walrasian auctioneer. It is a localized process implemented in sequential fashion by intermediators who specialize in collecting information for this purpose. This arrangement is a rational response to the costs of collecting and synthesizing information.

Coordination according to the voluntary principle implies that no one can be left worse off by any coordination plan. People must therefore be compensated for any of their resources that are placed at other people's disposal. There is no problem in satisfying this principle using an economy-wide plan of multilateral trade. Without the use of money, however, the principle is difficult to apply on a bilateral basis because of the well-known problem of barter trade: finding a 'double coincidence' of wants. The problem is resolved in practice by offering money as compensation in localized coordination plans. Without the use of money, localized coordination would hardly be a practical proposition. The economical use of money is in turn promoted by a banking system. In practice, therefore, the savings in information costs realized through local coordination are dependent on the quality of the banking system.

The role of the banking system can be neatly summarized by extending the wheel of wealth diagrams introduced in Chapter 1. In Fig. 2.12 a bank

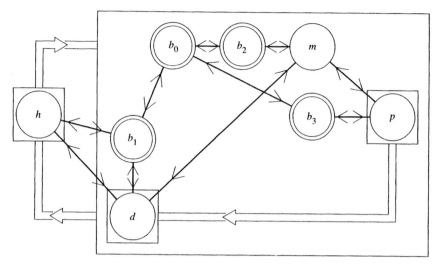

FIG. 2.12. *Role of banking in the wheel of wealth: the intermediation of payments*

is indicated by two concentric circles, which are supposed to represent the raised edges of a coin. The bank receives instructions from purchasers to make payments to suppliers by a transfer of funds between their accounts. To allow for the spatial dispersion of retail banking, it is assumed that inter-branch payments are cleared through a headquarters in the metropolis. In some cases a further stage of clearance may be required, involving a national central bank, but this is not shown in Fig. 2.12.

The flow of payments works in reverse direction to the flow of product. It is assumed that payments are made by cheque, although alternative forms of payments can be modelled using the same approach. To further simplify the diagram, the fact that cheques are normally handed over to the seller to be forwarded through the seller's bank to the purchaser's bank is ignored. The diagram simply shows the instruction to the buyer's bank that is written on the cheque, and the subsequent confirmation, on the seller's statement of account, that credit has actually been made. This corresponds to the legal position, that payment is made only when a cheque is cleared, and not when it is first received.

According to Fig. 2.12 the payment process begins when the local branch b_1 receives an instruction from the household h to pay the retailer d. The bank debits the household's account and credits the retailer's account. If the retailer banks with a different branch, however, then completion is effected by the intermediation of the headquarters b_0.

Headquarters can also back up the retailer when he pays the market-maker m for his supplies. The retailer instructs his bank b_1 to credit the market-maker's account with the bank b_2, which is a branch located in the metropolis. Since different branches are now definitely involved, headquarters is sure to intermediate. This is why b_1 and b_2 are linked only by information which flows through b_0.

Finally, the market-maker m instructs the bank b_2 to pay the producer p for his supplies, by crediting the bank b_3, located in an industrial area. This inter-branch transfer is also intermediated by headquarters. This underlines the fact that just as the market-maker intermediates the product flow, so the banking system intermediates the flow of payments that are generated by it. The figure confirms the importance of the flows of information handled by the banking system in the coordination process.

Because of the localized nature of coordination, the repercussions of any shock to the economic system tend to spread out slowly in wave-like fashion. The process is certainly not an instantaneous one. To help buffer the effects of shocks, inventories are held. Shocks propagate because when inventories are kept low people need to replenish them fairly quickly. Shocks propagate along particular channels. These channels are created by the substitution possibilities afforded by markets. Markets are not fully integrated, however, from an informational point of view. They are spatially segmented because of information costs. The sluggishness of adjustment means that individuals cannot count on trading opportunities arising as soon as they are required, and this explains why real inventories as well as money inventory must be held. The higher are information costs, the more sluggish is market adjustment, and the higher are the levels of inventory required.

A coordination plan that is novel in some respect qualifies as an innovation. Some innovations are large-scale, and may be sectoral in their scope even though they are not economy-wide. Innovations are not usually planned in great detail, however, in the sense that, say, the identity of individual buyers or individual suppliers would be known in advance. Indeed, such details may be deliberately left vague to strengthen the competitive threats that are subsequently available to the entrepreneur. The benefits of coordinating innovations seem to be much higher than for very localized coordination plans, and it is therefore strange that more is not done to take advantage of this. The obvious explanation is that the information cost of sharing such plans is very high, but this is explicable only in terms of the threat to secrecy. The absence of property rights in coordination plans makes secrecy an important appropriation mechanism. Entrepreneurs will therefore share information only if they trust other members of the elite. The culture of the elite therefore emerges as an important determinant of success in coordinating innovations.

The limitations of property rights in information are particularly acute where prospecting for new information is concerned because of the uncharted nature of the territory. Discovery takes place on 'common ground' and can lead to competitive conflicts when simultaneous discoveries are

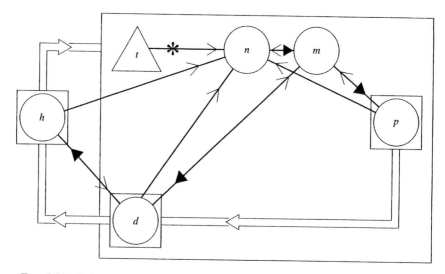

Fig. 2.13. *Role of innovation in the wheel of wealth: initiative based on feedback and synthesis of information*

made. The prohibitive cost of charting the territory, combined with the difficulty of identifying rival searchers and making agreements with them, distorts the allocation of resources to discovery. Whether the number of people engaged in prospecting is above or below the social optimum depends upon the balance of these opposing forces, and may vary from case to case.

The place of innovation in the coordination process is summarized in Fig. 2.13. Information is captured by the innovator from widely distributed sources. The innovator n taps into sources of scientific expertise indicated by the triangle t. The innovator may also get ideas from the households, h, the retailers, d, and producers, p. Much of this information may be fed back in the light of their recent experience. Households may complain about defective products they have bought, and suggest improvements in design; retailers may complain of lost sales, which could have been clinched with more reliable deliveries; whilst producers may complain of breakdowns in machinery which could be avoided by better technology. Above all, the market maker, m, reflecting on how the chain of production and distribution is working as a whole, may discern opportunities for improvement in pricing and logistics.

All of this information is put together by the innovator, n, who then takes the initiative by creating a new market, or modifying the organization of an existing market in a novel way. The solid arrow in the figure is used to indicate initiative: it shows a flow of information through which the process of coordination is initiated by a novel proposition being made. This proposition is then translated into proposals advanced by the market maker to the producers and the retailers concerned. In due course the experience gained in implementing the new proposal is fed back to make further refinements and instigate more new ideas.

3

The Nature of the Firm

3.1. Introduction

The theory of the firm has been one of the most exciting fields of economic research over the last twenty years. Yet despite a vast amount of work, no consensus has been reached on the subject. Theories of contracts, transaction costs, and entrepreneurship vie with each other to form the foundation for a truly comprehensive theory of the firm. Each of these theories has its own idea of what the key issue is, and naturally claims that it alone addresses this particular issue head on. This chapter sets out a general framework within which all the key questions in the theory of the firm can be brought together and discussed at once. It is inspired by the vision of the economy set out in Chapter 1, and builds upon the foundations of the theory of coordination set out in Chapter 2. The range of different issues discussed is summarized in Fig. 3.1: the pattern of the figure reflects the nature of the synthesis attempted in this chapter.

The framework is based upon the concept of volatility. It is supposed that the economic environment is continuously disturbed by shocks of both a persistent and transitory nature. Persistent shocks provide a stimulus to the formation of new firms or the radical restructuring of existing firms. Persistent shocks are intermittent and diverse, and are usually dealt with by improvisation. This improvisation is effected by the entrepreneur who founds the firm. By contrast, transitory shocks are repetitive and conform to a more limited number of types. They are dealt with routinely using procedures devised by the entrepreneur. Applying a division of labour to the implementation of these procedures creates the organization of the firm.

Information on shocks is costly to collect and communicate. The initial impact of shocks is localized and dispersed, which means that some people get to learn of them before others. Those 'in the know' buy up resources which have become more valuable as a result of the shock, in order to make a speculative gain. The gain is realized when the resources are deployed to a more profitable use. The most significant type of shock, so far as firms are concerned, is one which creates a new market opportunity. The shock could be a change in tastes, factor costs, technology, social values, or indeed anything that impinges on the gains from a particular type of trade. A firm

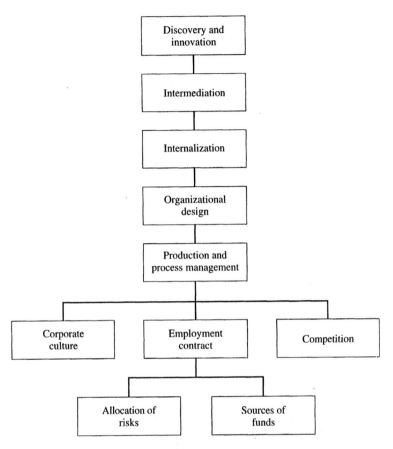

FIG. 3.1. *Related issues in the theory of the firm*

is created whenever an entrepreneur speculates that certain resources—including labour time—should be acquired in order to create a new market of some kind.

Market opportunities normally have to be realized through intermediation. Intermediation reduces transaction costs which would otherwise inhibit trade, as explained in Chapter 1. It is also a profit-extraction mechanism for the entrepreneur. The organization of intermediation has many different aspects, which are explained below; it is these different aspects that are followed up in different theories of the firm. Embedding all these issues in a common framework clarifies the connections between them. It also reveals a common theme—namely the importance of synthesizing information and of ensuring that the information that is synthesized is true. It is the synthesis of different kinds of persistent information that brings firms into being, and it is their skill in subsequently synthesizing transitory information which, together with the quality of the initial synthesis, governs their long-run success.

There are two main reasons, it seems, why this general framework has not been presented before. One is that economic theories of the firm have placed too much emphasis on production and too little on market-making. This in turn reflects an excessive concern with material flow in conventional economics, and too little concern with information flow instead. The second is that theories concerned with the formation of firms—such as theories of entrepreneurship—have remained somewhat divorced from theories of the routine operation of firms found in the literature on organizational behaviour and operational research. This has meant that the synthesis of persistent information discussed in the former theoretical tradition has not been integrated with the synthesis of transitory information considered in the latter. While the principle of synthesis is quite explicit in the former, it is only implicit in the latter, and so the connection has proved difficult to make.

3.2. Defining the firm

An unnecessary source of confusion in the theory of the firm stems from the lack of consensus on a suitable definition of the firm. Because of the sheer diversity of legal forms that a firm can take, a purely inductive approach to defining the firm is of little use. It is necessary to identify 'firm-like' qualities independently of what any particular real world firm happens to be like. From an economic point of view the most useful way of defining an institution such as the firm is in terms of the function it performs. 'The firm is what the firm does' in other words. But what exactly does the firm do?

According to Coase (1937), the firm is a co-ordinator. The market is a co-ordinator too, but unlike the market, where responsibility is dispersed through negotiations, the firm concentrates this responsibility upon itself. The firm may therefore be defined as an institution which specializes in coordination using a single locus of responsibility. Firms exist as 'islands of conscious power' in an 'ocean of unconscious cooperation' because, for some sets of activities, this approach to coordination is superior to others (Robertson, 1923, p. 85).

This definition needs to be amplified, however. The essence of coordination is decision-making. The firm is therefore a specialized decision-making unit. Specialization is effected when the firm takes decisions about resources which it does not itself supply and about resources which it does not itself consume. Unlike an individual worker, the firm does not decide how to allocate its own labour time; rather it decides how to allocate labour time purchased from others. In the same way the firm, unlike an individual consumer, does not decide how best to consume certain goods, but how best to allocate the goods it owns between the consumers who would like to purchase them.

But what is the point in an entity that does not work itself acquiring the rights to labour, and an entity that does not consume itself acquiring products whose value ultimately derives from consumption by other people? The answer lies in the improvement in the quality of the decisions that results when the firm rather than the worker decides how labour time shall be allocated and the firm rather than the consumer decides on the ultimate sources from which goods shall be procured.

But how does this improvement in the quality of decisions occur? It arises because the firm has information at its disposal that other people lack. Even if it does not have the information immediately to hand, it has the capacity to acquire this information when needed at lower cost than other people.

A methodological problem arises here, however, because decisions are actually taken by people and not by impersonal entities such as firms. What the firm can do, however, is to structure the activities of the different people who participate in the decision-making process, so that their individual contributions to the decision-making process are made in the most effective way. The firm, in other words, is essentially a structure designed to harmonize the decision-making efforts of a group of people who are focused on a single issue or set of related issues.

Where an individual is confronted with a one-off decision it may not be worthwhile to transfer the responsibility for the decision to a firm. The set up cost that is involved may outweigh any benefit to the individual from the support of the firm. Where recurrent decisions are required, however, the value of the prospective stream of benefits from improved decisions may well outweigh the set up cost. It becomes economic to vest decision-making responsibilities in a firm. Because the set up cost requires time to pay back, continuity of operation is one of the hallmarks of the firm.

The firm is more that just a structure, however. From a legal point of view the firm is a kind of fictional person which can acquire, hold and dispose of property in its own right. This legal fiction is a rational institutional response to the function of the firm. When the firm needs to acquire command of labour services in order to control their use it can do so by purchasing labour time. Likewise, when the firm needs to dispose of the product on which labour has done its work it can do so by selling it. In this way it generates revenue which can be used to cover the cost of the labour it hires.

But is this fiction really necessary, it may be asked. If the decisions are taken by a single individual, for example, can this individual not buy labour services and sell the product on his own account? Why does he need to operate inside the 'legal shell' of the firm? The answer lies in three legal privileges normally conferred by the corporate form, namely limited liability, indefinite life, and the right to set off purchases of inputs against revenues from output when assessing liability for tax. The advantages of limited liability to a risk-averse individual are fairly obvious, although there are disadvantages too: shifting risk to creditors could conceivably damage the financial reputation of the firm. Since limited liability is only an option, however, it is available to those who wish to take advantage of it without detriment to those who do not. The unlimited life of the firm allows its contractual rights and obligations to survive the death of its owner and so permits the structure to be perpetuated by his heirs or his trustees. So far as taxation is concerned, most tax systems aim to tax consumption. If an individual employed a worker in a personal capacity, the expenditure could be interpreted as a form of consumption. By employing the worker through a firm the employer makes clear that the expenditure must be set off against revenue so that only the profit is liable for tax.

In the light of this discussion, a firm may be defined as a specialized decision-making unit, whose function is to improve coordination by structuring information flow, and which is normally endowed with legal privileges, including indefinite life. There are, of course, many other common characteristics of firms, but these are best regarded as following from the implications of this definition rather than being elements of the definition itself.

3.3. The firm as a user of information

A person who takes a decision must be motivated to collect the information that is needed (see Chapter 1), and this means that they must bear some of the consequences of the decision. Thus the right to take decisions about a resource is normally ascribed to the owner of the resource. Thus people who have the relevant information already, or can collect it more cheaply than others, have an advantage as owners of a resource. They can afford to bid away the resource from others who lack this information or would find it more costly to collect. The advantage conferred on the firm by its structuring of information flow allows it to out-bid ordinary individuals for ownership of certain types of resource, and that is how these resources come to be within the control of the firm.

But why should certain people have better access to information than others? Information has the property of a public good, in the sense that supplying information to someone else does not reduce the supplier's access to it. Information is easy to share, in other words. In this case, why does everyone not have access to the same information?

The sharing of information is restricted in two ways. The first is by the cost of communication. When sources of information are localized and costs of communication are high, those who are closest to these sources can obtain information more cheaply than others (Hayek, 1937; Richardson, 1960). The second is a contractual problem. Sources of information may be costly to discover. In a private enterprise economy people can only specialize in the discovery of information if they can generate an income from this information. Selling information is extremely difficult, however, for the reason explained in Chapter 2.

But just as information incurs costs of communication, so ordinary resources incur transport costs when they are moved from the custody of one owner to the custody of another. Ordinary resources encounter contractual problems too. So why transfer the ownership of a resource to the person who has the relevant information rather than transfer the relevant information to the person who has the resource? In other words, why is the acquisition of resources explained by the distribution of information amongst prospective owners rather than the acquisition of information explained by the distribution of resource ownership instead?

The answer is that information is more costly to trade than most other resources. Resource ownership therefore moves to the information source, rather than the other way round. This is a special case of the more general proposition that ownership of resources is acquired by people who have a complementary non-tradable resource. This non-tradable resource is normally information-based; if it is not pure information then it is usually a related resource such as technological know-how.

In the short run this complementary resource may appear as a competitive advantage (Porter, 1980) or absolute advantage (Hymer 1960, Dunning 1977) possessed by the owner of the tradable resource. In the long run, however, the advantage possessed by the owner is best construed as a comparative advantage instead. Sustained competitive advantage or absolute advantage is achieved by investments of particular kinds. Anyone can, in principle, undertake investments of this kind, but in the long run only those with a comparative advantage in making such investments will find that it pays them to do so. In the long run, therefore, the ownership of resources is acquired by people who have a comparative advantage in investing in non-tradable resources. The prime example of such people are those who have a comparative advantage in collecting and processing information. These people will usually exploit their comparative advantage through the institutional framework of a firm.

Not all information is equally costly to trade, however. Communication costs are greatest for information of a tacit nature (Polanyi, 1964; Winter, 1988). Contractual problems are greatest for information that is difficult to patent and whose quality is difficult to assess (Buckley and Casson, 1976). Sustainable competitive advantage therefore rests on a comparative advantage in handling tacit information of uncertain quality which is difficult to patent.

A comparative advantage in scientific research satisfies some of these conditions, but not necessarily all of them. This is because some kinds of technology can be patented, which means that their information content can in principle be sold to those who already possess the resources required for their exploitation. Thus technology can be transferred to the owners of the resources, rather than the other way round.

Information about opportunities for trade, on the other hand, normally satisfies all the conditions for non-tradability. Opportunities for trade hinge on consumers' preferences and producers' opportunity costs. Information on such subjects is usually impressionistic, and therefore of a tacit nature. Unlike scientific inventions, such information cannot be patented, and because objective evidence to support it is difficult to obtain, its quality is uncertain. There is, therefore, no way in which such information can be adequately conveyed to the people who own the resources required for its exploitation; the costs of communication and the threat to appropriability are just too great. The resources required for exploitation must be purchased by the posessor of the information instead. It is, therefore, a capacity for acquiring trade-related information of this kind which is pre-eminent as the basis for the long-run comparative advantage of the firm.

3.4. Optimism and competence

Given that information is costly to trade, the exploitation of information is effected by allocating resources in a two stage process. In the first stage the resource is allocated to the appropriate owner and then the owner exercises his power of control to allocate the resource to a particular use. The first stage is based upon trade and the second upon the exercise of control. Trade is a voluntary process which involves the consent of both parties, whereas control is a more autocratic process in which the will of the owner prevails.

Not all ownership confers the same degree of control, though. If the resource can be used in only one way then the owner really has no choice to make. Only a versatile resource affords the owner control over how it is to be used. It is typical of firms that the resources they own are very versatile indeed. It is the importance of exploiting this versatility effectively that creates the demand for specialized decision-making that the firm is designed to meet. Labour time is the pre-eminent example of a versatile resource. Capital equipment is another example: though capital is less versatile than labour, the manager of a capital-intensive firm still has important decisions to make about the scheduling of equipment use. The third main factor of production, land, is versatile too—but only in the long run.

The information used by firms to control their versatile resources is of two main kinds: long-run information on permanent factors and short-run information on transitory factors. Permanent factors are exemplified by the long-run opportunities for trade alluded to the above. Transitory factors are exemplified by the impact of fashion on consumer demand.

Consider, for example, a unique physical asset that can be used to produce different varieties of a given consumer good. The permanent factor governs whether there is a market for the good. The transitory factor governs which variety is in demand in a given period. No individual can observe the permanent factor directly. Individual judgements about the state of the market are highly subjective, it is assumed. Some individuals—the optimists—believe that general conditions are favourable, but others—the pessimists—believe that they are not. The transitory factor can be investigated more objectively, but people differ in their competence. Some people can investigate it more easily than others.

In the course of the negotiations each person signals something of their own valuation of the asset to the other party. This valuation will be high if the individual is an optimist and low if they are a pessimist. It will also tend to be high if they are competent—i.e. they can observe the transitory factor easily—and low if they are not. Trade will proceed, if negotiations permit, when the buyer is more optimistic or more competent than the seller. If the seller is more optimistic or more competent than the buyer then no trade will occur. As a result, ownership is conferred on the more optimistic and/or more competent party.

The transitory factor can be investigated either before or after a bid is made. When the transitory factor is fashion, for example, the state of fashion will have a major impact on the style of the product that the manual worker is required to produce. When the transitory factor is highly volatile it pays to investigate afterwards because this ensures that the information governing the use of the resource is most up to date. If the value of the resource in its best available use is independent of transitory conditions then it also pays to defer investigation, since investigating beforehand does not significantly improve the quality of the bid. Both these conditions tend to be satisfied in the case of fashion: fashion trends are highly volatile, and the profitability of the most fashionable product may well be the same whatever the fashion happens to be.

A person who is optimistic about the permanent factor also has more incentive to investigate first, since they are more likely than a pessimistic person to finish up acquiring the resource. Thus optimistic people are likely to be better informed than pessimistic people when bidding for the resource. This explains why optimistic people do not make more mistakes on average than pessimistic people do—it pays them to invest more in avoiding them.

It is still possible for optimists to make a mistake, of course. Long-run success requires an individual to know when it is right to be optimistic, and when it is appropriate to be pessimistic instead. Because of the highly subjective nature of trade-related information, ownership of resources may be acquired by people who mistakenly think that they have a comparative advantage in handling such information, as well as by people who really do. Those who think that they have a comparative advantage, when they do not, squander resources through over confidence. Conversely, those who have a comparative advantage, but do not realize it, miss out on the profits they could make because they have too little confidence in themselves. It is only those who have a comparative advantage, and have sufficient self-knowledge to be confident of it, who benefit themselves (and society) in the long run.

This analysis can be extended in a straightforward way to include other attributes of the owner, such as their degree of risk aversion. Given the uncertainty that surrounds the permanent factor, risk-averse individuals will be reluctant to become the owners of resources, just as pessimistic or incompetent people are. Risk aversion may not affect owners so much as pessimism or incompetence does, however. It may simply provide them with a greater incentive to investigate the transitory factor before they make a bid. It is quite possible that a risk-averse individual, provided that he is optimistic and competent, may become the owner of a resource because, as a result of his commitment to investigation, he already knows before the negotiations begin that the transitory factor is favourable.

The implications of these results for the firm are seen by identifying the firm with the legal shell used by the owner of the resource who makes the decision on how it is to be used. The analysis identifies the owner of the firm as the optimistic and competent individual with low aversion to risk who acquires resources from other people because he believes that in the light of his better information he can put them to better use. He normally puts them to use by producing goods for sale. If his beliefs about trading opportunities are warranted then his venture in employing the resources will be a success.

3.5. The firm as employer

The preceding analysis unites three qualities in the owner of the firm: optimism, competence and tolerance of risk. But it may be a tall order for all three qualities to coexist in the same person. Is it possible to organize a division of labour in which different qualities are supplied by different people? It is indeed possible, and the examination of this possibility provides further insight into the nature of the firm. In particular, it elucidates the concept of 'employment' and the nature of the authority relation between employer and employee.

The basic idea is that a pessimistic but competent person may undertake to investigate the transitory factor on behalf of an optimistic but incompetent one. The incompetent optimist acquires the ownership of the resource and then hires the competent pessimist to carry out the investigation. The competent pessimist may even have been the person who sold the resource to the owner in the first place. The relevant resource may even be the pessimist's own labour time. The resulting arrangement resembles the employment relation—though not in every respect. The competent pessimist becomes the 'employee' of an incompetent but optimistic 'employer'. He investigates the transitory factor and is then directed to produce the appropriate product—i.e. he is directed to the appropriate use of his own labour time.

In the case of fashion, for example, the incompetent optimist believes that there is a latent demand for a new type of fashion product. He is not sure, however, exactly what style will be in fashion at any given time. He hires a worker, who is willing to sell his labour time because he is not so optimistic, and instructs him to investigate what the current fashion is likely to be. In the light of this the worker is told what style of product to produce.

A further division of labour may be effected which separates the manual and cerebral aspects of this work. Two 'employees' may be hired. One is hired to investigate the transitory factor and the other is hired to produce the appropriate output. The former is a pessimist with low information cost while the latter is a pessimist with high information cost. The former has a personal comparative advantage in investigation and the latter in manual work. This scenario may be elaborated by supposing that, to simplify communications, the owner tells the investigator what the implications of each observation is for product choice, and leaves the investigator to tell the manual worker what to do. This creates a simple hierarchy in which the owner prescribes a rule for the 'managerial employee' who observes the transitory factor and passes on the appropriate instruction to the 'manual employee'.

This analysis assumes that the investigation of the transitory factor occurs only after the manual worker has been employed. If the investigation is carried out beforehand then a somewhat different picture emerges. The role of the manager is now to advise the employer on his wage bid. More significantly, the employer is now in a position to state what particular use he intends to put the manual labour to.

In many cases the seller of a resource, like the manual worker, does not care to what use his resource is put because his alienation of ownership is complete. This is not generally true of labour time, though. The manual employee may care a great deal about how his time is used—he may very much prefer to produce one kind of product than another, for example. If the manual employee is averse to the risks connected with the job to which he may be assigned then on average it will be cheaper for the owner to recruit labour to a specified job rather than to make a general bid for his labour time. Defining a specific job means that the worker is no longer under the control of the manager in the way he was before (Simon, 1957).

The disadvantages of specifying the job in advance through prior observation of the transitory factor have already been alluded to, though. In particular, the volatility of the transitory factor favours carrying out the observation at the last possible moment, after negotiations are complete. The manual worker must therefore already be in place at the time the observation is carried out. This in turn means that the subordination of the manual worker to the manager's decisions is a necessary part of achieving a prompt response to news about the latest conditions.

The same kind of argument applies to a managerial employee who cares about the kind of instructions he is required to issue. Such a manager may wish to know the rules and procedures he must follow before he joins the firm. It may be difficult, though, for the owner to divulge this procedure if it is one that he has invented himself and that rival owners would like to imitate. He may wish to protect it through secrecy. To advertise the procedure as part of the job specification would be most unwise. It is far more prudent to build a requirement of confidentiality into the contract of employment which is already binding on the manager at the time he is told the procedure.

Furthermore, the procedure relating the production decision to the transitory factor may be complicated. Potential managers may decide that, despite their concern about the nature of the procedure, it is simply not worth the effort of assimilating it until they have already agreed to implement it. Because the complexity of the procedure raises the cost of communication, it is uneconomic to evaluate this aspect of the job in advance.

It can be seen that communication costs once again combine with the need for secrecy to create contractual problems. In Section 3.3 they created problems in the market for information by making the information itself difficult to divulge. Now they create problems in the labour market by making the procedure that the manager will be required to implement difficult to divulge. The confidentiality about the procedure has implications for the manual employee as well. Although the employee may not know to which job he will be assigned, he needs to form some expectation on the subject in order to evaluate the contract of employment he is offered. As explained in Chapter 1, a knowledge of the procedure would allow him to infer, from his own probability estimates of the transitory factor, the probability that he will be assigned to any given job. If he cannot know the procedure, however, then he must consider all the possible procedures that might be applied and attach a subjective probability to each. He can then rework his probability estimates, but the resulting degree of uncertainty about his job will be much greater than before. It is not just the manager, therefore, who is disadvantaged by the costs of divulging the procedure, but the worker too.

Another feature of the employment relation is its long-term nature. Because the costs of negotiation are mainly fixed costs, independent of the value of the contract, it is normally advantageous to substitute a long-term contract for a sequence of short-term ones. Fixed costs are important in other ways too; the manager may have to learn a complex procedure at the outset, while the manual worker may have to invest in habit formation to speed up his repetitive tasks. Screening costs must be taken into account as well (see Section 3.8).

A final feature of labour contracts is that they are often of an open-ended nature, allowing either party to terminate them by giving suitable notice. This has the unfortunate effect of allowing the party that terminates the contract unexpectedly to inflict considerable damage on the other. Where the damage would be great, open-endedness may discourage the parties from making appropriate commitments. There will be too little expenditure on non-recoverable set up costs, in other words. It is instructive to note that open-ended contracts are much less common where the hiring of machinery and other non-human resources is concerned. This peculiarity of labour contracts may be best explained, not in terms of efficiency, but as a custom which reflects a moral judgement about the inalienability of certain rights to labour. Further implications of moral judgements about the alienability of labour are considered in Section 3.8 below.

3.6. The firm as intermediator

It was suggested above that trade-related information is just as important as technological know-how—indeed, more important, perhaps—as a source of competitive advantage to a firm. While technological know-how is typically exploited through production, trade-related information is most naturally exploited through intermediation instead. Rather than sell the information directly, the possessor of it extracts rents from it by intervening in the market process—by buying goods cheap and selling them dear. Speculation and arbitrage are terms often used to describe such intervention, but these suggest, quite wrongly, that intermediation is usually an intermittent rather than a continuous process. Trade-related information is usually exploited on a systematic basis by organizing a market that did not exist before. The intermediator does not intervene in an already existing market so much as set up the market from scratch himself.

Markets need to be specially set up because the conduct of trade is fraught with difficulties. It may be difficult for prospective purchasers to get in touch with existing owners. Discovering the exact specification of what is on offer is another task. Then there is the problem of bluffing in negotia-tions. The essence of the market process is that each individual keeps his beliefs to himself. People do not share their beliefs, and come to a consen-sus view. Quite the contrary, indeed. Beliefs are encoded in price quota-tions and these quotations are intended to mislead other people as much as to inform them. The price quotations made at the outset of the negotiation process are likely to give a highly distorted view of the subjective valuations which underpin them. Even when a deal is eventually agreed, default is always a possibility.

Intermediation can reduce transaction costs of this kind. Contact can be made more easily if a middleman provides well-advertised and conveni-ently situated retail premises. Specification costs are also reduced if buyers can inspect samples of each product. Most importantly, the process of negotiation can be accelerated by having an intermediator intervene. The skill of the intermediator resides not in knowing exactly how the buyer will use the good he acquires from the seller, but in identifying the appropriate buyer and assessing the maximum he can afford to pay. Complementing this is a skill in identifying and making contact with the present owners of goods for which ready buyers can be found. The intermediator, in other words, trades on his special knowledge of valuations to reallocate goods to the people who can put them to the best possible use.

The intermediator exploits his own knowledge in the same way that the buyer and seller do—through negotiations. The essence of his strategy is to out-bluff both the buyer and the seller by claiming to the seller that the buyer can afford no more than the intermediator is offering to pay, and persuading the buyer that the seller will not accept less than what the intermediator is asking for it. (The intermediator needs to keep the buyer and seller apart, of course, to do this successfully.) By building a reputation for taking a hard line in negotiations the intermediator can effectively discourage haggling. At the same time, by setting realistic prices he can encourage buyers and sellers to regularly channel transactions through him.

A reputable intermediator can also eliminate default by creating a chain of trust in cases where the direct link between buyer and seller is very weak. Because the intermediator is a specialist, making his living by trade, he has an incentive to build up a reputation for integrity. Once he has acquired this reputation, he can require the seller to supply goods in advance of payment in a way that the buyer could not. Similarly he can require the buyer to pay in advance of delivery in a way that the seller could not. In this way he can guard himself against default by the parties lacking reputation, whilst pass-ing on the product between them.

Unlike the producer described in the previous section, the intermediator buys resources for resale rather than for use. His comparative advantage resides not in his knowledge of the use to which the good will be put, but his knowledge of who is the best person to put it to that use. Although the final users know this too, they do not know the sources of supply as well. The intermediator can obtain both the items of information required for coordination more cheaply than other people. He has the optimism that demand will be buoyant for the goods he has bought, and is not so risk-averse, or devoid of confidence, that he fears for the consequences of his judgement being wrong. That is why he becomes the owner of the goods that he re-sells.

3.7. The firm as an organization: a four-factor theory of the firm

A distinction was drawn in Section 3.4 between the permanent and transitory information used by the market-making firm. It was suggested that the firm typically used just one item of each kind. This is not generally correct: there are at least two items of each type. Both the long-run profitability of the market, and the short-run equilibrium of it, depend upon both supply and demand. It is a synthesis of information on supply and demand that the firm must make in each case. Other factors, such as transport costs, are important too, but including these would unduly complicate the analysis.

Permanent information on demand and supply is synthesized on a once-and-for-all basis. This is the synthesis that underpins the formation of the firm. Transitory information must be synthesized on a recurrent basis, however. Each period the intermediator faces the same problem of how to synthesize information on the demand factor and the supply factor in order to decide what output to order and what prices to quote. Because the problem is always the same from one period to the next it is advantageous for him to devise a procedure which routinely collects and combines the different items of information. Because information is costly to collect, however, it is not always advantageous to commit in advance to observing both demand and supply factors in every period. It is normally advantageous to adopt a sequential procedure in which the most volatile factor is investigated first.

It can also be advantageous to effect a division of labour in the implementation of the procedure. Two managers may be appointed: a marketing manager who observes demand and a purchasing manager who observes supply, each making observations that are a natural by-product of their other duties. The choice of procedure then governs the distribution of managerial power within the firm, as explained in Chapter 1.

If demand is more volatile than supply then the procedure will normally begin by investigating demand, and proceed to investigate supply only if the observation on demand is indecisive. This makes the manager who monitors demand more powerful than the manager who monitors supply in the sense that the demand information collected by this manager is used to decide whether to consult the other manager or not. The firm is therefore demand-driven (Casson, 1994*d*; Carter, 1995). Conversely, if supply is more volatile than demand then the manager who monitors supply becomes the more powerful one, and the firm becomes supply-driven instead.

There are many possible procedures by which information can be synthesized in order to take price and production decisions. These different procedures are analogous to the different techniques that may be used in an ordinary production plant. While the efficient choice of technique in a plant is governed by the available technology and by the relative prices of different material inputs, the efficient choice of procedure in a market-making organization is governed by the pattern of volatility in the market environment and by the different components of information cost—observation cost, communication cost, memory cost, and so on. Emphasizing the market-making role of the firm therefore gives a quite distinctive perspective on the issue of choice of technique.

3.8. The firm as a producer of market-making services: highly specific factors and the homeostasis of the firm

The analogy between intermediation and ordinary production may be pushed even further. Just as ordinary production transforms goods physically, so intermediation transforms their ownership instead. Intermediation is effected in a number of stages, just like the ordinary production of a good. Intermediation involves two activities—buying, and then re-selling—with possibly a third activity—such as quality control—in between. What is more, the different stages are complementary to each other. Like the different stages in the production of a good, they operate in fixed proportions.

Intermediation is produced, like ordinary goods are produced, by the utilization of durable assets such as capital and labour. The role of managerial labour has been alluded to already. Physical capital is exemplified by office equipment—fax machines, photocopiers, computers and filing systems, for example. Given that different stages of intermediation are complementary, the main threat to coordination comes from breakdowns—mechanical breakages, power failures, illnesses, and so on.

Breakdowns threaten the homeostasis of the firm (see Section 1.3). The incidence of a breakdown is a transitory factor—but it is a highly specific transitory factor relative to the other transitory factors considered above. These other factors were specific only to the market for a particular type of product, whilst a breakdown factor is normally specific to a particular asset. A firm which employs a complex portfolio of assets therefore faces a large set of different breakdown factors. The problems created by breakdowns can be controlled in two main ways. The first is by preventing breakdowns, or ensuring that when they happen it is not the firm's responsibility to put them right. The second is that when they do happen they are dealt with promptly and that 'knock on' disruption to other activities is minimized.

Every asset has certain hidden characteristics which govern whether it is prone to breakdown or not. Some of these qualities may be revealed through a screening process. Intermediators who have a comparative advantage in screening such assets will normally prefer to purchase them outright, whilst those who have a comparative disadvantage in screening may prefer to purchase the specific services of these assets instead. Thus a technologically sophisticated firm may prefer to own its equipment outright (and even buy it secondhand, which requires considerable skill), a less sophisticated firm may prefer to rent equipment on rolling short-term contracts, whilst a completely unsophisticated firm may prefer to purchase specific services under a contract which makes the supplier responsible when breakdowns occur. This is another example of the equilibrium described in Section 3.3: ownership of the asset, and the attendant responsibility for breakdowns, is vested in the person most competent to assess the risk, and most confident that the risk is low.

Where the asset concerned is labour, further complications arise. Because labour is inalienable (see Section 3.5), labour cannot be bought and resold like other commodities. Intermediation cannot occur in the labour market in the same way that it does in product markets (Spence, 1973). Speculators intermediate in capital and land; in the labour market, alone among the factor markets, intermediation can only be effected on a fee basis. Fee-charging intermediators, such as employment agencies, cannot be trusted to the same extent as normal intermediators because they do not directly bear the risks of their mistaken decisions. Transaction costs are therefore higher in the labour market than they would otherwise be. This discourages market-making firms from adjusting the composition of their labour force in response to shocks, and encourages them to adjust their use of other factors (notably capital) instead. Transaction costs are particularly high where skilled labour is concerned, since accurate screening is crucial in this case. For this reason many firms treat skilled labour (including managers) as a fixed factor of production so far as transitory fluctuations are concerned.

The second arm of strategy is to optimize the response to breakdowns. Sophisticated procedures are required. But the number of different combinations in which breakdowns can simultaneously occur makes it uneconomic to pre-plan the optimal response in every conceivable case.

To economize on information costs, slack may be deliberately built into the system. Holding precautionary inventories and maintaining spare capacity are obvious strategies for promoting flexibility (see Chapter 2). For example, ageing office machinery with high operating costs may be 'mothballed' for emergency use. Labour contracts may be written to allow the employer to insist on people working overtime if a crisis develops. This facilitates substituting labour for capital in the event of a mechanical failure.

Another opportunity for flexibility arises in the deployment of managerial labour between different jobs. This is a subject of considerable contemporary interest in view of recent Japanese successes in flexible production management (Geanakopoulos and Milgrom, 1991). Consider, for example, two employees on the same premises, each of whom has both a specialist skill and a general skill. The specialist skill is required by the activity to which the employee is allocated on a regular basis. The general skill relates to helping out the other employee when a breakdown occurs. A breakdown in either activity creates a crisis situation for the specialist concerned, which calls for an immediate response from the other employee. The need for rapid communication suggests that 'horizontal' communication from one employee to another may be more effective that 'vertical' communication—i.e. communication intermediated by another manager (Aoki, 1986). Moreover the difficulty of guaranteeing a pre-planned response requires good understanding between the employees themselves. It requires the employer to invest in employees who have general as well as specific skills and are willing to use these skills in order to help each other out. It also suggests that the employees should be drawn from a culturally homogenous group, or that some process of assimilation should be organized, in order to reduce the costs of communication between them (see also Section 3.11). In other words, an intermediating firm works best when it functions more as a family or as a social unit than purely as a collection of individual people.

3.9. The firm as the producer of the product it sells: the vertical integration of marketing and production

The advantage of the intermediator is that he has a wider vision of the situation than the buyer and seller with whom he trades. If the intermediator finds that the same buyers and sellers are dealing with him on a recurrent basis then it may be advantageous for him to acquire their resources and to become the permanent owner of them. Thus the buyers and sellers cease to be owners in their own right and become his employees. As his employees they no longer encode their information in the form of decisions whether or not to trade with him. They share their information directly with him (and normally with each other too). The intermediator structures their information flow in order to economize on the cost of communication. He replaces negotiations with a system for synthesizing information on a more centralized basis. The pure intermediator expands his activities into those of a fully integrated firm.

This only works, however, if the intermediator's customers and suppliers are other firms. The boundaries of the intermediating firm then expand by the firm taking over, or merging with, customer firms and supplier firms. This strategy does not work with individuals because the firm cannot commit individual customers to consume its product for life, nor can it commit them to supply labour for life—at least not in a free society.

A typical intermediator deals with fewer sources of supply than of demand. Sources of supply also tend to be more homogenous and more geographically concentrated than sources of demand—customer firms are often widely distributed and use a good in different ways. Because of the more limited diversity of supply, backward integration into supply is often more practical than forward integration into demand.

The theory of vertical integration is, of course, already well established, but it is most commonly applied to successive stages of ordinary production (see for example Bernhardt, 1977 and Carlton, 1979). Introducing market-making into the picture considerably strengthens the theory's relevance. Backward integration by an intermediator integrates market-making with the production of the product. The integration of production and market-making explains a prominent feature of many firms, namely the coexistence of a strong marketing department and a strong production department within the same firm. Internal conflicts between these two departments are a natural consequence of the internalization of the market for wholesale supply, which locks the two departments into each other.

Conversely, the possibility of disintegrating such a firm through the sub-contracting of production sheds considerable light on recent debates over the 'hollow firm'. More specifically, it shows that the hollowing out of a firm typically returns it from an integrated form to a pure intermediating role. It is only the mistaken belief that it is ordinary production rather than market-making that is crucial to the firm that leads people to perceive this as a paradoxical development.

What then governs the integration and disintegration decisions of the market-making firm? The structure of the wholesale market is one factor. If the market for supplies is basically competitive then an intermediator who is dissatisfied can always switch to a different producer. If switching is difficult, however, then the producer may realize that he enjoys a monopolistic position, and so the supply price may be set above the marginal cost of production. As a result the intermediator may wish to take steps to reduce the supplier's market power (Waterson, 1982).

Acquiring the seller is one approach, but this has the disadvantage that the monopoly rents accruing to the seller will be capitalized in the purchase price. In so far as the exercise of monopoly power is distorting allocation decisions at the margin, however, there will be efficiency savings even if the supplier is acquired at an 'inflated' price. The exercise of monopoly power by the seller only causes distortions of this kind, though, when the seller cannot extract his monopoly rents through price discrimination. Where the same seller is supplying a number of different customers, and resale between them is difficult to control because of information costs or legal constraints, then discrimination is difficult and distortion does indeed occur. Under these circumstances, therefore, the acquisition of a monopolistic producer may be effected purely to improve the coordination between production and final sale.

An alternative to acquisition is for the intermediator to build his own production plant in competition with his existing supplier. The disadvantage of this is that it may add unnecessarily to capacity in the industry. In any case, if extra capacity really is needed then it may be questioned why others have not entered the industry to build additional capacity already. One explanation may be that producers are less optimistic than the intermediator about the prospects for demand (for the reasons given in Section 3.4), and so are reluctant to invest. In this case the intermediator may invest as a speculation that his forecast of demand is better than theirs. If extra capacity is built then competitive forces will encourage the existing producer to cut his prices, which means that the intermediator may still wish to patronize that producer even though he now owns his own plant as well. Indeed if he delegates the management of his plant to people he does not really trust then he may find it advantageous to threaten them with switching production to an outsider unless they can produce more cheaply themselves.

There are three main reasons why, notwithstanding this, the intermediator may wish not only to invest in a plant of his own but also to rely on it exclusively for his supplies. Though logically distinct, they are related because they all apply with greatest force to the supply of newly innovated products. This makes the impact of the separate factors difficult to distinguish in practice, since they tend to appear jointly where innovative products are concerned.

The first concerns quality control (Casson, 1987, chapter 4). The intermediator may be unsure whether he can trust the producer to match the specification. He may not believe in the supplier's integrity, as noted above. But even if he trusts the supplier's integrity, he may not trust in his competence. With a new product whose production requires a modification of existing processes, the supplier may just not be up to the job.

To assure quality, the intermediator could, of course, insist on supervising the production operation. An independent producer is likely to object to this, however, because the information obtained as a result of supervision is likely to come as a package which contains some items of a confidential nature. A by-product of observing the production process may be a fairly accurate assessment of the production costs, for example. Use of this information in subsequent negotiations could improve the intermediator's bargaining power to the detriment of the producer. Again, the producer may have been selected for a special skill he has, which he needs to protect as a trade secret. Allowing supervision would divulge the secret to the intermediator and further encourage him to set up rival production of his own.

The second factor is sunk costs. The intermediator may require the producer to invest in specific equipment, or incur other forms of set up cost, in order to customize the product to his requirements (Klein *et al.*, 1978). Because of legal shortcomings, the producer cannot sell forward sufficient supplies to cover his costs before they are sunk. His consequent reluctance to customize the product obliges the intermediator to customize it for himself.

The third factor concerns the intermediator's desire to fully appropriate the value of his profit opportunity. In subcontracting the production of a new design the intermediator risks building up a competitor. Unless the design is patented, the intermediator's only method of excluding competitors is through secrecy. Even with a patent, the subcontractor may use his experience of production to improve the design and thereby render the original patent obsolete. For all these reasons, therefore, an intermediator launching an innovative product is likely to integrate backwards into its production.

3.10. Marketing, technology transfer, and horizontal integration

The integration of production and marketing need not be confined to a single market. The intermediator may have an idea so general that it has much wider implications than this. The design for the product may, for example, be relevant not to just a single market but to a whole set of markets. The limiting case involves a marketing concept of global relevance.

The exploitation of a general idea leads to a distinctive pattern of horizontal integration. Because the global market is spatially segmented by transport costs and tariffs, and by non-tariff barriers such as national safety standards, intermediation has to be replicated in different locations. In each town there may be a shop, in each country a warehouse, and in each trading bloc or supranational region a production facility. Within this framework, substitution possibilities tend to emerge. While each production facility normally sources its nearest markets, it is also possible for it to top up more distant markets if shortages develop there. Even within its own market area the firm can switch consignments between warehouses, and warehouses can switch consignments from one shop to another.

These internal substitution possibilities have important implications for the organization of the firm. The logic of synthesizing information is driven by the need to source each retail unit from the minimum cost location.

Under these circumstances it may be advantageous for each production unit, and each warehouse, to encode its report on local supply conditions as a price quotation. Price information is more explicit than most other forms of information, and is therefore cheaper to communicate; moreover it feeds naturally into an algorithm geared to identifying the cheapest source of supply. Internal markets with substitution possibilities may therefore be coordinated using transfer prices. Where complementarities continue to dominate, though, conventional procedures based on budgets matched to target quantities are likely to be used instead. Internal substitution possibilities are characteristic of large multinational enterprises, and it is in firms of this type that internal prices are most likely to be used.

Some of the most powerful general ideas relate not merely to market-making, but to the commercial application of technology as well. Schumpeterian innovation, for example, combines market-making intelligence with an assessment of the industrial potential of new technology (Schumpeter, 1934, 1939). Indeed, because technology is an internationally transferable public good, ideas for technological innovation are naturally global in a way that many ordinary market-making ideas are not. Technology transfer is thus an important aspect of the international operations of many firms.

Just as the production of a good, and the making of a market, involve a number of stages, so too does the development of a technology. Besides the 'value-chain' encompassing production and the distribution channel, there is the 'value chain' of research and development (R & D) as well. This involves, for example, basic research in the laboratory, scaling up to pilot production, and the replication of plants with suitable adaptations to the local environment.

The issue of vertical integration arises in connection with this R & D value chain as well as in the ordinary sequence of multi-stage production and distribution. The importance of technology is such that there is a strong case for effecting a vertical division of responsibility between its discovery and its exploitation. The natural way of effecting this separation is to create a market in which patented technology is licensed out for use. If licences were priced appropriately, and agreements were costless to enforce, then charging for use would not inhibit diffusion in any socially harmful way. This is because no-one would be asked to pay more than what they valued the information at, provided that this covered the cost of communicating it to them. If the licensing approach were generally applied, it would create two distinct types of firm: one that specialized in R & D, and another that specialized in exploiting the knowledge so produced (Buckley and Casson, 1976). The first type of firm would typically license a given idea to several different firms of the second type, each of which would make a market in a particular location.

Apart from the difficulties of licensing, noted earlier, there is a serious objection to this approach, though. Different licensees could easily dissipate the rents from the idea by 'dumping' in each other's markets. Export restrictions in the licence agreement can attempt to control this, but the most efficient method of rent extraction is to organize the licensees as a cartel. Covert price-cutting then becomes a major problem, however. If the licensees do not believe that this problem can be solved then they will reduce their bids for the licence. The sum total of the bids then becomes much lower than the maximum rent available and so, even allowing for his comparative disadvantage in exploitation, it pays the owner of the technology to integrate forward into the exploitation of the technology himself.

Obstacles to licensing thus encourage the internalization of the market for technology. This, in turn, creates further complexities for internal coordination. Besides the flow of materials from production through to distribution, there is now the flow of technical information that needs to be coordinated too. Experience from production and from customer use must be fed back to the research laboratories, while improvements effected in these laboratories must be fed back to production and explained to the customers. Additional flows of coordinating information are therefore required to coordinate the flows of technical information with each other and with material flow. This obviously adds further complications to the organizational procedures of the firm.

3.11. The firm as a social and cultural unit

The scope of the firm is ultimately constrained only by the scope of the owner's vision. Even if the owner lacks knowledge of crucial details required for implementation, he may be able to hire the expertise necessary to make good his own deficiencies. Multi-stage vertical integration may emerge if the owner has a vision of how an entire production sequence could be rationalized, with intermediate product flows being restructured and plants expanded or shut down. Conglomerate diversification may result from the owner having a vision of a new kind of lifestyle that consumers wish to pursue, involving the purchase of a complementary collection of novel household goods. In principle, horizontal, vertical, and conglomerate diversification can all occur together in the same firm.

Actual instances of this are fairly rare, however. The practical limit on the scope of the firm's operations stems from the increasing problems the owner encounters in recruiting staff with the appropriate competencies and in making sure they behave in an honest way. Skills in screening people for senior management posts are indispensable to the owner of a large firm.

Indeed, it may be said that in managing a very large firm it is the skill of recognizing other people who have the skill to recruit their own subordinates that is the most vital thing (Knight, 1921).

The larger is the firm the more complicated are likely to be the procedures that it uses. Wide-ranging integration means that many specific sources of environmental volatility impinge on the firm's operations. Managers must synthesize information from increasingly diverse sources in order to support decision-making. Although every member of the organization has some interest in its overall performance, the larger the organization becomes, the more remote the connection between overall performance and individual reward tends to be (Miller, 1992). Increasing complexity creates more and more opportunities for managers to pervert procedures in order to promote their personal interests (Milgrom and Roberts, 1992). With a fixed span of control, monitoring procedures involve an increasing number of administrative layers, and motivating people to monitor each other attentively becomes more difficult as a result.

The basic problem is that the decision-making procedures used in any organization are premised on people telling the truth. In a highly centralized organization this means quite simply that everyone reports their observations of transitory factors honestly to their superiors. In a decentralized organization, where different people are given their own particular rules to apply to the data they collect, it means that what they decide is based on applying the rule they have been given to the data as actually collected. The decision rules only make sense if they are correctly implemented and applied to honest data.

It is sometimes possible to check up on people after the event to see if their report was honest. But such monitoring procedures depend in turn on the supervisors following the procedures that they have been prescribed. 'Who will supervise the supervisors?' encapsulates the dilemma of the large firm. The answer is that only those who are really trusted can be permitted to supervise without being supervised themselves.

This points to an alternative approach to eliciting truth, which is to make everyone trustworthy as far as possible. Instead of having a small core of trustworthy people doing little else but supervising untrustworthy people, the untrustworthy elements are eliminated by making everyone trustworthy instead. The trustworthy people can then concentrate on taking decisions, since there are no untrustworthy people left for them to supervise.

But how can this desirable state of affairs be engineered? Trustworthy people, from the owner's point of view, are essentially self-monitoring. They check up on themselves and punish themselves with a bad conscience if they default (Casson, 1991a). They are motivated to check up on themselves because they believe in the objectives of the firm. These objectives enjoy a moral legitimacy which the pursuit of their own narrow material interests lacks. If the corporate objective is purely to maximize the owner's profit, however, then it is difficult to see why they should subscribe to it on ethical grounds. But if the maximization of profit is represented as something instrumental to the pursuit of a morally higher goal then individual self-interest may well be suppressed. More precisely, when self-interest is construed more broadly in terms of the satisfaction of helping to achieve this higher goal, material self-interest carries much smaller weight.

Engineering beliefs of this kind is difficult, however. Indeed, it is difficult to sustain such beliefs in the long run unless they really are true. How can a rational self-interested owner, who really wants to maximize profit, cope with the dilemma that he can only maximize profit by wanting to maximize something else instead? The answer is to appoint someone as a symbolic leader of the firm who really does want to maximize something else. It may be cheaper to allow this person to extract certain rents from the firm for the cause in which he believes than to do without this person and have numerous employees extract rents for themselves instead. There is, therefore, scope for a contract between an owner and a moral leader, allowing both to pursue the objectives—material and moral respectively—in which they believe (Casson, 1995a, chapter 6).

3.12. The foundation of the firm

Judgements about market prospects are essentially subjective. It was noted in Section 3.4 that opinions differ about the scope for profitable intermediation. Some people take an optimistic view and others a pessimistic one. This diversity of opinion about the permanent factors may be explained by the fact that the underlying market situation cannot be observed directly, but only through certain symptoms. Some people interpret the situation in terms of one symptom and others in terms of another. Each symptom is correlated with the true situation. Accurate symptoms are highly correlated with the true situation and the most successful owners use these. Others are more weakly correlated. Some symptoms may not be used at all because people realize that they are, on balance, too misleading.

Some symptoms may have a bias to optimism in the sense that while picking out good conditions very accurately they are quite likely to report bad conditions as good as well. Others may have a bias to pessimism in that they pick up bad conditions very accurately but are likely to report good conditions as bad too. Wrongly accepting good conditions as bad is less hazardous than wrongly accepting bad conditions as good, and therefore risk-averse people are likely to avoid using symptoms which are biased to optimism. Although the distinction between pessimism and risk aversion made earlier remains valid, it is also true that when people have a choice between alternative symptoms, risk aversion is likely to lead to pessimism because of symptom choice.

In principle, of course, people could reduce risks still further by combining information on different symptoms. The principle of synthesis, enunciated earlier in connection with transitory factors, would then apply to different symptoms of the permanent factors too. The subjectivity of opinion about permanent factors is almost certainly explained, however, by the fact that this cannot be easily done. Symptoms may be identified as a highly tacit form of information, each obtained from a quite distinctive source. No one who has not consulted a particular source directly can fully understand what the symptom shows, and the sources are too diverse for anyone to consult more than one symptom.

It is possible, for example, that the identification and interpretation of symptoms operates at a subconscious level. Each individual uses symptoms which their accumulated experience has taught them is useful in a particular type of situation. They may not know why they use this symptom or even be aware that they do so. The use of symptoms may be a highly pragmatic affair.

People can choose which symptoms to use only in the sense that by choosing a particular occupation and lifestyle they determine what kind of experiences they accumulate. Sophisticated symptoms are likely to be the result of a broad and varied lifetime experience. Because the use of symptoms is subconscious, people cannot share their expertise in any formal way. It is possible, though, to exchange life experiences through conversation, and quite a bit of business wisdom may be transmitted in this way. People may also find it easier to share their expertise when confronted with a specific situation. Each person examines particular symptoms in the situation and gives their opinion on the matter. Because these opinions may be difficult to justify by explicit reasoned argument, however, the weight that other people attach to a given person's opinion may depend more on their reputation and general social standing than on their ability to justify their choice.

The accuracy of the symptoms used is not the ultimate determinant of successful intermediation, however. If two or more people use similar symptoms to arrive at the same conclusions then rents from the exploitation of the general idea will be dissipated through competition between them. The loss is substantial because the costs of discovery are sunk costs and the marginal costs of exploitation are relatively low.

The combination of symptoms used to identify an idea therefore needs to be unique. This in turn suggests that the individual or group that develops the idea needs to be unusual—even eccentric—in some particular way. This makes them alert to opportunities which others simply fail to discover (Kirzner, 1973). Alternatively, it makes them aware that possibilities rejected by others really are opportunities, despite the fact that the others believe that they are foolish to go ahead with exploiting them. They are therefore able to preempt the opportunity and to invest in barriers to entry which will keep competitors out once they realize their mistake. Few barriers succeed in the long run, of course, but they may still be useful in prolonging the otherwise transitory period for which monopoly rents can be earned.

If an individual believes that he has recognized a change that others have not, and realizes that this is because of a special symptom that he has used, then he may well ask himself whether he may not be in the wrong and others in the right. He requires self-confidence to back his own judgement. Without self-confidence, moreover, he will probably be unable to get financial backing from others, as discussed below. Whether the individual is successful or not depends upon whether his confidence is well-placed (as noted in Section 3.4). People with good self-knowledge, who can assess their own competencies successfully, are more likely to achieve success because their degree of confidence will be matched to their true capability. People who lack confidence will never found a firm, while those who are over-confident are likely to found firms that fail.

3.13. Maintaining flexibility: the firm as an entrepreneurial unit

The opportunity for intermediation has hitherto been described as governed by permanent factors, but this is not strictly correct. The factors are certainly more durable than the transitory ones, but they are better described as persistent rather than permanent, as indicated at the outset. Opportunities for intermediation are certainly liable to change from time to time. This raises two issues, both of which are important for the nature of the firm.

The first is whether innovation in market-making is better effected by new entrants or established firms. Should the owner of an established firm continue to monitor the persistent factors by regularly updating his estimate of the gains from intermediation, or is it more efficient for him to leave this to others instead? If he leaves it to others then it is possible that his firm may not survive any change in long-run market conditions. Competitors who are more alert than the established firm will emerge when a change occurs, and if the established firm fails to recognize the competitive threat then it may fail. It may still be worth bearing this risk, to economize on information costs, if the owner of the firm considers that the market situation is basically very stable. Alternatively, the owner may believe that he has the flexibility to respond rapidly to any threat. In this case, the firm may be able to survive by free-riding on the information signalled to it by the behaviour of potential competitors. It relies on its established position to 'see off' any entrants.

If an established firm decides to retain an innovative capability of this kind then a second issue arises. This is whether the monitoring of market-making opportunities should be governed by a procedure. The handling of information on transitory factors is normally procedure-driven, as noted earlier. Should the handling of information on persistent factors be procedure-driven too?

Changes in the transitory factors are liable to occur each period. Information is frequently updated, and the costs of developing the relevant procedure are consequently spread over many successive applications. Moreover, the range of variation in conditions may be fairly narrow. So far as the persistent factors are concerned, however, change is more intermittent and the optimal frequency of observation is therefore low. The range of possible situations that can emerge is very wide and hence the probability that any one of them will ever occur—at least within the owner's lifetime—is very small. This argues against planning in advance how to respond to every conceivable change. Plans that are developed may never need to be implemented, and even if they are eventually implemented the cost of remembering them until they are required may be quite considerable. It is therefore more efficient, in terms of information costs, to wait till a particular situation reveals itself and then improvise a response in the light of the symptoms observed (Casson, 1996).

A change in the nature of the market-making opportunity implies a change in the procedures by which transitory information is synthesized. Indeed, if no change in these procedures is required then there may be little point in identifying the change in the first place. The implication is that changes in procedures are normally improvised—such changes are not themselves procedurally driven.

The responsibility for improvising procedural change may be set apart and allocated to a particular individual—typically the owner of the firm, but possibly a trusted employee instead. This responsibility for improvised decisions is the defining characteristic of the entrepreneur (Casson, 1982). The exercise of entrepreneurship reflects a fundamental division of labour within the firm between routine procedure-driven decision-making on the one hand and the improvisation of changes in procedures on the other.

This division of labour is not absolute, of course. Because changes in market-making opportunities are only intermittent, the act of improvisation is intermittent too. Although symptoms of the persistent factor need to be regularly monitored, this may not be sufficient to keep the entrepreneur fully occupied. It may therefore be advantageous for the entrepreneur to fill out his spare time by helping with routine work. This explains why entrepreneurship does not always correspond to a specific full-time job within the firm.

The kind of improvised response that is made to changes in the persistent factor is analogous to the decision made about the foundation of the firm. This is based on preempting the use of information about the persistent factor—information which would almost certainly have been exploited by someone else if the entrepreneur had not responded first. The same kind of entrepreneurship that is required to found the firm is also required to give it the continuing flexibility needed to survive. The firm is effectively 're-founded' each time its procedures change in response to a change in fundamental market conditions recognized by the entrepreneur.

3.14. The firm as a political institution

Given that the entrepreneur reserves the right to change the procedures of the firm at any time, it is open to employees to object that they did not anticipate such changes when they joined the firm. Notwithstanding the formal legal power that the owner of a firm possesses, employees might claim that he had reneged on an implicit component of the employment contract. It might be alleged that the procedures had been changed in a wholly unreasonable way.

It is, of course, possible to dismiss the entire problem on the grounds that only the explicit part of the contract of employment counts. But implicit contracts can often be useful in economizing on information costs, and cannot be dismissed altogether. It could be argued, however, that implicit contracts cannot emerge simply from custom, and that an employer who follows the same procedure for a long time does not morally validate employees' expectations that it will continue for ever.

One way of clarifying the issue for employees is to frame a constitution for the firm which sets out the range of permissible procedures. Given the enormous breadth of the range, it may be easiest to specify this set by exclusion—i.e. to specify what is not permitted rather than what is. Another possibility is to give the employee a right to be consulted over any change, or even to allow him to participate formally in the decision by giving him a vote that he can exercise along with other recognized 'stakeholders' in the firm. This is somewhat akin to a worker-controlled firm, or at least to a firm where management is overseen by a worker-controlled supervisory board. In this case the entrepreneur comes to resemble a political leader within his own firm, persuading employees to vote in favour of his recommended change of procedure.

The amount of protection afforded to the employee under such arrangements depends upon the nature of the voting system—thus majority rule affords the employee less protection than does a consensus rule, which confers a right of veto on any employee who believes he would lose by the change. The consensual approach has the desirable property—in theory at least—that it obliges the employer to compensate all losers and so ensures that the new procedure is a Pareto-improvement on the old one. It has the practical disadvantage, though, that it allows any one employee to hold up the change in return for extortionate compensation, and may precipitate the growth of factions, each determined to get a bigger pay-off for its members than the others do.

A more satisfactory solution from the standpoint of the entrepreneur is for him to constrain himself by the application of certain ethical principles. If these principles command the assent of the employees, and they trust the entrepreneur to act by them, then formal consultation may prove unnecessary.

It is obvious that the arbitrary exercise of power is an issue which arises not only in connection with the governance of the firm but also in conjunction with the state. There is, however, a difference between these two cases, in the sense that employees have more freedom to move between firms than citizens do between states. Competition between employers, even though it may be somewhat restricted, is normally sufficiently intense that those made discontented by a change in procedures can find alternative employment with another firm. In Hirschman's (1958) terms, because the 'exit option' is more attractive there is less need for the firm to invest in mechanisms for 'voice'.

Where key employees with job-specific skills are concerned, however, the exit option may be costly to the firm as well as to the employee. Costs sunk in training employees for their specific roles may be lost for good if discontented employees quit their jobs. The implicit contract between employer and employee is normally a reciprocal one in which the firm receives loyalty and hard work from the employee in return for steady career progression. An entrepreneur who instigates an adverse change in procedures without full agreement therefore risks undermining the loyalty and commitment of his employees.

In the light of all this, it may be asked why firms do not equip themselves with a formal constitution regulating changes of procedure. The answer is, quite simply, that the constitution would be costly to specify, and probably too costly to explain to employees as well. The probability of a change being required that, because of the absence of a constitutional process, will alienate key employees is quite small. From the employees' perspective, the opportunities for changing jobs are normally sufficiently good that refusing to work for a firm which lacks a formal constitution is hardly worthwhile.

Nevertheless, the costs and benefits of a constitution are very different when the constitution is standardized across all firms. The fixed costs of specification and assimilation are then spread more widely. Moreover, if established firms become more entrepreneurial—in response, for example, to the globalization of competition—then procedural changes may occur more frequently within any given firm. Under these circumstances it may be efficient for nation states (or, ideally, the international community) to establish a standardized corporate constitution as a response to the greater volatility now characteristic of the world economic environment. This standardized constitution need not be compulsory—it simply makes explicit the fall-back position should the firm not specify a separate constitution of its own. In this context the state is not directly regulating firms, and imposing unwanted uniformity upon them, but rather suggesting a convention, as a form of public good which employers can use if they wish.

3.15. The firm as a partnership of risk-bearers

It may seem obvious that the owner of a firm is a risk-bearer, but this is not inevitably the case. It is possible to imagine a firm which buys up all its supplies in advance and sells all its output forward too. It owns no resources, except those it can fully screen, but hires specific services instead. Flexibility is achieved by making forward contracts contingent on all uncertain events, or by negotiating separate insurance to cover these possibilities. Revenues and costs are carefully matched under each possible situation. It might, it is true, be advantageous to sink costs before negotiations are complete in order to discourage competitive entry into the market, but contingent contracts can, in principle, be extended to deal with entry threats as well, provided potential entrants can be identified in advance.

This scenario is not so far-fetched as it may seem. Many subcontractors do indeed supply their product to an intermediator under long-term arrangements, as indicated earlier. Furthermore, some sales, such as those in the defence industry, are made on a cost-plus basis, which effectively combines forward sale with insurance arrangements. The defence industry is unusual, however, in having a single dominant institutional customer—the government—with ready access to capital on account of its powers of taxation. In consumer goods industries, by contrast, forward sales are not really practical because the very large number of small orders involved, and the dubious credit status of the customers, means that transactions costs would be very high.

It is because forward contracts cannot be entered into that the profitability of intermediation becomes so uncertain. There are, of course, ways in which, in the absence of forward contracts, the set up costs of intermediation—and hence the down-side risks—can be reduced. For example, trade credit can be obtained by paying for supplies after they have been received. Indeed, if the entrepreneur is highly reputable then he may be able to obtain prepayment from buyers sufficiently early that he can pay for his supplies using the revenues from his sales (see Section 2.11). It is unusual, however, for a new enterprise to enjoy a reputation of this kind.

If the owner's personal wealth exceeds the firm's set up costs then there is no financial obstacle to starting the business. Otherwise the owner will have to dilute his role by borrowing from other people. Fixed interest loans may be obtained where suitable collateral is available—inventory for short-term loans and buildings for long-term loans, for example. But the main source of funds will normally be equity.

Since the ultimate power of control normally resides where the principal financial responsibility lies (Knight, 1921) equity holders will normally demand a right of veto on any proposed use of their funds. As a result the founder of the firm is likely to become part-owner and part-employee of his firm—delegated to use his discretion under the general supervision of a board comprising the major shareholders. The shareholders count on the fact that the arrangement does not significantly affect the motivation of the entrepreneur. In practice the major problem is likely to be not any dilution of effort by the entrepreneur, but rather his concern with other objectives—like growth—which may be at variance with the narrower interests of the other shareholders (Marris, 1964).

It is not necessary that the entrepreneurial function is performed by a single individual, though. The advantage of consultation in pooling relevant life-experiences was mentioned in Section 3.12. Major shareholders may wish to contribute their expertise in this way. In this case the deliberations of the board may actually strengthen the entrepreneurial role within the firm.

The willingness to share experience of this kind, and the need for honesty about what is shared, raise difficult incentive problems, however. The value of what a person contributes when they share their experiences is difficult to measure. The influence of a person's contribution to the emergence of a consensus on a particular issue—and their consequent responsibility for any mistakes—is also difficult to assess. For this reason, most firms use very simple rules to decide such issues. Each equity share, for example, carries a single vote, and conflicts are resolved by applying majority rule. In small partnerships shares may not be freely tradable, and the right to additional shares may be dependent on the senior partner's judgement of a junior partner's contribution to the firm. It is very difficult to justify these rules except as norms and customs designed to avoid the information costs which would be incurred if every aspect of joint ownership became the subject of negotiation.

No single rule can resolve all the incentive problems satisfactorily. Ultimately there is no substitute for a high degree of trust between the major partners in a firm (Buckley and Casson, 1988). Just as their rights in the firm are general rights of ownership rather than claims on specific services, so their obligations to the firm are general rather than specific too—to contribute all they know that is relevant to the firm, should there be a need for them to do so. It is therefore advantageous if they are drawn from a reasonably homogenous cultural group. They may well know each other personally, or know the entrepreneur. They must have sufficient in common to share a similar vision, and to have the same degree of confidence in it as does the entrepreneur.

Not every shareholder may wish to hold a substantial equity stake, however. The advantages of 'portfolio' diversification mean that some shareholders may simply wish to take a small stake as part of a policy of spreading their risks. Such share holdings can be encouraged by floating the firm's equity on a stock exchange. By reducing the transaction costs of both buying and re-selling equity, this not only markets the equity to a wider group of investors, but provides additional liquidity for the existing investors too.

The smaller shareholders will generally not wish to play an active role in managing the firm. This is because the costs of involvement in management are fixed costs, independent of the size of the shareholding. The small shareholders are in effect free-riding on the efforts of the larger shareholders to manage the firm (Grossman and Hart, 1980). The larger shareholders may have ways of extracting rents to compensate for their costs, however: management fees, capital gains from insider-trading, directing trade to other companies with which they are financially involved, and so on. The scope for abuse is obvious. There is, however, the sanction that once abuses are discovered the small shareholders may sell out to a takeover raider who disciplines the larger shareholders involved.

The potentially 'footloose' nature of small investments can damage the loyalty and effort of ordinary employees. It is one thing to call upon an employee to match the commitment of an owner who has sunk all his personal wealth into building up a firm, and another to call for the same degree of commitment on behalf of a diverse collection of anonymous speculative investors. The discussion in Section 3.11 suggests that the links between stock-exchange financing, ownership structure and company performance, which are currently receiving much public attention, have an important ethical dimension which has not been emphasized as much as it should.

3.16. Reflections on the 'ownership' theory of the firm

According to the theory presented above, ownership of a firm is an essentially speculative activity. The aim of the owner is to appropriate rents from what he believes to be privileged information. The information may relate to the hidden quality of some asset, as described in Section 3.8, but the most important case concerns an opportunity for intermediation, as described in Section 3.6. This opportunity may be associated with technological innovation, as described in Section 3.10, though this is by no means always the case. The owner cannot readily appropriate the rent from information by licensing its use to other people because property rights in ideas of this kind are insecure. The idea must be kept a secret until the opportunity has been preempted and, since it is difficult to sell a secret, he must preempt the opportunity himself.

Another way of appropriating rent from information is by placing a bet upon the subject with other people who are believed to be not so well informed. The rent is extracted when the truth is revealed and the bet is won. This is, in effect, what happens when a successful firm acquires resources from other people. The owner of the firm bets that his judgement of the situation is better that the judgement of those who sell their resources to the firm. The profit of the firm is his reward for being right.

Differences in judgement exist because different people use different symptoms to interpret the environment. People with wide-ranging but unusual experiences have the kind of entrepreneurial judgement which is at once both 'deviant' in terms of received opinion, and yet often correct. Other people who have confidence in the judgement of a person of this kind may contribute risk capital to the firm he founds. This helps to fund the indivisible sunk cost required to establish a new market. Major investors may also contribute their opinions on how the founder's idea is best exploited. Minor investors may be involved too; they essentially free-ride on the judgement of the principal entrepreneur and the major investors. All these investors count on the entrepreneur to exercise vigilance even though he may own only a modest portion of the equity.

The exploitation of an opportunity requires that once the relevant resources are acquired they are utilized in an appropriate way. Versatile resources confer power of control on the owner. An intermediator owns two main types of resource: the assets he uses to operate his business—office equipment and the labour-time of his employees—and the goods that he 'turns over' as a result of these operations. To fix price and output on the market that he makes, the intermediator requires a constant flow of information. This information is routinely collected by the office staff. Their role is to synthesize two types of transitory information, concerned with demand and supply. Information processed by stocks of resources of the first type is thus used to control the flow of resources of the second type. Control of the flows is effected using a procedure devised by the intermediator which is intended to achieve the appropriate degree of accuracy in decision-making at minimum cost.

Once he has devised this procedure, the entrepreneur must keep it under constant review. Should circumstances change, and another procedure become appropriate, he must beat potential competitors on speed of response. He has a natural advantage in his ability to feed back lessons from the use of the existing procedure, but vigilance is required to do this properly. To change procedures when circumstances require it is a prerogative of ownership, but there are also constraints on the extent to which this can be done without consulting, and if necessary compensating, loyal employees who are adversely affected by the change. While the formal contract of employment may seem seriously incomplete, it is 'completed' by the procedures, the constitution, and the culture of the firm.

Grossman and Hart (1986) offer a very different account of ownership, however. In their account, the emphasis on speculation is missing. According to them the owner seeks control, not in order to specify a decision-making procedure appropriate to the intermediation opportunity he has identified, but simply to gain the upper hand in a game of strategy played out with other people who contribute resources to the firm. Grossman and Hart lay great emphasis on the incompleteness of the employment contract. They argue that this creates an ambiguity which is resolved by allocating residual control—i.e. control over all the decisions not fully specified in the contract—to one particular party, namely the owner of the firm. Such an account of ownership is misleading because it overstates the incompleteness of contracts and thereby suggests much more scope for strategic behaviour than is possible in practice. It ignores the fact that the owner has committed himself to certain procedures and that although he can change these procedures, the probability that he will do so in any given period is actually very small. Moreover, his right to change these procedures in a manner which seriously damages the interests of other parties is constrained by the constitution of the firm. Should the owner breach the constitution he will lose the loyalty of key employees, who can inflict considerable damage on the firm if they quit.

The incompleteness of contracts certainly exists as a rational response to information costs. It does not, however, create a major ambiguity which strategic behaviour by a specialized residual claimant is required to control. Rather it creates a need for employees to acquaint themselves with the constitution and the procedures of the firm and to form rational expectations of how their conduct is likely to be regulated by these procedures on a day-to-day basis.

The only substantial way in which contracts are incomplete is that the owner retains the right to change the procedures in the light of changes he believes he has recognized in the environment of the firm. This is simply the entrepreneurial function. The owner is far too concerned with maintaining procedures that efficiently exploit his intermediation opportunity to be bothered, to any significant extent, with the strategic fine-tuning that Grossman and Hart discuss. Such fine-tuning may well occur, but it is the speculative factor that Grossman and Hart omit that is the principal factor governing of the ownership of the firm.

3.17. Reflections on the new institutional economics

The most influential account of the theory of the firm within the literature on management, broadly defined, is undoubtedly that of Williamson (1975, 1985). His account is based on three key assumptions of opportunism, bounded rationality, and asset-specificity. Opportunism is relatively clear and uncontroversial; it describes a phenomenon well known to all economists—the pursuit of material self-interest under conditions of asymmetric information. Bounded rationality is more controversial—to economists at least—and it is also more obscure. While it is easy to see what bounded rationality denies—namely the substantive rationality of full optimization—it is not clear exactly what it substitutes for it. Simon's (1947) alternative is procedural rationality, which is akin to the idea of using optimal procedures in a world of costly information. Williamson does not, however, develop a calculus of optimal procedures of this kind, as described in Section 3.7 above.

Williamson has accorded asset-specificity a central place in his analysis ever since Klein *et al.* (1978) highlighted its implications for vertical integration. An asset becomes specific when costs are sunk to customize the asset to the requirements of another party. Rendering an asset specific weakens the owner's bargaining position and encourages the other party to renegotiate the contract. Forward contracts are legally too fragile to prevent this, and so pooling the ownership of the assets is the natural response. The resulting concentration of ownership generates the vertically integrated firm. The key point in this argument is that asset-specificity reduces substitution opportunities and weakens competitive threats. The reduction in competition causes problems with bilateral market power.

It is noteworthy that Williamson's assumptions have played a rather limited role in the preceding analysis. Opportunism is endorsed, in so far as it underpins the strategic problems of assuring the quality of information. Yet the endorsement is limited by the possibility of assuring quality through a high-trust culture sustained by moral rhetoric. This point is underlined by the discussion of networks in Chapter 4, where it is shown that the engineering of high-trust relations makes opportunism of much less significance than Williamson suggests.

The assumption of bounded rationality has been replaced by an assumption that information is costly to collect and to communicate. This new assumption is both more powerful and more precise. It is more precise in the sense that it avoids ambiguity over exactly what deviations from substantive rationality are liable to occur. Thus Williamson considers bounded rationality to be a very serious problem when writing contingent contracts, but effectively ignores it when considering how the owner of the firm chooses between alternative boundaries for the firm. Indeed, in

Williamson's theory the principal role of bounded rationality is simply to explain why the employment contract is incomplete, along the lines of Coase (1937) and Simon (1957). In contrast, the alternative approach based on information costs does much more than this. It integrates the analysis of the employment contract with the analysis of the organizational structure of the firm, along the lines described above. This is why it is not only more precise, but more powerful too.

Asset-specificity has been endorsed in this chapter in the same manner as opportunism is endorsed—as a relevant factor, but one which receives too great an emphasis in Williamson's work. Indeed, it can be said that Williamson interprets the concept of asset-specificity so broadly in places that practically any asset can be made to appear specific when the argument requires it. Consider for example, technological know-how, which was mentioned earlier as a prime example of general information because it can be used anywhere in the world. Such versatility does not prevent it being highly specific in the special sense that the R & D expenditures are already sunk before the know-how can be licensed, and so the knowledge is highly-specific to the requirements of local licensees (Kay, 1993). Although the problems of licensing know-how are in practice caused by weaknesses in patent rights, and the difficulty of selling secrets, the rejection of the licensing option in favour of formal integration into production can therefore be explained superficially in terms of asset-specificity too. The problem with asset-specificity is that it is just too successful in accounting for vertical integration. The real challenge is to explain why vertical integration does *not* occur in the many cases where asset-specificity is present, rather than to account for why it *does* occur in a few of the many cases where asset-specificity can be found.

Williamson is undoubtedly correct in his contention that a comprehensive theory of the firm must draw upon the insights of Simon (1947), Commons (1934) and Coase (1937). His own analysis, while influential and insightful, hardly qualifies as comprehensive, though. Williamson has little to say about intermediation, and almost nothing to say about the role of entrepreneurship in the formation and the growth of the firm. A sense of the truly global dimension to the exploitation of general ideas is missing too. The problem seems to be that bounded rationality is too vague, and asset-specificity too ubiquitous, to build an entire theory on just these foundations. It has been suggested in this chapter that a better approach is to analyse the firm as a specialized intermediator created by an entrepreneur to routinely synthesize information about different sources of volatility. Information costs take the place of bounded rationality in this approach. Asset-specificity is supplemented by a number of other factors to provide a full account of vertical integration. The result is a theory that is entirely consistent with the principle of rational action employed in mainstream economics. It is these concepts of intermediation, synthesis, volatility and information cost—rather than opportunism, bounded rationality and asset-specificity—which turn out to be most crucial when economic principles are properly applied to the theory of the firm.

3.18. Reflections on resource-based theories of the firm

There is yet another approach to the theory of the firm that has gained prominence recently—a resource-based approach which emphasizes the competences or capabilities of the firm's management team. This strand of thinking originates with Penrose (1959) and Richardson (1960, 1972); its revival owes much to its synergy with recent evolutionary theorizing by Nelson and Winter (1982). When discussing the resource-based approach to the firm it is difficult to be sure whether there is one theory expressed in different ways by different writers, or several different theories which are broadly similar to each other.

Some writers, such as Loasby (1976) and Foss et al. (1995) lay great emphasis on the complexity of the real-world processes in which firms are involved. It is suggested that economic agents in general, and managers in particular, cannot behave rationally because they are overwhelmed by the complexity of the decision problems they face. People cope with this situation by relying upon procedures that are institutionalized through political power and social conformity instead (Hodgson, 1988).

This approach, with its emphasis on institutions and their internal organization, evidently asks the same kinds of question that are addressed in this book. The nature of the answers given is very different, however. Many resource-based theorists reject formal modelling altogether, and adopt the nihilistic stance that in a complex world any model of the firm will distort the analysis more than it illuminates it. This negative attitude runs directly counter to the positive thrust of this book, which attempts to rationalize institutions and their procedures in terms of a higher level of rationality— the rationality of choosing between alternative institutions and procedures in order to achieve the best possible trade-off between the quality of decision-making and information costs.

Writers who reject rationality are usually opposed to the equilibrium concept too. They argue that economic change is path-dependent (David, 1985; Langlois, 1984); in other words, the final stage that is reached depends upon the path of adjustment that is followed. Path-dependence then becomes an endogenous feature of real-world complexity with which individual decision-makers have to cope.

A key assumption here is that the path that the adjustment process starts down is essentially a myopic path. Thus in the later stages of the evolution of the system the path that is taken may involve dealing with contradictions thrown up by the inappropriate nature of the immediate response. Individuals find that they are 'locked in' by irreversible decisions made at an earlier stage (Dosi and Metcalfe, 1991).

Because the assumption of myopia is often left implicit, however, these writers rarely consider exactly why the myopic response arises in the first place. They also play down the related issue of whether the costs of myopia are really all that great. The information costs of considering all the possible scenarios that may emerge as a consequence of a given change may well be so high that it is, in fact, efficient to tolerate a certain amount of error, provided that the consequences are not too severe. This suggests that firms will tend to adopt far-sighted plans when alternative paths afford very different economic returns, but will allow strategy to evolve naturally when different paths afford fairly similar returns. In the first case the path will be optimal, both over time, and with respect to the risks that arise when commitments are made at each particular stage. In the second case the initial decision not to plan is rational in the light of information costs, and even though the subsequent evolution of events is not uniquely specified, the indeterminacy is of little economic consequence. Any disequilibria that emerge are therefore localized disturbances whose consequences are fully endogenized by the model. In both cases, therefore, the principle of equilibrium still prevails—the equilibrium is simply conditional on the structure of information costs.

Another significant feature of resource-based theories is the emphasis that is placed on the tacit nature of information (Fransman, 1995; Kogut and Zander, 1992). In particular, it is asserted that the ownership and competitive advantages of firms comprise tacit information which could not be transferred to another firm even if contractual arrangements would permit it. A sharp distinction is therefore made between resource-based theories on the one hand and the Coasian internalization theory on the other, on the grounds that the Coasian theory fails to identify the true obstacle to the diffusion of advantages to other firms. The distinction is, however, overdrawn; for example, Buckley and Casson (1976), in their application of internalization theory to this issue, clearly identify 'psychic distance' as a non-contractual obstacle to information flow.

Indeed, what is required is nothing less than a balanced synthesis of communication costs and contractual costs to provide an integrated account of the nature of the firm. This is what the present chapter provides. The concept of communication cost reduces tacitness to an economically relevant and measurable form, while the concept of monitoring cost addresses the contractual issues. Indeed, the present theory goes beyond this by emphasizing that managerial competence resides in handling information in a variety of ways—collecting it, assimilating it, disseminating it and storing it, as well as using it to take decisions. It avoids the rather restrictive emphasis on technological information characteristic of some of the resource-based literature (Cantwell, 1995) by recognizing the enormous variety of information associated with market-making intermediation too. In this way the questions raised by resource-based theories are addressed constructively by the methodology set out in this book. The theory of the firm, like managerial competence, benefits more from evolutionary changes of the kind described here than it does from a radical reconstruction of the kind that resource-based theorists propose instead. Radical reconstruction is always expensive, and often unnecessary—as in the present case.

3.19. Summary and conclusions

This chapter has provided a definition of the firm as a specialist decision-maker and then employed a small number of key concepts to examine several related facets of the firm. It has been suggested that previous writing on the firm has been essentially partial, with different writers focusing on different issues. A synthesis has been proposed which leads towards a theory of the firm centred on the entrepreneur as the founder and prime-mover within it.

The basis of this theory is that an entrepreneur monitors the environment in order to detect symptoms of change. This leads him first to found the firm and subsequently to effect intermittent changes in its procedures. These procedures synthesize information from two main sources of volatility— namely the demand factors and the supply factors in the market that the entrepreneur has set up. While shocks in the general environment tend to persist for a considerable time, shocks to the market, once it is set up, are of a more transitory nature. That is why routine procedures are an efficient way of dealing with them.

The managers who are delegated by the entrepreneur to monitor the volatile factors also have responsibility for implementing decisions. They are supported by administrative staff, who have to be in post before the decisions are made. The work of these staff is in turn disturbed by volatile factors of very high frequency. These disturbances arise from breakdowns, illnesses, and so on; they may be interpreted as very short-run production shocks, since they affect the production of intermediating services. Efficient response to these shocks calls for spontaneous cooperation amongst the administrative staff involved. This in turn calls for 'horizontal' information flow within a high-trust environment.

There is an asymmetry of information in the supply of the product to the intermediating firm. This raises problems of quality control which, together with other considerations, such as missing forward markets, may lead to backward integration in production.

General changes in tastes, and advances in technology, may require a global response. If the entrepreneur has the vision to recognize this, then the scope of the firm will extend well beyond a single market. In this case multiple sources of volatility will be encountered within the firm. Internal substitution possibilities are likely to emerge which require rather different kinds of procedures to those of a single market. In a single market complementarity between purchases and sales is the dominant consideration and information is most naturally encoded in quantity form. With multiple markets it may be advantageous to encode information in the form of internal prices instead, since the synthesis of price information is a natural means of coordinating interrelated substitution decisions.

The basic point about the firm is that all the relevant information on transitory factors is, in principle, shared within it. Some may be suppressed in the interests of economy, and some may be communicated in the form of orders, but at all times the main decision-making procedures are premised on the information being true. These procedures may be supplemented by monitoring procedures, or by moral rhetoric, both of which aim to validate this assumption of truth. The market alternative to the firm is very different to this. The market approach accepts that bluffing is likely and attempts to constrain it by competition. Factual information is simply encoded in price quotations, and coordination is then effected through negotiation. Competition and the law replace monitoring and moral rhetoric in the transition from the firm to the market.

Overall, the nature of the firm is most naturally explained in terms of the qualities required of a successful entrepreneur. The entrepreneur processes information on both persistent and transitory factors. He normally processes the former himself, albeit on an intermittent basis, and delegates the processing of the latter. Delegation is effected using procedures, some of which impose decision rules on managers and some of which allow improvisation instead. Where improvisation is allowed, entrepreneurship is partially diffused within the firm. The key to the firm's success lies not in specific business strategies, as suggested by Porter (1980), nor in specific ownership advantages, such as technology, as suggested by Dunning (1977). These are both short-run consequences of long-run decisions about organization and corporate culture taken previously by the entrepreneur. It is the quality of entrepreneurial judgement, as reflected in the correctness of these decisions, which holds the key to long-run success.

Good judgement involves correct interpretation of the symptoms of changes in the market environment. Some of these concern tastes (in respect of consumer demand) and some concern resource availability (in respect of product supply). Others concern technology; production technology is important in respect of product design and choice of technique, but information technology is just as important too. Changes in information technology—from the telegraph through to the Internet—alter information costs and so impact directly on the organization of the firm. Value change—in morals and social customs—must be considered too. The successful entrepreneur invests in building networks of trust between his employees, and the amount of investment required will depend on the degree of trust that already exists in the society in which the firm operates. Interpreting symptoms of value change is one of the most challenging areas of entrepreneurship because of the inherent subjectivity of the phenomenon.

As a firm grows, the range of symptoms that need to be interpreted grows as well. The entrepreneur must delegate more, and the screening of delegates then becomes a major task. Interpreting symptoms of personal competence and integrity in potential employees, and sustaining motivation amongst those recruited, become increasingly important skills. To take advantage of all the local opportunities offered by a truly global market-making concept, the firm may have to grow faster than the reinvestment of profits will allow. This requires the entrepreneur to take on equity partners too. In looking for partners who can also play an executive role, the entrepreneur must screen for a wide range of knowledge and experience complementary to his own, together with a willingness to share it without reserve. The selection of business partners raises issues similar to the selection of managerial delegates, but in even more acute form.

From a knowledge of markets, through to a knowledge of technology and a knowledge of people, it is the ability to interpret symptoms and synthesize results that emerges as the hall-mark of the successful entrepreneur. The only thing to add is that the successful entrepreneur requires self-knowledge as well. When backing his own judgement against that of others, he needs to be sure that his confidence is well-placed. Conversely, he must frankly acknowledge his own shortcomings, because it is these that dictate the nature of the complementary expertise that he must recruit. 'Know thyself' is not only a moral injunction, the theory suggests, but a key to entrepreneurial success as well.

4

Business Networks

4.1. Introduction

The concept of a network is widely used to describe relations between firms. Indeed, the term is employed so generally that it sometimes seems as if networking must be ubiquitous. The object of this chapter is to clarify the network concept. It is shown that the exchange of information is a crucial network function. The social bonds sustained by networks reduce the cost of both communicating information and assuring its quality. The consequent reduction in information costs encourages greater sharing of information. By reducing the incentive to secrecy, networks facilitate the exploitation of information as a public good.

Networks of local manufacturing firms are often identified as factors in regional economic development (Bergman *et al.*, 1991; Best, 1990)—particularly in textile districts such as nineteenth-century Lancashire and Yorkshire (Brown and Rose, 1992; Hudson, 1986) and the manufacturing districts of contemporary Italy (Brusco, 1982; Goodman and Bamford, 1989; Piore and Sabel, 1984). Regional and national networks were also important in financing the Industrial Revolution in Britain (Kirby, 1984; Pollard, 1981). Networks also figure prominently in accounts of the evolution of Indian and South-East Asian trade (Tomlinson, 1989; Brown, 1995) and the emergence of international banking (Gille, 1965). In contemporary policy debate the effectiveness of networks linking capital goods suppliers and their corporate customers is said to explain differences between countries in the rate of innovation (Von Hippel, 1988). Networking may also explain the unusual success of some Scandinavian companies in the international marketing of capital goods (Johanson and Mattsson, 1987). More generally, it has been argued that the loosely-coupled 'network' firm may be a more effective innovator than the conventional hierarchical firm (Chesnais, 1988).

Inter-firm networks are closely related to social groupings, and much of the literature on local business elites and 'economic groups' (Leff, 1978; Phipatseritham and Yoshihara, 1983) can be interpreted in network terms. Conversely much of what is said about networks can be reinterpreted in terms of groups. The reason why networking is so often ascribed to local communities, regional industries and ethnic groupings is that social groups work most effectively at a local level. In principle, though, there is no reason why social groups cannot operate at a national level—or even at the international level, for that matter. The essence of a network is that the different members of a network trust each other. Trust is naturally stronger within small groups than in large ones because the frequency of face-to-face meetings between members is greater. The range of trust can, however, be extended through appropriate moral and religious systems. In this sense it is quite feasible to view the national economy as a potential network, and to relate the economic success of a national economy to its ability to realize its network potential.

The discussion in the previous chapters indicates that the important thing about the structure of a network is not so much the flow of material goods and services within it, but the flow of information that is used to coordinate this material flow. Trust is a means of assuring the quality of this information at low cost. The essence of a network, from an economic point of view, is that it affords a distinctive high-trust method of coordination. From the standpoint of coordination, the network is essentially an institutional alternative to the market and the firm. This chapter clarifies the conditions under which the network emerges as the most efficient of these institutions.

4.2. Networks of trust

Because 'network' is such a slippery concept it is important to make clear exactly what type of network is being discussed. In general terms a network is simply a collection of linkages which joins up a group of elements. The set of connected elements constitute the members of the network. In the present context the elements are individual owners and managers of firms. The linkages are formed by regular flows of information between them. A defining characteristic of the network is that these linkages involve high levels of trust.

To define a network in terms of trust is alright as far as it goes, but it must be acknowledged that the concept of trust itself can be rather elusive. This chapter takes a strictly rational approach to trust. It defines trust as a warranted belief that someone else will honour their obligations, not merely because of material incentives, but out of moral commitment too. It is assumed that such moral commitment is rational because it generates emotional rewards. These rewards outweigh any short-run material losses that honouring obligations may entail. If two parties trust each other then each will respect their obligations to the other, and the other's confidence in them will be repaid. This generates a high-trust equilibrium; it is an equilibrium because expectations are fulfilled (so there is no need to revise them in the future) and it is high-trust because it is moral and not material

def

trust vs verifiable contracts that enforce prescribed action incentives which are critical to the way the two parties behave (Casson, 1991a).

The logic of the argument can be summarized in terms of the possibilities shown in Table 4.1. The right-hand columns distinguish two main mechanisms for engineering trust. The first relies on material incentives, and is exemplified by the legal system, which enforces contracts with a monopoly of coercion—threatening offenders with fines, imprisonment, and the like. The second relies on emotional forces, manipulated by social bonding and moral rhetoric.

The disadvantage of the legal system is that it requires a monitoring mechanism to detect defaulters and a legal system to weigh the evidence against them. Its advantage is that it is a relatively impersonal mechanism, and so works well over long distances, where people may not know each other very well at all. The advantage of the moral mechanism is that it does not require monitoring of this kind because people effectively monitor themselves. Its disadvantage is that, being dependent on the emotions, it works best in a localized environment where face-to-face contact is possible, and may prove unreliable where communication is remote.

It is sometimes suggested that it is possible to have the best of both worlds, by inculcating an emotional commitment to the law itself. This was indeed characteristic of Anglo-Saxon countries at one time, but it has proved a difficult commitment to sustain. For one thing the law is a rather impersonal thing for people to develop an emotional commitment to, unless such commitment is bolstered by symbolic devices and social rituals, such as popular monarchy, the veneration of the flag, and so on. For another thing, there is no disguising the fact that the law is ultimately coercive, and that miscarriages of justice can occur. People who are directly or indirectly threatened with the law are unlikely to feel that they are trusted, and will therefore experience little emotional attachment to those who use the law in this way. On these grounds it seems perfectly legitimate to see moral and material incentives as substitutes, and not as complements to each other.

Each of these two mechanisms requires a distinctive kind of investment, as indicated in the lower headings to the right-hand columns of the table. No investment of any kind will generate no trust at all. Too little investment

TABLE 4.1. *A typology of trust*

Intensity	Type of trust	Mechanism	
		Material based on monitoring and sanctions	Moral based on rhetoric and social bonding
Too Little	Unwarranted	Defective property rights	Naivety
Adequate	Warranted	Law	High trust relations

will generate unwarranted trust. People who are morally committed themselves, but naively optimistic about other people, will become victims of cheating, as the top right hand corner of the table shows. Those who trust in the law will find themselves let down by unforeseen defects in their property rights or in the enforcement system, as the top left hand corner shows. Only adequate investment in monitoring and sanctions creates a viable system of law, as indicated in the bottom left hand corner, whilst only adequate investment in social infrastructure generates the high-trust relation shown in the bottom right hand corner of the figure. It is this high-trust relation which is the model for the network relation described in this chapter.

4.3. The intensity of trust

Given that trust ensures that people honour their obligations, what kind of obligation is it that they honour? Where trust is of low intensity the obligations may be fairly minimal, whereas when it is of high intensity more extensive obligations may be involved (for a further discussion of the intensity of trust see Ring and Van der Ven, 1994).

Where networks are concerned, two obligations are of particular importance. The first is to agree a reasonable price, and the second is to abide by the contract. The obligation to agree a reasonable price reduces the *ex ante* transaction costs incurred before the contract has been made (see Section 1.4). It allows negotiations to converge quickly on a price which is a reasonable approximation to opportunity cost, and so sustains an efficient allocation of resources. The obligation to abide by the contract reduces the *ex post* transaction costs incurred after the contract has been agreed. It ensures that the buyer pays for the goods, that the seller delivers them and that the goods are of the specified quality.

The obligation to honour a contract is more fundamental than the obligation to agree a reasonable price because without the former the latter is quite useless, while the converse is not the case. The most basic kind of network, therefore, is one which simply assures the enforcement of contracts through moral mechanisms, and leaves individuals quite untrammelled over the negotiation of price. This basic network is exemplified by an organized commodity market (see the second line of Table 4.2). This market deals in the kind of contract which is notoriously difficult to enforce in law. It is not that the contract is entirely unenforceable, but rather that its complications make it difficult for laymen, such as judges and juries, to resolve disagreements satisfactorily. The contract is prone to default because the physical resources in which the property rights are defined may be geographically remote, and in some cases have an almost hypothetical status; futures contracts rarely mature to the point of actual delivery, for example. The opportunity for dishonest speculators to overextend their

TABLE 4.2. *Types of network supported by different intensities of trust*

Intensity of trust	Type of network	Honour contract	Compromise on price	Share cost information	Open-ended contract
Low	Ordinary market	*			
Moderate	Organised market	√			
Fairly high	Private network	√	√		
High	Communal network	√	√	√	
Very high	Commitment network	√	√	√	√

* In an ordinary market contractual compliance is assured by legal rather than moral means.

position is therefore considerable. By forming a network in which people feel a genuine sense of obligation to those with whom they trade the risk of default can be considerably reduced. Traders are therefore required to join the network before they deal with each other. Those who do not belong to the network must trade through those who do, which creates a demand for brokerage services. Brokers often spend a lifetime dealing in a single market, ensuring that the social bonds between them are disrupted as infrequently as possible.

The organized market normally relies on competition to fix the price. Competition is essentially a low-trust mechanism. A trader relies on the threat of switching his custom elsewhere to discipline his partner's market power. There is no sense of obligation to make a deal with a given partner on a regular basis. But in a market with a small number of traders competitive discipline may be quite weak.

In this case a spirit of compromise may be required instead (see the third line of Table 4.2). The parties accept an obligation to conclude a deal with each other. Shopping around is discouraged on the grounds that it wastes everyone's time to explore deals that will never be made, merely to strengthen bargaining power. The requirement to compromise may be accompanied by a requirement to return to the person with whom the last deal was made, provided that the compromise reached in that case is deemed, in retrospect, to have been satisfactory. This arrangement strengthens the incentive to reach a reasonable compromise in the first place.

What constitutes a reasonable compromise must itself be agreed, however. The most common principle of compromise is 'split the difference', but this still leaves scope for strategic behaviour in making the opening bid. There are two main ways of addressing this strategic problem. One is to require the parties to agree upon a customary price. The difficulty here is that the customary price may be inflexible. Knowing what price they will be required to settle on, one of the parties may withdraw from the transaction altogether, even though the transaction would be mutually beneficial at a slightly different price.

The alternative approach is to require both parties to divulge all the information on which their bids are based (see the fourth line of Table 4.2). If adopted, this approach radically changes the way that the market process works. Instead of people keeping their own information private, and strategically encoding this information in their opening bids, they communicate this information directly to the other party. The compromise is then reached on the basis of the opportunity costs themselves, rather than on the opening bids. If it can be properly enforced then this approach eliminates the strategic aspect of price formation altogether.

It requires a very high degree of trust, however, to share information in this way. This is underlined by the naming of the strategic options illustrated in rows three and four of Table 4.2. The former, based on a spirit of compromise linked to opening bids, is called a 'private network' because it is based on information on opportunity costs remaining confidential, whilst the latter is called a 'communal network' because it is based on information being shared.

The intensity of trust is relevant to another aspect of a network too, and that is to the nature of the obligations that are exchanged. The trust required for the honouring of a contract depends upon what the contract requires, and in particular on whether the obligations are of a general or specific nature. At one extreme is a contract which tightly specifies what each party owes to the other under every possible set of circumstances, where the set of circumstances that prevails is easy to check objectively. If it turns out that one of the parties cannot deliver the services that are required under the prevailing circumstances then the failure is the responsibility of that party alone and they can, in principle, be required to pay compensation to the other party for their default. The other party is thus insured against the possibility that the first party cannot do what they promised to do.

At the other extreme is a contract which specifies that each party will simply make every effort to achieve the desired outcome. The obligations here are of a very general nature. Each party must trust that the demands placed upon them by the other party are reasonable, and that their own demands will be accepted as reasonable, and met by the other party.

It obviously economizes on trust if contracts are tightly specified wherever possible. But where many different sets of circumstances need to be itemized separately, and circumstances are difficult to verify, it may be cheaper to seek out trustworthy trading partners than to negotiate an elaborate contract with a potentially untrustworthy one. One of the key characteristics of a network is the open-ended nature of the contracts, which is due to the general nature of the obligations that are exchanged.

It is normally only the very highest level of trust which will support the exchange of general obligations of this kind. It follows that such trust will normally support the sharing of information in negotiations too. For this reason Table 4.2 associates the exchange of general obligations with a 'commitment' network, shown along the bottom line, in which the contract is negotiated by sharing information. This reflects the highest possible degree of trust that can be found in business networks—as its name suggests, the mutual commitment of the parties is effectively complete.

4.4. The distribution of competence

Trust is not the only defining characteristic of a network. The members of a network are also independent in the sense that they own and control their own resources—they are not all employees of the same firm. If all the resources are under the control of a single firm then the concentration of ownership is very high. When resources are independently owned, by contrast, the concentration of ownership is low.

For the reasons explained in previous chapters, ownership is usually based upon competence. A wide distribution of ownership therefore implies a wide distribution of competence underpinning it. Optimism and tolerance of risk are important in ownership too, as noted in Chapter 3. If some people are distinctly more optimistic than others then ownership will tend to become concentrated on the optimistic, as they speculate by buying up resources from the more pessimistic members of the group. The same applies to risk aversion: if some individuals are less risk-averse than others then they will tend to buy up resources in order to insure the less risk-averse against uncertainties and fluctuations in their income stream.

A characteristic of the network, therefore, is the relative uniformity of its members, in terms of competence, optimism, and aversion to risk. This reinforces the uniformity which prevails in the moral dimension, which allows the individual members of the network to trust each other.

Combining the degree of trust with the distribution of competence gives the typology of firms, markets and networks shown in Table 4.3. The difference between the market and the network lies in the degree of trust involved, while the difference between the market and the firm lies principally in the distribution of competence instead.

An interesting feature of the table is that two types of firm emerge, rather

TABLE 4.3. *Firms, networks, and markets*

Intensity of trust	Distribution of ownership and competence	
	Diffused	Concentrated
High	Network	High-trust firm
Low	Ordinary market	Low-trust firm

Note: This table could be further refined using the additional levels of trust identified in Table 4.2, but the gist of the argument is best summarized using just the two levels shown.

than just one. Both the high-trust firm and the low-trust firm reflect a concentration of competence, but the high-trust firm coordinates people of different degrees of competence through mutual trust whilst the low-trust firm coordinates them through monitoring and supervision instead. This distinction can be related to a number of distinctions which have been made by other writers. In early twentieth-century Britain, for example, it was useful to distinguish between paternalistic (high-trust) and bureaucratic (low-trust) organizations—not just amongst firms, but in public services and government too. McGregor's (1960) differentiation of theory X and Y in managerial leadership highlights a similar phenomenon, as does the familiar distinction between American-type and Japanese-type firms (Ouchi, 1981; Aoki, 1986). This illustrates the important point, that will not be pursued further here, that high-trust linkages, analogous to networks, can be found within firms as well as between them. It raises the interesting possibility that firms with high-trust corporate cultures, which 'network' internally, may be better at networking externally too, because the strategies governing internal and external relations are then alike. Conversely, firms that have low-trust corporate cultures may have difficulty participating in inter-firm networks because the principles of networking are not well understood.

The diagrammatic technique introduced in Chapter 1 can be used to clarify these distinctions. Networks are potentially complex phenomena, and so when investigating them in detail it is appropriate to begin with the simplest possible configuration. Consider, therefore, the single link between adjacent activities illustrated in Fig. 4.1. This link between the producer p and the retailer r is abstracted from the economic system portrayed in Fig. 1.1. The production plant and the retail premises are indicated by squares, exactly as before, and the flow of product between them is illustrated by a double line. The two way flow of information is represented by a single line.

The innovations in the diagram are two-fold. The high-trust nature of the linkage is indicated by the double arrows used for the information flow.

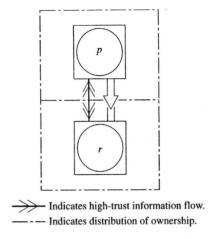

>>> Indicates high-trust information flow.
— · — Indicates distribution of ownership.

FIG. 4.1. *An elementary network*

Compared to the single arrows used in Chapter 1, a double arrow shows that the information flowing in that direction is reliable and can be trusted. It indicates the warranted trust of the recipient in the originator of the message. The degree of trust may be identified with that supporting a communal network as defined in Table 4.2. The distribution of ownership, which reflects the underlying distribution of competence, is indicated by the dashed and dotted line. The line represents the boundary between two different ownership units. Both the producer and the retailer feel competent in their own activities, and have no desire to surrender ownership of their facility to the other. Neither do they wish to surrender ownership to an intermediator instead.

This arrangement may be contrasted with that of the high-trust firm shown in Fig. 4.2. The inequality of competence in the high-trust firm is indicated by the strategic role of the market-making headquarters *m*. Information on supply and demand conditions is fed by the producer and the retailer to the intermediator at head office, who believes what he is told. He effects a synthesis, takes a decision, and issues instructions. These instructions are believed to be appropriate by the producer and the retailer, and the intermediator can be confident, without the need for monitoring, that the instructions will be carried out.

A low-trust firm would exhibit a similar configuration to the high-trust firm, but the quality of information would be assured in a different way. The producer and the retailer expect the intermediator to pay them their salaries because his reputation depends upon it. They expect the instructions he gives them to be appropriate because he is the principal risk-bearer and is therefore well motivated to make efficient decisions. The intermediator expects the producer and the retailer to carry out his instructions because

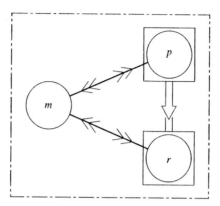

FIG. 4.2. *A high-trust vertically-integrated firm replacing an elementary network*

he is monitoring them, and holds sanctions based on the fact that they are paid in arrears.

The market alternative is also low-trust. The configuration may vary depending upon whether intermediation is involved. The law is the basis for expectations that contractual commitments will be met. As in the network, both the producer and the retailer are responsible for encoding their information into prices. Where they communicate directly considerable haggling may ensue, as each may believe that the other is attempting to bluff. Intermediation reduces haggling by allowing the intermediator to take a hard line on price. By quoting non-negotiable prices the intermediator forces the producer and the retailer to encode their information in quantity responses to given prices instead. This takes some of the initiative away from the producer and the retailer, and reduces the need for competence in negotiation. Unlike the firm, however, the intermediated market still requires a significant degree of competence to be demonstrated by the producer and the retailer.

A more elaborate configuration is illustrated in Fig. 4.3. There are now two producers, p_1 and p_2, and two retailers, r_1 and r_2, with four possible linkages between them. So far as each producer is concerned, the configuration describes a distribution channel, in which there are two retailers who can take delivery of the product. So far as each retailer is concerned, the configuration describes a supply chain in which there are two alternative sources of production. If the producers and retailers were distributed across different countries then the configuration could describe a trade diaspora in which each country either imports from, or exports to, two other countries.

The figure shows how each possible linkage is coordinated by a high-trust flow of information. Both producers and retailers are subject to local shocks. They share their information on these shocks in order to optimize

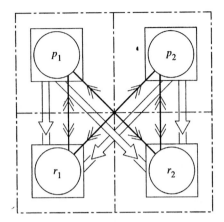

FIG. 4.3. *A distribution-supply network*

their overall response, and to distribute the proceeds in what they regard as an equitable way.

An interesting feature of Fig. 4.3 is that there is no direct communication between the producers p_1 and p_2, nor between the retailers r_1 and r_2. This is because there is no flow of resources for such communication to support. It is possible, though, that there may be opportunities for the producers, and for the retailers, to help each other out, and this could warrant such information flow. For example, if producer p_1 faces an unexpected shortage of raw materials, while producer p_2 has a temporary surplus, then it may be more efficient to transfer raw materials from p_2 to p_1 than to have p_2 expand its output and export more to r_1. Similarly if retailer r_1 unexpectedly loses inventory it may be more efficient, in the short run at least, to transfer inventory from r_2 than to increase r_1's supplies from p_1 and p_2. Focusing adjustments on transfers of this kind, instead of on the pattern of retailer sourcing, is particularly advantageous where production levels are costly to adjust, and where transport difficulties make cross-trades between p_1 and r_2, and p_2 and r_1, costly to set up.

The existence of a network may therefore make it possible to change the physical configuration of flows in a way which would not be viable in the absence of trust. A physical configuration typical of such a network is illustrated in Fig. 4.4.

Producer p_1 is the lowest cost source of supply for retailer r_1, and producer p_2 is the lowest cost source for retailer r_2. This is institutionalized in long-term relationships between p_1 and r_1, and between p_2 and r_2. This vertical flow of product, indicated by 1 in the figure, is supplemented by the two horizontal resource flows, indicated by 2 and 3. These flows occur at random when the producers and the retailers help one another out. The direction of flow 2 between the producers is dictated by which producer

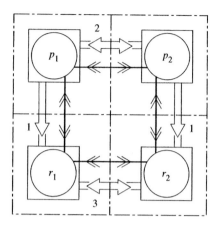

FIG. 4.4. *A high-trust network with both vertical and horizontal links*

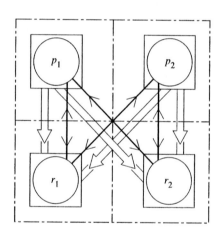

FIG. 4.5. *A market alternative to a network*

happens to be most in difficulty at the time. Similarly the direction of flow 3 between the retailers is dictated by which retailer happens to be in most difficulty. These flows are shown as bi-directional, although the flow only goes in one direction at any one time.

Contrast this with the relatively impersonal market illustrated in Fig. 4.5. This figure is similar to Fig. 4.3 except that communication is low-trust instead. Here the emphasis is on competition between rival flows of product. Neither the producers nor the retailers help each other out. Each producer strives to take advantage of the other's misfortunes, and so does each retailer. Neither retailer is loyal to any particular producer, and the producers respond to this by encouraging retailers to switch their allegiance wherever possible. Likewise the retailers encourage the producers to switch

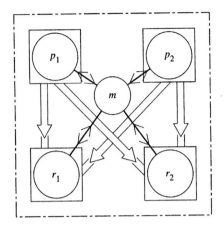

FIG. 4.6. *A low-trust firm*

their allegiance away from the rival firm. This threat of switching constrains the negotiating strategies of the parties. It is the basis of the competition which, as the number of rivals increases, leads the price to converge very quickly to its equilibrium level. In this competitive atmosphere the only guarantee that contracts will be honoured is provided by the law.

The corporate equivalent of this is shown in Fig. 4.6. It illustrates a low-trust firm that internalizes the market by owning all the facilities and monitoring the managers who control them. Notice how the headquarters, *m*, acts as a nexus of communications. Price negotiations are replaced by a centralized synthesis of the information on which the individuals previously based their negotiating strategies. Competition is no longer employed as a quality assurance mechanism for information, to drive prices into equality with underlying opportunity costs. Instead monitoring of costs and revenues is used to check directly on the accuracy of the information supplied to headquarters.

A high-trust firm has even more options at its disposal. It can switch supplies in the manner of the market and the low-trust firm, and it can arrange for producers and retailers to help each other out as well. The disadvantage of the high-trust firm is simply that it has so many options that it is difficult for headquarters to choose efficiently between them. To simplify decision-making at headquarters the high-trust firm may have to decentralize power, and this may create an intermediated network instead.

4.5. Intermediation

The larger a network becomes, the greater is the scope for intermediation in order to reduce communication costs. Yet because an intermediator is in

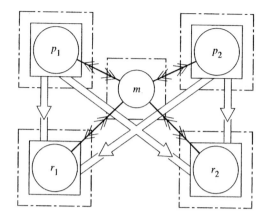

Fig. 4.7. *An intermediated network*

a privileged position, the symmetry that exists between members of a network on account of their uniformity of competence may appear to be undermined. The importance of the intermediator could suggest that someone of superior competence is required for this task. Within a network the difference in competence between the intermediator and the ordinary members may be quite small, however. Each member may retain considerable independence, and in consequence responsibility for the creation and adaptation of the network may also be diffused. For example, the network may be run by an assembly of its members, with the intermediator being elected, or the position being rotated on a regular basis. In this case it is individual voters in the assembly, acting collectively, rather than the intermediator alone, that controls the evolution of the network over time. Thus the membership as a whole may decide who is allowed to join the network and who is not. Intermediation may therefore have less strategic significance within a network than it does within an ordinary market or a firm.

An intermediated network is illustrated in Fig. 4.7. It is basically a dis-integrated high-trust firm. The dis-integration reflects the relative autonomy of the individual producers and retailers, which is mirrored in the fact that the intermediator has less executive authority than in the high-trust firm. The network structure is particularly suitable where there is little variation in the competence of members of the group, so that there is no one really competent to take on the responsibility of heading an integrated firm. It is also appropriate when transitory local shocks impinging on the producers and retailers are extremely varied, so that it is difficult to handle them purely by routine. This reduces the advantages of formal organization and favours the informality of the network instead.

4.6. Partnerships, business finance, and technological collaboration

The emphasis so far has been on the role of networks in supporting trade. Networks have another important role, though—in supporting the finance of economic activity through partnerships. Taking on a business partner is a potentially hazardous activity, since each partner shares in the consequences of the decisions that the other partners may make. In making these decisions the other partners are aware that some of the consequences have been shifted on to other people, and so they may not exercise as much care and attention as they would if they bore all the consequences themselves.

Networks provide an atmosphere of trust within which partnerships can be established. They also help to standardize the competencies of members of the network, in a manner described in Section 4.8. This reduces the risk of encountering an honest but incompetent partner. Finally networks provide an opportunity to learn in detail about both the integrity and competence of prospective partners, both at first hand and through reputation mechanisms.

Integrity and competence are crucial in partnerships because of the high level of commitment required. It is not just the sinking of financial capital into illiquid assets that is involved—in many cases there is also a commitment to supply whatever expertise is necessary to make the venture a success. This means that in the typical venture each partner must assess what special expertise his other partners possess, and whether they are willing to act in the spirit of partnership, which requires them to place this expertise at the disposal of the venture, whenever circumstances require it, without reservation. Operating within a network gives people the confidence to believe, first, that the typical partner is indeed honest and competent and, secondly, that they have the means at their disposal to check out prospective partners in advance if they wish.

The economic importance of partnerships depends on a number of factors, one of which is economies of scale. The larger the scale of the activity that needs to be financed, the more likely it is that the financial requirements will exceed the disposable wealth of any single entrepreneur. As the market grows and the technology matures in any given industry, so continuous flow mass production tends to take over from smaller scale batch production. This means that in each region or district in which the industry is concentrated, a network based upon trade between small production units is liable to be supplanted by a business partnership financing a single large production plant instead.

The transition is illustrated in Fig. 4.8. Flows of equity finance are illustrated using the 'spring' symbol, which indicates that the financier absorbs the financial consequences of the shocks impinging on the facility he owns. With two small-scale production plants financed by individuals f_1 and f_2, and

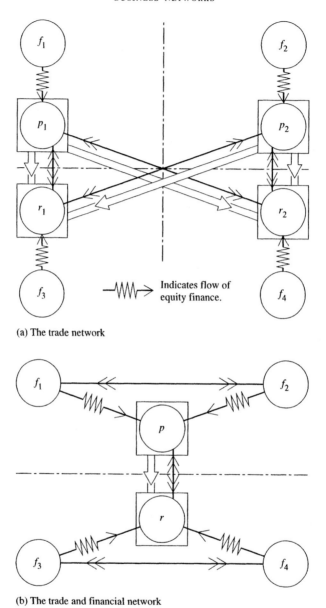

FIG. 4.8. *The transition from a trade network towards a financial network*

two small-scale retail units financed by individuals f_3 and f_4, coordination of the network is effected entirely through trade. When the two small scale production units are replaced by a single large plant, and the two small retail outlets by a single large outlet, then the financiers combine to form two partnerships. Coordination is now effected partly through trade and partly through the financial arrangements.

Economies of scale can, in some cases induce vertical integration, since the exploitation of scale economies at adjacent stages of production creates problems of bilateral market power. Within a network, however, such conflict may be peacefully resolved through sharing information and compromising over price. It is possible, though, that there may be administrative economies afforded by centralised information synthesis, and this may induce vertical integration even where there is trust. This creates the situation shown in Fig. 4.9 where the four financiers collaborate to found a high-trust firm controlled by the chief executive *m*.

Another important factor driving the formation of partnerships is the need to combine complementary forms of expertise (Buckley and Casson, 1988). In recent years this has emerged as an important motive for international collaboration in R & D. The range of different scientific disciplines required to research modern product innovations has widened, and the costs of development programmes have risen in the light of the demand for globally acceptable products that meet health, safety, and other regulations in all major countries. The combination of diverse research expertise and high development costs has encouraged even large firms to search for joint venture partners. The commitments made by the firms to such projects are often limited to the expertise available from one particular subsidiary company or project team. There are few firms that trust their

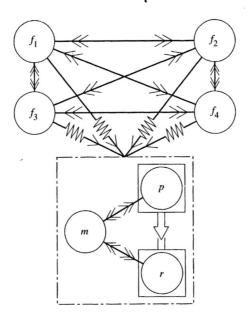

FIG. 4.9. *A financial network supporting a high-trust firm*

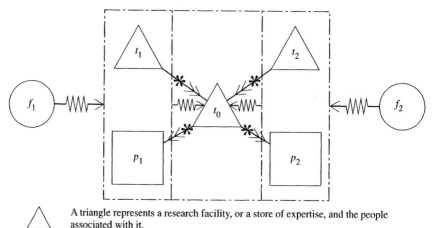

△ A triangle represents a research facility, or a store of expertise, and the people
   associated with it.

✳⟫ A flow of trustworthy expertise (the information flow required to coordinate this flow
    of expertise is not shown separately in order to simplify the diagram).

FIG. 4.10. *Financing of a research-based joint venture between two firms*

partners well enough to commit the expertise of their entire group to any single collaborative project. Subject to this qualification, however, business partnerships between major firms are now a distinctive feature of the world economy.

The way that networking may support collaborative research is illustrated in Fig. 4.10. The two business partners are firms which are separately owned by the financiers f_1 and f_2. The financiers supply risk capital to the firms which is then passed on to the joint-owned research facility indicated by the triangle t_0. The research is supported by flows of expertise emanating from the wholly-owned corporate research laboratories t_1 and t_2. The flows of expertise are indicated by asterisks, to distinguish them from the ordinary flows of information used purely for coordination. The flows carry double arrows, to show that the information provided by the experts can be trusted. Instead of feeding their research results directly to the production plants p_1 and p_2, the two laboratories contribute expertise to the jointly-owned facility t_0. The results generated by the facility are shared between the plants p_1 and p_2.

Because new technology is a public good, neither plant loses directly from the fact that the results are made available to the other plant as well. There is, however, a potential competitive threat if the two partners seek to exploit the same knowledge in similar ways. It may help to build trust if the partners are interested in slightly different applications of the results, or if because of geographical segmentation they are likely to be supplying different markets. Indeed the firms may enter into agreements for this reason—a collusive agreement to fix prices, or to partition markets into non-overlapping segments, or perhaps a specialization agreement to ensure that the products are sufficiently different that customers cannot substitute between them.

4.7. The emotional dimension

Partnerships can be a source, not only of material rewards, but of emotional satisfactions too. This is undoubtedly true of partnerships between individuals, although its implications for joint ventures between firms are not so clear. For individuals, participation in a partnership may be not only a means to an end, but also an end in itself. Four aspects of this are relevant to network behaviour.

The first is that people are very interested in what their own level of competence is. Status is often related to competence—in the professions, for example—so that people are interested in their competence as a guide to what level of status they can aspire to achieve. To realize their true competence they may need a challenge of some kind. But the most worthwhile challenges often involve ambitious tasks which require the support of other people. The spirit of competition often stimulates people to the most sustained effort when it is organized as competition between groups rather than as competition between individuals (Casson, 1995a, chapter 3). The partnership therefore provides a suitable environment in which people can discover their true potential, and hence learn something about their favourite subject—namely themselves.

A related point is that people often wish to leave behind themselves some kind of legacy—it provides a kind of immortality, they believe. For this legacy to be on a suitably impressive scale, the cooperation of other people is required. This cooperation could be obtained under a variety of different contractual arrangements. Given that people may lack confidence in certain aspects of their ability, however, the mutual assurance provided by a partnership makes this arrangement particularly attractive. The partnership is therefore a natural mechanism for creating monuments on a collective basis.

The third aspect is a sequel to this. For most adults the natural legacy is children, and consequently the natural model of partnership is the family. Since almost everyone has experience of family life during their childhood, the family is the natural archetype of the partnership, in business as elsewhere. The open-endedness of the mutual commitment is particularly striking in the case of marriage, since people pledge their lives to each other in an almost unconditional way. The emotional satisfactions of marriage are also highly rated—indeed the correlation between the depth of the commitment and the size of the emotional reward may be nature's way of correcting for some of the risks involved. Even the most hard-headed and cynical economist is likely to concede that material rewards alone cannot account for altruistic behaviour within the family. Although such intensity of reward cannot be replicated within a business partnership, the experience of such rewards may encourage people to approach business partnerships in a positive way. The link between family ties and business partnerships is a well-established one. Although the connection can be readily explained in terms of the lower screening costs and wider range of sanctions that exist within the family's own capital market, the existence of enhanced emotional rewards is almost certainly a factor too.

A further point about the family is that the terms of the marriage contract are normally dictated by custom. Negotiations may, of course, take place over the size of a dowry, heritable estates may be entailed, and so on. But these are essentially modifications to, rather than replacements of, the principle that the resources of time and money are pooled within a marriage. A custom of any kind is, of course, useful in reducing transaction costs (Schlicht, 1993). This particular custom does have a certain rationale, however, in the sense that human resources of the kind committed in marriage, being of uncertain quality, are difficult to value. Relying upon people to signal their self-valuation through a negotiation process is likely to be inefficient whenever the owner of the resource, being unsure of their competencies, does not know the value themselves. In the absence of strong evidence to the contrary, therefore, a custom which imposes pooling has much to recommend it. This probably explains why the principle of pooling is so widespread, even in business partnerships, where the 50:50 equity joint venture is one of the most common forms.

4.8. The social embeddedness of business networks

Because business networks are so dependent on the integrity and competence of their members, the question naturally arises as to whether these qualities have to be developed entirely on the initiative of the business community itself. The answer is that they do not. The business community can 'free ride' on the activities of numerous social groups which constitute the fabric of society as a whole (Granovetter, 1985). Table 4.4 identifies seven major types of social group observed in advanced industrial societies. These groups have an important role both in legitimating moral values and in developing people's technical competencies too. This is because all the groups contribute in some way towards their members' education. The members go out from these groups with values and skills rather different from those they entered with.

In order for a social group to support business operations through a network it is necessary for the members of the group to be in a place where the business operations require them. The economic logic of the business

TABLE **4.4.** *Economic significance of different types of social group*

Institution	Moral education	Technical education	Affiliation strategy
Family	Provides basic moral teaching Inculcates respect for age and experience	Passes on tacit business skills useful for self-employment Inheritance system develops useful concentrations of business capital	Marry in Become adopted protegé
Church	Legitimates morality Encourages concept of personal accountability to ancestors, God, etc. as well as to peers Perpetuates tradition	Reading of scriptures improves literacy	Conversion
School, university qualifications	Inculcates loyalty (in both pupils and alumni) Emphasizes achievement through hard work Values ability and competence	Develops analytical decision-making skills	Study to gain entry (where appropriate)
Military service	Teaches discipline, respect for authority, and how to cope with risky situations	Teaches tactical and engineering skills	Conscription or volunteering
Trade unions, professional associations, etc.	Promotes craftsmanship and professional standards Values solidarity		Gain appropriate work experience, through apprenticeship, take vocational examinations, etc.
Clubs (sporting, charitable, hobbies, etc.)	Value of teamwork (in team sports) Value of caring (in charitable activities)	Self-improvement through friendly competition Develops management skills by participation in collective decision-making, etc.	Attain sufficient proficiency, respectability, etc.
Political party	Encourages vision, and interest in major long-term issues Negative 'partisan' effect	Make contacts linking public and private sectors Acquire 'charismatic leadership' skills by standing as candidate	Very easy to join

Source: Adapted from Casson (1995*b*), chapter 3, pp. 55–6.

operations will normally dictate where members of the group need to be placed, rather than the other way round. If a group is to fulfil a business role its members therefore need to display a degree of mobility. The mobility required is, of course, much greater to operate an international business network than, say, a purely local one.

It may be questioned whether a business network can really be effective over long distances, because opportunities for face-to-face contact will be very limited. The answer is that many of the social groups used for business purposes were formed when people who were once together later disperse. The emotional intensity of their togetherness is sufficient to bind them together for a considerable time after they have left. Once they have revitalized their association for business purposes, the limited contact experienced in the normal course of business dealings may then be sufficient to keep the bond intact indefinitely.

Each of the social groups distinguished in Table 4.4 provides a structured framework within which members meet regularly over a significant period of time, after which they tend to disperse, carrying their affiliation with them. Since different types of group have different functions, many individuals will choose to belong to at least one group of each type. Multiple affiliation is possible with some types of group, but not others. Thus while a person may switch by conversion from one religion to another, they cannot credibly adhere to two different religions at the same time; by changing affiliation they distance themselves from the group to which they originally belonged. On the other hand, a person can quite credibly belong to two different local clubs or societies, and may indeed perform a valuable service in brokering between what might otherwise be two non-overlapping social groups.

Multiple affiliation is important in the development of business networks by entrepreneurs. The wider the range of an individual's affiliations, the greater will be his personal network of trusted contacts. This applies particularly to people with varied work experience and leisure interests ('playing hard' may be as strategically important as working hard where the 'networked' entrepreneur is concerned). There is, of course, a trade-off between breadth and depth of attachments—people who change jobs frequently, or spread their leisure time thinly across several societies, are unlikely to become as strongly bonded to their colleagues as those who maintain steady allegiance to a small number of social groups. So far as business networking is concerned, however, a wide range of relatively superficial attachments can always be strengthened by subsequent social contact in the course of business negotiations.

Some institutions tend to discourage dispersal of their members—for example, families which instil in children an obligation to care for aged parents discourage long-term migration. On the other hand, institutions such as Victorian public schools, which educated people for colonial government, positively encouraged long-term migration. Similarly religions which stress individual faith and world-wide mission encourage migration, in contrast to those which stress collective ritual centred on local traditions. Finally, professional institutions which accredit individual competencies based on standard criteria encourage worker migration, compared to most trade unions, where loyalty to the local work group is stressed instead.

Dispersal of a group is sometimes an unintended consequence of the group's beliefs, as when a religious group is dispersed through persecution. It was noted above that multiple affiliation is more difficult in the case of religion than in the case of, say, local clubs. Differences in religion therefore tend to create factions, with limited opportunities for brokering between them. Where different religions coexist in a territory, it is usually the nation state that has the job of managing conflict between them. This is usually done by an ethic of religious toleration on the one hand, and an ethic of national unity on the other. A nation state so weak that it cannot enforce toleration may precipitate the dispersal of minority religious groups at the hands of the most numerous or militant group. As an alternative, the state may exalt nationalism as a religion of its own, with much the same effect so far as strongly committed religious groups are concerned.

So far as business networks are concerned the conclusion is somewhat paradoxical. By promoting the enforced dispersion of emotionally-bonded groups, a combination of strong religious convictions and weak national governments may actually promote business activities on a global scale. It could be added that since the development of religious conflict is often the result of turbulent changes which encourage the emergence of new (often fundamentalist) sects, such change acquires a dynamic of its own. By creating conflict which precipitates the dispersion of these sects it encourages the spread of their ideas, and helps to build business networks which become future engines of economic change.

4.9. Leadership in networks

It was noted in Table 4.1 that the engineering of trust requires investments in moral rhetoric and social bonding. This investment is undertaken in social groups. The question arises as to whether this investment can be deliberately planned in order to encourage networking, and thereby improve the economic performance of the group. More generally, it can be asked whether intermediation, which is so useful in the organization of trade, can be applied to the engineering of trust as well. It is suggested here that leadership can be employed as a form of intermediation to create not only trust, but also competence within a group.

Most groups evolve a division of labour in their social organization. Even the most primitive societies generally have a division of labour between the leader and his followers, and their members tend to identify a good group with one that has a good leader. As a society develops, so priests, philosophers, politicians and teachers may emerge as part of a differentiated leadership elite. Such an elite can disseminate moral exhortations conducive to trust. However strong their moral rhetoric, though, some criminal elements will remain immune to it, so a system of law is required to back up the moral rhetoric.

The division of labour applies to the law as well. Advanced societies tend to have a quite elaborate division of labour in the legal domain. For example, responsibilities for legislation, adjudication, investigation, and the implementation of sanctions may be devolved respectively to parliament, the courts, the police, and the prison service. The rationale for this lies not only in the efficiency gains from functional specialization, but the political importance of imposing a division of powers on what might otherwise become a monopoly of force.

A key element in Western culture is a belief that such a 'balance of power' is necessary for political freedom. Some commentators, however, have wrongly concluded from this that the law is itself sufficient for building up trust and that when there is ready access to the law moral commitment is no longer required. Even where the need for morals is recognized, there is a tendency to think that moral pluralism is to be favoured over moral uniformity, on the grounds that moral pluralism, like political pluralism, safeguards freedom. The economic need to engineer trust indicates otherwise, however. Legal enforcement is so costly that a cheaper alternative is usually required, and this alternative calls for a consensual commitment to integrity. It is moral uniformity, centred on functional values like integrity, that is required to engineer trust. Moral pluralism creates uncertainty about other people's commitments, so that trust is no longer warranted, and people are reluctant to trade.

The standardization of a group on appropriate functional values is a natural role for a leader. Such a leader intermediates between the followers, not by intervening directly in trade between them, but in influencing them so that they can trade more easily amongst themselves.

Different styles of leadership are conducive to different types of organization. A dogmatic and authoritarian style may be conducive to corporate organization, in the sense that it legitimates a concentration of responsibility at the top of an organization. A relatively impersonal, yet democratic style of leadership may be appropriate to a market system. A personal and consultative style of leadership is most appropriate to a network organization, since it emphasizes the value of personal bonding on the one hand, and the competence of the individual members on the other, in the sense that they are all expected to have some information of value to contribute to a strategic decision.

It is not only morals that a leader can disseminate, but theories, concepts, and information too. A leader can encourage individual entrepreneurship by giving people a mental framework with which they can analyse situations for themselves. Equally, he can inhibit entrepreneurship by encouraging the majority of people to avoid responsibility for decisions and concentrate simply on implementing other people's rules. The entrepreneurial approach is conducive to markets and networks, because they diffuse responsibility, whilst its opposite is conducive to corporate organization instead.

4.10. Networks and national economic performance

The contribution of networking to economic development is more often discussed at the regional level than at the national level. This is partly understandable on the grounds that social interactions are often more intense at the regional level than at the national level. Where isolated or peripheral regions are concerned there may be little social contact between the region and the rest of the country. Besides regional groupings, however, most countries have national elites centred around a major metropolis or the capital city (the two are not always the same). The higher echelons of each regional community may belong to this elite. This can generate a kind of federalism within the social structure, with negotiations between the leaders of the different regions being intermediated by the leader of the national elite.

It goes without saying that the more enterprising the elite, and the greater their success in engineering trust, the more successfully the economy is likely to perform. A prerequisite for success, however, is that the elite can successfully bind together the different interest groups in the country. It is not just regional factions that are important here. A society can split into factions in many different ways, and once it splits rent-seeking conflict over the distribution of income can quickly undermine coordination (Olson, 1982).

One possibility is that society becomes stratified into different layers, corresponding to different levels of status. If status is ascribed on the basis of income then in a free-enterprise economy there may be considerable mobility between the layers, so that networks can actually operate across the boundaries of status groups as well as just within them. Conversely, in a society where status is ascribed on the basis of parentage, status mobility may be low and networking may be confined to non-overlapping segments of society. The resulting distrust between the different social layers may generate a form of class conflict which inhibits overall coordination.

Another kind of factionalism is based upon institutionalized specialization. This has become particularly prominent amongst Western professional groups in recent years. It is seen by many as a rational response to the growth of scientific knowledge, which calls for an ever-greater division of labour in teaching and research. The premature socialization of potentially creative people into narrow professional groups, each with its own distinctive concepts and its own intellectual 'territory', may well inhibit the development of imaginative solutions to practical problems, however. If intellectual specialization is combined with an elitist attitude that stratifies societies horizontally by ability too, then the implications for coordination may be very serious indeed.

4.11. Victorian Britain as a national network

An interesting historical illustration of national networking can be found in mid-Victorian Britain. One of the striking characteristics of Britain in the period 1850–80 was the energetic nature of its national elite. This elite invested heavily in all of the different social institutions listed in Table 4.4. The family was promoted as the bastion of middle-class respectability. It provided a social foundation for the paternalistic family capitalism which was characteristic of mid-Victorian enterprise. Sunday church-going was an important ritual element in respectable family life. The Church of England underwent a spiritual revival in mid-century under the twin influences of the Evangelical movement and the Oxford movement; the cool deism of the late eighteenth century was replaced by emotional commitment and missionary zeal. This had implications not only for national development, but for imperial development too. Missionary activity played a major role in legitimating imperial expansion. Where trade developed, the missionaries followed, and this in turn fostered colonization.

Schooling was also high on the Victorian agenda. Compulsory attendance was introduced, and new schools built to accommodate the additional children. The Sunday School movement, re-inforced by city church-building and revivalism, had a major (if short-lived) impact on the working classes. Of greatest significance for imperial development, however, was the emergence of the public schools inculcating the virtues of leadership through self-discipline (Wilkinson, 1964). Intense social bonding at school created the phenomenon of the 'old school tie'—an allegiance formed in youth which could be exploited for business purposes throughout a person's career. The school, the church, and the family all provided links between those in the colonies and those at home which allowed business transactions to proceed in a high-trust atmosphere even though the parties concerned were thousands of miles apart.

The role of the armed forces should not be overlooked either. Many explorers and business adventurers had a military background and could call on their former colleagues for capital when suitable opportunities arose. The armed forces themselves were glamorized by their part in the rituals of imperialism. Whig historians placed the military successes of the early nineteenth century into a broader context of national progress. Parallels were drawn between economic and social progress under Queen Victoria and national revival under Queen Elizabeth I three centuries earlier.

The existence of this social infrastructure shows that in Victorian Britain the business network was a viable alternative to the integrated firm. Contrary to the claims of Chandler (1977, 1990), where social networks are already in place it may be more advantageous for businesses to 'free ride' on them than to create large hierarchical organizations instead. Even if hierarchy was advantageous in mass-production manufacturing industry, networking was almost certainly the right approach in other important sectors. The expansion of London as an international financial centre in the late nineteenth century, for example, owed a great deal to networks built around the public schools. These networks proved extremely useful in solving the problem of monitoring at a distance where the export of capital to colonial territories was concerned (Jones, 1992). Indeed, by stressing the colonial mission of spreading British democratic traditions to frontier territories, the public schools encouraged great geographical mobility. The result was the emigration of many talented people whose skills, though primarily in government, were sufficiently general to be applicable to finance and commerce as well. The study of the economic problems of the Greek and Roman empires proved very rewarding in building the British one!

The emphasis on history and the humanities, however, meant that technological skills had to be obtained from a rather different source—namely from consulting engineers drawn, in part, from the ranks of upwardly-mobile artisans. Thus finance and technology were never married as effectively in Britain as they were, say, in Germany; two different social networks were involved, and as the nineteenth century progressed differences in status between them seem to have widened, with finance gaining respectability and engineering losing it. It is perhaps no accident that this growing social factionalization—mirrored, too, in industrial relations—emerged at about the same time that Britain's relative economic performance began to decline.

4.12. International comparisons of networking

The development of business relationships in the USA seems to reflect a different pattern. Within a country of immigrants, there were few social networks already in place in the growing industrial centres of Pennsylvania, Ohio, Indiana, Illinois, etc. With no networks to free-ride on, hierarchical organization based on formal monitoring was the natural response. Relations between firms were based on carefully written arm's length contracts—businessmen trusted the legal process more than they trusted their peers. Although attempts were made to organize cartels and to 'manage' competition, these had only short-run success. Cartel-cheating meant that formal trusts were more effective than informal price-fixing agreements (for as long as they were legal). Informal price-fixing did, of course, occur, but usually under the influence of a dominant firm's price umbrella—so that material sanctions were readily available to punish under-cutting.

The tendency of migration to select the most entrepreneurial people—particularly noticeable in the first wave of nineteenth-century European migration to the USA—means that considerable entrepreneurial resources were available in the USA at that time. It is therefore somewhat paradoxical that the earliest nation-wide firms adopted hierarchical forms of organization in which entrepreneurial subordinates were given so little responsibility. Four factors mitigated this problem. The first was the emphasis on freedom of entry into business, which made self-employment a relatively easy option for the frustrated entrepreneurial employee. The second—which only came much later, after World War I—was the evolution of multi-divisional structure—which is an appropriate innovation for a low-trust society. Thirdly, experience with formal low-trust monitoring procedures endowed US businessmen with transferable skills in managing low-skill labour on mass production lines. Finally, the emphasis on measurement, engendered by the need to base contracts on objective quantified requirements, also facilitated the application of laboratory science to industry. After World War II this package of skills was transferred to Europe and other developed areas through US foreign direct investment. The disadvantage was that the formal procedures were also applied, in many cases, to headquarters-subsidiary relations. European managers were not used to being treated as if they could not be trusted by their superiors. Overall, therefore, the hierarchical control of overseas subsidiaries was not a success, compared with other aspects of the process.

By the 1970s it was evident that European foreign investors, who relied more on socialization amongst top managers, were on average performing better. In Europe, socialization is often undertaken before people join the firm—it is reflected in recruitment procedures which implicitly discriminate in favour of people with particular educational, religious, political affiliations, etc. Weaker socialization in the USA means that more has to be done after people have joined the firm. Recognition of the need for change led many large US firms to invest heavily in engineering a corporate culture designed to enhance internal entrepreneurship and managerial flexibility (Kotter and Heskett, 1992). The engineering of corporate culture is, however, a difficult task when, for example, employees think mainly in terms of individual career progression rather than life-time loyalty to the firm. Unlike Japan, for example, there is no previously established concept of loyalty which the employee can transfer to the firm. Recent efforts at engineering corporate culture have therefore generated mixed results (Casson *et al.*, 1996). It is interesting to note, in this respect, that the socialization effected by leading business schools (Marceau, 1989) has inculcated very little concept of loyalty to the employer, possibly because of the influence of US values on the curriculum.

The conclusion, therefore, is that differences in methods of business organization reflect a rational response to underlying patterns of trust established by social institutions. Deficiencies in British manufacturing industry around the turn of the century are more likely to be explained by negative cultural attitudes to industrialization and the application of science than to an inefficient choice of organizational structures. Conversely, the success of the British economy in the financial services sector is more likely to be explained by the 'cultural infrastructure' of its elite educational system than by the absolute superiority of the particular organizational arrangements which it employed.

An important policy implication is that social institutions are of enormous economic significance: they affect both the absolute level of performance and the comparative performance of different sectors. Since these institutions have moral rather than profit objectives, the strength of the moral commitment of their founders is probably more important to the national economy than their conventional entrepreneurial skills. An economy needs to encourage social leadership in order to build and maintain social institutions that engineer trust. A society that emphasizes the pursuit of profit to the exclusion of other objectives is therefore likely to suffer in the long run as it will damage these institutions and so be unable to exploit contractual arrangements that require high levels of trust. Profitable business does not therefore require an exclusive emphasis on the pursuit of profit; but rather a balanced moral system in which profit considerations guide the choice of efficient means by its firms and business networks, but which is ultimately driven by the not-for-profit ends of its social institutions.

5

Imitation and Instability

5.1. Introduction

When discussing the role of information in coordination it seems natural to suppose that more information is always better than less. It also seems natural that a wider diffusion of information will improve coordination. Better coordination should in turn contribute to the stability of the economy. Yet there is a paradox here—namely that some of the most information-rich economies also seem most prone to instability. This instability is often attributed to excessive investment, or the excessive bunching of investments, which in turn is attributed to financial speculation.

The resolution of this paradox, it is suggested below, is that information is often interpreted in a misleading way. Unsophisticated decision-makers may use oversimplified models of their environment, which produce mistaken inferences. Unscrupulous sophisticated decision-makers may exploit the situation to take advantage of this. Although everyone may act rationally within the content of the mental models they employ, some mental models may be more accurate than others. No society has yet advanced to the point where all the inappropriate models have been eliminated. Until they have, the more sophisticated may continue to manipulate the less sophisticated by deliberately feeding them with information calculated to make them behave in an exploitable way.

An easy form of information to feed to people, and one that is very prone to misinterpretation, is information encoded in behaviour. Previous chapters have discussed the way that information may be encoded in prices or in quantities, but the possibility that information is encoded in actions has not been explicitly discussed. Yet it is obvious, on reflection, that because decisions are based on information, the actions that result from these decisions embody information too. For social 'outsiders', who are denied access to proper information, reversing out the information content of 'insider's' decisions is a way of remedying their information deficit. The problem is that such reversing out is difficult to do, and the outsiders may be the very kind of people for whom the difficulties are particularly great. Under such conditions it is easy for a sophisticated person to conjecture accurately how other people will interpret his actions. By performing an action that he knows will be misinterpreted it is easy for him to tell a lie without actually saying anything that can later be proved to be untrue.

One reason why advanced economies are prone to speculative instability is that lower information costs not only facilitate the communication of price and quantity information but encourage wider imitation too. If such economies also had a strong ethic of integrity, which discouraged people from performing actions that they know are likely to be misconstrued, then the consequences of this might not be too severe. Regrettably this condition is rarely satisfied in practice, though. Nevertheless, there are some measures that can be taken to curb the manipulative power of a sophisticated elite. One is to educate the less sophisticated in the methods employed by the more sophisticated. Another is to tackle the root causes of social exclusion. Should these prove, for any reason, to be deeply entrenched, there could be a case for restricting certain activities—in particular those of a speculative nature—to people with appropriate qualifications, to prevent unsophisticated imitators from damaging themselves. Some sacrifice of individual freedoms may be the price that must be paid for greater economic stability until the problems of misguided imitation can be tackled at source.

5.2. The concept of imitation

Imitation has received less attention in conventional economics than it deserves. One reason seems to be that it is regarded as a non-rational phenomenon. Imitation tends to be viewed as a human instinct, a natural habit, or some other form of programmed behaviour. But it can equally be regarded as an optimal response to a particular type of uncertainty. Indeed the rational basis of imitation is quite simple and straightforward. Because imitation is such a fundamental social process, the implications of a rational action approach to imitation are wide-ranging.

Most analysis of imitation in the economic literature takes place in the context of technological diffusion (see e.g. Mansfield *et al.*, 1981). This chapter, by contrast, is concerned with imitation as a more general social phenomenon, in which technological diffusion is subsumed as a special case. Building upon the important recent work of Sinclair (1990), it considers the implications of imitation for organizational behaviour, entrepreneurship, financial market stability, and business cycles.

The underlying rationality of imitation was first explored systematically by Conlisk (1980) who contrasted the cheapness of imitation with other more costly ways of obtaining information. His insights have recently been developed by other writers in a variety of different contexts (for example Banerjee, 1992; Bikhchandani *et al.*, 1992; Welch, 1992). A major concern of the later literature has been that the threat of imitation may induce originators to underinvest in discovering information. The focus of this chapter, by contrast, is on the general principles underpinning imitation, and their implications for the stability of the economy. Its concerns are more general, and the discussion more wide-ranging, than previous literature on the subject.

Imitation occurs when one economic agent copies the action of another. This copying may take place with or without the consent of the other party. This distinction is not always sufficiently emphasized in the literature. The focus of this chapter is on imitation without consent—in other words, with the case in which one agent simply follows what another agent does without obtaining their permission first.

Imitation without consent within the social sphere is often presented by economists as a response to a very radical form of uncertainty which defies proper analysis. Imitation is the chosen strategy, they argue, simply because the situation is too fuzzy to be analysed properly (Shackle, 1979).

An appropriate metaphor is that of a person in a car who has lost their way to a party in the fog. Whilst parked at an intersection, studying their host's instructions, they are passed by another car. It is possible that the driver of the other car is going to the same party and, wherever he is going, at least he seems to know the way. So the person decides to follow the other car. By imitating the other driver, he expects to be led to the party.

The usual interpretation of this story emphasizes the fog, as representing uncertainty about the physical environment. This is a mistake. It is more helpful to focus on the driver of the other car instead, and the issue of whether he is going to the same party. If he is, then both people are in the same situation. The other driver seems to have better information— perhaps he has a proper road map of the area. The lost person could return home to collect a proper road map, but this would be an expensive and time-consuming way of acquiring the missing information. He cannot ask the other driver because the other driver is already ahead of him in his car. But what the driver knows is reflected in where he takes his car. The easiest way of gaining access to his information is to just follow him instead.

The thrust of this analysis, therefore, is that the lost driver has a model of the distribution of information even if he does not have a model of the environment to which this information refers. If this model allows him to identify someone else who has a model of the environment then he does not need a model himself because he can 'free ride' on theirs. His decision to imitate is therefore entirely rational because he does not actually require the model of the physical environment that he does not have.

5.3. Basic principles

Five main principles were implicit in the preceding metaphor. They may be stated explicitly as follows:

(1) *The similarity principle.* Different people are often in similar situations.

(2) *The principle of differential information.* Because sources of information are localized, some people have more information than other people who are in the same situation.

(3) *The public good principle.* Because information can be shared and the discovery of information is costly to replicate it is advantageous for the less-well-informed to learn from the better-informed.

(4) *The revelation principle.* The information people possess is reflected in the decisions they make.

(5) *The observation principle.* Other people's decisions are often easier to observe than their information is to acquire.

It follows that the imitation of behaviour is often an effective substitute for other ways of obtaining information. It is better than discovering the information for oneself, and it is also better than acquiring it directly from the other people involved.

To understand more fully how the five main principles work, consider two people in identical situations. Their environment is the same, their preferences are the same, and so the structure of the incentives they face is the same. One of them, however, has already obtained some information which the other does not have. The situations are independent in the sense that the exploitation of information in one situation does not affect the value of the information in the other situation (this assumption is relaxed in Section 5.6 below).

The value of the information, v, is the increase in the expected value of the outcome that is achieved by using the information. Because the situations are identical and independent, the value of the information to each person is the same. It is known to both parties. Both people also know the distributions of information—i.e. who has it and who does not.

The less-well-informed individual has a choice between four main strategies:

(1) rediscovery;
(2) assimilation;
(3) imitation; and
(4) ignoring the information altogether.

He knows the key cost parameters involved. It costs him c_1 to rediscover the information himself. It costs c_2 to obtain the information from the other party and assimilate it. It costs c_3 to simply observe what the other person does and imitate it.

Being rational, the less-well-informed individual maximizes the difference between the value of the information (if obtained) and the cost of acquiring it. This determines his optimal strategy as a function of c_1, c_2, c_3, and v.

If $c_1 < c_2, c_3, v$ then the discovery of the information will be replicated.

If $c_2 < c_1, c_3, v$ then the information will be obtained from the better-informed party instead.

If $c_3 < c_1, c_2, v$ then imitation will occur.

If $v < c_1, c_2, c_3$ then there is no point in imitation, assimilation, or rediscovery. It is better to remain uninformed and risk the consequences of a mistaken decision.

It follows from this that the propensity to imitate is highest when the value of the information is high, the cost of rediscovering it is high and the cost of communicating it is high, but the cost of observing other people's decisions is low. This suggests a number of practical predictions about the incidence of imitation.

When information is complex and technical its costs of discovery are particularly high, and the waste involved in replication of discovery is correspondingly high as well. Other things being equal, therefore the complexity and technicality of information favours imitation over rediscovery.

Explicit information is easier to assimilate than tacit information. Tacit information can only be assimilated easily when people come from similar cultures. Information of a novel or speculative nature tends to be tacit, and complex technical information is often tacit too. Because tacit information carries a high cost of assimilation, tacitness is conducive to cross-cultural imitation.

Other people's decisions are easiest to observe when they have large-scale physical manifestations and require many people to be involved in their implementation. Investments in plant and equipment exemplify these conditions. This explains why imitation is considered the natural mechanism of information diffusion where industrial innovation is concerned, whereas assimilation is considered more natural for intellectual innovations where the physical manifestations are few. This emphasis on imitation is particularly true of innovations of a complex, technical, and tacit nature, which are copied by members of a different cultural group.

5.4. Accuracy, availability and relevance of information

The preceding discussion assumed that the better-informed person always had additional information, that this information was always correct, and that it was always relevant to his decision. In general, of course, this will not be the case. The consequences of relaxing these assumptions are not quite so serious as they may seem, however. This is because the previous analysis depends only upon the expected value of whatever information of whatever quality and whatever salience the better-informed person happens to have in his possession. Exactly how this expected value is calculated is irrelevant to the analysis. So long as the information that the less well-informed person could discover for himself would be no different to that available from the better-informed person, the expected value of the information remains independent of who discovers it. Thus despite the limitations of the information, the decision to imitate still hinges on comparing this expected value with the cost parameters, and on nothing else.

Consider the question of error first. If the better-informed person is fully aware of the probable errors in his information then this will affect the weight that he puts upon it himself. Thus the imitator can rely on the fact that the information has already been discounted to allow for this. It is only if the imitator believes that the other party has over-estimated the accuracy of the information that he needs to worry. If he believes that systematic overestimation is likely, however, then he may decide not to imitate the other party.

If the better-informed person only occasionally has additional information then his decision will only occasionally differ from what the less-well-informed person would have done anyway. Yet the less-well-informed person still incurs the cost of observing the other person every time. The less often the better-informed person obtains information, therefore, the less worthwhile imitation becomes.

The same point applies to the relevance of the information. If the information in the possession of the better-informed person only occasionally affects the way he behaves, then most of the time he will behave just as the less-well-informed person would have done. The more infrequently he behaves differently, the less worthwhile imitation becomes.

In all these cases the limitations of the information lower the value v. Since the cost parameters remain unchanged, the incentive to imitate rather than to assimilate or rediscover the information remains unchanged. All that changes is the incentive to use information at all. Once the value of v falls below the minimum of c_1, c_2, and c_3 the information ceases to be worth obtaining by any means from any source. It is better to act in ignorance of it instead.

5.5. Dissimilarity and the limits of imitation

One reason why the analysis is so robust is that the principle of similarity is so powerful. So long as similarity applies, other things do not matter much. But what happens when the assumption of similarity is relaxed? The answer, not surprisingly, is that imitation is discouraged. Assimilation is discouraged too. It becomes more efficient for the less-well-informed person to investigate his own situation for himself.

Suppose, therefore, that the two situations are no longer identical, but just loosely connected. The environment in which each person is situated can be in one of two states—labelled 'good' and 'bad'—and there is a positive correlation between them. When the correlation is imperfect, inferences drawn from the other environment—whether by assimilation or imitation—run a risk of error. The costs of the assimilation and imitation strategies are therefore inflated by the expected cost of this error. The expected cost is greater the lower is the correlation and the more serious are the consequences of making the wrong decision. Low correlation and serious consequences of error therefore encourage the less-well-informed individual to abandon imitation and investigate the situation for himself.

The same sort of effect will be observed if the discrepancy between the skills of the originator (the better-informed individual) and the imitator (the less-well-informed individual) is reduced. The correlation between the *apparent* state of the originator's environment and the *actual* state of the imitator's environment will fall, and the imitator will switch to investigating his own environment to avoid importing errors from the originator.

Greater similarity in the competencies of the parties thus reinforces the effect of greater dissimilarity in their environments by discouraging imitation and encouraging discovery for oneself.

5.6. Imitation with consent

So far imitation has been discussed from the imitator's point of view. But what does the originator think of the process? The originator is presumably unsympathetic to other people 'free riding' on his initiative. He would like them, at the very least, to pay for the privilege wherever possible.

Two cases may be distinguished. In the first, the situations of the originator and the imitator are independent, as assumed above. The way the imitator uses the information does not affect the rents that the originator obtains from his own situation. The originator's only interest is in appropriating as much as possible of the rents obtained in the imitator's situation in addition to the rents accruing in his own situation.

In the second case the two situations are interdependent. The most common form of interdependence involves potential rivalry between the originator and the imitator. This rivalry will lead to the dissipation of rents in both situations unless there is coordination in the use of the information. Such coordination must normally be effected by a cartel-type arrangement. If a cartel is difficult to organize and enforce then the second-best solution is normally for the originator to control the entire situation himself. In this case the originator is opposed to imitation altogether.

The interplay between the strategic interests of the originator and the imitator may lead to imitation occurring by consent. There are two main cases in which this can happen. In the first, the originator holds a patent which can be readily enforced. The only way the imitator can legally use the information is to acquire a licence. The originator is willing to grant a licence either because he perceives no threat of rivalry or because he believes that this threat can be eliminated through a cartel. Provided the transactions costs involved in negotiating a licence are not too high, both parties will consent to the licensing arrangement and, where appropriate, a cartel will be set up.

In the second case no patent is available, but the imitator would like to receive training to make his imitation more successful. Although the imitator does not require the consent of the originator, he implicitly asks for it by offering to buy training services from him. If the originator is unconcerned about the possibility of strengthening a rival, then he may see the supply of training as a mechanism for appropriating some of the rents from the imitator's situation that he would otherwise lose altogether. Implicit consent is given when training is supplied.

It is not only the imitation strategy that stands to benefit from consent—assimilation may benefit too. The imitator may wish to do more than just copy the originator; he may wish to absorb his information too. He not only requires 'know-how' but 'know-why' as well. Provided the originator is not too worried about the long-term consequences of sharing his more general 'know-why' as well as his more specific 'know-how', he may be willing to 'educate' the imitator in the information as well as 'train' him to copy his behaviour. By potentially strengthening both training and education, consent improves the efficiency of the information diffusion process, provided that the transaction costs involved are not too great.

5.7. Secrecy

The most obvious case in which consent will not be given is where the originator lacks patent rights (see Chapter 2). When information is not protected by a patent it is natural for the originator to resort to secrecy as an exclusion device. Licensing a secret is possible in principle, but difficult in practice (Casson, 1979). It is difficult for the licensor to devise a contract and conduct negotiations without revealing what the information is. It is also difficult for the licensee to be sure that the information is accurate when no patent has been filed. Thus the transactions costs incurred in licensing a secret are usually prohibitively high. If both parties recognize this then a licence will be neither sought nor given.

If secrecy does not allow the appropriation of a licence fee then the originator must décide whether secrecy is worth maintaining at all. If the situations of the two people are truly independent then there is little point in the originator incurring the cost of maintaining secrecy since the imitator's use of the information will not affect his own returns. He may as well adopt an open access policy instead. Only if there is rivalrous interdependence is secrecy worth persisting with.

If secrecy is maintained then, of course, support services will not be provided. As a result, the effectiveness of any assimilation or imitation that occurs is likely to be reduced. But if an open access policy is adopted then support services can still be provided if desired, and the efficiency of diffusion maintained.

The degree of secrecy maintained by the originator will influence the follower's choice between imitation and assimilation. Recall the earlier suggestion that it is usually cheaper to imitate behaviour than to assimilate information. This point related to an open access situation. Within an atmosphere of secrecy the advantage to imitation is even greater.

Secrecy also impacts on the choice between imitation and rediscovery. It raises the cost of imitation relative to rediscovery, and so encourages the imitator to try to find things out for himself instead.

In terms of the cost parameters described earlier, secrecy increases c_2 relative to c_3, and increases both c_2 and c_3 relative to c_1. The first change promotes the substitution of imitation for assimilation, while the second promotes the substitution of rediscovery for them both. The net effect on imitation is therefore ambiguous. But if, as seems likely, the margin of substitution with assimilation is the more active one, then the impact of secrecy on imitation will on balance be a positive one.

5.8. Deciding who to imitate

Suppose now that there are several people whom the imitator could follow, and some of them are doing different things. How does a rational imitator decide whom to follow?

If their situations really are similar then the differences between these candidates for imitation must be attributed to the information at their disposal. Some people's information must be better than others. An obvious way to find out who has the better information is just to wait and see who proves successful. The problem with this approach is that the wait may be rather long. This is particularly important where the imitator wants to act quickly in order to preempt his rivals (see Section 5.9 below).

If the imitator is impatient then he may decide to act on the basis of individual reputation. He looks at people's records of previous successes and failures. On the implicit assumption that some people are permanently connected to reliable information sources and others are not, he attempts to discriminate between them.

If the previously successful people are unanimous in what they are doing then he follows them. It is a reasonable inference that their sources are all reporting the true situation to them. Occasional lapses from unanimity may be explained away by intermittent faults in some of their connections to their sources. Thus near unanimity may also suffice for imitation.

When no unanimity can be observed, however, a likely explanation is that the records of success and failure are chance phenomena. With no systematic differences to rely on, the imitation decision hinges on who has the best information on this particular occasion.

In some cases there may be direct evidence on this. A particular individual may have been witnessed consulting a definitive source—conducting a key technological experiment, for example, or receiving a 'tip-off' from insiders working for a regulatory body. Chance 'eavesdropping' of this kind seems unlikely to be a common phenomenon, however.

In the absence of direct evidence, the revelation principle (referred to above) may be invoked. Access to information is inferred from observed behaviour. Someone is seen to have made a decision that no rational person would make unless they possessed a key item of information. The inference is that the other person knows something that the imitator does not. If no one else has followed suit then it is simply that no one else has access to this information. For example, the other person has made a large irreversible investment in some industry (see e.g. Caplin and Leahy, 1994) and the inference is that they know that demand for its output is going to increase. The very fact that the investment seems risky to the imitator is taken to imply that the investor must know something that the imitator does not.

This signalling mechanism may be elucidated as follows. Suppose that, as before, each person's environment is either good or bad. In a good state, investment is warranted whereas in a bad state it is not. The probability of a bad state occurring is sufficiently high that in the absence of any specific information on the current state the expected value of the 'investment' strategy is lower than the expected value of the 'no-investment' strategy. Everyone faces the same incentives and, in addition, they all make the same assessment of probability when they are ignorant of their environment.

Given these assumptions, a no-investment strategy indicates to other people that the person either has no information or knows that the state of the environment is bad. An investment strategy, on the other hand, clearly signals that the person knows that the state of the environment is good. This implies that everyone else should invest as well. Thus if just one person invests, the imitator will follow suit.

This argument assumes, of course, that the information people possess is correct. If information is liable to error then the imitator must assess how likely it is that a solitary investor has correct information. If he can be sure that the solitary investor has also asked himself this question, and answered it correctly, then it is still safe to imitate him, for the reasons indicated in Section 5.4. It is only if the investor has overestimated the reliability of his information that special caution is required.

If several people pursue the same risky strategy then this reinforces the view that the information is correct. With imperfect information it is quite possible that one of them may be wrong, but most unlikely that they would all be wrong at the same time. Thus if a group of people pursue a risky strategy other people are more likely to follow suit. This point is followed up in Section 5.10.

5.9. Imitation and asset-price volatility

So far it has been assumed that an originator will attempt to appropriate rents from information principally by licensing its use, and perhaps by supplying some education and training too. There is, however, another method of extracting rent from information which is potentially very powerful, but which is often neglected because it is considered rather fanciful. This involves betting against less-well-informed people (Casson, 1982, chapter 5). Although betting on some kinds of information is indeed a fanciful idea if taken literally, the principle of betting provides important insights into the effects of imitation on the stability of asset markets. It is therefore worth examining the principle carefully before discussing its practical manifestations.

Suppose, therefore, that the better-informed person knows that the state of the general environment is good, whilst the less-well-informed person attaches a positive subjective probability to the possibility that it is bad. There are certain odds at which the less-well-informed person will bet against the possibility that the environment is good. The amount he will bet at any given set of odds depends upon his subjective probability, his degree of risk aversion, and the amount of wealth at his disposal. By choosing an appropriate set of odds, the better-informed person can specify a bet that is acceptable to the other person and which will maximize his winnings when his own beliefs turn out to be correct.

The value of these winnings bears no relation whatsoever to the value of the information as defined in Section 5.3. At one extreme, if the information is valuable but people are risk-averse then only a small amount of the value may be appropriated in this way. At the other extreme, if the information is worthless but people are willing to gamble heavily because of low risk-aversion then a signficant surplus may be appropriated—exploiting inside information on a horse-race is a case in point.

Straightforward betting along these lines tends to incur high transaction costs, however. It requires an honest stakeholder who can hold the money that has been pledged until the outcome is known. It also requires an honest judge to determine what the true situation really is. But what is more to the point, it requires a degree of anonymity for the better-informed person. For if he is recognized as being better-informed then the way he bets will signal his information, along the lines indicated in the previous section. Other people will revise their beliefs and the odds will shorten to the point where no profit can be obtained. Thus opening a 'book' on a special situation and then placing bets oneself not only incurs high transaction costs but also gives the very kind of signal that the better-informed person wants to avoid.

It is far easier for a better-informed person to enter an existing market to bet on something which is only indirectly connected with his privileged information. The price of assets is a case in point. If demand is about to increase in a particular industry, for example, then assets used intensively in that industry are likely to appreciate in value—especially if they are unique to the industry and are relatively inelastic in supply. An originator who cannot license his information about demand because of the limited coverage of the patent system may still be able to appropriate value by acquiring appreciating assets instead. Thus the owner of a firm who anticipates buoyant demand can benefit not only by increasing his own capacity in good time. He can also secretly acquire shares in other firms in the industry so that when their own profits increase as a result of the increase in demand the gains accrue to himself.

Indeed, using the cloak of anonymity that asset markets provide the speculator may be able to do even better than this. He may be able to exploit the imitation process to make further gains. These gains are made at the expense of the imitators themselves. They are achieved by retaining ownership of the assets beyond the point where their price reflects their true value in the light of the privileged information.

The process works as follows. The originator is aware that because he has disguised his intervention in the asset market the potential imitators may not realize that he has already appropriated almost all the real gains that are to be had from the increased demand. The only gains that remain come from increasing individual firm's production capacities in line with their market shares. But the imitators believe that gains from asset appreciation still remain to be had, and the originator knows this. Because they lack a full model of the industry environment the imitators cannot correctly value the assets for themselves. All they have is a model of the distribution of information in which the originator has signalled an increase in demand. Underestimating the strategic sophistication of the originator because of the naivety of their models, they fail to appreciate that asset prices already incorporate the information that he has signalled to them.

The imitators therefore enter the asset market, bidding up prices against each other until they reach a level at which even they judge that no further gains can be made. Only at this level are they able to acquire the assets. This is the level at which the sophisticated originator is prepared to sell. The imitators do not realize that they have just acquired the assets, not from their initial owners, but from the originator who secretly acquired them beforehand. By retaining the assets the originator has been able to resell the assets at a price well above what they are really worth. It is only when the expected profit stream implicit in this asset price fails to materialize that the imitators realize their mistake and the asset prices fall back to their true value.

The strategic use of imitation by a sophisticated originator can therefore provide a simple account of asset price volatility. The cycle of rising and then falling prices effects a redistribution of income from naive imitators to a sophisticated originator, and is, indeed, engineered by the originator for this very purpose. The key to the engineering is quite simple. The originator deliberately publicizes his capacity expansion to signal increased demand, whilst using the cloak of anonymity to disguise the fact that he has pre-empted the use of this information in asset markets. He then exploits the fact that the imitators use a social model of their environment rather than a physical one to lure them into acquiring assets at inflated prices. Because the originator has both a physical model and a social model at his disposal, therefore, he is able to take advantage of imitators who have only a social model available to them.

5.10. The diffusion process

The preceding model assumed that the originator was directly in touch with all potential imitators. He secretly acquired all the assets in the industry and then sold out at the last moment to all the imitators involved. This approach can be questioned on two counts.

First, it is unlikely that a single originator can acquire all the assets in an industry. For a start he will require external financial backing, and to obtain this backing he will have to convince his backers that his idea is sound. Once they are convinced of this, they can put his idea into effect themselves. Since they have the funds and the originator does not, they can cut out the originator altogether. Thus to avoid creating competitors the originator will normally have to limit his speculative activities to what his own personal wealth will sustain.

Another reason why the originator cannot acquire all the assets is that not all the assets are continuously on the market. Sellers normally bring to market only a small proportion of the total asset stock in any given period. Thus the faster the originator moves to keep ahead of the imitators, the more he must take the initiative in advertising for sellers. This not only raises his transaction costs; it increases his risk of losing anonymity too. Thus even without financial constraints the optimal pace of acquisition may be relatively low. The combination of limited financial backing and sluggish acquisition means that, in practice, at the time the first imitators enter the market preemption of the profit opportunities will be incomplete.

The second count on which the model can be questioned is that is is unlikely that the originator will know who all the potential imitators are. He is likely to know only those who are closest to him. Each of these people is then known to others. This means that imitation will diffuse in stages. The originator is monitored by a given number of first-stage imitators. Each of these, in turn, is monitored by a similar number of second-stage imitators. These second-stage imitators are not in touch with the originator. The first-stage imitator that they follow acts as the originator so far as they are concerned.

Imitation therefore spreads out from the primary originator along a series of wave fronts. At each point on the wave front there is a secondary originator who is imitated by local people, who will in due course become originators themselves. Because the observations made by the imitators take time to complete, there will be lags in the diffusion process. The wave front will therefore propagate at finite speed (Hagerstrand, 1969; Rogers, 1983). Thus the wave front will be spreading out whilst the process of preemption is underway.

The situation is illustrated in Fig. 5.1. Following the conventions established in Chapter 2, each individual is noted by a circle, the flow of information by a line, and the direction of propagation by a solid arrow. The fact that information diffuses by imitation rather than by ordinary communication is indicated by the 'eye' symbol, which represents the imitator's observation of what the originator does. The information is discovered by the originator 0, whose behaviour is then imitated by individuals 1–4. As imi-

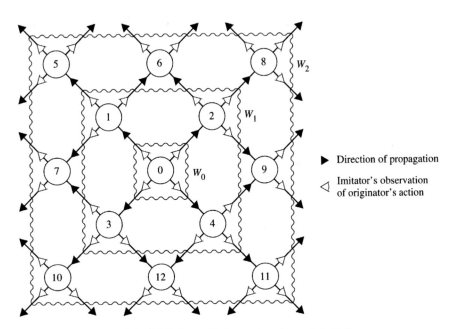

FIG. 5.1. *Diffusion of information through imitation*

tation proceeds the wave front W_0 moves out to W_1. Individual 1 is then imitated by individuals 5, 6, and 7; individual 2 by 6, 8, and 9; individual 3 by 7, 10, and 12; and individual 4 by 9, 11, and 12. It is evident that some individuals—namely 6, 7, 9, and 12—have two people they can imitate. This reinforces their behaviour since they have two examples to follow rather than just one. During the second round of imitation, the wave front moves out to W_2. As imitation proceeds the wave front expands even further until, in the limit, every individual is imitating the originator 0.

Because this process is more complicated than the previous one there is even more scope for imitators to misunderstand what is going on. Indeed, two distinct levels of misunderstanding are likely to be involved. The first level involves a fundamental misunderstanding about the relevance of imitation to speculation which afflicts only the most naive of the imitators. The second involves a more subtle misunderstanding amongst the sophisticated imitators who are trying to take advantage of the others' naivety. What these people see as their own sophistication blinds them to their own naivety about where they are placed within the overall diffusion process.

The fundamental misunderstanding is that in a speculative market where imitation is diffusing at the same time as preemption is underway, two of the key principles of the imitation process are violated. The similarity principle and the revelation principle no longer apply with full force, yet naive imitators behave implicitly as if they did.

With preemption progressing continually, the imitator and the originator are no longer in similar situations. There is a superficial similarity in that both have an opportunity to speculate in the asset market. But there is now a fundamental difference in that the originator was able to buy assets at a lower price than the imitator can, because by the time the imitator gets to recognize the opportunity preemption is further advanced.

Furthermore, the originator who conspicuously invests in additional capacity is only revealing one aspect of his behaviour. He is actually disguising another aspect—namely his acquisition of the assets of other firms. Thus although the information is still revealed in behaviour, the revelation is calculated to mislead so far as its speculative implications are concerned.

The more subtle misunderstanding concerns the place of the imitator in the diffusion process. There may be a systematic bias by which imitators believe that they are placed at an earlier stage of the diffusion process than they really are. Hence they underestimate the amount of preemption that has already occurred and consequently run the risk of acquiring assets that are already over-valued.

The problem is that each imitator may attempt to pass himself off as the primary originator when dealing with those who are imitating him. It is difficult for the other imitators to check out his claim, since they have no contacts further up the chain. If they believe his claim they will believe that preemption is less further advanced than it really is. This will encourage them to take a speculative position of their own.

The imitator has two incentives to act in this way. The first is a financial incentive. Any imitator who is trying to 'play the system' knows that he will have to sell out at some point for as high a price as possible, and his own imitators, and those who imitate them, are part of his potential customer base. Indeed, if the asset market is segmented, so that trade in assets is also confined to the social groups within which imitation occurs, then they constitute the whole of his customer base. It therefore pays him to 'talk up' the unexploited opportunities that remain whenever circumstances allow it, because this will maximize the price at which he can sell out. The natural way to do this is to claim to have made the original discovery for himself.

The second incentive is an emotional one. For reasons explained in Section 5.13, origination usually conveys high status (Casson, 1995a, chapter 9). Within each group the imitators will tend to defer to the originator, and the closer a secondary-originator is to the primary originator the more deference he will receive. If deference affords emotional rewards, then emotional rewards are maximized by passing oneself off as the primary originator.

But since everyone is doing it, it may be asked, why should anyone believe anyone else's claims? The answer may be that a rational imitator who values subjective self-esteem may be willing to accept the claim of their local originator to be the primary one because this places them closer to the primary originator than they would otherwise be. This raises their own perception of their status and so enhances their own emotional rewards. It also affords a useful fall-back position if their own claim to be the primary originator is challenged. They can then claim, with subjective conviction, that although they are not in fact the primary originator themselves, the person they are imitating really is. The material risks of self-deception on this score may therefore be compensated for by emotional rewards based on perceived proximity to primary origination. These rewards may be reinforced by the ability to defend one's actions later, if challenged by one's imitators, by claiming honestly that one was duped by other people oneself.

5.11. Bandwagon effects and the propagation of imitation

The idea that each secondary imitator is mistaken for the primary originator may well explain how speculative acquisition acquires momentum, but it is somewhat implausible as an explanation of how this momentum is sustained. By the time that half the potential imitators, say, have made their move, it would be surprising if the remaining half were not aware of the scale of the phenomenon. For in contrast to the analysis in the previous section, where each imitator monitors a single local originator, imitators can in practice monitor a variety of different people, as noted in Section 5.7. Social groupings overlap much more than the strictly hierarchical diffusion model of the previous section allowed.

There are four distinct reasons for believing that imitation may continue even though the imitators realize that they have many competitors in the field.

The first is that imitators believe that multiple origination has occurred. Imitation is confused with origination on a grand scale. Each new imitator believes that he is confronted with a set of people who have independently discovered the same information from different primary sources. He does not realize that all but one of them are imitators drawing upon a single primary source. Instead, because the seemingly independent sources cross-check, he believes that the risk of error in the information these people are using is very low. The chances of imitating people who are completely wrong are therefore significantly reduced. Thus the diminished opportunity for preemption is compensated for by the enhanced subjective quality of the information involved.

The second reason is that some of the potential imitators lack confidence in their own judgement, and seek safety in conforming with the majority view (Leibenstein, 1950; Galbraith, 1958). Insecure people are very concerned to avoid the affective penalties associated with 'loss of face'. They fear being challenged to justify their actions. Because they do not have a model of their physical environment they cannot justify their actions in terms of the particular situation they are in. If they were to claim that they possessed privileged information themselves then they would expect other people to dismiss this claim out of hand. The only model they claim to have is a social model of 'who knows best'—and if they fail to follow the majority's lead then even their grasp of this model may be called into question. Following the majority view therefore becomes a safety-first strategy of legitimating one's actions to one's peers.

The same argument also applies—and with particular force—to people who act as 'agents' to 'principals' who have a low opinion of the people they employ (Milgrom and Roberts, 1992). If principals do not attempt to appraise their agents' performance carefully, but merely require them to keep abreast of 'informed opinion', then imitation becomes the safest way for agents to keep their jobs (Scharfstein and Stein, 1990). This applies, for example, to salaried fund managers, who may become imitators rather than originators simply because origination may be too difficult to justify to the fund's trustees. As such, this argument is a variant of the commonly heard complaint about short-termism in financial markets. The root of the problem is that people who are delegated with decisions feel that they are not trusted, and so respond in a finely-tuned way to the naive methods by which they are appraised.

The third reason is quite simply that the people who are the last to learn about new trends are also likely to have the most naive models of the social environment. Indeed, if they had better models they might well be able to use these models to place themselves at an earlier stage of the diffusion process. Those who are the last to imitate are therefore most likely to imitate on very naive grounds such as social conformity or trend extrapolation of asset prices. This highlights a more general point which needs to be developed in future research: that while the basic principles of asset price volatility apply at all stages of the cycle, there are distinctive aspects of the cycle associated with particular stages of the diffusion process.

The final reason is that once it is evident to everyone that a majority of people are following the trend, the remaining people may fear that should the trend prove mistaken they will be penalized by having to help the majority out of trouble. The majority may use their political power to claim subsidies—in other words to be financed out of taxation levied on the prudent people who did not join the trend. Once such subsidization of failure becomes likely, the advantages of following the trend become much greater, because the down-side risk is much reduced. This mechanism has the distinctive prediction that once a critical level of support for the trend has been attained, it will accelerate quickly and everyone will participate in order to avoid being called upon to subsidize other people at the end. It also predicts that should the bubble burst in the short time elapsing between the critical point and saturation being attained then subsidies will indeed be claimed by those who have lost from the bubble.

5.12. The psychology of imitation and the business cycle

The preceding account of asset price volatility has obvious affinities with psychological theories of the business cycle going back to Pigou (1927), Keynes (1936) and even earlier. The explanation of business cycles remains one of the major unresolved issues in economics. The regular recurrence of the wastage associated with unemployment and idle capacity has proved persistently difficult to analyse in terms of rational action.

The idea that some people may substitute models of their social environment for models of their resource environment suggests a possible way forward. It has been shown above that the use of a social model allows the majority of the population to 'free ride' on the resource models used by a sophisticated minority. Free-riding renders people vulnerable to strategic manipulation, however. In the long run people will tend to free-ride only so long as the expected saving in their information costs outweighs the risk of their being exploited by the better informed. The more difficulty people experience in handling information about their physical environment, the greater are the risks of exploitation they are prepared to run. When people are confident in the judgements made by the better-informed, and trust them not to use their information in an exploitative fashion, then they will be happy to imitate what they do. But when the reputation of the better-informed becomes tarnished, and their integrity compromised, people will be reluctant to imitate them and be more inclined to check out primary information sources for themselves. The following discussion suggests that these two phases may be identified, respectively, with the boom and the slump of the business cycle.

Imitation-driven asset price volatility impacts on the real economy through investment demand. When asset prices are driven up above the level that is appropriate given the available information, production of new investment goods is boosted to excessive and unsustainable levels. To see how this works, consider an initial shock caused by an increase in consumer demand. Some additional investment will be called for just to increase the capital stock to its new equilibrium level. Production in the capital goods industries will increase to the point where the supply price of new capital goods is equal to their capitalized value in use. If this capitalized value is driven up further by speculation then even more capital goods will be produced. Managers of over-valued firms who do not invest in additional capital goods will be perceived by their shareholders to be wasting opportunities to further enhance the value of the firm. Even if the shareholders recognize the long-term risk of excess capacity, they will be planning to sell out before share prices fall. Managers who fail to invest therefore risk losing their jobs. Because of high investment the capital stock will rise too far, and when the economy returns to normal there will be excess capacity. This will eliminate the demand for replacement investment until some of the existing stock wears out. As a result, fluctuations in real investment are amplified. This accords with Keynesian theory, which places considerable emphasis on investment as a source of volatility. It elaborates this theory, however, by spelling out in detail a mechanism by which imitative speculation may amplify investment fluctuations.

Asset price volatility impacts on consumer demand as well. As asset prices are driven up by speculation, people become subjectively wealthier and as a result their consumption rises. This comes at a time when investment is already high. Thus labour demand increases sharply—the unemployed are offered jobs and overtime increases. Conversely when asset prices collapse later, consumer confidence is undermined at the same time that investment falls, labour demand falls sharply and unemployment rises again.

Although unemployment can, in principle, be avoided through wage flexibility, it is important to emphasize that considerable flexibility is required to compensate for speculative volatility in asset values. It seems unreasonable to require workers to continually renegotiate their wage rates to accommodate the latest speculative whim in the equity markets. If the basic problem is asset price volatility then it is better to try and address this issue head on rather than to rely on wage flexibility to mitigate its worst effects. Moreover, unemployment is not the only problem caused by asset price volatility—unnecessary shifts of labour between consumption good industries and investment good industries are also involved, and the age composition of the capital stock is distorted too, leading to 'echo' effects in replacement investment later on.

Imitation can impact on business cycles in other ways as well. Chari and Jagannathan (1988) have shown, for example, that imitation can lead to a run on a bank which precipitates a panic and undermines the financial liquidity of the economy.

5.13. Social aspects of imitation

Business cycles are certainly not the only application of the theory of imitation. The concluding sections of this chapter consider some of its wider ramifications, beginning with the implications of imitation for the evolution of social hierarchies.

Imitation is very obviously a social process in the sense that it involves interaction between people that is not mediated by the market. It is not so social as direct communication, though, because unless consent is required the originator and the imitator do not actually have to talk to each other. But in some respects its social repurcussions can be more far-reaching than those of ordinary communication.

Many societies confer status on originators to compensate them for their inability to appropriate rents from imitators. Although origination is potentially profitable when imitators can be licensed, or exploited through speculation, there are areas such as art, basic research and voluntary welfare provision where origination is important but appropriation of rents is difficult. In these areas an alternative system of rewards is necessary if an efficient level of origination is to be sustained. To address this issue, leaders of societies commonly offer originators public recognition and honorific titles to generate emotional rewards as a substitute for the missing material rewards.

Because imitation often diffuses in stages, as described above, the dynamics of imitation create a hierarchy of status. At the top of the hierarchy is the primary originator, while at the bottom of the hierarchy are those who are the last to imitate what he does.

New entrants to a group often start with low status, because they have to learn the customs by following what other people do. They gain status by being seen to imitate originators quickly. In other words, they have to become dedicated followers of fashion in order to work their way up the hierarchy. Only when they are close to the top of the hierarchy can they risk originating anything themselves.

These social mechanisms can be harnessed by originators in various ways—for example, to promote sales of fashion goods. Young people are particularly vulnerable to fashion because they are striving to gain status within a peer group that they have recently joined. Endorsements of products from high status people (pop stars, etc.) are therefore very effective in launching new products to young consumers. (Older more confident consumers often prefer endorsements from more conservative figures who will reassure them about the quality and craftsmanship of the product instead.)

Imitation is important in creating fashions in policy-making too. For example, politicians in different countries regularly borrow policy packages from one another. Indeed, it is quite remarkable, in view of the great structural diversity amongst different economies, that so many of them are governed by similar policies at the same time. Imitation rather than assimilation certainly seems to be the more important factor, given that the politicians who espouse the fashionable policies often do not seem to understand how they are supposed to work. The policies are simply judged to have been successful in other countries. These countries are deemed to be similar to their own because the underlying differences are not apparent to the casual observer.

5.14. Imitation, precedent and habit

So far the emphasis has been on contemporaneous imitation. But it is useful at times to imitate behaviour which occurred in similar situations in the past. These situations are said to create precedents for the present one. Although the basic principles of imitation are the same for situations in the present and situations in the past, there are important differences of detail too.

To begin with, the importance of preemption is much reduced when the other situation occurred some time ago. Any profits from the exploitation of privileged information have already been appropriated. This means that there is not the same need to act quickly. It also means that sufficient time will have elapsed to know whether the strategies employed were a success. The risks of imitation are reduced on these grounds: there is time to evaluate with hindsight just how successful a given strategy really was.

There is a new source of risk that must be considered, though. When the precedent occurred some time ago it is a rather brave judgement to suppose that nothing has changed since. There may be important differences of detail, and these may have been obscured by the imperfect, and often highly selective memories of those involved. This is where written records are very useful, and where historical analysis of them can pay dividends in identifying those 'lessons of the past' which are still relevant today.

In some cases, however, those who acted in the previous situation, being aware that their decisions might subsequently be taken as a precedent, may have recorded salient details. Thus in institutions where there is regular recourse to precedents, decisions which should not create a precedent are often carefully identified as such. Many institutions do in fact operate on the basis of precedent—notably the English common law—so that solving problems by an organized search for precedents is a prominent feature of their institutional life. In such institutions it is most important that those who take decisions in unprecedented situations should record the details and state their reasons clearly, so that should an apparently similar situation occur again the relevance of their precedent can be assessed in a reliable way.

Another point is that the use of precedents affords opportunities for self-imitation. The decision-maker may recognize that he has been in the same situation before and that all he needs to do, therefore, is to repeat his previous action (see Casson, 1995b, chapter 6). This is a particularly low-cost strategy, for it is easy to verify the similarity between the present situation and the previous one when one is directly involved oneself. The details of the other situation can be retrieved from personal memory without any further observation.

Overall, therefore, imitation of precedents rather than of contemporaneous events has three distinctive features: dissimilarities caused by preemptive behaviour are less significant, dissimilarities caused by the passage of time are of greater significance, and opportunities for self-imitation are much enhanced.

On the whole, imitation of precedents makes very efficient use of information, and that is why it is used in so many different kinds of institution. The existence of useful precedents that can be accessed through the memories of colleagues is an important resource, especially for an institution operating in a stable environment, where the present is very similar to the past.

5.15. Implications for entrepreneurship

Entrepreneurs are people who specialize in exercising judgement; they take decisions concerned with unique—and therefore unprecedented—situations, usually of a complex nature (Casson, 1982). The natural way to take such decisions, it would seem, is to build a model of the situation concerned,

collect the relevant information and use this information to appraise alternative courses of action.

On this view the entrepreneur definitely comes into the category of
originator rather than imitator—as it seems natural that he should. Nevertheless, it seems rather harsh to dismiss all those businessmen who imitate
others as not being entrepreneurs. This raises the question of whether
entrepreneurship may include significant elements of imitation—and there
are indeed, reasons to believe that it may.

An unprecedented situation may not be unlike all other situations in
every respect. Although there is no other situation exactly like it, there may
be one situation that is similar in one respect and another situation that is
similar in another respect. It may therefore be possible to devise an eclectic
imitation strategy, which combines different aspects of other situations
according to the different similarities that are involved. Although the entrepreneur does not construct a model of his actual environment, he employs
a relatively sophisticated model of his social environment instead. This
model distinguishes different dimensions of the situation, along which similarities or differences may arise, and identifies for each dimension the
relevant people to follow when similarities exist.

It was noted in Chapter 3 that entrepreneurship can be carried out
collectively by a board of directors, each member of which contributes
expertise they consider relevant to the issue at hand. This may be a practical
manifestation of the eclectic approach, in which the experiences of different
people are pooled on the basis that each contributor believes they have
experienced a similar type of situation before.

This eclectic approach may be contrasted with the more analytical approach outlined in Chapter 1, which instead of combining different aspects
of behaviour synthesizes different items of information instead. The revelation principle suggests that these two approaches could, in fact, be equivalent. For each aspect of behaviour combined by the eclectic entrepreneur
may correspond to a particular item of information synthesized by the
analytical entrepreneur.

The problem with this argument, however, is that it assumes that all of
the information required on a given dimension of the situation can be
inferred from the behaviour that has been selected for imitation. This may
not be correct. While a given item of information uniquely determines
observed behaviour, the relationship between information and behaviour is
not necessarily one to one; the same observed behaviour may emerge as a
rational response to several different kinds of information. The information
required for synthesis may be more precise than what can be inferred from
observed behaviour. Thus a synthesis effected by eclecticism may be an
imperfect substitute for an analytical synthesis of the information itself. The
disadvantage of eclecticism, therefore, is that it generates knowledge in a

somewhat compartmentalized form, and may therefore prevent an effective synthesis from taking place.

This compartmentalization generally prevents eclectic entrepreneurs from performing as well as analytical entrepreneurs, except in those cases where the costs incurred by the analytical entrepreneur in assimilating information from diverse sources are unusually high. The model of the eclectic entrepreneur is nevertheless extremely useful because many entrepreneurs who are not major innovators seem to function in this way. This is particularly true, it may be suggested, of the owners of low-growth small and medium-sized firms. These entrepreneurs often seem to solve problems by imitating the strategies of larger higher-growth firms in related areas, using different firms as models for different aspects of strategy. Because these entrepreneurs have no analytical model of their environment, their thinking is genuinely unsophisticated and so they often find it difficult to explain and justify their actions to outsiders. This may also be linked to their typically low level of formal education and to their desire for 'independence'—an independence which obviates the need to justify what they do in analytical terms.

5.16. Imitation and on-the-job learning

The analysis of imitation also has implications for the role of the firm as a social group. Because it is easy to be misled by imitating people who cannot be trusted, it is advisable for complete novices to confine imitation to a secure social group. This group contains reputable people who can be adopted as role models—it is not only safe, but positively desirable to imitate what they do. Indeed the group may be divided into leaders and followers, with the leaders being experienced and successful people whom the followers imitate. The obvious metaphor is parenting within the family—indeed, the role of the family as a metaphor for intra-firm relations was noted in Chapter 4. In the context of the firm this means that new employees are apprenticed to experienced employees, and acquire job skills by following what their masters do. This is reinforced by the role of the master as a tutor and a mentor, who positively encourages the imitation of what he does. The master is willing to pass on his skills in this way because his job is relatively secure. Custom dictates that the full master's wage must be paid once the training is complete, so that wage and salary competition from the trainee is ruled out. This custom is sometimes underpinned by collective agreements negotiated by trades unions or professional associations. These agreements are the analogues of the restrictive clauses in the licensing agreements which protect the interests of the licensor when technology is diffused between firms.

Self-imitation is another important factor in raising productivity within the firm. A worker who memorizes how he carried out a task can carry out that task more quickly when he has to perform it a second time. Proficiency increases further with more repetition, but at a decreasing rate. This generates a learning curve, which relates productivity to the cumulated level of output (Arrow, 1962; Klein, 1973).

Workers who operate in teams, and are able to observe each other, may be able to augment this habit-driven productivity increase by picking up useful ideas from colleagues as well. These ideas might be very difficult to explain in conversation, but they are easy to transmit when embodied in physical activity. This reinforces the point made earlier—that imitation is particularly effective as a substitute for tacit communication. It also reinforces the argument in Chapter 3 that the theory of information costs can illuminate important issues in resource-based theories of the firm, which emphasize learning processes of this kind.

5.17. Summary and conclusions

This chapter has presented a simple theory of imitation and considered its applications in two main fields—namely the role of asset-price volatility in the business cycle, and the impact of imitation on entrepreneurship and the social organization of the firm. It has been shown that imitation has a vital role in exploiting the public good properties of information in a world of high communication costs.

The key point is that many people work with a model of the information diffusion process, rather than with a model of the resource environment itself. Working rationally within a model of this kind, they see that they can economize on information costs through imitation. Intuitively grasping the five basic principles set out at the beginning, they realize that although they do not have a model of the resource environment, they can free-ride on information about this environment collected by those who do. They need to be sure, though, that the people they are imitating are in the same situation as themselves. Imitation is particularly useful when the other people are acting on the basis of complex tacit information which is very difficult for them to explain. Imitation is also very useful when these people cannot license their information, because of inadequate patent protection, but cannot readily keep it secret either.

Unfortunately, however, people often assume that things are similar just because they do not have definite information to the contrary. There is a certain logic to this: the principle of Occam's razor suggests that unnecessary distinctions should not be drawn. But on the other hand, it is prudent to recognize that important differences can be hidden, and that things may not always be so similar as they seem.

This need for caution is particularly important where the imitator and the originator are in a potentially rivalrous position, for the originator may have preempted opportunities that the imitator believes still exist. It is also important where the originator is sufficiently sophisticated that he not only has a good model of his own resource environment, but a good model of his social environment too. In this case he may be able to anticipate, and so endogenize, imitators' responses to his own behaviour. He may recognize that, according to the revelation principle, certain aspects of his own behaviour may be used as signals by other people. By publicizing some aspects of his own behaviour and concealing others—notably through the cloak of anonymity that is available in asset markets—he may be able to outwit his imitators and, indeed, profit substantially at their expense.

It has been suggested that sophisticated originators may start up speculative bubbles with this strategy in mind. Speculative bubbles can have substantial real effects because they induce excessive investment at the same time that they boost consumption through subjective wealth effects. Unless wage rates are sufficiently flexible to adjust in line with volatile asset prices, aggregate employment will vary according to the intensity of speculation.

Imitation also has a bearing on a number of issues connected with entrepreneurship—the distinction between eclectic entrepreneurship and analytical entrepreneurship, the role of fashion effects in the marketing of consumer goods, and the use of precedents as part of the 'collective memory' of the firm. Unfortunately, it has only been possible to skim the surface of these topics within this chapter. Because imitation raises fundamental issues about how decisions are made, much more still remains to be done to develop its practical applications.

6

Information: Factual and Moral

6.1. Three problems of communication: misunderstanding, incompetence and dishonesty

A recurrent theme of the preceding chapters has been that successful coordination depends upon adequate information. There is a tendency, though, to think that the relevant concept of information is simply factual information. This is misleading, however. The information required by the coordination process is of several different types. This chapter explores these various types, relates them to each other, and examines their different roles in the coordination process.

Information can vary in quality as well as in quantity. A good deal of the information used in the coordination process is collected in order to assure the quality of other information. The other information is used directly to decide the allocation of resources; the information collected to corroborate it is not.

Information can be obtained either directly, or second-hand from other people. It is secondhand information that raises the greatest doubts about quality. These doubts are of two main kinds. The first is whether the information has been understood properly given that the other person was telling the truth. The second is whether the other person really was telling the truth or not. These two issues may be termed misunderstanding and misrepresentation.

Misrepresentation can in turn occur in two different ways. The informant may be incompetent, or they may be dishonest. Consider the issue of competence first. Facts by themselves do not signify much; it is only when they have been interpreted that their significance becomes clear. Because strings of facts are tedious to communicate, it is usually interpretations of facts that are supplied instead. The competence of the supplier depends upon the quality of the framework used to interpret the facts. Concepts are employed to decide what to look for at the outset, and to guide the classification of the results obtained. Heuristic theories, or even formal models, are used to determine what conclusions should be drawn. Such concepts and theories are themselves a form of information. Like ordinary factual information, they can be communicated and memorized. The key difference is that unlike factual information they are not the result of direct observation. At the very least they are the result of reflection upon observations, and the discernment of patterns in them. In some cases they may be the result of pure introspection.

The process of interpretation is rather like the process of synthesis described in previous chapters, in which different items of information are combined in order to produce a single item of sufficient significance that the allocation of resources is changed. In a simplified account of synthesis it may be supposed that only factual information is concerned. In fact, however, it is often conceptual information that is crucial. Emphasizing conceptual information enriches the concept of synthesis quite considerably. It is not an alternative to the view that synthesis combines factual information, for conceptual input is particularly crucial when factual material is combined. Rather it highlights the parity that prevails between factual and conceptual information, and the importance of considering the two types of information together.

Now consider the issue of dishonesty. Someone who believes that they could be misled may ask for corroborating evidence. The evidence will be factual information too, though normally of a more detailed kind. There is another way of tackling dishonesty, though. The recipient may attempt to forestall any deception by explaining why deception is wrong. This may be done in general terms, by articulating a universal moral obligation to tell the truth. Alternatively, it may be done in specific terms, explaining the importance of the use to which the information may be put and the social consequences of any mistakes. The supplier of the information may, for example, be told of a social mission to which the users of the information are committed, and invited to share that commitment by joining the group.

The information content of moral judgements has been questioned by philosophical sceptics, but from the standpoint of coordination, moral judgements have an important role (Wolfe, 1989). The nature of the evidence by which moral judgements are supported may well differ from that used in respect of factual information, but that does not mean that the evidence is any less valid. It is just different, that is all.

Even if the informational status of moral judgements is accepted, a sceptic could argue that honesty simply cannot be engineered through moral rhetoric of this kind. It may be suggested, in particular, that the ethos of a market economy simply does not permit it. It must be recognized, however, that the entire basis of a market economy—namely an individual's right to private property—is based on a moral precept, and that if people were so cynical as to disregard this precept then the security of property—and thus the entire market system—would be undermined. Enforcing property rights by law within a moral vacuum is a hopeless task, since without morality there is no guarantee of judicial integrity, and no assurance that judicial decisions will be honestly forced. Given that morality is fundamental to markets, the question is not whether moral rhetoric has any place within the market system, but simply what kind of moral rhetoric is used. In a successful economy the moral rhetoric will promote coordination, rather than inhibit it, and coordination is promoted by encouraging people to tell the truth.

Not everyone is equally susceptible to moral rhetoric, however. Where its effectiveness is in doubt, and corroborating evidence is difficult to obtain, it may be appropriate to investigate the source more carefully. Suppliers of suspect information can be screened by checking out their qualifications, cross-examining them in interview, and so on.

Screening can also be effected indirectly through reputation mechanisms. Because reputational information is obtained from other people, however, there may be doubts about its quality too—are other people really competent to judge, for example, and do they have a grudge against the person concerned or, alternatively, are they loyally protecting a fellow member of their clique?

This leads into the final issue of misunderstandings in communication. Because it is not raw facts, but interpretations of facts, that are communicated, it is important for the person who receives the message to know something of the way that the sender interprets factual information. To take the right decision it may be necessary to decode the message to recover the original information. This suggests that the concepts and theories employed by the sender should be understood by the recipient, and vice versa.

6.2. Conceptual frameworks: uniformity or diversity?

There are two ways of achieving this. One is to standardize the concepts and methods employed by people who are in regular communication with each other. People who need to communicate regularly may be given common education, so that they learn to think alike. Each person implicitly knows how the other person thinks because in practice they think like themselves. This standardization of the conceptual framework may be reinforced by pressures to conform: individuals who express deviant opinions, or who employ unfamiliar concepts in their arguments, may be shunned, or sanctioned in some other way.

The alternative is to encourage people to understand how other people think, on the basis that everyone thinks differently, and that differences in conceptual frameworks are valuable. This emphasis on conceptual diversity is characteristic of the contemporary West. It is a more expensive way to effect communication than is standardization because it requires everyone to learn everyone else's framework. It is difficult enough to understand one framework, let alone several, and far more difficult to understand frameworks that are alien than the framework one has been brought up with.

However, the advantages of diversity are considerable, even though the costs may be great. Any one conceptual framework is inadequate to explain all of the relevant features of an individual's environment. That is why it is often useful to interpret a conceptual framework as a guide to the things that should be noticed, and conversely to the things that can safely be ignored. When the unexpected happens, however, it may be the things that are being ignored that hold the key to a correct decision. Familiarity with another conceptual framework, used by someone else, may prove very valuable in these circumstances. For example, the other person may operate in an environment where such events are much more common, and where the conceptual framework needs to give such events a more central role. Openness to alternative frameworks may therefore raise the quality of decision-making by allowing individuals who are confronted with unusual situations to borrow concepts they have picked up from other people.

A further advantage of diversity is that it generates outward-looking rather than inward-looking attitudes. Standardizing the conceptual framework of a group makes all non-members of the group seem alien, and their behaviour inexplicable. The standard becomes the norm and the norm becomes a moral absolute. Thus non-members appear to be morally inferior too. Relations with other groups deteriorate, and potential gains from inter-group coordination are lost. Considerable savings may be effected in intra-group coordination, but losses in inter-group coordination must be offset against them.

6.3. Moral standards and conceptual diversity

One way of reducing the costs of conceptual diversity is to replace ordinary communication with a highly structured exchange of summary information instead. This is effectively what the core institutions of the market economy do. People who have good ideas for coordination do not bother to explain these ideas to other people. They implement the ideas themselves. They may, for example, code up their knowledge in the form of price quotations for a particular product, which they disseminate through the media to a completely anonymous group of listeners. The price of a product is intelligible to most people whatever their conceptual framework happens to be. People who are interested in the coordination opportunity respond by placing an order for the product. This order is expressed as a numerical quantity, and even the product itself may be identified by an item number too. The routine operation of the market does not require conceptual diversity at all.

Where conceptual diversity matters is in identifying the opportunities for coordination in the first place. Here diversity can be a source of strength, simply because it allows a very high proportion of the available facts to be interpreted in one way or another, instead of many facts having to be discarded because they do not fit neatly into the prevailing standardized conceptual scheme.

Similarly, within private firms—the other core institution of the market economy—information is encoded in instructions to subordinates instead of being patiently explained to everyone else in the firm. Subordinates may sometimes be given reasons for decisions, to enable them to improvise sensibly when there is no time to refer an issue to a higher level of authority. In many cases, however, reasons may be given for decisions simply to motivate subordinates to implement them conscientiously, as suggested by the discussion of motivation in Chapter 3.

By side-stepping the problems that conceptual diversity creates for routine coordination, the market system does not, however, resolve the problem in its entirety. Conceptual diversity may, for example, impede coordination between entrepreneurs. Opportunities for simultaneous innovation in complementary activities may be forgone because the entrepreneurs responsible for the individual activities cannot communicate effectively with each other (see Chapter 2). More generally, there is the problem of informal non-market coordination which has to go on in any market economy side by side with the market activity. Motorists need to show courtesy to each other, and neighbours need to respect each other's privacy. There is little point in promoting trade if the transport of goods endangers lives, or if the consumption of goods by one person merely creates a nuisance for other people.

Non-market coordination highlights two related points about conceptual diversity in a market economy. The first is that neither the firm nor the market is designed to create the mutual understanding of, and respect for, other people's conceptual frameworks on which the continuing vitality of the market system depends. The role of educating people in other people's concepts, and in fostering understanding generally, is typically delegated to the not-for-profit sector. This sector is dominated by voluntary organizations and charities. These organizations do not sell their services in the manner of the market sector. They rely on voluntary contributions, of time, talents, and money.

Their ability to elicit these contributions depends upon the moral obligation that people feel to support their work. This obligation in turn reflects the moral content of the conceptual framework that people use when deciding how to employ their own resources. This raises a further point, which is whether the diversity of conceptual frameworks that can be tolerated extends to diversity of moral values too. The way that moral judgements are woven into the fabric of conceptual frameworks suggests that diversity in one necessarily implies diversity in the other. Against this, however, is the view that certain moral values, such as respect for property, and respect for the truth, are embedded in the constitution of the market system itself. It is difficult for a system to support a degree of diversity so great that it threatens the minimum moral consensus around which its institutions are built.

If this moral constraint on conceptual diversity is accepted, then it shows that the roles of moral information and conceptual information are intertwined. They are important not only for the interpretation of factual information, and for its quality assurance, but for the practice of entrepreneurship, and the foundations of the market system itself.

6.4. The classification of information

While information flow supports a division of labour in the material dimension, information flow itself benefits from a division of labour too (Babbage, 1832). Intermediation is just one example of specialization in the handling of information. Specialization also leads different kinds of organization to concentrate on handling different kinds of information. To understand the range and diversity of the different types of organization found in an advanced society it is necessary to understand all the different kinds of information that such a society can generate.

The classification of information is not a simple matter. Table 6.1 illustrates a first attempt at the task. The two columns distinguish between factual information and conceptual information, along the lines described above. The rows distinguish between descriptive and prescriptive information, which corresponds to the distinction between the factual and the moral aspects of discourse noted above.

Neoclassical economics is mainly concerned just with the top left hand element of the table, which deals with factual information. This information tends to be viewed as objective—the subjectivity that is inherent in the use of concepts and theory to interpret raw data is ignored (O'Brien *et al.*, 1983). It is also perceived as being objective in the sense that it is held to be free of value-laden assumptions. A rigid dichotomy separates the positive and normative aspects of the economy, and the information pertaining to them, so far as neoclassical economics is concerned.

The neoclassical view, indeed, would tend to suggest that there are just two types of information rather than four. One type—factual information—

TABLE 6.1. *A simple typology of information*

	Factual	Conceptual
Descriptive	Factual information	Theory
Prescriptive	Law	Moral values

is objective, and the other, defined as a residual type, includes all forms of subjective information. The weakness of this approach is exemplified in the bottom left hand corner of the table by the role of law. Law is objective, in the sense that it is a fact as to what the law happens to be on any particular subject, but it is also moral, in the sense that it prescribes what should happen rather than describes the way things are (Werin, 1990). The fact that conventional neoclassical theory is so naive in its treatment of law, taking it simply as given in most cases, reflects its inability to deal with the interplay of the factual and the moral in the economy as a whole.

The classification shown in Table 6.1 is relatively crude because it does not distinguish the different kinds of information that are found in each category. The analysis in previous chapters has highlighted the importance of the distinction between transitory and persistent information. Transitory information is typically handled using routine procedures, whereas persistent information is not. Another important distinction concerns the level of aggregation at which the information is expressed. Highly specific information relating to individual households, for example, is typically handled by retailers, whereas information of a higher level of generality, concerning fashion trends and other systematic factors that influence households as a group, tends to be handled at a market-maker's headquarters instead. The market is not, by any means, the highest level of generality at which information can be reported, though. Some information, such as reports on legislation, apply at the national level, and cover trade in all the markets in the country. Yet other information, such as technological know how, is potentially universal in its scope (Lamberton, 1988).

Table 6.2 identifies four different types of factual information. The emphasis is on the kind of information required by an intermediating firm. General information of a persistent nature, indicated in the top left hand corner of the table, is the kind of information that underpins the recognition of a market-making opportunity. It may relate to a scientific breakthrough, or perhaps to a political breakthrough that liberalizes trade. At the other extreme is specific information of a transitory nature, indicated in the bottom right hand corner, which affords a short-run opportunity for speculation or arbitrage, or helps a firm to identify a new customer with an urgent requirement that rival firms cannot fulfil.

TABLE 6.2. *A typology of factual information*

Level of aggregation	Persistent	Transitory
High	Market-making opportunity	News of fashion change affecting demand
Low	Individual customer's credit rating	Order placed by specific customer

The more interesting cases, though, are those represented by the off-diagonal elements in the table. The top right hand corner concerns transitory information of a high level of aggregation. This is typical of the kind of information routinely used by a marketing-led firm to set its output (see Chapter 3). The firm faces volatile demand, which varies on account of systematic factors such as macroeconomic fluctuations in disposable income, change in fashion, and the like. The firm regularly monitors these determinants of overall market demand, using transitory information of a lower level of aggregation merely to fine-tune its strategy.

Perhaps the most unusual combination, though, is that of specific information of a persistent kind. There is a lot of this kind of information about—people's names and addresses, for example, and timetable information for buses and trains. Because much of it seems intrinsically boring, its significance for coordination is often ignored. It is important to note, however, that it is information of this kind whose handling has been most transformed by the information technology revolution. It is far cheaper to communicate this information, and to store it in a readily accessible way, than used to be the case. Moreover, when it does occasionally need updating, it is now much easier to make the alterations too.

The significance of this information for coordination is twofold. First it is important in retailing products which need to be advertised selectively and delivered personally to the customer. Until recently, retailing revolutions had been confined mainly to mass-advertised mass-produced products which relatively anonymous customers collected for themselves. Customized retailing, being information-intensive, was still very much conducted face-to-face. The advent of databases, however, has allowed the vast amount of information required for personalized retailing to be collected and processed impersonally. This has had a major impact on the retailing of banking, insurance, and other personal services.

The second point is that reputational information tends to be of the persistent but specific kind too. Much of this information is still stored by individuals rather than by computers, and exchanged face-to-face by gossip rather than by remote communication. There are concerns, though, that more of this information will move on to databases, as has already happened with credit rankings. In academic life, and in competitive sports, for example, there is a tendency for computerized rankings to take over from personal judgements as the basis on which reputations are formed. As a result, reputations may become more widespread, because of the cheapness of communication inherent in computerized ratings and rankings. Some of these reputations may become distorted by biases in the ratings procedures, however, and in particular by the ability of unscrupulous individuals to acquire misleading reputations by discovering and exploiting loopholes in these procedures. There will, therefore, remain a role for the well-informed social group in correcting such biases, although the ability of such groups to engineer biases of their own in outsiders' perceptions of their general standing will be more circumscribed in the future than it has been in the past.

Table 6.3 attempts to integrate Tables 6.1 and 6.2. It might be expected that this would generate a $4 \times 4 = 16$ element table, but because conceptual information is of a persistent nature the actual number of elements is only 12. Two main points emerge from this table which have not been made before.

The first concerns the importance of fictional worlds in accounting for much of the informational flow in a market economy. A high proportion of leisure activity is concerned with living in fictional worlds, whether it is in reading novels, watching television drama, visiting theme parks, or escaping into history which has been specially romanticized for the purpose.

The world of fiction is not merely a world of entertainment, though; it is a source of education too. Dramatic story lines provide parallels with eventful episodes in ordinary lives, and can suggest to people ways of coping with their problems. Other stories take the form of parables, which are object lessons in popular morality. The world of fiction is therefore rich with metaphors and moral meanings for everyday life. It has a key role in supplying both the conceptual framework and the moral values which were shown to be so important in the earlier discussion of coordination.

It is necessary to distinguish clearly the overtly fictional worlds of literature and drama from the real but unobservable world of religion. Positivists who identify reality with observability may well insist that the world of religion is fictional, but this is, in fact, a metaphysical claim (about the non-existence of a metaphysical world) and cannot be used consistently to classify the religious world as fictional when that is not what it claims to be. Just as some scientific theories resort to 'explaining' the behaviour of observable variables in terms of unobservable ones, so religions explain selected aspects of the observable world as a whole in terms of another unobservable one.

The second point that emerges is the very wide significance of prescriptive information, not only in the general and persistent form exemplified by morality, but the specific and transitory form associated with individual rights and obligations: the obligation to carry out a particular order from a superior, or to make a payment for some goods that have just been delivered. This is the specific and transitory analogue of the legal information discussed above. It is both factual and prescriptive. It is factual in the sense that it describes exactly what the obligation is, and who is obligated to whom, and prescriptive in the sense that it says what they should do rather than describes what they have actually done.

Information of this kind is, in fact, 'bread and butter' information so far as the market economy is concerned. When a price is quoted by a firm, for example, an obligation is created to accept orders at that price. When an

TABLE 6.3. *An integrated typology of information*

| | Factual | | | | Conceptual | |
| | Transitory | | Persistent | | Persistent | |
	Specific	General	Specific	General	Specific	General
Descriptive	News of changes to individual's circumstances	Market price, quantity traded, etc.	Individual names and addresses	Practical know-how	Literature, drama	Scientific theory Religious belief
Prescriptive	Orders, commitments, credits and debits	Crisis measures by governments, etc.	Individual reputations, credit ratings, etc.	Legislation, constitution	Parables, political argument on particular issues	Moral values

order is placed, a further obligation is created to supply the good as specified and within a reasonable time, while a reciprocal obligation is incurred by the buyer to pay for the good when the order has been fulfilled. As the trade is completed, by delivery of the product and the receipt of the payment, these obligations are annihilated and nothing remains of them at the end of a successful trade. It is only if one party defaults that the obligations remain outstanding.

Transitory information on rights and obligations therefore flows continuously through the system, being created when a coordination opportunity is identified and annihilated once it is successfully exploited. Creation and annihilation are not quite instantaneous because most trades take time to complete. There is, therefore, a small amount of such information held at any one time, on account of transactions still in progress, or of transaction failures still unresolved, but the stock of this information is very small compared to the volume of trade going on.

6.5. The storage of information

An important distinction between transitory and persistent information lies in the economics of storage. The storage of persistent information is more viable than the storage of transitory information, even though records of transitory information may be useful for historical purposes. Inventories of goods are most valuable when goods are durable, and the same applies to inventories of information.

Storage separates the collection of information from its use. Observations can be made and filed without the pressures created by demand for immediate use. Conversely users do not need to get involved in generating their own observations because they can obtain the information they need from the store. Just as an inventory of goods buffers supply and demand, so an inventory of information buffers the production of information from its use.

Another way of putting this is that storage of information facilitates the exploitation of inter-temporal economies of scope. But for these economies to be large, the information must be regularly consulted. If no one ever consults the information it is clearly not worth storing it, whether it is persistent or not. The urgency with which information is required is another factor affecting the demand for storage. If spur-of-the-moment decisions are required, and information is time-consuming to collect, then it is advantageous to have the information already to hand in a store. This is the analogue of the precautionary demand for inventory, which arises where ordinary goods are concerned.

There are two main situations in which information is regularly consulted. The first is where there is a single recurrent user who needs the information on a regular basis. The information is stored in files simply to save the user the trouble of storing it in his head. Files may be more reliable than ordinary memory and, if the user is a specialized decision-maker, he may be too preoccupied with other things to remember details easily.

The second situation is where there is a variety of users, each of whom uses the information on an intermittent basis. The difference between the two cases lies principally in the question of access. It is easy to make access convenient for a dominant user by locating the file store close to him. Moreover, as a regular user he will soon become familiar with the arrangement of the filing system, so that the administrative cost of access will be small as well. With multiple users, however, a mutually convenient location for the file store may be hard to find. Furthermore their personal use of the store may be so infrequent that they need to re-familiarize themselves with the store each time they access it.

This second situation is more likely than the first when the information is of a general rather than a specific nature. As noted in Chapter 3, information expressed at a high level of aggregation summarizes a situation which is likely to be relevant to a considerable number of people, whereas information expressed at a low level of aggregation may be of interest to only one person. This is not invariably the case, however. Information on a very unusual subject—a rich and successful person, for example, or a turning point in history—may attract multiple users. Reputational information also falls into this category—everyone who trades with a particular individual has a potential interest in their competence and integrity.

The benefits of storing information must be set off against the cost. The alternatives to storing information are really twofold: to collect the information on demand, as and when required, or to do without the information altogether. The first comparison is the most instructive, although the second should not be overlooked entirely.

The case for collecting information on demand is strongest where transitory information of a specific nature is concerned. Because it is transitory, it is possible that it can be stored without ever being used, simply because the situation changed yet again before any new decision came to be made. The more intermittent the use of the information, the more likely is such waste to occur. Because specific information tends to have only a single user, the chances that different users would replicate the collection of the same item of information when it was unavailable from a central store are somewhat remote.

The converse of this, of course, is that the case for storing information is strongest where persistent general information is concerned. This point is not quite so obvious as it may seem. This is because the costs of accessing information need to be considered too. Mutual convenience will encourage the location of the store at a 'central place', such as a transport or telecommunications hub. This is not just because such location offers an efficient compromise to the conflicting requirements of users at different locations. It also permits users to undertake 'one-stop shopping' for all their information requirements. All information of a general nature can be stored at the same central location. To find their way around this store, however, users will require guidance. Files need to be indexed, and in the case of paper rather than electronic storage, shelves need to be labelled and directions signposted too. Considerable skills in reference services are needed to keep the costs of access down to an acceptable level (Casson, 1990, chapter 8).

It is not just access that creates administrative difficulties, either. The depositing of information can be costly too. Where persistent information is concerned, deposit is essentially a once-and-for-all activity. Its costs are one-off sunk costs which can be spread over all subsequent users. This is not the case with transitory information, though. The costs of depositing transitory information are usually spread over very few users—and in extreme cases, over no users at all, as the previous discussion made clear. The depositing of transitory information needs to be a very simple process to be economic. Since by its very nature transitory information has to be frequently updated, this means that a streamlined routine for the deposit of transitory information is crucial.

The updating of transitory information affords a choice as to whether the previous information should be destroyed. Should the files be over-written, so that no record of the previous entry remains, or should the previous entry simply be transferred to a back-up store? What is the value of an archive of obsolete information, in other words?

There are two main ways in which an archive can be of value. The first is as a repository of data that can be analysed to test out theories and models, or to identify historical trends. It is important to emphasize that although such an archive may contain information of a transitory and specific nature, the archive as a collective entity may be of persistent and general value. This is because the theories that can be tested using the archive are a form of persistent and general information, as indicated above. Moreover the people who generate new theories to test, or come with ideas about historical trends, may be very diverse. An open archive may therefore attract multiple use. Even though the current information in the archive may be of value to just a single user in respect of his day-to-day decisions, it may be of multiple use once it becomes obsolete and is added to a longer run of historical data.

These issues apply at many different levels. They can be applied at the national level, in the context of, say, the place of research libraries in a national innovation strategy. The strategic issue here is how to determine an appropriate level of investment in stores of economic and scientific information. How can entrepreneurial firms who have collected information of this kind be encouraged to deposit it where other firms can make use of it too? Should firms be paid for information they deposit in order to compensate them for any reduction in the monopoly rents that may ensue as a result of this? Would a system of payment encourage firms to collect information of more general use in the first place? Should users be charged for information, and if so how exactly should access to research libraries be controlled? Should distinctions be drawn between basic research and applied research, or between academic research and commercial research, in regulating access? Are such distinctions relevant, and are they enforceable in practice? Should access be entirely open, on payment of the appropriate subscription or fee, or should a vetting procedure be used as well? Is it possible to prejudge whether the use of the library by a particular person with a particular idea in mind is likely to be in the national interest or not? Should foreign-owned firms, for example, be discriminated against in access to national scientific archives? Or is the concept of such a national archive an anachronism in the contemporary globalized economy?

Issues of the same kind also arise at the regional level, and at the level of the local community. Business networks of the kind discussed in Chapter 4 face issues of this kind as well. Should members of the network club together to create a library as a central resource? Is it sufficient to share information at meetings, or is it desirable to intermediate this process by creating a central store of information too? Should intermediation extend to collecting information from outside on behalf of the group, or should it be confined to pooling information that has been collected individually by members of the group? Should all members of the group be obliged to join, and how should the subscription be set? Should there be a flat fee, or a fee related to ability to pay or frequency of use? Should deposits of additional information be accepted *in lieu* of a fee?

Finally, these issues also apply at the level of the firm itself. They are particularly acute in respect of multi-plant production firms, and of market-making firms of the kind discussed in Chapter 1. In such firms information is generated at different locations, and used at different locations too. This raises the question of whether information storage should be centralized geographically or not.

Different levels of the hierarchy have a need for different types of information. But information whose primary use is at one level may have secondary uses at other levels. This raises the question as to whether different stores of information should be held for the use of different levels of the hierarchy, or whether all levels of the hierarchy should have access to a common store. If there is a common store, should access be restricted, and if so, on what basis should the restrictions be applied? How important is confidentiality, and how important is it that superiors should have privileged access compared to their subordinates? A full answer to these and other important questions can only be provided when further research on the organization of information storage has been done.

6.5. Value shocks and moral disturbances

It has been emphasized throughout this book that information processing is a continuous process because the economy is continually being disturbed by shocks. Although the shocks are most frequent where transitory factors are concerned, persistent factors are intermittently affected too. All the types of information described in Table 6.3 have to be updated from time to time in the light of shocks which occur.

Economists are inclined to think of shocks to the economy in resource terms or monetary terms, but to fully understand the role of information in the economic system the concept of a shock needs to be interpreted more widely than this. It is not just a matter of considering the impact of the weather on food supplies, for example, or even the effect of changes in the money supply on the price level, but the effect of scientific advances on technology and of changes in religious thinking on moral values too.

It is not just the direct effects of these shocks that need to be considered, moreover, but their indirect effects as well. Scientific advances, in particular, have a very wide range of effects indeed. Scientific advance is not just a question of improvements in production technology, but the reduction of transport costs as well. Reductions in transport costs widen the markets that firms can serve. Larger markets feed back on production to allow the exploitation of greater economies of scale, and this in turn encourages further technological advance.

The division of labour becomes more sophisticated too. Because intermediate products are easier to transport, different stages of production become concentrated at particular locations suited to the particular type of work involved. The coordination of the division of labour over long distances is facilitated by reductions in information costs which also stem from general scientific advance. Advances in information technology often arise from improvements in components, such as cables and switches, which originated from research directed to lowering ordinary production costs instead.

Scientific advances have religious and moral implications too. The demise of popular Western belief in the Biblical account of creation and of the origin of humanity, due to research on evolution, has encouraged scepticism about traditional sources of moral authority. It has led to a search for more secular justifications for morality—a search which has been only partially successful (Whiteley and Whiteley, 1964). This has in turn undermined traditional Protestant values of integrity, thrift, and hard work. Given the importance of honesty in assuring the quality of information, a weakening commitment to honesty in ordinary affairs tends to undermine coordination by raising transaction costs. The spread of moral scepticism has been accelerated by the application of science to the diffusion of information through the media—television, satellite broadcasting, and so on.

The net result of this is that each individual within society is now sub-jected to far more sources of volatility than in the past. When production was primitive, transport was slow, and mass communication virtually un-known, life consisted of long periods of uneventful monotony, punctuated by intermittent crises caused by war, plague, failure of the local harvest, and so on. Now, with sophisticated production, rapid transport, and instantane-ous access to mass communication, individuals are buffeted with a continu-ous stream of shocks, supplemented by numerous reports of shocks that have impinged on other people. Shocks are transmitted rapidly from one part of the world to the other through global markets. The world economy is now so interdependent that the ultimate sources of the shocks that impinge on people may be so remote that they are extremely difficult for them to discover. For example, many industrial workers who lose their jobs because of competition from cheap imports have little idea of the condi-tions under which those imports are produced, the technologies that are being used to cheapen production, and the social and political changes that have allowed the exporting countries to emerge as new economic powers at that particular time. Media reports confirm the impression that people like themselves are being overwhelmed by wide-ranging changes which no one really understands. Even policy-makers now often 'wash their hands' of the problem. The channels along which shocks are propagated in a highly interdependent world economy are so many and varied that insulating any country from their effects appears to be a hopeless task. Politicians who are used to guaranteeing the preservation of local jobs to their constituents have become discredited because it is now clear that even national govern-ments cannot control situations of this kind.

It appears that the demands placed upon coordination by the modern globalized world economy may have become excessive. The problem does not lie principally in the factual domain, because the capacity of the system to handle factual information has been much increased by new information technology. The problem lies more in the conceptual domain. It is the difficulty of finding an intellectual framework within which all of the differ-ent aspects of the situation can be understood that seems to be crucial. Without such a framework it is difficult for entrepreneurs to interpret current trends in order to identify future market opportunities correctly. But much more significant is the fact that without such a system it is difficult for ordinary members of a society to see what future shape their society will have. As a result they lose their commitment to the society and to the traditional moral values on which coordination depends. As the global economy integrates different nations, so the nations themselves disinte-grate because the social and moral difficulties raised by the domestic conse-quences of international integration are too great.

The solution to this problem lies, essentially, in an improvement in the quality of intermediation in the moral domain. Much has been said in this book about the role of intermediation in improving the structure and quality of information flow in a market economy. The focus of this discussion has been mainly on factual information, though. The issue now under discussion concerns conceptual information instead. The role of leaders as intermediators in the moral domain was considered in Chapter 4, but the focus was rather narrower than the present one. Nevertheless, it was suggested there that national economies need to recover the high-trust culture that many of them once had, but which is now found only in smaller groupings at the regional or local level. In the past organized religion was able to transcend local communities in order to engineer trust at national level. In the late nineteenth century nationalism emerged in Europe as a secular substitute for organised religion. Nationalism is now itself discredited—at least in intellectual circles—but only because of its devastating military consequences, and not because a superior secular system of values has emerged.

6.6. Moral leadership

Successful moral intermediation requires leaders who are personally committed to the traditional values that promote coordination—honesty, loyalty, and hard work. The problem of where the supply of such leaders is to come from remains unresolved, however. Since people typically acquire their values from the social groups to which they belong when young, a higher level of investment in suitable social groups would seem to be desirable. Suitable groups are those that give young people a vision of a good and just society which they can serve during their subsequent working lives. Groups that have a practical orientation can also teach the important economic truth that the successful pursuit of social and moral goals requires efficient coordination. Efficient coordination in turn requires both respect for authority, and a willingness to improvise where circumstances require it.

Since most people are born into a family, the quality of moral leadership shown by parents is clearly an important influence on social attitudes. Apathetic parents, who have made no moral commitments of their own, are obviously a poor example to their children, as are parents who are locked into conflict over where authority in the household should lie. Poor parenting is always liable to occur in some families, however, and so the availability of supplementary sources of authority is important too.

Some of the alternative sources are heavily institutionalized—notably schools and churches—whereas others—such as youth clubs, sports clubs, and so on—are less so. The less institutionalized groups often rely on unpaid volunteers, who work in their spare time. Many of the most effective youth leaders are likely to have other jobs, including a paid job which makes major demands on the time. Unless their employers are prepared to support them, they may find the commitments to their voluntary work difficult to fulfil. The voluntary sector is therefore dependent on the private sector not only for ordinary donations, but for cooperation in allowing employees a high degree of autonomy in the use of their 'leisure time'. Unless there is consensus amongst competing employers that employees should be allowed such autonomy, participation in voluntary activities may be impaired by long hours of work.

The nature of the problem is illustrated in Fig. 6.1. This figure builds on Figs 2.12 and 2.13 which were used to discuss the principles of coordination earlier on. The economy is shown as comprising a production sector p, a market-making sector m, a retailing sector d, a banking sector b and a technological elite, t. Such an economy cannot function without a sense of moral obligation which encourages people to work hard, respect property rights and tell the truth. This sense of obligation is instilled by the rhetoric of the moral leader a. This leader personifies the values of the ruling elite— for example, the ideas of intellectuals, endorsed by religious leaders and communicated with passion by politicians. His moral rhetoric impacts on the economy and on society both directly, through individual emotions, and indirectly by providing a moral framework for the law.

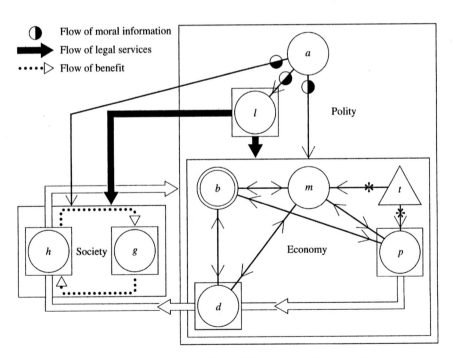

FIG. 6.1. *Flows of factual and moral information for coordination*

Flows of moral information are indicated in the figure by the half-black half-white circles, symbolizing the sharp distinction between good and evil embodied in moral rhetoric. The flow of legal services is represented differently—by a solid black line. The thickness of the line is the same as that of the double lines representing material flow. This indicates that physical services are involved in apprehending and punishing offenders. The law exists to deter those who are insufficiently sensitive to emotions aroused directly by the leader's moral rhetoric. The law is ultimately coercive, which is why the physical services emanating from the legal system l are distinguished from the ordinary factor services emanating from h and the products emanating from p.

The practical significance of moral values is appreciated most fully by those who participate in the social groups g that make up society. As indicated above, most of these groups operate on a non-profit making basis. Individual members of households contribute their time and talents to these groups, as indicated by the line of dots in the left hand sector of the figure, flowing clockwise from h to g. Individuals also derive benefits from membership of these groups—better physical health from belonging to sports clubs, better psychological health from belonging to churches, and so on. This flow of benefits is indicated by the line of dots running clockwise back from g to h. In some cases the link between contribution and benefit may be indirect. Thus many groups have a charitable function, which means that some of those who benefit have not contributed, because of the redistribution of resources that is involved in charitable work.

Social groups are also subject to the law, but the impact of the law is much weaker in the case of society than it is in the case of the economy. It is no accident that economic growth through the division of labour does not normally 'take off' until a society has evolved a fairly formal system of law. Thus the single line running to society from the leader a is of greater significance than the solid line running from the legal system l; in the case of the economy, by contrast, the two lines from a and from l are of roughly equal significance.

Participation in society increases the competences of the households and so improves the quality of the labour services—both manual and cerebral—that they supply to the economy. This is because, as noted in Chapter 4, group membership provides technical training as well as moral training. This technical training is effected partly by the close proximity of the old and young, which enables skills to be transferred through imitation, according to the mechanisms described in Chapter 5.

Increased competence in the household sector is important not only for the economy but for the polity too. It is of particular significance for the leadership function because it is from the household sector that leaders are recruited. This is indicated in the figure by the way that the flow of factor services from the households is directed not only into the economy but into the polity as well. An effective society, with flourishing group activities, is likely to generate effective leaders who can sustain the moral basis on which the system as a whole depends. Conversely, a society where group activities are dormant may fail to incubate leadership skills, creating a weak economy and a fragmented polity, which interact to precipitate decline.

6.7. The moral weaknesses of Anglo-Saxon individualism

An interesting sidelight on this issue is provided by the decline of traditional sources of moral authority in the West during the twentieth century. For many leaders in the making, the most immediate sources of such authority were the schools and the churches. Unlike other social groups, schools and churches have their own professional workforces, and in the twentieth century these workforces have developed a distinctive culture. This is particularly true of the USA and the UK, and to some extent of Scandinavia too. The nature of this culture is crucial for the economy because it determines the values that are systematically imparted to the young.

Because of the intellectual nature of their work, attitudes in schools and churches reflect modern intellectual trends. Fashion may exert a weaker influence on churches than on schools because of the greater importance of tradition in religious belief. Religion does not operate in a cultural vacuum, however, and respect for tradition may mean that the churches simply respond to intellectual fashions with a longer time lag. In the case of both schools and churches it is easy to criticize the rather lax easy-going individualism which has flourished in the post-war period as a result, respectively, of 'child-centred' education and liberal theology. Certainly any system which encourages young people to think in terms of their rights rather than their obligations is likely to create problems of insubordination that undermine coordination. Likewise the identification of a just society with an unworkable form of socialist welfare state is likely to create social divisions between an academically-oriented minority that aspires to join the technocratic elite, and the majority which is resigned to becoming the manual workers and subsidy-claimants that are dependent on it.

Arguments like this are not new of course. Indeed throughout the 1980s party politicians of the 'new right' made accusations against educational sociologists and liberal theologians along these lines. While they have been quite successful in destroying some of the more absurd beliefs that surfaced during the 1960s, members of the new right have been less successful in providing an acceptable set of beliefs to put in their place. Right-wing critics have basically promoted a low-trust view of society in which competition under the rule of law becomes the exclusive coordinating mechanism. The new right believes that individual selfishness and greed can be condoned provided the law is in place. They fail to take account of the information costs of the legal system, and the fact that as traditional morality weakens, increasing dependence on the law causes these information costs to escalate. No-one can believe what anyone else says unless they check up on them first, and the diversion of time and effort into checking means that much less information can be handled than would otherwise be possible (Casson, 1993).

The overview of information and coordination provided in this book suggests that some kind of synthesis of the ideas of the 'old left' and the 'new right' may be possible. A satisfactory synthesis can only be achieved by introducing a further dimension, however, which is connected with high-trust culture. Within a high-trust framework it is possible to see that all of the ideas discussed above have some part to play, but that each idea becomes counter-productive if it is exploited in isolation, and thereby taken to extremes. Child-centred education is useful in giving people the confidence to improvise, liberal theology has its place in restating traditional moral values in a post-Darwinian world, and the 'new right' has a point in emphasizing the value of law and competition in situations where moral values are expensive and liable to fail. The current challenge is to synthesise these ideas in a logically consistent and parsimonious manner, rather than just as an eclectic collection of folk wisdom.

In view of the amount of time that has been spent by party politicians in debating issues of this kind, it is disappointing to see how little progress they have made. The modern party politician seems far more interested in exploring the weaknesses of his opponent's view than in recognizing its strengths and synthesizing these with his own point of view. Indeed, it seems to be a maxim with the more ideological party politicians never to recognize any validity in their opponent's point of view at all. Since the evolution of a new moral synthesis, restating traditional values in a modern form, is essentially an intellectual exercise, this anti-intellectual stance is quite counter-productive. It raises the question as to whether the current framework of party political rivalry conducted through representative assemblies and the popular media brings to power people who in fact lack the very leadership qualities that their responsibilities require. It is possible that the principles of democracy based upon a universal franchise have become so corrupted that people with the leadership qualities required by this system actually avoid political life because of the low moral standards that now prevail there. The vested interests which lie behind the party conflicts have become so powerful that they resist any attempt at intellectual synthesis on the grounds that such a synthesis would concede too much to the opposition.

The urgent need at the present is for a restatement of traditional Western liberal values that is sufficiently inspirational to motivate people to honesty, loyalty, and hard work, and sufficiently realistic that it does not become discredited by the failure of specific policies. It is hoped that the analytical framework developed in this book may provide some help in formulating a value statement of this kind. There may already be a broad consensus that some such development is desirable. The intellectual challenge is to provide a solution which transcends conventional party political divisions, and provides a workable moral standard which both leaders and their followers can make a serious effort to maintain.

PART II

EXTENSIONS AND APPLICATIONS

7

Industrial Districts

7.1. Introduction

It is widely recognized that although networking is an attractive metaphor, the practical application of the metaphor is quite difficult (Easton, 1992). Chapter 4 has argued that business networks should be analysed from the standpoint of economic efficiency. Networks should be viewed as a decentralized high-trust institutional arrangement for coordinating flows of goods and services. They afford an effective way of handling information, and are a potentially attractive alternative to both the market and the hierarchy (Blois, 1972). *def*

Competition between alternative institutional arrangements will in the long run tend to select the most efficient arrangement. What is most efficient depends upon the circumstances, however. Economic analysis of coordination indicates the circumstances in which networks are most efficient. Such analysis can be used to predict where networks will occur and where they will not. *cond.*

In practice, network configurations can be very complicated. Diversity amongst networks arises from differences in their size of membership, and differences in the way that relations between members are configured. *charact* Chapter 1 introduced a simple diagrammatic scheme which can be used to summarize the economically relevant aspects of a network configuration, and this was further developed in Chapter 4. The present chapter employs this scheme in a more ambitious way. It compares and contrasts two alternative forms of networking. The first is the local network used for internal *types* co-ordination in an industrial district; in this context the major role of the network is to sustain a flexible and relatively informal system of subcontracting. The second is the long-distance network associated with overseas economic development, which supports the transfer of technology, capital, and skilled labour from a core geographical area to a peripheral one.

These two types of network have certain things in common, but they exhibit important differences too. In the case of subcontracting, for example, the key players are typically merchants handling exports of finished products and, to some extent, the procurement of raw material imports too. These merchants control the flow of intermediate products between the subcontractors. In the case of long-distance technology transfer, the key players are typically company promoters in the core area, and the professional experts (consulting engineers, etc.) who work for them. The promoters combine capital and technology to exploit natural resources in the peripheral area. The long-distance network is potentially more sophisticated than the local network, because it cannot rely simply on frequent face-to-face contact to make it work. Moreover, the long-distance network normally feeds into local networks at either end. The analysis of a long-distance network is therefore potentially more complicated than the analysis of a purely local one.

The specific focus of this chapter is a comparison of the role of local networks and long-distance networks in two industrial areas—the textile district of Prato in northern Italy and the iron-making and coal-mining district of Merthyr Tydfil in south Wales. The period chosen for study in each case is the one during which the district excited most comment from outside observers. Since Prato has been widely used as an example of a Marshallian industrial district (Becattini, 1990; Marshall, 1919), it is studied with respect to the 1970s when its recent prosperity was at its height. The key developments in Merthyr Tydfil, however, occurred much earlier, at the beginning of the Industrial Revolution. Merthyr Tydfil is therefore studied over the period 1750–1850.

7.2. Modelling material flow in an industrial district

The methodology employed in this book is to distinguish clearly between the *flows of resources being coordinated* and the *flows of information needed to coordinate them*. Both are important, but they need to be considered separately before they are integrated.

The flow of resources being coordinated can be of three main types. Each type is a consequence of a particular type of division of labour. The three types are:

(1) *flows of materials* created by a physical division of labour in production;
(2) *flows of knowledge* created by a division of labour in research, in which a technical specialist generates know-how and diffuses it to other people;
(3) *flows of equity finance* created by a division of labour in risk-bearing which leads to the emergence of a speculative investor class.

In an industry with a *mature technology* and *low sunk costs* the division of labour in physical production is the dominant factor, and so coordination of material flow is the key determinant of network configuration. The Prato case study illustrates this situation. Historically, this case exemplifies the system of mercantile capitalism (beginning in the fourteenth century) in which goods are traded over long distances but sources of technology and equity are local.

Conversely, in an industry with *innovative technology* and *high sunk costs* it is the division of labour in knowledge and in risk-bearing that holds the key instead. In fact, innovative technology and high sunk costs often go together because new technology is usually embodied in costly and highly specialized equipment. This generates a distinctive kind of situation. It is exemplified by the exploration and exploitation of deep mineral deposits, as described in the South Wales study. Historically, this case is related to the growth of industrial and financial capitalism in the eighteenth and nineteenth centuries, in which the sources of technology and equity finance became international, and the long-distance aspects of economic networks increased in importance.

7.3. The textile industry of Prato

In 1981 48,000 people were employed in the textile industry in the province of Prato. There were 11,000 firms, of which about 9,000 were run by self-employed artisans. Thus the average size of firm was very small: 4.3 employees. Most of the small firms were subcontractors working for *impannatore*—entrepreneurs with no fixed capital of their own who procured raw materials, and put them out, using a special contract, for them to be made up into finished products according to their own designs. A typical *impannatore* would put out work to a favoured group of main contractors, each of whom would in turn subcontract to smaller firms who were already known to them.

Prato has been a textile centre since the Middle Ages (Origo, 1957). Its system of subcontracting has many traditional aspects, which can be found in other fashion textile centres too. The immediate antecedents of its system are rather unusual though. In the second half of the nineteenth century Prato was known world-wide as the 'town of rags' (*citta' degli stracci*). It recycled rags and remnants to produce a fibre used in the production of woollen fabrics. By the inter-war period production was concentrated in a small number of large vertically integrated mills (*lanifici*) which converted the raw material into plaids, wool shawls and blankets, cotton clothes and flannels (Tamburini, 1945; Dei Ottati, 1993). These highly standardized products were suitable only for low-income export markets such as India, China, and South Africa (and for military corps demand during World War II).

Close to the *lanifici* there were some small firms specializing in particular stages of the textile process, such as burling, weaving, and spinning. These firms acted as subcontractors to the smaller woollen mills. They also worked for the *impannatore*, making up 'fantasy' fashion fabrics, woven of different coloured reconstituted threads, and sold in the Italian women's wear market (Piore and Sabel, 1984, p. 214).

After 1945 both the export market and the military demand for standardized woollen textiles declined, and the *lanifici* laid off workers. They rented them looms and other textile machinery so that as self-employed artisans they could use their special skills acquired at the mill to fulfil orders either from the *lanifici* themselves or from the *impannatore* instead. This generated a flexible competitive system which allowed the *impannatore* to increase production of high quality goods for the fashion market, using labour and machinery released from standardized production. Competitive forces were, however, constrained by a collective agreement on 'fair' charges between the artisans and the industrial entrepreneurs who employed them (Brusco and Sabel, 1981, p. 109; Piore and Sabel, 1984, p. 272). As export demand for fashionable designer textiles increased, Prato—like other textile centres in Northern Italy—had achieved considerable prosperity by the 1970s.

The system has continued to evolve, with competition from newly industrializing countries putting greater pressure on prices and wages and eroding some of the cooperative spirit characteristic of the 1970s. Dependence on rags has steadily diminished, and the use of synthetic fibres has steadily increased, reducing the ability of the Prato industry to benefit from its traditional sources of expertise (Bellandi and Romagnoli, 1993). Vertical integration has re-emerged, driven, it would seem, by changes in the nature of demand: intensified consumer-driven concern over quality control, and the increased market power of major wholesalers and multinational retail chains (Trigilia, 1989; Gandolfo, 1990; Bellandi and Triglia, 1991).

7.4. Modelling the coordination of material flow in an industrial district

A highly stylized account of the woollen textile industry of Prato is presented in Fig. 7.1. It identifies four stages of processing: the sourcing of rags, symbolized by R; upstream production U (including carbonizing, carding, winding, and the dyeing of yarn); downstream production D (including weaving, finishing, and the dyeing of cloth); and the consumption of the cloth through household use, C.

Figure 7.1 follows the usual convention of portraying sequential activities in the vertical dimension (so that 'vertical integration', when it occurs, really means what it says). To incorporate a spatial dimension, different regions are represented in the horizontal dimension, so that where transport is involved the material flow acquires a diagonal form. As shown, the rags originate (on the left) in the hinterland of Prato, they are processed entirely within the Prato district (in the middle) and finished cloths are exported all over the world (on the right).

The flow of information for coordination purposes is illustrated in Fig. 7.2. To avoid confusion with Fig. 7.1, information flow for coordination purposes is illustrated by a single line, as compared to the double line used

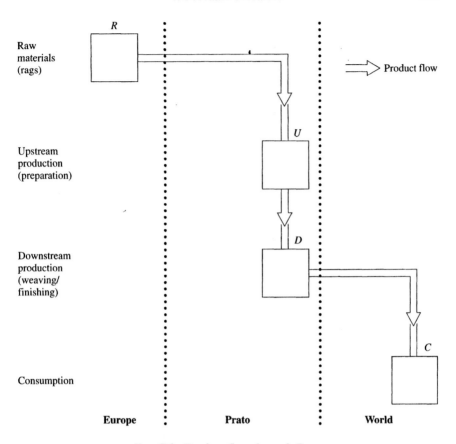

FIG. 7.1. *Product flow through Prato*

for material flow. Three points about information flow are relevant at this point, and are recalled from Chapter 1:

(1) Information flows between *people* rather than between *plants*. To highlight this, people are identified by *circles*, in contrast to plants, which are identified by *squares*.

(2) Information flows are normally *two-way*, unlike the material flows illustrated in Fig. 7.1. This is illustrated by the two-directional arrows in Fig. 7.2.

(3) Flows of information are often *intermediated*. Entrepreneurs are key intermediators so far as coordinating information is concerned. The presence of intermediators is indicated by the presence of *circles (people) which have no corresponding squares (plants)* in Fig. 7.1.

In Fig. 7.2 each individual is identified by an ordinary letter, in contrast to the capital letters used to identify the plants in Fig. 7.1. Where an individual manages a particular plant, the letter by which they are identified is the same as the one used to label the plant. Thus individual *r* manages the

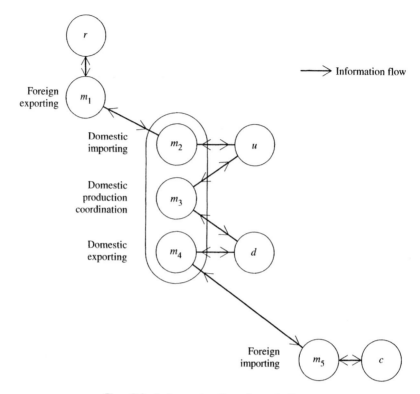

Fig. 7.2. *Information flow through Prato*

sourcing of rags, individuals *u* and *d* manage upstream and downstream production, whilst individual *c* is a representative consumer.

Intermediation is effected by merchants. Five different merchanting functions are identified in Fig. 7.2. The individuals responsible for them are labelled m_1 to m_5. Three of these functions are, however, performed by the same person in the case of the Prato woollen industry. This is illustrated in Fig. 7.2 by the oval line drawn around the circles m_2, m_3, and m_4, indicating that the same person is involved. The person concerned is the *impannatore*. As the figure shows, the *impannatore* acts as

(1) an importer of rags
(2) a 'putter out' of materials to a sequence of independent sub-contractors, and
(3) an exporter of woollen cloth.

The intermediators can be identified visually by the fact that when Fig. 7.1 and 7.2 are overlaid, as in Fig. 7.3, there is no plant to which the intermediator corresponds. The intermediator is concerned with the flow of information rather than with the flow of materials themselves.

Reality is, of course, more complex than this stylized account suggests.

The *impannatore* do handle the materials, for example, in the sense that they inspect them for quality and arrange for their security during transportation. Nevertheless the simplicity of the diagram helps to illustrate the key point—that the coordination of material flow, both locally and over distance, relies extensively on intermediation by an entrepreneurial merchant elite.

All products face problems of quality assurance. As emphasized in Chapter 3, these problems are particularly acute in the case of coordinating information. Are people bluffing in the prices they quote? Will people honour their promises, paying on time and delivering the quality of good that is specified in the contract? As in Chapter 4, a flow of reliable information is indicated by a double-headed arrow, to distinguish it from a flow of ordinary information which continues to be indicated by a single-headed one.

Networks solve the quality assurance problem by allowing people to signal to each other that they belong to the same social group. People

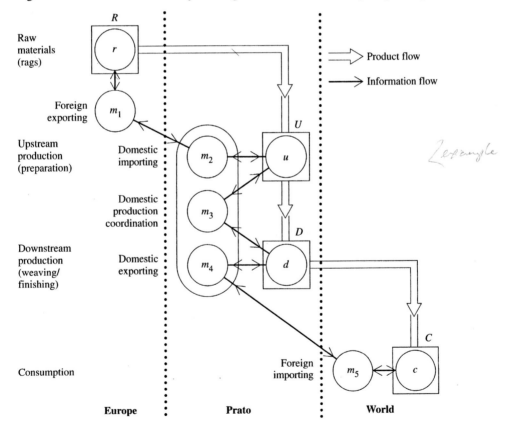

FIG. 7.3. *Product flow and information flow through Prato*

belonging to the same group, it is assumed, can trust each other, but those in different groups cannot. Thus in Fig. 7.4 the double arrows link members of the same social group; single arrows link members of different social groups.

Figure 7.4 identifies three social groups. Group I is a business community of rag merchants which is involved in organizing the supply of rags. The merchants in Prato deal with merchants in other parts of Tuscany and further afield. By regularly trading with the same partners mutual confidence is built up, and individual merchants acquire reputations which they are anxious not to lose. This assists in the negotiation of prices for rags, and encourages compliance with contracts. Importers can therefore be confident of the quality of the rags and the timeliness of their delivery.

Group II is the business community of Prato itself. This community helps to assure the quality of information passing between the *impannatore* and their subcontractors. Special contracts are written for this purpose, but the flexibility of the system depends crucially on compliance with unwritten understandings as well (Putnam, 1993). Local institutions in Prato not only strengthen reputation mechanisms but generate emotional obligations between the parties too.

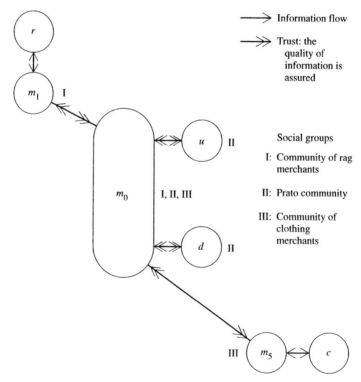

Fig. 7.4. *Social groups that sustain high quality flows of coordinating information on the Prato textile industry*

The relevant institutions include:

(1) *industry associations*, which meet regularly with each other to set a standard scale of charges for subcontracted work;

(2) *trades unions* who meet regularly with the industry associations to set wages;

(3) *professional associations* which provide accounting services (especially for artisans), economic information, training, and marketing services;

(4) *local banks* who finance the *impannatore* using local savings;

(5) *political parties* (particularly left-wing and ex-Communist parties) which sustain a shared ideology;

(6) *local government,* which during the 1970s invested heavily in both industrial infrastructure (including transportation and pollution control) and social services (including nursery schools and family-care centres which facilitated labour force participation by women);

(7) *technical schools* (such as the Technical Institute for Textiles) which not only transmit specialized competences between generations but also serve to socialize people—developing bonds between them which will prove useful later in business life;

(8) *large families*, which not only create emotional bonding between their members but provide a forum for the exchange of economic information, and an 'internal capital market' through which the savings of parents can be recycled to provide finance for the expansion of their childrens' businesses.

The relative permanence of large families, and their extended nature, is in marked contrast to the situation in Merthyr Tydfil described below. The dominance of such families in the working population of northern Italian towns has, however, diminished somewhat since the 1970s owing to substantial immigration from the countryside and also from the south of Italy (Bull, 1992).

Finally there is group III, which is the community of clothing merchants which organizes the export trade. This is an international community which includes managers of major multinational enterprises as well as self-employed merchants such as the *impannatore* themselves. This community is perhaps the least personal of the three, in the sense that face-to-face communication is often confined to meetings at trade fairs, and so on. Nevertheless introductions, once made, can lead to lasting relationships simply because of the cumulative confidence acquired through repeatedly successful trades.

7.5. The iron industry of Merthyr Tydfil

It is interesting to compare the essentially localized coordination of material flow effected by the *impannatore* with the long-distance coordination of technology transfer and equity finance effected by the iron-masters of Merthyr Tydfil at the end of the eighteenth century. The iron industry of Merthyr Tydfil was at the cutting edge of the Industrial Revolution. It has been persuasively argued by several historians (following Nef, 1932) that the reason why the Industrial Revolution began in Britain has less to do with the Lancashire cotton industry than with the large deposits of coal and iron ore found conveniently near the British coast. Iron was the material and coal the fuel that made the steam railways possible and stimulated the growth of a national market for consumer goods. Moreover it was mining that first encouraged the development of the railway concept, and prompted the innovations of Newcomen, Trevithick, and Stephenson that provided the technology for steam power in transport and industry.

Iron was of considerable strategic importance for the armaments industry, but until Abraham Darby of Ironbridge developed a technique of smelting iron using coke in 1709, the iron industry was dependent on charcoal, obtained by burning wood. The industry was driven away from the south-east of England in the seventeenth century because wood was also required for shipbuilding, which was of local strategic importance to the navy. Darby's invention was absolutely crucial in liberating the production of iron from the ecological constraint created by limited domestic supplies of wood.

In 1750 Merthyr Tydfil was a remote parish near the head of the Taff Valley in South Wales. Welsh-speaking farmers reared sheep, but there was little local processing of agricultural exports (Davies, 1933). Unlike England, Wales had few major market towns. Brecon, fifteen miles to the north of Merthyr, was the local social centre for the English speaking gentry, but it had little industry (see Fig. 7.5). For commercial purposes, the port of Bristol, on the opposite side of the Severn estuary, was the local hub where the major merchants and provincial bankers were based.

It is the South Wales coalfield that holds the key to the story. Coal outcropped on the sides of valleys and could be collected quite easily by local people for domestic heating purposes. Before 1750 copper was smelted in the Swansea and Llanelli area where the coal seams came closest to the coast (Symons, 1979). Ore was shipped up the Bristol Channel from Cornwall, and later on down the coast from Amlwch in Anglesey. The logic of this was that coal was bulkier and more fragile than copper ore, and was required in greater quantities, so that it was easier to bring the ore to the coal rather than the other way round.

Unlike the north-east of England, where a substantial export trade in coal had developed from Newcastle more than a century earlier, South Wales was remote from major markets and its infrastructure poor (Flinn, 1984). South Wales coal could not compete for the London market in domestic heating (and later in gas making) because of the roundabout shipping route and the lack of efficient overland transportation.

Fig. 7.5. *Key places in the development of the iron industry*

In Merthyr Tydfil deposits of iron ore and coal occurred together, and this made it the natural place to exploit Darby's invention. Moreover the coal was of the same type as that used by Darby, so no adaptation was required to transfer his technology.

Outside entrepreneurs were crucial to the development of the Merthyr iron industry (John, 1950). John Guest, a neighbour of Darby's son, who had learnt the technology, became manager of a local ironworks. A London merchant, Anthony Bacon, who had begun his career exporting coal from Whitehaven in Cumberland to Dublin, and subsequently built a small fortune provisioning the navy, became involved in the supply of cannon to the Admiralty (Namier, 1929). He utilized a precision technique for boring cannon developed by John Wilkinson of Broseley near Ironbridge. Bacon identified Merthyr as a suitable place to produce cannon. He was the classic entrepreneur, bringing together capital and technology to exploit natural resources which previously, because of their remoteness, were of very limited use.

When Bacon retired, his estate was split up and other outside entrepreneurs such as Richard Crawshay and Samuel Homfray took over. Mass production techniques came into their own as the scale of production expanded in the build up to the Napoleonic wars.

As the mines went deeper, the risks of flooding increased and the new energy-efficient pumping engines of Boulton and Watt, manufactured in Birmingham, were installed. To handle geological problems, and to advise on ventilation techniques, colliery viewers from the north-east were employed as managers and as consultants.

Problems over the drainage of mines led to disputes between the iron masters when one person's mine drained into another person's workings. Disputes also arose concerning the diversion of rivers used to power water-wheels and to feed canals, and over pollution caused by the disposal of waste. In some cases these disputes developed into pitched battles between gangs of workers from rival plants, each defending their master's interests (Evans, 1993).

As the demand for workers expanded up to 1800, labour was drawn in from the rural areas of south and west Wales (notably Cardigan), and from Ireland too. Some of the Welsh workers only came during the off-season for agricultural work. Others were full-time, but essentially transient. Merthyr was a mining town to which young men would often go to earn high wages and then return to their roots elsewhere. There were also miners who had moved on from other areas where coal seams had been worked out.

7.6. Modelling the flow of resources in the iron industry

The flow of resources in the Merthyr Tydfil iron industry is indicated in a highly stylized form in Fig. 7.6. There are two important differences between this diagram and Fig. 7.1. The first is that factors of production are explicitly shown: labour, N, from west Wales, land, L, in the form of mining concessions and wayleaves to build tramways across the local gentry's land, and capital equipment, K, as exemplified by Boulton and Watt's pumping engines.

The second is that flows of technological know-how are also shown. The source of technology, T, is indicated by a triangle (as distinct from a square), whilst the flow of technology is indicated by a single line with an asterisk along it (as indicated in the key to the figure).

Two flows of technology are indicated in Fig. 7.6. The top flow refers to technology *embodied* in capital equipment, whilst the lower flow refers to *disembodied* technology used in colliery management. The source of this expertise is different from the source of capital equipment. The expertise

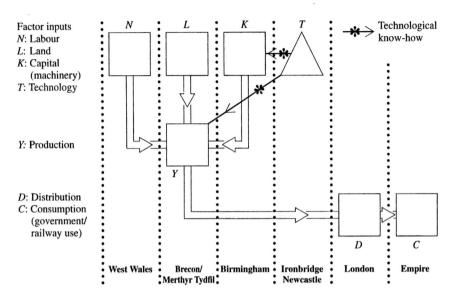

Fig. 7.6. *Product flow and technology flow in the Merthyr iron industry*

originates in Shropshire (as indicated above) and also in the coal industry of north-east England, centred on Newcastle.

The factors of production are combined in the plant Y which represents a vertically integrated system of coal mines, ore mines, and smelting furnaces. The rationale for this vertical integration is not difficult to discern. High transport costs of coal and ore lock in each works to its nearest sources of mineral supply. In addition, vertical integration is a way of internalizing some of the environmental externalities concerned with the draining of mines, the disposal of waste, and so on.

Finished product such as cannon are transported to the London area, where they are tested and then distributed (D) by the navy to outposts of the British Empire around the world where they are utilized (C).

Once again the flow of information is crucial to the coordination of resource flow. This is illustrated in Fig. 7.7. Coordinating flows of information are again represented by a single line. But now the figure also incorporates details of the flows of equity finance. As in Chapter 4, the symbol for equity finance is a spring, placed midway along a single line; the symbol is chosen to indicate that equity owners buffer the firm by absorbing the shocks of changes in its profits.

The intermediation of information flow is no longer centred on the production locality, as in the case of Prato. The key intermediator is the company promoter, p, based in London. The promoter taps into the market experience gathered by the merchant, d, who is in charge of the distribution of iron. The promoter passes on selected summary information to the

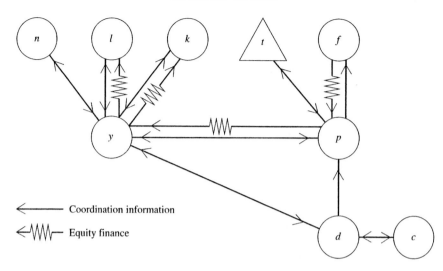

FIG. 7.7. *Information flows and financial flows in the Merthyr iron industry*

speculative financier, *f*. It is the capital-intensity of large-scale production in the coal and iron industries that generates this need for finance. Thus much of the capital raised is used to purchase capital equipment; later on in the nineteenth century quite a bit went to the purchasing of concessions, but these were relatively cheap in the early years because only a handful of entrepreneurs recognized the opportunities for large-scale production and landowners did not realize the value of the mineral rights they possessed.

Quality assurance of information in the Merthyr iron industry was effected by four main groups: the family dynasty of the iron-master himself, I,—perhaps best illustrated by the Crawshays, with the father based in London and the son managing the works in Merthyr; the metropolitan elite, II, linking the London-based promoter with his customer (in this case the Admiralty), and his financier; the professional technologists, III, comprising the colliery viewers and smelters on the one hand and the manufacturers of specialized equipment on the other; and the local gentry, centred on Brecon, IV, to which both the landowners and the iron-masters belonged.

Figure 7.8 illustrates these four groups. It shows how the promoter, *p*, the local producer, *y*, and the technological consultant, *t*, are crucial in knitting the four groups together. It is the way that these three individuals each share allegiance to more than one group that enables them to broker between different groups and so sustain the overall network of trust on which successful coordination depends.

Note also that the functions of merchant and promoter are combined in the same individual—just as the *impannatore* combined different roles in the previous case. This highlights the important point that combining different functions in the same individual is an alternative to coordinating them within a social group. Conversely, as functions become increasingly differentiated and complex, so that one person cannot do them all, effecting the division of labour within a social group avoids the worst effects of splitting them up between different people.

The family dynasty (group I) is important because it can operate effectively over distance. The bonding between father and son effected by parenting sustains a subsequent business relationship in which they remain far apart. In a pattern that was repeated in many fields of British overseas development, the father begins the operation outside of London in his youth and then moves (or returns) to London in middle age, sending out his son (or in some cases leaving him behind) to take over the management of the local operations under his general oversight.

The professional technologists (group III) also constitute a group that works effectively at a distance. Here the bonding may emerge from apprenticeship to a common master, or simply from a shared curiosity and enthusiasm sustained by scientific correspondence. Membership of certain religious sects that were inspired by a scientific view of creation (for example Unitarians and Deists) also seems to have been a factor in bonding technologists in some cases.

The local gentry (group IV) seem to have been very weak in the case of Merthyr. Common membership of this group was insufficient to resolve differences between the local iron-masters arising from the external costs they imposed upon one another. Although they contributed jointly to the

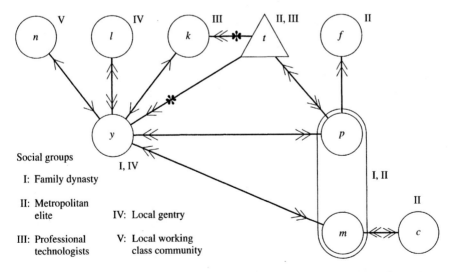

FIG. 7.8. *Social groups that sustain high quality flows of coordinating information in the Merthyr iron industry*

financing of the Glamorganshire Canal, opened in the 1790s, which conveyed their iron to the port of Cardiff, there were disagreements about the route of the canal and subsequent difficulties over its operation too.

Of the two local groups, the metropolitan elite seems to have been the more important. The merchant, m, who enjoyed good relations with his customer, c, gained access to exclusive social circles where he made contact with wealthy individuals, f, who regarded speculative investments as an alternative to gambling—betting on the value of a mining concession seems to have been just as much fun for them as betting on a horse, and potentially more remunerative too. The merchant, m, having gained social acceptance, could thereby develop into a promoter, p, generating the situation illustrated in Fig. 7.8.

Unlike the situation in Prato, there was little sense of community in Merthyr. The industrial workers (shown in Fig. 7.8 as group V) were never fully integrated with other local groups. This led to poor industrial relations, particularly since some of the English-speaking managers could not readily communicate with their mainly Welsh-speaking workforce. The class antagonisms that developed from this became visible at the end of the Napoleonic wars, when the armaments boom came to an end and the masters implemented a series of wage cuts, setting off strikes that culminated in an infamous populist rising in 1830. The Merthyr Rising was directed not only against the masters but also against the English-speaking shopkeepers and tradesmen of Merthyr, to whom many workers had become indebted. The workers particularly resented the repossession of their goods through the local courts (Williams, 1978).

The basic problem was that even by 1830 Merthyr had not achieved the status of a town. Although larger than either Cardiff or Swansea, its local government was primitive. The paternalistic iron-masters were to some extent a law unto themselves. The shopkeepers and the iron-masters were regularly in conflict over who should pay the Poor Rate (i.e. fund local social security). There was conflict amongst the workers too, with the Welsh looking down on the Irish, whom they expected to do only unskilled work.

Like many mining towns throughout history, Merthyr was a town of factions (Carter and Wheatley, 1982). Most of the factions had a high degree of economic rationality to them. The core of skilled workers who had settled in the town with their families wanted to discourage unskilled workers without dependents from flooding into the town because of the increase in crime and drunkenness, and because their competition might depress wages too. The tradesmen were anxious to ensure that they had good security for items sold on credit, but wanted the iron-masters to help pay the costs of upholding the law. Narrow economic rationality is also apparent in the payment of workers. Wherever appropriate, workers in both the iron works and the coal mines were paid by the piece. A 'butty' system was often used, in which a worker would contract to do a certain job and then recruit his own team to carry it out. Wage rates were highly graduated according to skill, and the most skilled workers could negotiate individual deals on the basis of offers they had received from rival entrepreneurs. With conditions in a continual state of flux, alliances between the different factions in Merthyr were continually changing. There was no investment in institutions to integrate the factions in an effective way.

7.7. 'Internal colonialism' in South Wales

One of the reasons why so few people took an active interest in developing amenities in Merthyr Tydfil seems to be that Merthyr was regarded by many people from the outset as an essentially transitory settlement. It was basically a mining town, doomed to collapse once the mineral deposits ran out. Unlike the north-east of England, where coal and iron ore were also found together, there was no tradition of craftsmanship or yeoman agriculture to suggest that diversification into other lines of activity would be possible later on (Evans, 1989).

Merthyr was not the sort of place that people who had made their money would be happy to retire in. Although the iron-masters built quite impressive mansions, these mansions were close to their works and some of them (at Dowlais, for example) were quickly covered in soot. The countryside to the north of Merthyr was desolate and barren, the social possibilities of neighbouring towns like Brecon and Cardiff were rather limited and, until the construction of the first Severn Bridge, and later the Severn Railway Tunnel, the area was relatively isolated.

Few craftsmen making precision engineering products were tempted to move from Birmingham or Bristol to Merthyr, for they would have been too far away from their markets. In many respects, therefore, Merthyr might have been thousands of miles away from London, rather than about the 140 miles that it actually is.

This view is consistent with what happened to Merthyr after 1850. When the demand for iron declined, the area was slow to switch to the production of the preferred substitute—steel. Once again it was an outsider who showed the local industrialists the way in this respect. As the local industrial use of coal declined, however, the export of coal developed—especially of steam coal from the nearby Rhondda valleys. Cardiff docks were enlarged, but disagreements over the transport of coal from the valleys and its loading onto ships were continually occurring and eventually a rival port was developed at Barry, south-west of Cardiff. As local coal reserves diminished and demand for coal declined with the onset of recession during the 1920s, Merthyr went into steep decline, recording the highest level of unemployment of anywhere in Britain in the early 1930s. It was even suggested at this time that the entire population of Merthyr be relocated to new settlements.

The movement of capital and technology from the metropolitan core of Britain to its periphery in Merthyr foreshadows by about a century the massive export of labour, capital and technology from Britain that occurred at the end of the nineteenth century. Indeed, patterns of labour migration to south Wales suggest that historically people have migrated there as an alternative to emigration to North America (Thomas, 1973).

The closest analogy with Merthyr is provided by colonial mining ventures in Africa (and to some extent Latin America). In the latter half of the nineteenth century many so-called 'free-standing companies' were formed to finance overseas mining ventures using equity raised in London (see Chapter 8). The promotion of these companies was organized by the London elite along very similar lines to those described above. Indeed, it can be argued that this elite acquired much of its expertise from domestic financing of the Industrial Revolution in the previous century in areas like north-east England and South Wales.

The London elite had a durability that the local elites of mining towns lacked. The locational advantage of a metropolis as a centre for commerce tends to be more permanent than the locational advantage of a mining town, which in most cases is eroded as deposits became exhausted. Few mining towns have successfully adapted to other industries because of the long-run environmental costs that mining creates. A metropolis too can go into decline, of course, if its entrepôt trade deserts it, if a royal court or national government on which it depends goes into decline, or if congestion or overpopulation undermine its quality of life. Throughout the eighteenth and nineteenth centuries, however, London consolidated its metropolitan position both nationally and internationally, strengthening its international networks in the process.

During the latter half of the nineteenth century the London elite increasingly relied on the public schools to socialize new members of its network. This allowed the sons of successful merchants to mix with the landed aristocracy and the officer class to create the combination of complementary functions identified in Fig. 7.8. Local networks too developed in provincial and colonial towns—but to a more limited extent. Both churches and freemasonry seem to have played an important role in the provinces. The growing reputations of key professional groups—solicitors and accountants, for example—allied to the growth of international family dynasties, enabled the local networks and the international networks to join up and operate effectively together.

Thus where economic opportunities were of a long-term nature, substantial investment in social infrastructure occurred. In agriculture and manufacturing towns local networks often developed in step with international networks, creating an effective system of imperial trade. But in mining towns local opportunities were often perceived as too transitory to warrant substantial investment in networks, and so long-term integration between local and international networks never occurred. Flexibility in the allocation of resources was maximized at the international level rather than at the local level in these cases.

7.8. Summary and conclusions

This chapter has sought to demonstrate the economic logic of the networks that developed in the northern Italian textile industry of the 1970s and the South Wales iron industry 1750–1850. An important aspect of this economic logic is that networks can adapt to the circumstances of each case. It has been shown that the local networking of the Marshallian industrial district is well adapted to the demands of the fashion-oriented sector of the textile industry. Conversely the long-distance networking that links a metropolitan elite to a local elite is well adapted to the demands of large-scale ventures in basic industries.

This rather simple point has a number of significant implications. First, it shows that the mere existence of a district that is heavily industrialized does not qualify the place as an 'industrial district' in the Marshallian sense. From a purely geographical point of view, nothing could be more clearly defined than the boundaries of the Merthyr industrial district because it was so isolated from other centres of population and industry. Yet Merthyr was never an industrial district in the social sense, for it did not develop a community strong enough to coordinate local economic activity effectively in an informal way.

The explanation does not lie in the different time-frames of the two case studies. Prato had many of the characteristics of an industrial district in the fourteenth century as well as in the nineteenth century. Conversely there are many towns of the nineteenth and twentieth century which resemble Merthyr in their failure to evolve an effective community on a narrow industrial base.

It is not the time-frame but the industry that is important, it would seem. It is the transitory nature of the locational advantage associated with mineral deposits that discourages investment in social infrastructure. The problem is not just that mineral deposits become exhausted. Newly discovered minerals often seem to be depleted at an excessive rate. The population of a mining town grows quickly through massive immigration, but declines again almost as rapidly later on. Furthermore the demand for minerals is highly cyclical because it is derived from the demand for durable goods, which is naturally more volatile than the demand for perishable ones. This creates a scenario in which a transient population periodically groups into various factions to fight over the issues that economic depression invariably brings—wage cuts, collection of debts, financing local taxes to cover social security costs, and so on. Such divisions quickly undermine any sense of community that might evolve during a period of prosperity.

Yet industry alone is not the entire explanation. Geography is important too. The absence of rich agricultural land, coupled with the remoteness of the location, meant that there was no other economic basis for networking in the Merthyr area. Unlike the north-east of England, there were no pre-existing relationships on which the iron and coal industries could free-ride. Space rather than time therefore holds the key to the emergence of networking, it would seem.

The insights gained from this comparative study confirm the claims that have been made for the utility of the diagrammatic approach on which the comparison is based. Without a suitable set of conventions with which to portray—albeit in stylized fashion—the complex flows of product, information, technology, and equity finance, the key points in each case study could not have emerged with the same clarity.

The diagrammatic approach is also important in representing explicitly the role of the entrepreneur. Because entrepreneurs do not necessarily handle the resources that they control in a physical sense, they do not naturally appear in any account of a network that focuses exclusively on the physical aspects of an industrial process. It is where flows of information are concerned that entrepreneurs come into their own. They are intermediaries who act as a hub within the information network. By separating the schematic representation of information flow from the schematic representation of material flow, the diagrammatic method reveals more clearly this intermediating role of the entrepreneur.

The diagrammatic method is sufficiently flexible to illustrate quite clearly how different social networks, based on allegiances to different groups, interact with each other in sustaining quite subtle patterns of resource flow. This point is very important where long-distance resource transfers are involved, for here long-distance networks and local networks interpenetrate. Once again the entrepreneur emerges as a crucial figure, since it is typically the entrepreneur who belongs to two or more groups and is therefore able to broker between them. The name by which the entrepreneur is known may well depend upon the kind of industrial system in which he is embedded—he may be a merchant, a promoter, or the organizer of a subcontracting system. But the diagrammatic analysis will reveal the basic similarity between all these roles: the entrepreneur is a specialized coordinator who brings together high-quality information from different sources. It is, therefore, not only specific historical and geographical insights that emerge from the diagrammatic approach, but more general analytical insights too.

8

Free-standing Firms

8.1. Introduction

The free-standing firm was to some extent the natural successor of the long-distance network which supported the export of technology and capital from London to the provinces in the seventeenth and eighteenth centuries, as described in the previous chapter. The greater sophistication of the nineteenth century business operations, necessitated both by the greater distances involved and the greater complexity of the technology transferred, required a more formal and more specialized type of organization. This type of organization was the free-standing firm.

The free-standing company flourished in the age of high imperialism, 1870–1914. It was a company typically based in London or some other European financial centre, which owned purely overseas operations. It undertook no domestic production operations at all. It was a distinctive form of international business enterprise, admirably adapted to the economic needs of empire-building, as perceived by the imperial power.

The economic rationale of the free-standing firm has been the subject of much recent debate. A key issue is whether all free-standing firms are direct investors or not. In particular, there has been debate over whether the internalization theory of international business (Buckley and Casson, 1976) needs to be extended to incorporate financial flows in order to explain the free-standing firm. This chapter argues that internalization theory is perfectly adequate as it stands to explain the boundaries of the free-standing firm, although because of the peculiarities of free-standing firms it needs to be applied with particular care. The relationship between internalization and financial flows can be elucidated using the schematic technique developed in this book. Application of this technique demonstrates that the free-standing firm can take a variety of forms, some of which correspond to direct investment and some of which do not. These different forms are associated with different patterns of information flow within the firm. It is shown that a fuller understanding of the free-standing firm can be achieved by taking the theory of the firm set out in Chapter 3 and embedding it in the context of nineteenth-century European imperialism. The main mistake that has led to confusion over the free-standing firm is to analyse the free-standing firm along the same lines that Chandler (1977, 1990) and Vernon (1966) have used to explain the growth of US multinationals in the mid-twentieth century. This is to misconstrue the rationale of the free-standing

firm. Unlike the modern US multinational, its rationale was not to disseminate the technology of mass production and the skills of mass-marketing,
but to create an infrastructure of transport, utilities and services which
would support export-oriented agriculture and mining in developing colonies. It is the 'imperialist' template, rather than any other, that best fits the
free-standing firm.

8.2. The historical controversy

According to the product cycle theory of foreign direct investment
(Vernon, 1966) successful overseas operations hinge on the exploitation of
competitive advantages first developed in the home market. From this
perspective the free-standing company appears paradoxical because it has
no domestic operations from which it can derive competitive strength. This
has suggested to some writers that the free-standing company is inherently
weaker than the kind of multinational enterprise described by the product
cycle theory. The free-standing company may be just a transitory phenomenon, it is suggested, called into being by speculative bubbles on the stock
exchange, and doomed to failure in the long run. It has been further alleged
that the nineteenth-century free-standing firm was a typical product of
European capitalism, in that it lacked professional management, and so
failed to exploit economies of scale and scope in the way that US multinationals subsequently did (Wilkins, 1988). The apparent decline of the
free-standing firm after 1914 is cited in support of this view.

  It is possible to challenge this interpretation on several grounds. First, the
product cycle theory is not a general theory of foreign direct investment,
but merely a generalization of specific post-war US experience (Hennart,
1996). It takes the spread of overseas branch plants exploiting new technology and converts it into a general account of foreign investment. In fact
there is no reason why, in general, a firm's competitive advantage has to
derive from its domestic operations, and hence no reason why a firm's
overseas operations have to resemble its domestic ones. There is therefore
no paradox about the free-standing company, and so no reason to allege a
competitive weakness either. Secondly, although the free-standing form
was far more conspicuous amongst European investors than amongst US
investors, the existence of significant US free-standing investments in
Mexico and South America belies the idea that the free-standing company
is just an inferior culturally-specific form of multinational firm. The free-
standing firm appears to have been important wherever particular types of
investment—notably the project-oriented investments typical of mining,
agriculture and utilities—needed to be organized. When there was a frontier to be explored, an imperialist drive to exploit it, and infrastructure to be
created, the free-standing firm usually had an important role. During the

age of high imperialism frontier activity was focused on Africa, Australia, and the American West. The first two were European spheres of influence, while the third frontier was, of course, internal to the USA. The fact that the frontier was in the interior of the country is one simple reason why it is European firms rather than US firms which appear as leading free-standing foreign investors in the period 1870–1914.

The main sources of information used to establish the number of free-standing companies based in a particular country are company registrations and (less frequently) stock exchange handbooks. These sources are not particularly informative about the nature of the company's operations, and certainly reveal little of its internal management structure. Until more archives have been located, the overall picture concerning the organization and management of these companies will remain difficult to discern. Although there are business histories which provide secondary source material on some of the larger and more successful companies, their coverage is too patchy to permit reliable generalizations. This deficiency of primary material has made it difficult to resolve theoretical controversies by a direct appeal to the evidence.

Even where the evidence is abundant, though, there is still a problem for business historians in reconciling their inductive approach, based on business records, with the deductive approach, based on theory (Corley, 1993). Steps have already been taken to interpret the available evidence on free-standing companies using international business theory, notably by Wilkins (1988, 1996) and Hennart (1994a). This chapter contends, however, following Casson (1994c), that these interpretations are unduly speculative, and that the conclusions to which they point may be premature. It develops an alternative schematic approach which, it is suggested, provides historians with a useful technique for future research.

The approach also helps to clear up a confusion about whether all free-standing firms are direct investors or not. According to Wilkins (1988), they are. At first sight this view seems quite reasonable, since the free-standing firm maintains an equity linkage between home and overseas countries. Equity is normally assumed to confer control, and the exercise of control over foreign operations is the defining characteristic of direct investment so far as international business theory is concerned. But then, in her infamous reference to 'brass nameplates', Wilkins goes on to argue that in many cases effective control was not exercised from the head office at all. It would appear that in these cases equity was issued in the home country, not because it was intended that control should be exercised from there, but for some other reason instead. But what might this other reason be, and what bearing does it have on whether the investment was direct or not?

The issue is clearly important because, as Corley (1994a) has noted, the existence of an unrecorded concentration of managerial control in London, transmitted abroad through free-standing firms, would substantially alter the common perception of the declining competitiveness of the British economy after 1870. If such control existed then the statistics of British foreign direct investment should clearly be revised upwards, by reclassifying indirect portfolio investments as direct ones. But, if no such control existed then the previous classification of these investments as indirect would seem to be correct, and there is no reason to reevaluate the standard interpretation of declining competitiveness in post-1870 Britain.

Unfortunately the issue has been further clouded by Hennart's (1994a, b, 1996) claim that the internalization theory of international business supports Wilkins's view. He claims that direct investment occurs whether active managerial control is concentrated in London or not. Free-standing firms internalize equity markets, he asserts, and this is a sufficient condition for direct investment.

It is argued below that Hennart's interpretation of internalization theory is incorrect. It is suggested that a correct application of internalization theory would focus on the export of information or technology instead. It is shown that this approach identifies four main types of free-standing firm. Type A exports both information and technology, Type B exports information but not technology, Type C exports technology but not information, and Type D exports neither. Types A and B are direct investors but types C and D are not. Types A and C are the most interesting from a theoretical perspective, and Type D is the least interesting of them all. Unfortunately, most of Hennart's examples relate to Type D.

The point of most immediate relevance to the historian is that Types C and D are typically embodied in wider business networks in which other kinds of firm—notably managing agencies—are involved. In these cases it is the other firms that supply the information and managerial expertise that the free-standing firm itself lacks. In this sense the term 'free-standing' is somewhat misleading, because although the foreign operation is free-standing in the sense that it is independent of any domestic operation it is not free-standing in the sense of being independent of other firms (Chapman, 1992; Jones, 1995). Indeed, the more 'free-standing' is the firm in one sense, it could be argued, the more likely it is to be embedded in the other sense. In this respect the term 'free-standing' represents a rather unfortunate choice of words.

Because Types C and D are not direct investors, they are not covered by conventional theories of the multinational firm. This suggests that conventional international business theory is too narrow a perspective from which to examine the free-standing firm. A broader perspective can, however, be developed, in which indirect investments may be analysed as well. This perspective is provided by the analysis of information flows in the earlier chapters of this book. This makes it possible to consider why individual free-standing firms are of a particular type, and why certain types may be concentrated in certain industries. This perspective is set out in the schematic analysis presented later on.

8.3. The concept of control

As indicated above, the defining characteristic of foreign direct investment is the exercise of control over local operations from a foreign headquarters. A free-standing firm that exercises no control from its headquarters cannot be a direct investor.

The significance of control for the foreign direct investment literature is illustrated in many ways. The treatment of multinational holding companies is one. Most previous empirical work has excluded holding companies from measures of foreign direct investment for the simple reason that they do not exercise significant control from headquarters. For similar reasons banks which hold a major proportion of the equity of a foreign company have not been regarded as foreign direct investors. Because a bank is a corporation, it would be possible to regard firms owned by a bank as subsidiaries of the bank, but because of their 'hands off' approach to the management of their equity investments banks are usually regarded as indirect portfolio investors instead. The emphasis on control is also reflected in the political economy of foreign direct investment, where debates usually centre on the 'branch plant syndrome'—the fear that control exercised at a distant headquarters may impinge adversely on the plant because of managerial ignorance or simple disregard of local interests.

Unfortunately, however, control is a potentially ambiguous concept because of the various stages through which the exercise of control can pass. Nominally, control is conferred by the shareholder's right to vote. Votes can in principle attach to any kind of share, but in practice they usually attach to equity. Some firms have various tiers of equity, though, with shares in a higher tier having more rights than others. Some equities may even have no votes at all.

Voting rights are to some extent residual rights, in the sense that they do not apply to matters on which the firm has already surrendered control through contractual commitment (Grossman and Hart, 1986). The equity-holders cannot vote to suspend payments to bond-holders in order to increase their dividends, for example. In some cases, indeed, bond holders may restrict the rights of equity holders by giving themselves the right to manage instead. Some Chinese railway bonds, for example, conferred on bond holders the power to appoint the railway's general manager, in order to prevent the principal equity holder—the Chinese Government—from attempting to influence operational matters (Huenemann, 1984, p. 58). In other cases committees representing bondholders have taken over effective control of firms which have failed to meet their interest payments. These examples illustrate quite nicely the general point that possession of equity is not synonymous with the right to control.

Most shareholders simply vote on the election of board members, and on any capital reconstructions, mergers, etc. that may occur. In effect, they delegate day-to-day control to the chief executive, who in turn delegates to managerial subordinates, and so on. While control ultimately resides with the shareholders, therefore, *de facto* control over operations usually resides with managers on-site. Whatever instructions or guidance these managers are given, they can, in the short run at least, ignore them and do exactly as they please. The really interesting question is how control is allocated within these limits. This is the key question for the organization of the free-standing firm, just as it is for any other kind of firm.

There is some confusion in the economic literature, however, about how far delegation really can occur. According to Frank Knight (1921) control is always located where responsibility ultimately lies. Financial responsibility clearly rests with the equity shareholders, since they bear the residual risks—that is, those risks that have not been shifted on to other people through the firm's contractual arrangements. (Creditors too bear risks, arising from the bankrupty of the firm, but this complication is ignored.) Since financial responsibility rests mainly with the equity owners, Knight argues that they will collectively exercise control.

Collective control by the shareholders is obviously a myth, though. In practice shareholders normally trust the managers to take decisions on their behalf. If the shareholders cease to trust the managers then they simply sell out, provided that there is a good secondary market for their shares. It is actually a quite different principle that governs where control is really located. Control is located where competence and integrity reside. Here competence refers to the ability to access and interpret relevant information about the firm's environment in order to make correct decisions. Integrity refers to the way that the decision-maker is trusted to keep the shareholders' interests at heart.

The question then becomes one of where the relevant competence is located. This may vary from one industry to another, and even from one stage of the firm's existence to another. If strategy is dominated by the timing, location, and design of an initial investment project then the relevant competence may reside in one place (say the headquarters country), whereas when strategy is dominated by efficient utilization of the completed investment then the relevant competence may reside elsewhere (overseas, for example).

Hennart is implicitly a follower of Knight: he construes control as virtually inalienable by the equity holder. Yet he also asserts that managerial competence was often located entirely overseas (Hennart, 1994*b*). The inescapable conclusion is that in free-standing companies control resided where competence was lacking, violating the fundamental principle of efficient delegation enunciated above. The organization of free-standing firms was thus obviously very poor. Hennart's proposition therefore runs directly counter to the general stance of internalization theory—which he claims to support—that competitive pressures will select efficient organizational forms. It is interesting to observe, however, that his view accords quite closely with Chandler's (1990) view of European firms as being inefficient because they lacked professional management. Hennart's analysis supports the view that enterprising individuals overseas were let down by the weakness and incompetence of the firm's headquarters in Europe. It remains an enigma, however, as to how the world's most sophisticated capital markets tolerated such apparently incompetent management structures for so long. It is little short of a miracle that any free-standing firms were successful, given the conditions suggested by Hennart's theory.

Hennart's dismissal of British managerial competence leads in nicely, though, to his alternative explanation of why free-standing firms were headquartered in London—namely to gain access to its equity market. Hennart notes that free-standing firms procured capital in London in order to transfer it to another location where it would be used. Hennart's analysis of the advantages of London as a source of equity funds is quite standard. What is unusual is that he claims that equity raised through a company office there must be classified as direct investment, whereas in fact it could just as well be indirect investment instead. Hennart claims that the transfer of funds effected by the firm constitutes the internalization of an international market in capital and so, by appeal to internalization theory, turns the free-standing firm into a direct investor.

To an economic theorist there is something suspect about this argument. For a start, capital is a factor of production and not an intermediate product. According to internalization theory it is intermediate product markets that are internalized, and not factor markets. Factor markets link households with firms, and cannot normally be internalized, whereas intermediate product markets typically link one firm with another, and can be internalized quite easily.

Initial doubts over Hennart's approach are reinforced when it is recalled that the function of a market is coordination (see Chapter 2). Markets and hierarchies are alternatives because they are different methods of coordination. Coordination by a market involves reconciling the plans of the buyers and the sellers. Internalization brings the market within the firm, and allows management to draw up an integrated plan instead. This coordination process is quite distinct from the transfer of the intermediate product itself. The truck driver who actually takes the product from the upstream plant to the downstream plant is not a coordinator—the coordinator is the manager responsible for deciding how much product is to be transported in the first place.

In the case of the free-standing company, it is the equity market that determines how much equity capital will be subscribed to the firm. Coordination is effected by a market process that drives the equity price to its equilibrium level and thereby determines the amount of the funds that the firm can raise through a given issue of shares. The subsequent transfer of these funds overseas may be little more than a simple banking operation. Their transmission is merely a 'truck driver' activity, in other words. All the key decisions have been taken by the participants in the external equity market. Indeed, Hennart's own reference to 'transfers' in the title of his paper (Hennart, 1994a) conflicts with his contention elsewhere that it is *markets* and not mere *transfers* that are internalized by the firm. The principles of internalization, as set out by Hennart himself, clearly indicate that the internal transfer of equity funds is not the same thing as the operation of an internal equity market.

Another way of expressing this criticism is to say that the free-standing company as described by Hennart functions rather like a special type of holding company. It is special in the sense that it normally holds only one investment in its portfolio. It has already been noted that holding companies are normally excluded from statistics of direct investment on the grounds that they do not exercise significant control. Yet even a normal kind of holding company can decide whether to reinvest the earnings from one project in a different project or not. In this sense a normal holding company has an internal capital market of sorts, though it is technically not an equity market. But a typical free-standing company does not even have this option because, having only one project, there is no other project to consider investing in. Its only decision is whether to distribute dividends or to reinvest profits instead. A free-standing company as described by Hennart therefore has even less of an internal market than a normal holding company would have.

Hennart does not claim that the London office of a free-standing company did absolutely nothing at all. He notes, quite correctly, that head offices fulfilled a useful function in selling equity to speculative investors through the use of prestigious addresses and the recruitment of eminent or titled people to the board. He recognizes that incorporation under English law enhanced the perceived security of the shareholders' claims against the company, whilst the depth of the London equity market conferred a liquidity on the shares far in excess of the real liquidity of the assets in which the funds were invested. Moreover, despite the limitations of Knight's approach, it remains true that a power of monitoring resided at head office, and reserve powers of intervention in a crisis were located there. But the literature on foreign direct investment has a well developed code of practice, according to which such activities, even in total, do not constitute an exercise of active control. The role of London as a capital market is not sufficiently compelling to turn all of the free-standing firms located there into direct investors, as that term is commonly understood.

8.4. Multinationality and direct investment: traps for the unwary

A peculiar feature of the free-standing company is that the usual connection between foreign direct investment and the multinational enterprise breaks down. A multinational is conventionally defined as an enterprise that owns and controls activities in more than one country (Buckley and Casson, 1976). It tends to be assumed that a multinational enterprise necessarily engages in foreign direct investment, and that foreign direct investment is necessarily carried out by a multinational firm. The two concepts are therefore often employed in an interchangeable way. This is incorrect, however. The point at issue here concerns the second part of the proposition, namely whether foreign direct investment is necessarily carried out by multinational firms: the first part of the proposition is considered later.

The foreign direct investment concept is concerned with the location of control relative to the activity being controlled. The multinationality concept on the other hand is concerned with whether two activities in different countries are under common control, wherever that control is located. Thus if an activity located in country B, which has no analogue in country A, is actively controlled from a headquarters in country A, then foreign direct investment occurs even though the firm is not a multinational enterprise.

This problem does not arise in the context of 'product cycle' investments because control is normally exercised from the country in which production first begins. (Indeed, the traditional emphasis on product cycle investments probably explains why the problem is so often overlooked.) The problem is a serious one in the case of the free-standing firm, however.

The problem can be overcome by classifying the headquarters as a separate activity. Because the headquarters is in A and the main activity is in B, the firm now has activities in both A and B. Both activities are controlled from A, and so foreign direct investment is now once again effected by a multinational firm. This approach involves an element of circularity, though. For A, as headquarters, now controls A as activity. The approach only works on the convention that each headquarters controls itself.

While a fudge of this kind may suit the empiricist, it creates theoretical difficulties. So far as internalization theory is concerned, it means that orders given by headquarters to affiliates become information flows that are internalized by the firm. Thus an internal market in information is created quite independently of any other markets that the firm may have internalized too. This then raises the question of where the coordination of this new internal market is located, and if this locus of coordination also qualifies as a separate activity as well. To justify the fudge, the condition must be imposed that all coordination of internal markets in information is effected by one of the activities that handles the information (normally the activity that sources the information, though this is not necessarily the case).

In the interests of clarity it is best to adopt the convention that being a headquarters is not an activity, so that a headquarters office is not an activity unless it performs some other function as well. The obvious candidate for an additional function is the provision of technological advice or some other intangible service. Such services have always played a crucial role in rationalizing the existence of multinational firms. Analysing an internal market in services of this kind does not raise the problems of circularity discussed above. The advantages of coordinating an export of services from the location that generates them are fairly self-evident, and can be explained in terms of conventional internalization theory.

Internalization theory therefore makes clear the importance of distinguishing an export of information, embodied in the exercise of control, and an export of technology embodied in a supply of intangible services. The interaction of information and technology flows creates a typology of free-standing firms that is formally presented in Table 8.1.

The Type A firm, that exports both information and technology would, under the recommended conventions, qualify as both a direct investor and as a multinational firm. It takes information from sources close to headquarters, synthesizes this with information received from the foreign plant, and encodes it in the form of orders sent overseas. It is a direct investor because it exercises control and a multinational firm because its headquarters qualifies as a separate activity.

The Type A firm was discussed in Casson (1994c). It was argued that the typical firm of this type exported project management services. These services related to the planning and execution of major infrastructure investments. Empirical support for this view was found in the concentration of free-standing companies in industries such as mining, railways, harbours, and oil, where infrastructure investment has a crucial role. The role of the headquarters, it was suggested, was to take an initial entrepreneurial idea— to sink a mine or to build a railway for example—and refine it. The headquarters teamed up specialists on engineering, marketing, property law, and procurement to generate a detailed specification which enabled the project to be completed on time and within budget.

In terms of the more conventional interpretation of international business theory within a manufacturing context, a suitable analogy is between project management and R & D. While R & D produces a detailed specification for a new product or process, project management produces a detailed design for an infrastructure investment instead.

TABLE 8.1. *Typology of free-standing firms*

| Export of information | Export of technology | |
	Yes	No
Yes	A multinational direct investor	B direct investor
No	C quasi-multinational	D —

The analogy is not exact of course, but the differences involved are, in fact, the very differences that explain the unusual features of the free-standing firm. For a start, the output of R & D has potentially global application, while the output of project management is specific to one particular site. This explains why R & D-intensive firms operate in many overseas locations while free-standing firms normally operate in only one. Secondly, R & D is a continuous activity which feeds back information from regular operations to refine and improve the product or the process; by contrast project management is a once for all activity because its output is embodied in equipment and infrastructure which is difficult to alter later on. This explains why R & D-intensive firms are long-lived firms with a continuing capacity for innovation whereas free-standing firms are often short-lived firms whose innovative capacity dries up once their projects have been completed. Finally, R & D-intensive firms typically commence their feedback of information using their domestic operations, which are closest to the laboratory. Free-standing firms, however, cannot feed back information so easily because their operations are usually tailored to the unique geography and resource endowments of the overseas location which has no exact parallel at home. The home-based skills used by the free-standing firms are the general skills possessed by the scientific community and exploited through consulting firms, rather than the specific skills found amongst employees in the domestic industry. This explains why R & D-intensive firms expand by replicating domestic operations overseas while free-standing firms do not.

The Type B firm exports information but not technology. It is a direct investor because the information exports are encoded in the form of orders, but it is not a multinational because its headquarters, being specialized entirely in coordination, does not qualify as a separate activity. The Type B firm illustrates quite nicely the kind of semantic paradox that a free-standing firm can create. A Type B firm is created when, for example, it is found to be easier to manage at a distance than to manage on the spot. A plantation on the West African coast may be managed from London because the local environment is not congenial for managers to work there for long periods of time. Information generated by the London commodity markets may also be of greater strategic importance to the firm than information obtained in Africa itself.

To understand firms of Types C and D it is necessary to consider the first part of the proposition with which this section began—namely that a multinational enterprise is necessarily a foreign direct investor. The issue concerns whether the exercise of control can be externalized or not. It has already been shown that control can be delegated. The managing agency system, described below, demonstrates that control can in fact be delegated to independent agents, provided that a contract with suitable performance incentives can be drawn up. Of course, the owners still retain residual rights not to renew the contract (indeed, they may also have rights to terminate the agreement if certain minimum performance norms are not met). The externalization of control raises the possibility that a company might be a multinational owner, in the sense of owning outright activities in several different countries, without exercising multinational control. It would not be a true multinational, for this by definition both owns and controls, but it could be described as a quasi-multinational instead.

The Type C firm exports technology or project management services, but without the responsibility for coordinating them. The coordination is arranged by consultants or managing agents who have an arm's length relationship with the firm. It is not a direct investor, and is only a quasi-multinational firm. There is evidence to suggest that a number of Type C firms were actively promoted by managing agents—particularly those operating in Asia—as a device for expanding their operations without diluting the partners' control of the agencies themselves.

The Type D firm exports neither technology nor information. Its role is basically to own overseas assets which other people manage. The reputation of the independent management is crucial to this arrangement. The logic of it also hinges on the fact that there may be little that the management can do to influence the performance of the activity, apart from carrying out routine operations in a professional manner. The value of the asset—such as an open-cast mine—may be subject to economic fluctuations according to the state of business confidence, and all that is required is a large and diversified group of investors who are prepared to tolerate the speculative exposure that such assets invariably create.

The Type D firm is neither a direct investor nor even a quasi-multinational firm. Unfortunately it seems to be this type of firm on which Hennart places the greatest emphasis. He may be correct in his judgement that this type of firm is statistically well represented in the population of free-standing firms, but all this really shows is that there are a large number of firms which have been classified as free-standing which are of very limited economic significance. They are of limited theoretical interest since they are merely a device for marketing equity in risky projects, and of limited historical interest since the real coordination was done elsewhere—by the people who promoted the firms in fact, and the agents who managed the operations on a regular basis. It has also been suggested that Type D firms may have been 'shell' companies for tax-avoidance, or even devices for 'laundering' illegal funds. Firms of this kind have existed ever since company law afforded loopholes which could be exploited in this way; it would seem rather disappointing if the study of free-standing firms were to degenerate into a study of such operations, when there are more important issues connected with the other types of firm that warrant immediate investigation.

Hennart himself seems unaware of the distinction between direct investment and multinationality in his application of internalization theory to the free-standing firm. The distinction is important for his purposes, though, because internalization is first and foremost a theory of the multinational firm. It explains why two distinct activities in two different countries are brought under common control. In analysing the Type D company, Hennart identifies the head office as one of the firm's activities, because he considers the sale of equity to be an important function so far as his theory is concerned. In this way Hennart turns the Type D firm into a multinational. According to Hennart, this head office is set up on the initiative of individuals overseas, who deploy it to access funds that could not be obtained through local equity sales. In many cases this account of type D firms' origins may well be accurate. But it implies that the overseas firm is actually making the direct investment in the home country rather than the other way round. Foreigners or ex-patriates are investing in a registered London office, for example, in order to procure additional funds. They control this office from overseas. What Hennart actually explains, in terms of his own approach, therefore, is foreign direct investment in Britain by overseas firms, to the value of the office premises that they use. He employs the concept of multinationality in such a way that he generates, not a large British direct investment overseas, as Wilkins claims, but a small overseas direct investment in the London office property market instead. Such direct investment almost certainly did occur, but is this what the free-standing firm is really supposed to be all about?

8.5. A schematic analysis of the free-standing firm

To account for the behaviour of all the firms identified by Wilkins, a theory is required which encompasses both direct and indirect investment. The approach taken here is to embed the analysis of the free-standing company within a more general view of the imperial system of which it formed such an important part. The free-standing company is viewed as part of a larger international business system, in which other types of company—notably the managing agency—also played a role. Free-standing companies of the type emphasized by Hennart—which were not direct investors in the normal sense of the word—appear in this model as adjuncts to the managing agencies. They allowed the more reputable agencies to raise large sums of money on the security of relatively illiquid assets. This was an alternative to floating shares in the agencies themselves, which would have created large high-risk firms and would have led the partners in those agencies to lose their overall control.

The concept of imperialism used in this analysis is an economic rather than a political one. It certainly embraces the classic forms of imperialism, such as the British in India, but it includes the US in Latin America too. There is a widespread view that imperialism is a specifically European vice, but from an economic perspective the subsidization of a pro-Western government in a 'banana republic' has much the same consequence for foreign investment as overt political control by a colonial power. The analysis therefore not only addresses the role of British and Dutch investments in Asia and Africa, say, but US investments in Mexico too. The distinctive features of European investment, as compared to US investment are explained within the model—they are not prejudged at the outset.

The analysis begins by distinguishing three different types of international flow (a fourth type is introduced later). The 'imperial template' suggests that an appropriate illustration of resource flow would be a raw material which is exported from a colonial mine to a smelter in the home country. (To apply the model properly, the term 'colony' needs to be interpreted very broadly, to include not only self-governing dominions, but any country that is heavily dependent on overseas trade and capital for its development.) A flow of this kind is illustrated in Fig. 8.1. The conventions used in this and the subsequent figures were explained in detail in Chapter 7. The upstream production plant—i.e. the mine—is denoted Y_1 and the downstream production plant—i.e. the smelter—is denoted Y_2. For future reference, the ship in which the mineral ore is transported is also shown, indicated by V. It is a convention that production plants and physical equipment such as ships are noted by squares and that the product flows that link them are indicated by double lines.

The export of mineral ore is coordinated by a flow of information. This information flow informs the decisions which govern the quantity of material that is shipped at any one time. Information flows are indicated by single lines in the figure. Unlike the material flow, which is one way, the information flow is two-way, as indicated by the arrows pointing in each direction (see Chapter 1).

Information is processed by individuals—individuals are indicated by circles to distinguish them from production plants. When an individual is based at a plant—as in the case of the production managers y_1 and y_2—then they are shown as circles within the corresponding squares. The coordina-

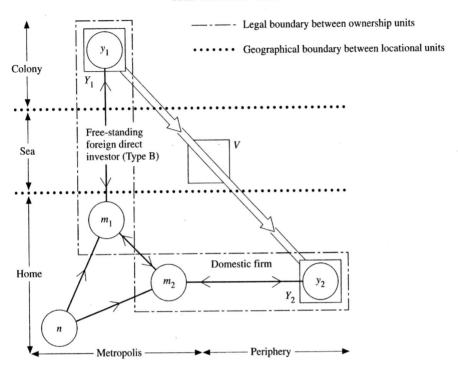

Fɪɢ. 8.1. *Intermediation in the coordination of a raw material export flow*

tion of product flow is not necessarily effected by direct communication
between the managers of the plants, however. When modelling information
flow it is crucial to recognize that information flow is often intermediated by
third parties. If the same firm owned both plants, so that the product flow
was internalized within a vertically-integrated multinational, then both production managers might well report to a single intermediator—namely the
senior production manager at headquarters.

The free-standing firms were not of this type, however. When a free-
standing firm exported to its home country then the product was usually
sold to an independent local firm for further processing. In this case the
intermediation typically involved two parties who were linked by a market
transaction. This is the case illustrated in Fig. 8.1. The intermediator m_1—an
import merchant at the free-standing firm's headquarters in the home
country—negotiates with the intermediator m_2—his 'opposite number' who
purchases on behalf of the smelter firm, and who is typically based at the
smelter firm's headquarters. Once these two merchants have fixed the price
through their negotiations, the quantity information is transmitted back to
their respective production managers. The mine manager y_1 sets an appropriate level of output, and the smelter manager prepares to adjust his own
output ready for when the consignment of ore arrives.

Figure 8.1 also shows the location of the various plants and people. In particular it shows that both intermediators are located in the home country. Intuitively this captures the tendency for intermediation to be concentrated in the metropolitan centre in the home country where organized markets for products are most likely to exist.

The two-way flow of information between y_1 and m_1 does not, of itself, identify m_1 as being the headquarters, since it does not indicate which direction of flow is the most important. The importance of m_1 relative to y_1 is determined by the fact that m_1 also has access to the supply of news n which y_1 lacks. The managers m_1 and m_2 are agglomerated in the metropolis not only so that they negotiate face-to-face (and avail themselves of organized markets), but also because they get privileged access to the news. To some extent, of course, they are themselves a source of this news because they are helping to form the prices of products which are later reported to others. But by agglomerating in a locality that has specialized information workers, such as journalists, they gain priority access to information collected more widely than their own social contacts would permit.

It is because m_1 can combine information on overseas production conditions obtained from y_1 with the general news n, that he is better placed than y_1 to take decisions. The manager m_1 encodes his synthesis in instructions given to y_1, rather than the other way round, because m_1 has superior access to information. This is why authority runs from m_1 to y_1 and why m_1 is therefore the headquarters of the firm.

Because control over colonial operations is based in the metropolis the firm is a direct investor but because the headquarters does nothing but coordinate it is not a true multinational firm. It therefore corresponds to the Type B firm described above. This is the type that illustrates the apparent anomaly of the free-standing firm most clearly.

Besides the flow of materials and the flow of information, the flow of equity finance is also distinguished. Equity finance is the third of the flows mentioned above. Such flows are identified in Fig. 8.2 using the notation of a spring introduced in the earlier chapters. This rather unusual notation is used to suggest that the equity holders buffer the firm against fluctuations in its profits. They insure the firm's creditors by absorbing all shocks to the profit stream through changes in their dividend stream or through changes in the value of their undistributed reserves.

The ultimate source of equity finance is individual savers—particularly those of a speculative disposition—who may live either at home or overseas. They prefer to channel their funds into assets using companies incorporated in the metropolis because of the greater security and liquidity that this affords, as explained above. Funds are therefore transmitted to the metropolis for this purpose. The managers at the headquarters incorporate themselves into a legal entity with limited liability by promoting the firms r_1 and r_2. The funds collected from the sale of equity are then channelled to

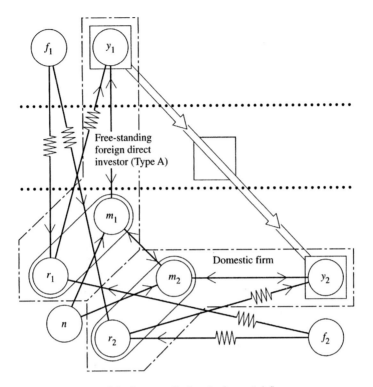

FIG. 8.2. *Intermediation in financial flows*

the plants. In the case of the smelter they are channelled to a peripheral region of the home country where heavy industry is located—near to the coast and close to a major coalfield, for example. In the case of the mine they are simply channelled overseas.

It can be seen that each headquarters intermediates not only in the coordination of the intermediate product flow but in the flow of equity too. Such a dual role, though not inevitable, is very likely, given that the two types of intermediation are so closely related.

By setting the model up in this way the mine and the smelter are put into roughly symmetric positions. Both are engaged in the raw material market, and both are recipients of capital raised in the metropolis. They are both constituents of the empire too. They just happen to be in different countries within the empire. This demonstrates that the free-standing firm which owns the mine may well be an international analogue of the domestic firm that owns the smelter. The arrangements relating to the former may be deemed to have evolved directly from the arrangements that related to the latter, as explained below.

This suggests that even though the product cycle model does not apply in the physical sense that domestic plants are replicated overseas, it may apply in the organizational sense that patterns of intermediation, exemplified by the free-standing company, that have proved themselves in a domestic context are later used for the organization of overseas activity. Just as the bureaucratic structures of post-war US investment may be traced back to the managerial revolution begun by the transcontinental US railroads, so the lean and flexible structures found in the London-based free-standing companies may be traced back to the speculative enterprises used to finance the early industrial revolution in Britain (for the formal analogy see Chapter 7).

8.6. Maritime operations and the managing agency

No account of the imperial system would be complete without some discussion of maritime activity. Voyages of discovery played a crucial role in the foundation of the Spanish, Portugese, French, and Dutch empires, whilst a combination of the search for a northern passage to the Orient and organized piracy created the early momentum for the British Empire. Before the start of the industrial revolution the maritime sector was instrumental in developing a consumer society in Europe, based on the conspicuous consumption of imported luxuries. Later on—during the years of the scramble for Africa—it brought the raw materials to feed the heavy industries of Europe.

Of particular relevance to the free-standing company is the way that the joint stock principle of finance developed in the maritime sector, both in the ownership of ships and in the financing of voyages. For example, one-sixty-fourth shares in ships were widely traded by the sixteenth century (Scott, 1912). One way in which a shipping company can be factored in to the imperial system is shown in Fig. 8.3. The vessel V is controlled by the master, or captain, v, who coordinates the arrangements for the voyage with the manager of the shipping company m_3. The manager is appointed by the director of the company r_3 who controls the equity funds subscribed by the shareholders f_2. As shown, only domestic shareholders own the shipping company, although there is no reason in principle why colonial investors could not be involved as well.

The shipping company r_3 occupies a line of intermediate position on the spectrum between the free-standing direct investor r_1 and the domestic company r_2. The company is domestically financed, like r_2, but its asset base is not confined to domestic territories in the sense that the ship it owns can sail to foreign ports. In so far as the ship is domestically registered, however, the company technically remains a local investor like r_2. If, however, the ship were foreign-registered, in order to use cheaper labour, for example, then the company would technically become a free-standing direct investor like r_1.

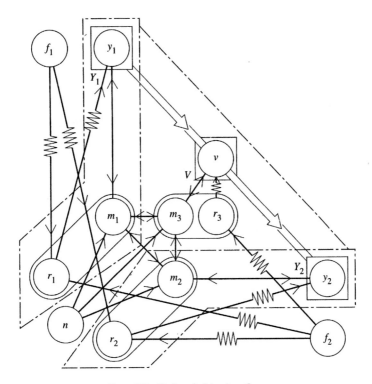

FIG. 8.3. *Role of shipping firms*

In fact the organization of maritime activity did not evolve in quite this way. Instead of having a few shipping companies with substantial fleets, each ship was typically organized as a separate company in order to control the financial risks involved. It neutralized the 'domino' effect which the loss of one ship could have on the finances of other ships in the owner's fleet. Ships have always been amongst the largest, least divisible and most risky assets in which people can invest. Merchant ships are floating containers, and economies of scale encourage them to be built as large as possible, compatible with access to port facilities. Financial risks are great not only because of the risks of loss at sea, but because charter rates are highly volatile on account of the durable nature of the fleet and sensitivity of international trade to the state of business confidence—particularly where raw material shipments are concerned (for further discussion see Chapter 10).

With many small shipping companies, each owning a single vessel, it became quite common for the owners of a ship to vest the management of it with an agent. The agent, for example, could arrange to charter out the ship on their behalf. The agent would be rewarded by some combination of salary and commission. The agent had to enjoy a good reputation for competence and integrity, however, because he personally carried only a very small proportion of the financial risks associated with the vessel's operations.

To make efficient use of a specialized ship agent's time, it was necessary for an agent to manage several ships. This, of course, allowed agents to accumulate enormous expertise. To capitalize on this—in other words, to exploit the economies of scope afforded by their general knowledge of the shipping trade—they could take on junior partners to expand their agency provided, of course, that they could also procure the finance to buy more ships. This induced reputable agents to promote the building of ships (or in some cases the acquisition of secondhand ships), incorporating a new company for each additional ship, and inviting wealthy speculators to subscribe equity. Although the historical details are sometimes rather sketchy, it seems clear that the subscribers often included merchants who were interested in chartering the vessels for themselves.

The intelligence gathered by the captains of these ships would inform the managing agents of business opportunities overseas—in particular opportunities for procuring larger return cargoes by developing mines, plantations, etc. Individual shipping routes tended to be highly competitive because, unless they were controlled by a charter monopoly that was effectively policed, vessels could easily be switched on to routes where existing operators were enjoying profits higher than elsewhere. Vertical integration into the procurement of export cargoes made little sense, therefore, when the arrival of ships to collect the cargoes could not be accurately predicted, where the export products were difficult to store, and where it was costly to vary the rate of production at short notice. It was far better to ship the exports on the first available ship than to try to coordinate production and sailings within the constraints of using only vessels from a particular owner's fleet. These features of the shipping market still apply today (Boyce, 1995).

Managing agents seeking to develop an export trade would therefore find it advantageous to promote a company that invested in a mine or plantation quite independently of the shipping companies that it might otherwise control. By analogy with the shipping company, the mining company or plantation company would be promoted on the basis that management would be effected by the agency rather than by the company itself. The shareholders would have the residual right to take the management of the company out of the agent's hands if it performed persistently badly, but it was anticipated that such action was most unlikely to occur.

The resulting situation is illustrated in Fig. 8.4. The separation between ownership and management effected by the managing agency system is shown schematically by separating the plant or vessel, denoted by a square, from the individual manager of the plant, or captain of the vessel, denoted by a circle. The managers and the captains are under the control of intermediators in the metropolis, just as before, but these intermediators now work for a managing agency whose activities are coordinated by a senior partner m_0. This senior partner is networked to the major private sources of news, and takes policy decisions based on this news which are communicated to the more junior partners who deal with the individual firms. The owners of these firms—the investors f_1 and f_2—channel their funds through the company headquarters r_1, r_2, and r_3 into the plant and equipment Y_1, Y_2, and V which provides their main collateral. As Hennart has noted, the highly speculative nature of this collateral explains why equity finance rather than bond finance is normally required. The 'downside' of these investments is so large—their entire value could be wiped out—that there is no effective way of protecting ordinary creditors such as bondholders.

The separation between the ownership of the company and the management of its headquarters is shown by separating the two circles involved. The circle r_1 represents the owners acting as a corporate body, while the circle m_1 indicates the independent agent to whom they have delegated control. The line enclosing them indicates that they are linked by a management contract. The shape of the line is different from that in Fig. 8.3 because the agent is no longer an employee of the firm.

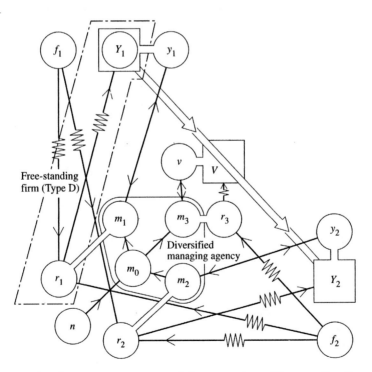

FIG. 8.4. *The managing agency and the promotion of free-standing firms*

The separation between ownership and control explains the lack of control which Hennart so eloquently describes in his discussion of the Type D firm. The registered office of the Type D firm is indeed merely a conduit through which the capital raised from f_1 and f_2 is transferred to the overseas plant, Y_1. This is because coordination of product flow, drawing on the news, n, is being effected by the merchant, m_1, and not by the registered office, r_1. Management has been externalized by the contract between the free-standing firm and its agent.

The free-standing firm is not a direct investor in this case because control has been placed in other hands. It is possible, though, that the managing agency may qualify as a multinational firm. This multinational dimension of managing agency operations has received little analytical attention so far. It is clear, however, that if the managing agency, m_1, also holds responsibility for the management of the mine, Y_1, so that the manager, y_1, is an employee of the same firm, then multinational operations are in principle involved. The agency is internalizing the market for information between m_1 and y_1 just as the Type B firm did before.

It goes without saying, of course, that the mine and the smelter used in these examples have been chosen only for purposes of illustration. The model applies to other industries too. It may, for example, help to explain Scottish investments in the Indian jute industry, and English investments in Brazilian agriculture. In both these cases managing agents appear to have played an important role in a major export trade. The link with managing agents is not ubiquitous, though. It is certainly the case, as Hennart has argued, that some free-standing firms in mining were quite unconnected with managing agencies based in London. It is well known, for example, that many free-lance concession-holders took up temporary residence in London to attempt to float companies there—though often with little success. Similarly, not all managing agencies originated in the maritime sector—many of them were ordinary merchants or factors who diversified out of commodity trading when the innovation of the telegraph and liner shipping rendered their short-term speculations obsolete. The picture given here is for expository purposes only—it is not claimed to portray a situation that is fully representative of free-standing firms as a whole, or any given export trade in particular.

8.7. The role of technological expertise

It must be recognized that even the most speculative investor is unlikely to subscribe shares in an asset such as a mine or smelter—particularly one that is overseas—unless they are reasonably confident that the technology exists to operate it properly. In the case of underground mine workings, for example, it is important to understand the geology of the seams, to arrange

the shafts to provide adequate ventilation, and to install pumping equipment of appropriate capacity (see Chapter 7). Specialized scientific knowledge must be obtained from geologists, mining engineers and mechanical
engineers to ensure compliance with these requirements. The source of this
technological expertise is indicated diagrammatically by the triangle in the
bottom left hand corner of Fig. 8.5 labelled *t*. The flow of technological
knowledge is indicated by a single line with an asterisk along it. It is a single
line rather than a double line to indicate that it is a flow of information
rather than materials, whilst the asterisk is used to indicate that it is not
ordinary coordinating information such as prices and quantities that is
involved, but know-how instead.

The know-how is shown as being supplied to the companies themselves
rather than to the managing agencies. This is because the information is
vital to reassure the shareholders. The technological assessments are more
in the public domain than the private one—summaries may well appear in
the company prospectus, for example. In the early stages of the venture,
therefore, while the company is being launched, and immediately afterwards, the headquarters of the company may well have an active role to

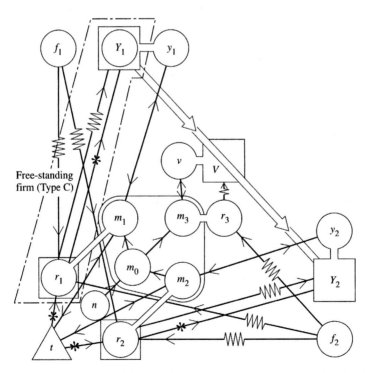

FIG. 8.5. *Technology and the supply of project management services by the
free-standing firm*

play. But once the innovations have been completed, and the funds supplied by the shareholders have been allocated to their purposes, the headquarters may assume a purely passive role.

The technology acquired by the firm is not purely for public consumption,
however. It will be passed on to the overseas operation too. A synthesis of
the various kinds of expertise required by a complicated project qualifies as
an activity in its own right. A square has therefore been drawn around the
circle that represents the company to indicate that so far as internalization
theory is concerned, a proper activity is now under way in the home country. The input, synthesis, and onward transmission of the expertise remains
coordinated by the agent m_1 however.

In this case the free-standing firm is of Type C. It is a quasi-multinational
because its headquarters generates exports of technology embodied in
project management services. Because all coordination is in the hands
of the managing agency, however, no direct investment is involved.
As indicated earlier, the export of technology may cease once the initial
project is complete, in which case the firm becomes Type D, as illustrated in
Fig. 8.4.

The final possibility is that the free-standing firm is actually akin to a
conventional multinational, with the qualification that it just happens to
lack domestic operations similar to its foreign ones. Like a conventional
multinational it exports technology from the country in which it is
headquartered, and controls is own operations too. This is the case of the
Type A firm shown in Fig. 8.6. Because the internal structure of the firm is
slightly more complicated than in the previous cases, the firm has been
abstracted from its environment to give the diagram greater clarity.

Because the Type A firm is so conventional, it fits not only with internalization theory but with Dunning's eclectic theory (Dunning, 1981) too.
Hennart has claimed, in the light of his own analysis, that free-standing
firms did not have ownership advantages of the kind described by Dunning,
but Type A firms clearly do. Certainly their ability to convert technological
expertise into project management services can be construed as an ownership advantage (or, equivalently, a competitive advantage) in Dunning's
terms. This underlines the fact that Hennart's analysis overstates the differences between free-standing firms and conventional ones. It is not necessary to reject Dunning's eclectic theory in order to explain the free-standing
firm, but only the product cycle theory. Dunning's theory can be criticized
on other grounds (Casson, 1987, Ch. 2) but it does not seem to be at fault in
this particular case.

It is worth noting that much of the technological expertise available in
London during the nineteenth century had been accumulated in the operations of domestic companies such as the one portrayed in the figures above.
The Newcastle coal industry, the Shropshire iron industry and the Birmingham precision manufacturing industries, for example, all incubated prag-

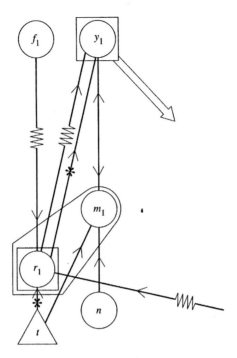

FIG. 8.6. *The Type A multinational direct investor*

matic expertise which gave birth to the professional engineering consultancy firms on which the free-standing companies drew. Because many such regional industries were financed, at least in part, using London funds, these domestic firms may be seen as progenitors of the free-standing firms in respect of both technology and capital. The organizational methods incubated in the shipping industry were refined in domestic industries such as coal and iron before they were exported to the colonies in the nineteenth century by the free-standing firms.

So far as the free-standing firm is concerned, this analysis suggests three things. First, that the free-standing firm forms part of a system predicated on arm's length contracts rather than on vertical integration. It is this that explains why, in the example discussed, the mining company and the smelting company are not just different divisions of a multinational enterprise of a conventional type.

The second is that the separation of ownership and management effected by the managing agency system is designed to distribute the enormous risks involved in the process of colonial and imperial development as widely as possible. It avoids concentrating too many large and speculative assets in the hands of the same firm. Thus any difficulties encountered in one area of the managing agency's operations—a particular colony, or a particular export trade—cannot bring the whole company down and disrupt the entire process of imperial development.

Thirdly, despite the contractual separation of ownership and management, quite a lot of management activity was carried out in the imperial metropolis, even though it did not necessarily take place in the headquarters of the firms that the agents managed. A great deal of trading activity was managed in London on a day-to-day basis because of the importance of accessing commodity markets—for example to hedge commercial risks by buying futures. Access to the financial markets was also important not merely for raising equity finance, but for the important function of raising and then arranging for the discounting of the bills of exchange by which trade was financed.

8.8. Summary and conclusions

This chapter has claimed that the classification of all free-standing companies as foreign direct investors is unsound. The way in which researchers trawl through data on company registrations in search of free-standing firms makes it inevitable that a rather varied assortment of firms will be caught in the net. It is hardly surprising that the resulting firms turn out to be of different types. Labelling them all simply as free-standing firms tends to obscure important differences between them that merit further study. Following the pioneering work of Wilkins and Hennart, it therefore seems natural that the next step should be careful differentiation of types and a close examination of each type.

To understand these types it is important to realize that the seemingly straightforward concepts of foreign direct investment and multinational enterprise present a semantic minefield for the unwary researcher. The concept of foreign direct investment relates to the *location* of control whereas the concept of multinational enterprise is concerned with the *breadth* of control. It is much more important to keep these issues distinct when analysing free-standing firms than it is when analysing the more familiar type of product cycle investment.

Rather than stretch these concepts to breaking point in an effort to clarify the nature of the free-standing firm, this chapter has pursued an alternative strategy based upon the schematic techniques developed earlier in this book. These techniques are well suited to analysing the internal organization of the free-standing firm, which is an issue of considerable historical interest. The analysis they support serves to embed the free-standing firm in a wider context. In this context the boundaries of the firm emerge quite naturally from the partitioning of ownership within a complex system. This partitioning generates other complementary types of firm as well. The overwhelming historical evidence for the existence of these complementary types suggests that the analysis is basically along the right lines.

The schematic technique relates material resource flows to information flows, technology flows, and financial flows. It also highlights the importance of intermediation—particularly in information flows. The comparative advantages of different locations in the intermediation of information flows explains the location of control, and hence have an immediate bearing on the direct investment issue. Locational comparative advantage in organization explains, for example, why the headquarters of a free-standing company is typically in the home country and not the colony, and therefore explains why the home country is a direct investor in the colony and not the other way round. The comparative advantage of different locations in the intermediation of finance explains why equity is sold from the home country and not in the colony, and hence why the registered office of the company is in the home country too.

The home country, in other words, normally has a comparative advantage in both forms of intermediation: organization and the provision of finance. A key reason for this is that the home country has many organized markets. These markets are supported by a large amount of face-to-face contact between merchants, and this is in turn associated with economies of agglomeration in a metropolitan area. A conventional firm based in the metropolis will intermediate both information and finance from a registered office which is also its operational headquarters. The greater need for flexibility associated with the distinctive types of investments in which free-standing companies were involved, however, favoured the specialization of these intermediating functions with separate firms. The firms were therefore distinct even though they were both headquartered in the same place.

The fundamental rationale for this special type of institutional specialization can be found in the economies of scope afforded by the information available in the metropolis. The European empires of Britain and Holland were based on global trading systems coordinated by market rather than by hierarchy. International trade was not coordinated by vertically integrated enterprises with a single locus of control, but by disintegrated enterprises linked through the metropolitan markets. The price information used for coordination purposes was basically common knowledge to those participating in the markets. By combining this information with information received from explorers and adventurers in the colonies it was easy for entrepreneurial merchants to identify profitable opportunities overseas. To avoid the diseconomies of managing a large diversified conglomerate, the most entrepreneurial merchants chose to establish each new project as a profit centre, bringing in consultants at critical stages, such as start-up, to temporarily strengthen their management team. Moreover, to facilitate the financing of their expansion, they chose not to issue equity in a conglomerate company but to adopt the principle of raising mortgages on the assets associated with each project. Because of the highly speculative nature of the investments, however, it was deemed prudent to raise the mortgage using equity rather than fixed interest debt. Given the popular euphoria over imperial expansion in the late nineteenth century, there was little difficulty in raising funds in this way, provided that endorsements from reputable non-executive directors and consultant engineers could be obtained. Indeed, many entrepreneurs, given their superior knowledge, may have been quite sceptical about the long-term value of these investments. They recognized, however, that under the terms of their management contract their short-term returns were secure, and that even if the business failed later, the equity-holders, unlike bondholders, were not creditors and so could not forcibly liquidate the investment.

The French and German empires were less reliant on disintegrated firms and on metropolitan markets, with foreign investments being perceived much more as elements in an organized strategy for imperial self-sufficiency. Their greater dependence on integrated structures may explain the relative paucity of free-standing firms in these countries.

It is quite misleading to perceive British free-standing firms, with their lean management structures, as symptomatic of the weaknesses of unprofessional family capitalism. Free-standing firms were a key component—though not, in themselves, the driving force—in a dynamic imperial system.

Within these systems control resided where competence lay—namely with the merchant entrepreneurs. If there is a question mark about the system, it lies perhaps in the question of whether competence was always linked with integrity too. The system of management contracts created potential moral hazards, and it is possible that some of the managing agents placed short-term gains ahead of long-term viability. The system was also heavily committed to the principle of vertical disintegration in trade. As production and transport technology changed, and the imperial dream lost political legitimacy, the system as a whole began to collapse. Weaknesses in the free-standing companies were not the cause of this collapse. The companies went into decline because they were specifically adapted to the needs of the system, and the system itself was no longer well adapted to altered economic circumstances in the aftermath of World War I.

9

Chartered Trading Companies

9.1. Introduction

Chartered companies dominated a number of important maritime trading routes from the seventeenth to the nineteenth centuries. Because of their investments in warehouses and other port facilities, and their propensity to integrate backwards into export production from time to time, they were clearly multinational firms (Carlos and Nicholas, 1988; Carlos and Kruse, 1995). Moreover in their joint stock status, their large number of managerial employees, and their use of quite sophisticated accounting techniques they were surprisingly 'modern' in their organization. The sheer diversity of their activities, which included government and military operations as well as production and trade, makes their analysis complex, however. This chapter uses the schematic technique developed in the previous chapters to clarify the relationships between the different activities of the typical company. It analyses key issues such as the boundaries of the firm, the role of social networks and the impact of competitive threats on the survival of the firm.

The chartered trading companies make an interesting case study of the 'market-making' firms described in Chapter 1. They were firms engaged principally in the organization of trade rather than the organization of production. They encapsulate very neatly the vision of a firm as an information processing system. They also illustrate the role of entrepreneurship in the formation of a firm, and show how important efficient organization is to the realization of the plans of the entrepreneur.

The chartered trading companies were major innovators of their time. Innovation in a production firm normally involves the introduction of a new technology. Innovation in a trading company means the pioneering of a new kind of trade. In his discussion of innovation, Schumpeter (1934) mentions not only the introduction of new technologies and new products, but the opening up of new export markets and the discovery of new sources of supply. The chartered trading company was certainly an innovator in this sense: it discovered new sources of novel and fashionable products—tobacco, spices, beaver pelts for hats, and so on—and developed new markets for these products in emergent metropolitan centres such as London and Amsterdam.

Indeed, the charter conferred on the company can be regarded as the equivalent of a patent conferred on a technical invention. It rewarded pioneers who collected valuable information about new overseas sources of supply and who built ports and fortified settlements from which goods could be despatched home. Private reward would have been dissipated by competition if a charter monopoly had not been conferred, although some tacit knowledge and experience would undoubtedly have remained as a competitive advantage of the company.

Substantial private rewards were required to compensate for the considerable costs that were sunk in collecting this information—indeed 'sunk costs' had a very literal meaning where the early chartered companies were concerned; in the initial voyage of the Russia Company's fleet, for example, only one vessel returned home safely (Willan, 1956).

The charter was important in excluding foreign interlopers from the trade—whether they were chartered companies of rival nations, private opportunists, or simply pirates. Exclusion was vital, given that the trade was potentially very profitable and that underpricing a monopolist is an easy way to make money. Commercial intelligence was well advanced at the time, despite poor communications, with foreign ambassadors having an important role in collecting information about the trading strategies of rival states. Thus the threat of competitive entry was very real.

The backing of the state, with the implication that naval forces might be placed at the disposal of the company, was particularly important in enforcing the monopoly because of the turbulence of international relations at the time (Furber, 1976). The discovery of America by Columbus had given traditional European rivalries a new imperial dimension. While the Spanish exploited the resources of the Caribbean and Central-South America, the Portuguese and the Dutch developed the spice trade with the Orient. The English Elizabethans entered this new arena of international business by harassing the Spanish with state-sponsored piracy. At the same time they continued to explore north-eastern and north-western routes to the Orient. This led to the formation of the Russia Company and the Hudson's Bay Company respectively. Failure to find an alternative route to the Orient required the English to challenge the Dutch and Portuguese directly on the route to the Orient via the Cape, through the efforts of the East India Company. Although it seems that the state was often reluctant to intervene when asked to do so by the companies, this may not have been known to rival nations at the time, and so the infrequent nature of intervention may be construed, to some extent at least, as successful entry deterrence.

The charter could be deployed against domestic interlopers too. The company could capture interlopers abroad and return them for trial in the home country. The interlopers could expect to be punished severely because the sovereign had a direct interest in the continued prosperity of the company. Not only did courtiers, including the sovereign's own family in some cases, have investments to protect, but the company was also a useful source of soft loans and *ad hoc* imposts at a time when alternative sources of state revenue were limited because of the administrative costs that were involved.

There was a long-term strategic dimension to the enforcement of the charter too. Newly discovered territories afforded opportunities for colonization. In some cases, such as Virginia, the immediate prospects were good, whereas in other cases, such as Panama, even the long-term prospects were bad, as the Scottish Darien Company learnt to its cost. In the middle of the spectrum, however, were resource-rich locations in cold climates, where lack of infrastructure made colonization a distant aim. In such cases the short-run expedient was to 'plant the flag'. It was in the national interest to support the company in maintaining a trading post with an appearance of permanence (Cain and Hopkins, 1993; Mommsen, 1981). A simple picket fence around a seasonal settlement could create a 'fort' which could act as a symbolic 'outpost of empire' when territorial rights came to be contested later on. The rivalry between the French and the English around the Hudson River, the St Lawrence River and Hudson's Bay exemplifies the dual role of forts: as collection and distribution points of trade, and as assertions of sovereignty too.

Another aspect of Schumpeterian innovation is the creation of a new institutional form. The chartered trading companies qualify as innovators in this respect as well. Unlike the regulated companies, such as the Merchant Venturers, the chartered companies were organized from the outset as joint stock companies. Although domestic joint stock companies had been formed in England before many of the chartered trading companies were established, they were the first to adopt this form in international trade. Merchants who were members of a joint stock company were equity investors and did not trade on their own account. Agents in overseas ports were employees of the company, and bought and sold on behalf of the company as a whole, instead of acting as the partners of individual merchants in the home country (Carlos and Nicholas, 1988). Although agents were often required to place a bond—particularly when they were collecting and remitting large sums of money—their contract of employment was analogous to that of an employee of a modern multinational firm. A company would normally have a full-time secretary and a governor elected from the members of the company. It had premises which it owned or rented in the metropolis, which represented a nascent form of international headquarters, in the sense that overseas correspondence was conducted from there.

Chartered trading companies were precursors of the modern multinational in the sense that they were sometimes vertically integrated too. They owned warehouses at the ports, and sometimes processed goods prior to export, usually in order to preserve them or to reduce their weight and bulk (rope-making, for example). In the light of all this, it is surprising that economic analysis of them has been so neglected. There is a wealth of archival material, much of it readily accessible—indeed there is a surfeit rather than a shortage so far as minutes and correspondence are concerned (Rich, 1958; Chaudhuri, 1965, 1978).

Early historical interpretation tended to focus on the political and cultural aspects of the companies, rather than on their economic performance. Thus more has been written about the influence of the East India Company's oriental imports on eighteenth-century English taste than about the management of the company itself. Moreover, what has been written on the economic aspects has often been written from an ideological point of view: to demonstrate that managed trade is superior to free trade from the home country point of view, or to argue from the standpoint of the colonies that the companies simply siphoned off economic rents rather than promoted local development.

One explanation of this neglect is that until recently historians of modern business perceived only discontinuity between the 'traditional' trading enterprise on the one hand and the 'modern' multinational created by the 'managerial revolution' on the other. There is now growing recognition that the origins of multinational enterprise must be pushed back beyond the 'managerial revolution' to include the free-standing companies in the nineteenth century, as noted in Chapter 8. But the strength of these free-standing companies derived in turn from the sophistication of the London capital market, where a vast amount of technical and legal expertise, and accumulated international experience, was available on a contractual basis. This was the legacy of the chartered trading companies. Indeed, the competitive strengths of contemporary British multinational firms in food, retailing, shipping, and finance can be traced back, through these free-standing firms, to the skills developed in the early operations of the chartered trading companies.

Another factor may be the economists' fixation with the management of production rather than the management of trade that was noted in Chapter 1. Certainly there is a widespread view that the competitive strengths of modern multinationals derive from their harnessing of advanced technology to mass production rather than from their skills in managing trade. What this view neglects is the obvious point that products have to be marketed because they do not just sell by themselves. One of the most remarkable features of the managerial revolution in the USA was the emergence of mass marketing and mass distribution. Firms actively created demand for their branded goods. The fact that they integrated production with marketing disguises the fact that they were, like the chartered trading companies of an earlier epoch, essentially marketing-driven firms. In many cases their skills resided more in the design of the goods, in predicting their demand and in pricing them appropriately, than in their production *per se*.

This is even more true today than it was before because many companies now subcontract production that they once carried out themselves. Physical production has been progressively divested, leaving behind what some commentators refer to as the 'virtual firm' or the 'hollow firm'. These terms are misleading because they suggest that when production is missing there is nothing of substance inside the firm. In fact these firms possess a pure entrepreneurial organization as their core (D'Cruz and Rugman, 1994). This entrepreneurial organization manages global trade in the firm's branded product and its components. The firm exploits a knowledge of product demand and factor supply conditions in a manner exactly analogous to the chartered trading company. The brand rather than the charter is the source of the firm's monopoly, its product is assembled from high-technology components rather than just packaged or processed from natural materials, but it is managed according to the same economic principles as was the chartered trading company.

Perhaps the major reason why chartered companies have been so neglected, though, is simply the enormous diversity of the issues they raise. Economists are discouraged by the sheer complexity of the problem, and in particular by the intrusion of apparently non-economic issues, such as the political rivalry between the imperial powers and the consequent emphasis on the provision of defence. Few issues turn out, on closer examination, to be entirely devoid of economic aspects, however. The defence of a firm's overseas assets has, indeed, already been discussed as an economic problem in the international business literature, where the firm's home government is seen as a specialist subcontractor, providing defence in return for corporate taxes (Casson, 1987, chapter 9). Chartered companies—most notably the East India Company—indicate that the converse can apply as well, with the company providing civil government in the colony as a subcontractor to its government at home. This can be viewed as a straightforward internalization issue—albeit in an unusual context. As such, the economics of internalization can be used to explain when and where the firm provides its own defence, and if it does so whether it supplies defence on behalf of other institutions too.

This suggests that the problem of complexity lies not so much in the mixture of economic and non-economic issues, as in the difficulty of keeping the different economic issues distinct from each other. It is useful to have a conceptual framework in which different aspects of the company's activities are distinguished, and in which the various connections between these aspects are indicated separately. A framework of this kind has been developed in the earlier chapters of this book. Its schematic method allows the representation of the firm to be built up in a number of stages. Thus although the final form of the representation may be quite complex, it remains intelligible because of the step-wise approach through which it is developed. The exposition therefore proceeds through a sequence of diagrams. Because it is concerned with chartered companies, the focus is on flows of trade. In line with the previous discussion of trading firms, a clear distinction is drawn between the flow of the physical product and the flow of information that is used to control the volume and direction of trade.

The discussion begins by outlining the functional requirements of a trading system so far as information flows are concerned. The firm is only introduced once these functional requirements have been set out. The aim is to show how the firm structures information flow as an efficient response to these functional requirements. As a result, when the firm emerges it is seen to be embedded in a wider institutional context in which other types of institution, notably domestic government and colonial government, have an important role as well.

9.2. The schematic approach

The basic idea of the schematic approach is to separate out the flows of resources in a system from the flows of information that are used for coordination. As explained before, material resources, denoted by double lines, flow between plants (denoted by squares), while coordinating information, denoted by a single line, flows between individuals (denoted by circles). An individual who manages a plant is indicated by a circle drawn inside the corresponding square. On the other hand, a merchant who coordinates product flow but does not manage a plant is indicated by a circle which is quite apart from any square.

A trading system typically decomposes into subsystems (see Chapter 7). The two main kinds of subsystem are the local system, which collects up goods at one end and distributes them at the other, and the long-distance trunk system which links the local systems. As indicated above, chartered trading companies were involved with both these types of subsystem.

A typical local system, feeding goods into a trunk system, is illustrated in Fig. 9.1. The producer y delivers his goods to the warehouse manager x at the port on the orders of the merchant m. The product flows directly from the factory to the port, as indicated by the direction of the arrow on the vertical double line. Coordination is effected by the merchant m. Since the company itself has not yet been introduced into the analysis, the merchant may be considered at this stage to be either self-employed, a member of a partnership or an employee. The merchant arranges for the producer to make the good and for the warehouse manager to receive it. These arrangements are effected by two flows of information, as indicated by the two-way arrows on the single line. Thus while the product flows directly from the factory to the warehouse, the information flow is channelled through the merchant instead. This emphasizes the more general proposition, alluded to

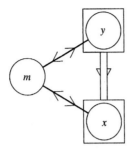

FIG. 9.1. *Schematic illustration of a local feeder system*

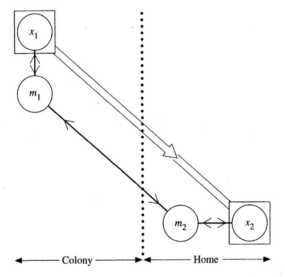

FIG. 9.2. *Schematic illustration of a long-distance trading system*

in earlier chapters, that information flows tend to be intermediated even where product flows are not.

A long-distance system typically involves the carriage of large consignments of goods. Large consignments are consolidated from smaller consignments at the point of departure, and are unpacked to recover their constituents at the destination. Large consignments tend to have lower unit costs than small consignments because of economies of scale in vehicle design. This is particularly true of the ocean-going ships which dominated colonial trade, where economies of scale in transport were significant from the outset, and became more so as naval technology advanced (due, for example, to better rigging and, later on, to the use of steam).

In pre-colonial times it was quite usual for merchants to sail with their cargoes around the Mediterranean or the Baltic in order to keep their merchandise secure. By the seventeenth century, though, it was more usual to entrust the sale of goods and the procurement of a return cargo to the captain or, once a colony had been discovered and settled, to an agent in the colonial port. This is the situation illustrated in Fig. 9.2.

The export of a product from the colonial port, x_1, to the home port, x_2, is indicated by the double line. The line is diagonal because it connects plants at two different locations, as indicated by the labels at the base of the figure. Coordination is effected by communication between the merchants, m_1, m_2, at each port. These merchants in turn communicate with the warehouse managers at the two ports. Because of the long distance involved the intermediation is now a two-stage process.

The feeder system illustrated in Fig. 9.1 is connected to the long-distance system illustrated in Fig. 9.2. The latter is in turn connected to a distribution system which unscrambles the consolidation of consignments effected by the feeder system. The entire system is shown in Fig. 9.3. Colonial production y feeds into the colonial port, x_1, from where it is consigned to the home

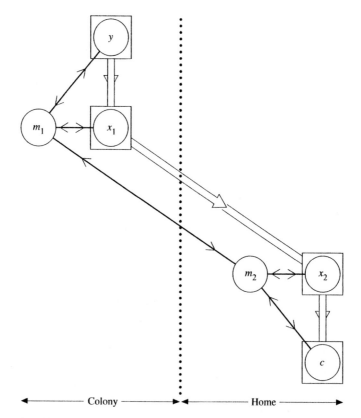

Fig. 9.3. *A long-distance trading system with feeder and distribution subsystems*

port, x_2, for distribution to domestic customers c. The merchant, m_1, who coordinates the feeder system is also in communication with the merchant, m_2, who coordinates the distribution system. Thus it is the two merchants who are alone responsible for the coordination of the entire system. This illustrates another general point which is reinforced by the subsequent discussion: namely, that although specialized intermediation may appear somewhat superfluous where very simple systems are concerned (such as those illustrated in Figs 9.1 and 9.2), it affords quite significant economies where more complex systems are concerned. As system complexity increases, the number of different channels of communication feeding into the intermediator's hub increases too, giving the intermediator an increasingly powerful role in system coordination.

In the early years of the chartered trading companies an important factor in system complexity was the provision of defence. The preceding discussion emphasized the need for defence against rival Europeans but in some cases defence against the indigenous people was important too. Initial relations were often friendly because native peoples valued the trade goods that the company's fleet brought with it. The sovereign would send presents and a letter of greeting to the native leader, in the hope of receiving a grant of land, a concession to trade, fiscal privileges or immunities, and a right to settle disputes amongst the colonists subject to the laws of the colonial power. Only where diplomacy failed, as a rule, would conquest be used to establish an absolute form of colonial government, or to install a local 'puppet' regime. Because of the unsettling effects of colonial economic expansion on the native people, however, diplomacy often did fail in the long run (or, at any rate, was deemed to have failed by the colonial power). Thus attempts to exercise direct control by the colonial power became increasingly common by the mid-eighteenth century.

A typical arrangement for the provision of defence is illustrated in Fig. 9.4. The illustration is highly stylized and is elaborated further later on. It begins with a group of merchants in the metropolis of the colonial power, m_2, approaching their sovereign, s_2, for support in the provision of defence. The sovereign already controls the army and navy, d_2, which defends the home port, x_2. When granting the charter the sovereign also agrees, if necessary, to garrison the colonial port, x_1, using the defence force, d_1. The provision of defence is illustrated in Fig. 9.4 by the thick lines with black arrows. The thickness indicates that defence is a material resource and not just a flow of information. It is, for example, not merely a threat announced to potential enemies, but a commitment to fight if necessary. The use of black serves to distinguish a flow of defence services from an ordinary flow of product.

The sovereign s_2 is in contact with his 'opposite number', s_1, in the colonial territory. This may be a native ruler or a governor appointed by the sovereign himself. In the former case the defence of the colonial port is in

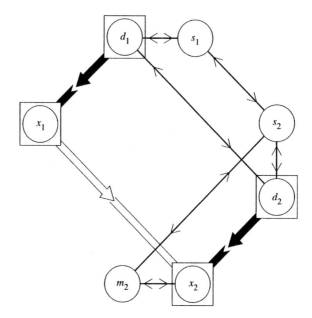

FIG. 9.4. *Provision of defence*

the hands of forces loyal, in the first instance, to the native ruler, whereas in the latter case they are in the hands of forces directly loyal to the sovereign. In terms of Fig. 9.4, the first case implies that the forces d_1 are controlled by a local leader s_2 communicating diplomatically with the sovereign s_1, while in the second case they are controlled by the sovereign himself, who gives orders through his military headquarters d_1.

It should be emphasized that routine security at a fort was usually maintained by the company itself. Its employees often had a dual role as managers and military officers. Some officers were quite experienced but, with notable exceptions, such as India, they were equipped more for local skirmishes than full-scale campaigns. Figure 9.4 illustrates the underlying balance of military power rather than the way that power was exercised on a day-to-day basis.

9.3. Maritime technology

An important omission from Fig. 9.4 is the defence of shipping. National maritime supremacy was crucial to the success of the chartered trading companies. More generally, maritime technology was an important source of competitive advantage to a country. It was not just the luck of discovering new territory ripe for development, and the entrepreneurial drive to take advantage of the opportunity that mattered in the long run, but above all the ability to build, operate, and defend the large merchant fleet required to appropriate the gains from trade. Maritime technology held the key to protecting long-run monopoly rents through entry deterrence.

Maritime technology was useful not only in equipping the navy but in allowing merchant vessels to be operated economically. It was important in ship design: a vessel is basically a floating container, and the shape of its hull is particularly important in maximizing the volume of cargo that it can carry—subject, of course, to the strength of the prevailing winds, the depth of water in the ports, and so on. The design of the rigging is important too, in making a ship fast and manoeuvrable. Other relevant expertise includes cartography, which is vital in recording and codifying information obtained on earlier voyages of discovery.

Maritime technology was arguably as important in the seventeenth century as production technology became in the nineteenth century. Although maritime technology was not patented in the seventeenth century in the same way that production technologies were in the nineteenth century, rents could still be extracted indirectly through the trading companies that exploited the technology. Indeed, in the context of Restoration England it may not be too fanciful to interpret some of the money advanced to the sovereign by the companies as compensation for their access to maritime technology developed on the initiative of the state.

The coordination of the supply of maritime technology is shown schematically in Fig. 9.5. The key to the figure is the triangle, t, representing the emergent scientific elite carrying out research into maritime affairs. A triangle has been chosen as the symbol for this elite because a triangle has been used to symbolize research and development in previous chapters. This elite supplies the technology used by both the merchant mariners v and the naval officers n. The flow of technology is represented by a single line with an asterisk placed along it. A single line is used to show that it is information rather than physical product that is generated by the activity t. The asterisk is used to distinguish this flow from an ordinary flow of information used for coordination purposes. The activities of the scientific elite depend partly on the patronage of the sovereign s_2. This is indicated in Fig. 9.5 by the two-way flow of coordinating information between the sovereign and the scientific elite.

The explicit introduction of the merchant vessel means that the coordination of the vessel's sailings must be made explicit too. The lines of information flow between the merchants m_1, m_2 and the captain of the vessel, v, represent this. Notice how the merchants—and in particular the home merchant m_2—are strengthening their 'hub' activities in intermediating information flow. The merchant m_2 is now in touch not only with the agent at the port x_2 and with the colonial merchant m_1, but with the sovereign s_2

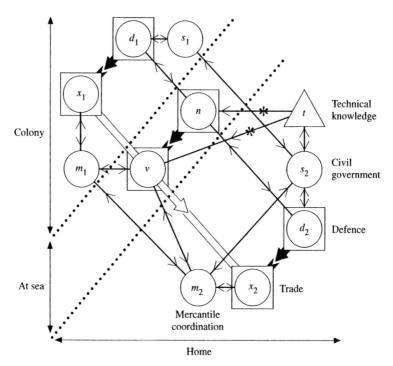

Fig. 9.5. *Role of maritime technology in international trade*

(as noted in Fig. 9.4) and with the captain *v*. The economizing effects of intermediation are thus becoming quite conspicuous.

The introduction of maritime activity into Fig. 9.5 means that a third location must now be distinguished, namely 'at sea', as indicated at the bottom of the vertical axis. The coastlines of the colony and the home country are symbolized by the lines of dots. Although this refinement increases the complexity of the figure, a distinctive pattern is still discernible. This pattern is indicated by the labelling of the diagonals which run from the top left-hand corner to the bottom right-hand corner of the figure. The labelling reveals five distinct kinds of activity linked by information and resource flows: the provision of technical knowledge, government, defence, trade, and mercantile coordination. It is a useful feature of the schematic approach that the relations between so many different activities can be illustrated in a single diagram.

9.4. Financing the chartered company

The scheme is not yet complete, however. A major omission is the provision of finance. Finance is an important factor in all forms of voyaging, whether for trade or discovery. Finance was required both to charter the vessel and to provision it. In exceptional cases, as with the earliest voyage of the Russia Company, the vessels were newly built for the task because of the special requirements of the route involved (though the actual requirements were poorly anticipated). This of course added to the initial outlay. Sometimes labour costs could be reduced by pressing sailors into service, but this was not always possible.

Whilst a trading voyage might afford fewer risks than a voyage of discovery, it incurred the additional cost of the merchandise carried for export. The more valuable was the return cargo at its point of purchase, the greater the outlay required at the start of the voyage. Thus the working capital requirements of a trading voyage might well be just as high as for a voyage of discovery, even though the duration of the voyage might be shorter and the risk of total loss smaller too.

The merchants who combined to promote the trading company would undoubtedly expect to contribute much of the capital from amongst themselves. If they were trading as merchant adventurers in an ordinary regulated company then they would certainly expect to have to lay out a considerable sum for stock in trade. A similar sum might naturally be subscribed in shares in the joint stock trading company. But in addition to this the merchants would hope that the confidence of the sovereign, as expressed by the grant of a charter, could encourage wealthy individuals from outside the merchant community to subscribe as well. In particular, members of the court—including the landed aristocracy who, if necessary, could mortgage part of their estates to raise the cash—might be expected to subscribe. The lawyers involved in the incorporation of the company might well subscribe too, taking advantage of the inside information that came their way.

The situation is illustrated in Fig. 9.6. The merchants, m_2, acting in concert, promote the company r which holds a charter from the sovereign, s_2. They advertise the company to speculative financiers f who subscribe shares even though they do not expect to play an active role in the running of the company. The supply of risk capital by the financiers is indicated by a line with a spring symbol on it. This follows the convention adopted in earlier chapters; the symbol indicates that the owner of an equity share 'buffers' fluctuations in the company's profits by accepting variations in the dividends that he receives. The capital is supplied in the first instance to the company as a whole, as indicated by the flow from f to r.

The capital is then directed, under the direction of the company's board, or court of governors, to the financing of the voyage and also, most likely, to the establishment of warehouses at home and overseas (where port improvements may be financed as well). The capital requirements of the voyage depend on whether the fleet is chartered or whether the vessels are purchased outright. This distinction is formalized by introducing ship-

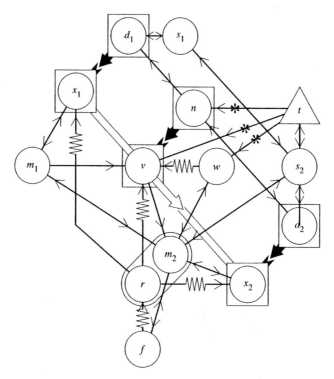

FIG. 9.6. *Provision of equity finance to international trade*

ownership into the diagram. The diagram illustrates the role of an independent ship owner, *w*, in financing the construction of a ship that will be chartered to the company. The ship-owner draws on maritime technology, *t*, in preparing the design, and also communicates with the merchants m_2 to negotiate the agreement. The ship owner in Fig. 9.6 is independent because he is shown as providing a separate source of risk finance. If the chartered company owned its own ship then there would be another line in the figure, connecting *r* to *w*, indicating that ownership was being financed from equity subscribed to the company. It is because the chartering of vessels was the most usual arrangement that this case is the one illustrated in Fig. 9.6.

The introduction of ship ownership refines the figure by making explicit the fact that the utilization of a ship is a key input into a voyage. It also helps to differentiate the ways that maritime technology is used in a trading voyage. The direct link from *t* to *v* represents the use of technology in the operation of the vessel—for example, charts and navigational instruments—whilst the link that is intermediated by *w* represents the contribution of technology to the design of the vessel itself.

A further refinement of the figure would be to introduce the shipbuilding industry that constructs the vessels acquired by the ship owner. The efficiency of the domestic shipbuilding industry was undoubtedly an important factor in the success of colonial enterprise (and so too, to a lesser extent, was the subsequent ability of the colonies to develop a ship-building industry of their own). It would, however, be too much of a digression from the main theme of the chapter to pursue this further here. (For interesting developments of this theme see Pollard and Robertson, 1979, and Ville, 1987).

9.5. Competition and monopoly

The rationale for a chartered monopoly offered in the introduction was based on the company's need to recover the sunk cost of discovering a new trade route. As exploration advanced, however, the amount of exploitable territory remaining to be discovered began to diminish. At the same time the costs of international communication began to fall. This particular rationale was weakened as a result. By the time that Adam Smith (1776) wrote about the issue, the case for abolishing charter monopolies and allowing free trade seemed increasingly strong. Free trade would expand the total volume of trade, and also provide an external check on administrative inefficiency that was suspected of absorbing the chartered companies' monopoly profits.

There was, however, a diplomatic argument for retaining the monopoly. It allowed the arms trade to be more effectively policed. Competition could degenerate into warfare if competing companies were able to arm rival tribes in the colonies in an effort to expand their area of trade by force. On balance the political arguments carried the day during the eighteenth century, and most companies survived political challenges to the renewal of their charters.

Even though the charter might be renewed, though, the pressure of competition on the companies was inexorable. For a start domestic markets became increasingly saturated as the discovery of new territories provided alternative sources from which European markets could be sourced. London could be sourced by re-export from Amsterdam, for example, and Amsterdam by re-export from London. Of more immediate danger to the company, however, was the discovery of a new out-port for the same inland sources of supply. As the export trade developed, and colonial settlement expanded into the hinterland of each port, new production locations emerged. Initially this was very much to the company's advantage: not only did the increased aggregate volume of export afford economies of scale in warehousing and transport, but the ability to play off different suppliers against each other increased the company's bargaining power. But the marginal producers at the more remote inland locations could strengthen their positions by finding outlets for their products at other ports further along the coast. In some cases the port might be in the hands of an established rival, as where British and French firms were competing in the North American fur trade. In other cases it might be a newly discovered port, as happened in the Russian trade in the seventeenth century. If the company failed in its attempt to expel its rivals then the value of its monopoly would be constrained by competition at marginal locations roughly equi-distant between the ports. A similar consequence would follow from the failure of legal moves to extend the monopoly to a newly discovered port, for in this case independent merchants from the same country could move in to develop the trade as well.

As the number of territories and ports multiplied, trading routes became increasingly complex. Triangular trade replaced bilateral trade—for example, the slave route between Bristol, West Africa, and the West Indies and the tea route between London, Calcutta, and the Treaty Ports of China—making it necessary to either extend the range of the monopoly, or to abolish the monopoly altogether. The extension of the monopoly was often the immediate statutory response, but in the long run the evolution of multilateral trade and round trip voyages calling at many ports was bound to undermine the monopoly position. The monopoly simply became increasingly difficult to administer, because of its complex logistics, and increasingly costly to enforce as well.

The more astute companies realized that with so much competition between routes the real monopoly profits were no longer to be made by controlling a particular route but by developing the entrepôt potential of the principal ports through which they operated. Creating a highly competitive environment at a particular port would develop its potential as a hub for the consolidation, transhipment, and (where appropriate) intermediate processing of goods. The company would then prosper indirectly from its share of the growing long-distance traffic to and from the port, and would benefit directly if it owned land or other assets in the port which would appreciate in value as a result of the growth of traffic.

The evolution of competition in trade is illustrated schematically in Figs 9.7–9.11. Because of the multiplicity of production locations and ports that became involved, it is vital to retain the simplicity of the original scheme. To this end some new notation is introduced which allows a large amount of information to be summarized in a parsimonious way.

Figure 9.7 illustrates the implications of increasing competition in the procurement of export production in an expanding colony. In Fig. 9.7a the port x_1 is sourced from two locations y_1, y_2 instead of just one. This strengthens the bargaining power of the company since its agent, the merchant m_1, can play off the rival sources against each other. In particular the emergence of a second source of supply means that the producer y_1 can no

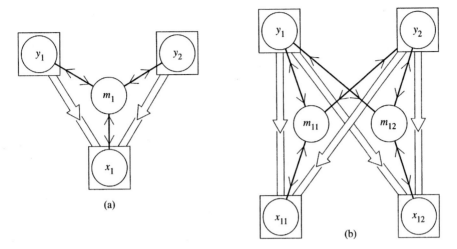

FIG. 9.7. *Implications of local competition for the export trade of a colony*

longer stipulate for a price in excess of y_2's cost of production. Although y_2's costs may well be higher than y_1's because, for example, of its more remote location, competition from y_2 will still constrain, even though it cannot eliminate, the economic rent available to y_1.

Matters may not remain like this for long, however. A new port may be opened up, giving both y_1 and y_2 alternative access to the export trade. This generates a variety of cross-trading possibilities, as indicated in Fig. 9.7b. The opening of a new port is likely to favour y_2 more than y_1 because if y_1 is more remote from the original port, now denoted x_{11}, then it is likely to be nearer to the new port, denoted x_{12} (this is not inevitably so, however). Some benefit will also accrue to y_1, though, because y_2's new opportunity to export through x_{12} raises the price that he can demand for his exports through x_{11}, and so reduces the intensity of the price competition that y_1 faces from y_2. Thus the company will lose out one way or another: its merchant, now denoted m_{11}, will have to pay higher prices. These prices will be settled through duopolistic rivalry with the merchant m_{12} based at the other port.

It is obviously going to be difficult to incorporate schematically a subsystem as complex as this into a scheme such as Fig. 9.6, which is already quite complicated enough. Fortunately it is possible to summarize a system of the kind illustrated in Fig. 9.7 using the N-notation introduced in Fig. 9.8. The N-notation can be employed whenever there are substitution possibilities involving alternative sources of supply, or alternative sources of demand. Where several alternative sources are connected to the same activity, it is possible to draw just a single representative source and to label this representative source with the letter N. The letter N is an index which can, if desired, be set equal to the actual number of sources involved (for example, $N = 2$ in Fig. 9.7a). It is often useful to leave N unspecified, however, indicating that there is, quite generally, a multiplicity of sources, so that competition between alternative sources is likely to be quite intense. The appearance of N does not guarantee that there will be competition of course, because the various sources may be able to collude. But because the notation N is applied only to sources which are substitutes, and never to sources which are complements, it always indicates a tendency to competition, even though full competition may be obstructed by other factors in the situation.

The N-notation can be applied both to plants, which are sources of material product flow, and to individuals, who are sources of information. Thus in Fig. 9.8a, which applies the N-notation to Fig. 9.7a, the N applies both to the product flow emanating from the plant and to the information flow emanating from the manager of the plant. Because there is only a single port in Fig. 9.7a, however, and only a single merchant too, the N appears only where the flows emanate from production y, and not where they are received at the port x_1 or by the merchant m_1.

Contrast this with Fig. 9.8b, which summarizes the structure shown in Fig. 9.7b. Here there are multiple ports as well as multiple production plants, and there are multiple merchants too, although there is still only one merchant per port. The N-notation now applies to the flows of materials received at each port, and also to the information received by each of the merchants involved. The relevant Ns are positioned above the box x_1 and above the circle m_1 respectively. There are still no Ns along the communication link between m_1 and x_1 because, as indicated above, there is, by assumption, still only one merchant at each port. Only if the chartered company lost its monopoly at its own port, so that other merchants set up there, would the N-notation apply to this link as well.

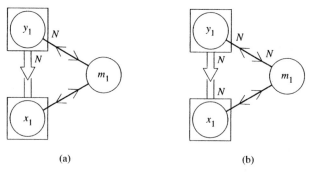

(a)   (b)

FIG. 9.8. *Use of N-notation to summarize the substitution possibilities within a trading network*

9.6. Triangular and multilateral trade

To analyse the growth of triangular trade it is necessary to consider in a little more detail the way that return freight on a voyage is obtained. So far the analysis has focused exclusively on the organization of the colony's export trade. These export earnings are used to purchase imports, however. Under simple bilateral trade the colonial imports will be carried on the outward leg of the round-trip voyage from the home country. This ensures that the ship does not have to travel outward in ballast to collect the colony's exports. For example, earnings from colonial exports of tobacco or spices may be used to purchase household goods, farming equipment and luxury items from the home country. The colonist's purchases of home-country goods are paid for, in real terms, by their exports of agricultural produce and raw materials.

This has implications not only for the organization of international trade but for the organization of the company's colonial operations too. It means that the company is engaged not only in the collection of export production but in the distribution of imported goods too. It also means that competition from out-ports that impinges on the procurement of exports is likely to impinge on the sale of imports as well.

Given that the company enjoys a monopoly of both exports and imports through the port x_1, it is natural to entrust the coordination of both exports and imports to the same agent m_1. There may be a case for a division of labour in the export and import trades when the volume of trade becomes large—for example, to give specialist attention to the management of retailing through the company's general stores—but this complication is not considered here. The integration of the export and import trades by

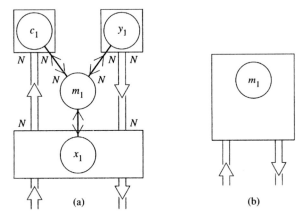

FIG. 9.9. *Simultaneous coordination of colonial export and import trade by a company's local agent*

the merchant m_1 is shown schematically in Fig. 9.9a. The box denoting the port has been 'stretched' sideways to accommodate the portrayal of the import trade as well as the export trade. The principal innovation is the introduction of the representative colonial consumer c_1. The N-notation introduced in Fig. 9.8 is now used to show how the different colonial consumers compete to purchase goods from the company's retail stores. The company, however, faces competition from other stores who obtain their wholesale supplies through ports that the company does not control.

Figure 9.9a also shows that the same port facilities x_1 are used for both the export and import trades. It is the same ship in the same dock that delivers the imports and loads the exports, and it may well be the same warehouses that are used for storing the imports and exports too.

For the purposes of analysing international trading patterns it is useful to regard the local system as a 'black box' subsystem which interfaces with the international system at each of the company's ports. Figure 9.9b shows the symbolic way in which the subsystem in Fig. 9.9a can be represented, while Fig. 9.10 shows how this symbol is used to summarize alternative patterns of international trade.

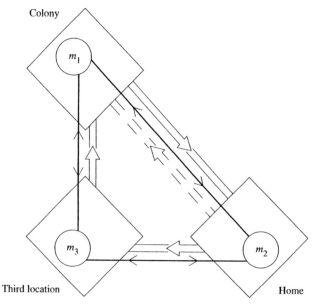

FIG. 9.10. *A comparison of bilateral and triangular international trade*

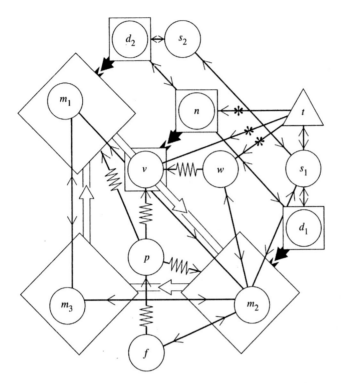

FIG. 9.11. *An integrated view of the operations of a chartered trading company engaged in triangular trade*

Bilateral trade is indicated by the two way flow of product between the colony and the home country, with the broken double line representing the exports of durable goods and consumer specialities from the home country. An alternative trilateral arrangement is indicated by the set of solid double lines making up the three sides of the triangle. According to the arrangement shown, vessels call at the third location on the outward leg of their journey. Under an alternative trilateral arrangement they would call at the third location on their homeward journey, however. More complex arrangements are also possible involving four or more locations.

A complete picture of triangular trade, with competition between ports in the collection of exports and the distribution of imports, is given in Fig. 9.11. The figure shows that on their outward voyage to the colony the ships deliver cargo to a third country which, as indicated here, is not a full part of the colonial system because it is not governed or defended by the home country. The ships reload with additional cargo and sail on to the colony. On arrival at the colony most of the cargo collected from the third country is unloaded, though some may carry on for the return voyage to the home country, together with the cargo loaded at the colonial port.

Some through cargo from the home country, which was not unloaded at the stop on the way out may be unloaded at the colony. In the age of sail it was often convenient for ships to sail either mainly clockwise (as here) or mainly anticlockwise to take advantage of the trade winds. With the advent of steam, two-way journeys became relatively easier and the amount of freight shipped indirectly via an intermediate port could be reduced.

The company would normally have a full-time employee acting as its agent in the third country port. Its investment in port facilities there was likely to be lower, however. Competition on the route between the third country port and the home country port was also likely to be more intense, unless the sovereign would agree to separate provisions—such as navigation acts—to exclude foreign ships from using the home country trade. In practice such restrictions were often enforced, so that the company's monopoly power on the route was partially preserved.

9.7. The boundaries of the firm

The importance of the schematic approach employed in this chapter is not just that it makes it easier to conceptualize the colonial trading system in a rigorous way. It also helps to explain where the boundaries of the chartered company were drawn.

As noted earlier, the scheme distinguishes sharply between the flows of resources within the economic system and the flows of information used to coordinate the movement of these resources. For effective coordination it is important that the information used is reliable. Each individual must feel able to trust the information provided by others, and this trust must be well placed.

If a product is totally homogenous, its quality is easy to inspect, and it is supplied under competitive conditions, then the amount of trust that the buyer has to place in the seller is relatively low. The only way in which the seller can easily cheat the buyer is not to supply the product at all, and the buyer can address this issue (at least in part) by refusing to pay in advance. The buyer only pays when he has checked that the product has been delivered in full amount. By holding back his payment in this way he creates an incentive for the seller to deliver full measure.

Many of the chartered trading companies were in the fortunate position that the information they obtained from their colonial producers was basically reliable. They were dealing in natural products whose quality, though variable, was easily assessed on delivery to the colonial port. So far as agricultural products such as sugar and tobacco were concerned, technology was still fairly basic, so there were few questions to be asked about the production methods employed. Despite the existence of large plantations there were sufficient colonial settlers to sustain competitive markets in which price broadly reflected long-run marginal costs.

Quality is not just a matter of defects in the product, however. Timeliness of delivery is also important. This has been brought home to contemporary firms by the success of Japanese just-in-time production methods in reducing inventory costs. Similar considerations were important to the chartered trading companies. Some export products were liable to deteriorate if stored for a long time, since the technology did not exist to control temperature and humidity in a reliable way. Moreover voyages were often confined to a single sailing of the fleet during the summer, and if goods missed the sailing then the ships sailed empty whilst the warehouses became prematurely full for the following season. Where it is difficult to penalize suppliers for the consequences of late delivery, too many coordination failures of this kind may occur. Backward integration into supply offers a potential solution to the problem.

Most trading companies appear to have begun with a fairly high level of integration, and then to have divested themselves of various activities as their methods of operation were refined. Figure 9.12 illustrates a typical sequence; although it does not correspond exactly to any one particular case, it incorporates a number of features common to most of them. The boundaries of the company in its earliest state are indicated by the outer perimeter of the shaded area. As before, lines of dashes and dots are used to indicate the boundaries of the firm, but in this case shading has been added, because of the complexity of the figure, to give the boundaries greater clarity.

The company quickly divests itself of ship ownership as private ship owners respond to the increasing demand for larger ocean-going vessels by financing the construction of more vessels of this type. Backward integration into colonial production becomes less important as the frequency of sailings increases with the growth of colonial trade. Colonial production is therefore divested as concern over the timeliness of supplies diminishes. Eventually the provision of defence is divested too. Integration into defence becomes increasingly costly as colonization spreads into the more remote part of the hinterland, creating a frontier with the native people which is long and increasingly difficult to police. Defence therefore comes under the control of colonial government instead.

The pattern of progressive disintegration of the firm is quite common even today—it is certainly not peculiar to the chartered trading company. The underlying logic is fairly straightforward. Whenever an entrepreneur—or a group of entrepreneurs, as in the case of a chartered trading company—effect an innovation, the full realization of their entrepreneurial vision may require not just one facility but a number of different facilities (see Chapter 3). As Fig. 9.12 indicates, the opening up of a new trade route, for example, requires shipping, port facilities, and a reliable source of

Colonial production

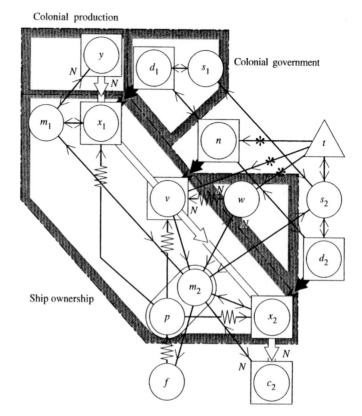

FIG. 9.12. *The changing boundaries of the chartered company*

export production. If each of these facilities needs to be specialized in some way then no suitable facilities may be available 'off the shelf'. Independent provision of these facilities may be difficult to arrange because potential providers do not share the entrepreneurial vision of the innovators. Indeed the innovators may not wish other people to share this vision until they have had a chance to preempt the most valuable opportunities available.

Because the users of facilities value them more highly than the potential providers do, the users finish up owning them themselves. This has the disadvantage, though, that the capital requirements for starting up the enterprise are increased. (Even today it may be difficult to obtain a mortgage on the security of specialized and highly speculative assets.) As the business succeeds, however, the requirements for working capital relentlessly increase, and although the growing reputation of the business makes the raising of additional capital easier, it is tempting to liquidate fixed capital by selling off facilities to independent firms, and to reduce overheads by shifting expenses onto government wherever possible.

Of course, the actual reasons for divestment vary from case to case. In the case of the East India Company, the increasing difficulty of combining trade, defence, and diplomacy proved to be a major catalyst for change. Diplomatic and military issues multiplied at the same time that the administrative demands of trade increased. Reconciling the company's interest and the national interest became more and more problematic (Lawson, 1993). Corporate objectives became fuzzy, and changed each time a new governor assumed power. The separation between the company and the colonial government of India effected in 1858 was the logical conclusion of a protracted process of reform. It effected a much needed financial specialization which eliminated many of the conflicts of interest which had bedevilled the company up to that time. Unfortunately it came too late to restore vitality to the company's trading operations in India, which by that time had become overshadowed by those of the ordinary private companies. It is interesting to note that the company's China trade, which involved fewer diplomatic complications, seems to have been economically more successful too.

9.8. Engineering trust

So far as the chartered trading company is concerned, the seriousness of these incentive problems varies from case to case. Each particular link in the chain, beginning with colonial production and finishing with home consumption, raises its own particular issues.

The strategic difficulties encountered in any link depend not only upon tangible factors, such as the nature of competition, the frequency of voyages and the ease of inspection of the product, but also upon less tangible factors such as the degree of trust between the people involved. As explained in previous chapters, trust is absolutely vital in business relationships. Where transactions belong to the same social group, reputation mechanisms and shared morality may combine forces to overcome incentive problems. Contracts are negotiated using norms of fairness and quality maintained through a sense of obligation to the buyer. Traditional values serve to mediate sophisticated commercial arrangements.

The existence of a social and mercantile elite based in the home country metropolis was a crucial factor in the formation of most of the early chartered companies. So far as the analysis of trust is concerned, the distinctive feature of an elite group is that its members trust each other, and that they are also trusted by other people who do not belong to the elite. These other people do not necessarily trust each other; they share, however, an awareness of the reputation of the elite, and their ability to recognize the members of it.

Figure 9.13 illustrates the pervasive influence of the metropolitan elite in

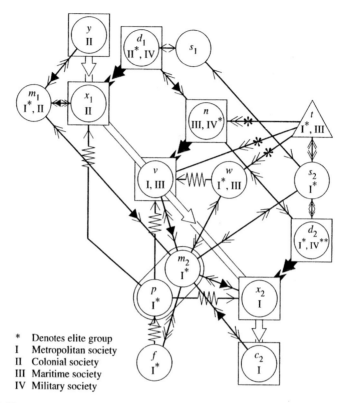

* Denotes elite group
I   Metropolitan society
II Colonial society
III Maritime society
IV Military society

FIG. 9.13. *Social groups that engineer trust in the formative period of a chartered company's operations*

Note: The *N*-notation has been suppressed in the interests of clarity.

the formation and early operation of a typical chartered company. It can be seen that the elite is quite diverse in the range of skills it includes. The absence of narrow-minded professionalization is very important in making the group work effectively. The sovereign, s_2, is the symbolic leader of the group. The wealthy merchants, m_2, and the more passive financiers, f_2, drawn from the ranks of the courtiers and leading gentry, also belong to the group. So too do the major ship-owners, w, and the scientific elite, t, who possess the knowledge required for designing ocean-going ships and navigating to distant parts.

The ship owners and the scientists also constitute an elite of the maritime community, which includes ship's captains and the naval officers. The trust placed by captains and officers in the maritime elite facilitates the dissemination of maritime know-how, and encourages seafarers to place confidence in the ships and navigational instruments with which they are equipped on potentially dangerous voyages.

The colonial elite comprises the merchant community m_1 and the garrison commanders d_1. It may also include the local ruler s_1, depending upon who exactly the local ruler is. If he is appointed by the sovereign, or elected by the colonists, then he will certainly be a member of the elite. If he is a native ruler then he may belong to the elite if he is assimilated to colonial culture, but not otherwise. He may be downright hostile to the colonists in some cases. This is why the local ruler s_1 has not been identified in Fig. 9.13 as a member of any one particular group.

Military society also constitutes a distinct grouping. It is typically a very hierarchical one. This is indicated in Fig. 9.13 by the existence of two distinct levels of elite. The naval commanders, n, constitute an elite with respect to the garrison commanders, d_1, because they convey instructions to them from naval headquarters in the home country. But they in turn are subordinate to the chiefs of staff, d_2, in the home country, who also belong to the metropolitan elite.

When members of an elite deal with other members of the same elite then, as noted above, there is mutual trust between them. But when they deal with other members of the group, the trust is one way in the sense that the members of the elite do not trust the others. This means that they can only deal with them by having some sanction against them. For example, the merchant who deals with an ordinary member of the local community—whether in the colony or the metropolis—is trusted by the ordinary member to keep his part of any deal because he belongs to the local elite. Thus the consumer c—an ordinary member of the metropolitan community, I, trusts the merchant m_2, whom he recognizes as a member of the metropolitan elite, I*. Because the merchant does not trust the consumer, whom he regards as his social inferior, he requires the customer to pay in advance for the goods that he purchases. Thus the merchant holds the goods hostage to prevent default by the customer. The customer is only allowed to pay in arrears if he too is a member of the elite. Similarly the colonial producer y—an ordinary member, II, of the local community—is willing to trust the colonial merchant m_1 to pay in arrears because he recognizes the merchant as a member of the local elite II*. The merchant insists on paying in arrears because he does not trust the quality of the goods the producer supplies because the producer is not a member of the elite.

The existence of trust is indicated in Fig. 9.13 by a double-headed arrow (as explained in Chapter 4). The second arrow indicates that the information flowing in the direction indicated by the first arrow is accurate, and can therefore be trusted. This accuracy reflects the recipient's confidence in the competence and integrity of the source of the information. When information cannot be trusted, a sanction, such as the placing of a hostage payment, must be put in place instead. The existence of a sanction is indicated by the use of a solid black arrow rather than an ordinary arrow. Thus in the top left hand corner of Fig. 9.13 it can be seen that the producer places a hostage with the merchant, by delivering the product in advance of the payment, but does not require a hostage himself, since he trusts what the merchant says. There is recognition on both sides that the merchant can legitimately demand to be trusted while the producer cannot.

Of course, not all producers lacked reputation in practice, any more than all the metropolitan customers did. In the days of the Virginia company, for example, the principal producers included ex-English aristocracy who were clearly members of the local elite. Similarly many consumers of imported luxuries in the metropolis were members of the local elite. The fact that producers or consumers were not members of the elite did not necessarily prevent them from receiving loans from the wealthier merchants either. But these loans were often offered as part of the merchant's banking activities, or as part of a deliberate strategy by the merchant to extend the base of his trade; they did not indicate the merchant's willingness to relinquish sanctions over the creditor because of social solidarity.

If the network of trust created by social groupings were complete then there would be little need to have a chartered company at all. Everyone could deal with whomever they needed, either by mutual trust or by offering a hostage to a member of their group's elite. From this perspective, the chartered company is called into existence because of the need to supplement natural groupings by an artificial one designed with the promotion of trade specifically in mind. Just as the military (group IV in the figure) functions as both an organization and as a social group, so the chartered company can do so too.

The different patterns of integration discussed in the previous section, and portrayed in Fig. 9.12, can therefore be thought of as differing institutional responses to potential weaknesses in the natural pattern of relationships described in Fig. 9.13. A particular source of weakness is the link between the colonial merchant m_1 and the metropolitan merchant m_2 which, though crucial to the entire enterprise, depends critically on a suitable person being available overseas. If the colonial merchant concerned is not a true member of group I, and does not recognize the metropolitan merchant as an honest person, then he may behave dishonestly. The incorporation of a company gives the metropolitan merchant control over the appointment to this post, allowing people who are clearly from the appropriate group to be chosen for it. Furthermore monitoring and appraisal procedures (based, for example, on the submission of detailed annual reports) can be introduced, and managers who are discovered to be unreliable can be removed and replaced by others.

9.9. Conclusion

This chapter has extended the insights of Carlos and Nicholas (1988) into the economic rationale of the chartered trading company. It has exploited recent theoretical developments to make explicit the structure of these companies by extending the schematic technique developed in previous chapters. In the interests of brevity the analysis has focused on a case which is typical of all the companies, but in detail resembles none. It claims only to be an analysis of the 'representative' company. This representative company is somewhat abstracted from time and place, but it can nevertheless serve as a useful benchmark for more detailed studies of individual companies in their historical and geographical context.

The analysis represents the chartered trading company as part of a system in which different varieties of institution—the firm, the military, the government, and even the emergent scientific societies—all played distinctive roles. In the early days these roles were not fully differentiated. The evolution of the trading companies can indeed be explained by the progressive differentiation of institutional forms as other more specialized institutions took over activities previously performed by the companies themselves. The larger the scale of their international operations became, the greater was the imperative to hive off different activities to other organizations.

The schematic approach also helps to clarify the relations within the private sector between the different varieties of company involved at various times in the colonial trades. As colonial economies developed, new ports rose to prominence and new shipping routes became available. This attracted competitive entry which tended to undermine the statutory monopolies on which the early chartered companies were based. With the rise of economic liberalism, the perpetuation of monopolies became not only increasingly unenforceable but ideologically unacceptable too. New types of firm began to appear in the colonial trades—merchant houses, managing agencies, and later the free-standing firms mentioned in Chapter 8 (Chapman, 1992; Wilkins, 1988).

It is difficult to analyse these various types of firm in isolation from each other. However, by viewing the trading system in its totality each type of firm is seen to specialize in performing certain functions of particular value to the others. Its distinctive features are explained by its adaptation to this task.

10

The Historical Significance of Information Costs

10.1. Introduction

This final chapter returns to the general issue of the logic of institutions discussed in Chapter 1. It addresses the historical question of how far institutional evolution can be explained in terms of changes in information costs. The basic idea is that institutions can be analysed as though they had been designed in an optimal way. They allocate decision-making power, and structure information flow, in a manner which is efficient given the pattern of volatility in the environment and the level of information costs they face. Following North (1981), it may be postulated that as circumstances change, organizational structures will adjust (albeit slowly) to their new optimal form. If volatility increases, for example, then, as explained in Chapter 1, more flexible and consultative organizational structures will replace more rigid and autocratic ones.

The particular focus of this chapter is the implications for organizational structure of a fall in information costs themselves. It is postulated that there has been a long-term secular decline in information costs and that, as a result, the institutional framework of the market economy has evolved along a distinctive path. In broad terms the path of adjustment represents an efficient response to this change. But many individual firms— and individual societies for that matter—have failed to adjust as they should. This is because they have remained wedded to inappropriate values and beliefs, or have adjusted their values and beliefs in an inappropriate way. The efficiency-driven response to falling information costs has therefore tended to operate by favouring those firms and societies with appropriate values and beliefs, and punishing those that lack them. Thus as the lowering of information costs has increased the intensity of global competition, competitive forces have selected in favour of firms and societies with functionally useful cultures and against those with functionally unhelpful ones.

Even in the absence of cultural constraints, though, institutional adjustment would not be fully optimized to environmental conditions at every moment of time. The theory of information cost itself predicts that institutional structures will tend to adjust intermittently and in discrete jumps rather than through continuous change.

There are several reasons for this. The first is the prohibitive cost of continuously monitoring the pattern of volatility in the environment and of continuously monitoring changes in information costs themselves. When observations are intermittent rather than continuous there is bound to be some delay, on average, between the occurrence of a change and the response to it. Secondly, because many of the costs of organizational change are fixed costs—incurred by small changes as well as by large ones—it pays to wait until the need for change has reached a threshold level before the implementation of the response actually occurs. Thirdly, changes in the environment may be either transitory or persistent, and it is difficult to filter out the persistent changes that require procedures to be altered from the transitory ones that do not. The symptoms of transitory and persistent changes are frequently mixed together, and unscrambling them may take considerable time. It may be necessary to wait to see whether changes do indeed persist, and this will lead to delay in adjustment. Finally, much of the information needed to optimize organizational structure is general information on the environment which is of relevance to all institutions, rather than specific information which is relevant to just one. This means that institutions have an opportunity to free-ride on other institutions by imitating the changes they make. When the environment changes, therefore, the initial response may be deferred while each institution waits for one of the others to collect the relevant information and make their move. Once the move has been made, there will be a rush to follow in order to capitalize on the information revealed by the first-mover. The urgency of imitation will be greater when the change affords a positive opportunity which the early movers can preempt (see Chapter 5).

To fully analyse the effects of a secular decline in information costs it is necessary to distinguish different components of information cost. As well as the cost of collecting information, for example, there is the cost of communicating it and using it in decisions. The costs of storing and retrieving it need to be considered too. As different components of information cost decline at different speeds, so the relative costs of different structures of organization change as well. Thus changes in organizational structure over time may be caused not only by absolute falls in information cost but by relative movements in different components of information cost as well.

10.2. Basic concepts

From an evolutionary perspective, concept of information cost is seen at its simplest in a Robinson Crusoe economy. If information is very costly then it is uneconomic for Robinson Crusoe to resolve the uncertainties that he faces. It is better for him either to abandon risky projects, or to accept that what he does may turn out to be a mistake. As the cost of information falls, however, it becomes economic for him to dispel some of the uncertainties by collecting information before he makes a decision. This means that when he decides to commit resources there is less chance of a mistake. This in turn means that Robinson Crusoe can undertake more projects within a given overall tolerance of risk. Cheaper information therefore encourages investment, by reducing the risk that any given investment will turn out to be a mistake.

Now suppose that Robinson Crusoe is joined by Man Friday. The economist naturally supposes that they both have different preferences and different resource endowments, so that they will wish to participate in trade. But if information on their respective wants is difficult to communicate—because, for example, they have no language in common—then trade may be prohibitively costly to set up (see Chapter 2). It is not just trade that may suffer because of information costs, though. Opportunities for teamwork—for example, in helping one another to build a house—may be passed up too. Damaging externalities may also fail to be avoided: thus each may pollute the other's environment when, with a little adjustment on both sides, each could avoid harming the other. As communication costs begin to fall, however, and they learn to speak in sign language, so trade and teamwork will both increase and the incidence of negative externalities will fall. Thus lower communication costs will improve coordination in a variety of ways.

An important feature of information costs, noted above, is that they are usually fixed costs independent of the value of the project or the value of the transaction to which they refer (Casson, 1982). This means that information is normally worth collecting only on larger projects or higher-value transactions. It is better to either pass up the opportunity to undertake smaller transactions because the risks are not worth resolving, or simply to proceed with them and risk making a mistake. It is only large transactions that are systematically investigated and undertaken only when conditions are judged to be good.

Small transactions can, of course, be turned into large transactions by making them less frequent. One can buy small amounts of ripe fruit every day or larger amounts of not-so-ripe fruit every week, for example. High information costs therefore encourage periodic rather than continuous transactions. Conversely, as information costs fall, small frequent transactions become more economic. The frequency of transactions increases and their average value falls. The increased frequency of transactions in turn makes inventory-holding less important. For a flow of given intensity, the average inventory holding varies inversely with the frequency of transaction. Thus lower information costs encourage people to substitute information costs for storage costs. They increase the frequency of their transactions, thereby handling more information, but reducing their inventory levels.

This means that working capital requirements fall as information costs decline. It is interesting to combine this observation with the earlier one that the riskiness of investment projects falls at the same time because uncertainty is cheaper to resolve. This impacts selectively on the larger projects which are worthy of investigation. Large projects of this type normally involve fixed investments in plant, buildings, and machinery. Lower information costs are therefore likely to encourage fixed investment. Thus so far as the economy as a whole is concerned, a decline in information costs is likely to encourage the substitution of fixed capital for working capital. This is, of course, the kind of substitution that occurred in many industries during the Industrial Revolution. Stocks of raw materials, work in progress and finished goods diminished in importance relative to plant and machinery as industries such as textiles and ceramics switched to mass production. Although there are other, more obvious, explanations of the same phenomenon, such as the reduction in inventory effected by increased speeds of transportation and the role of steam technology in raising the productivity of fixed capital, it would be interesting to investigate whether there are any specific aspects of this change in capital structure where the effect of lower information costs can be easily discerned. Although case study evidence is available on this subject (for example, Hudson, 1986), historical statistics of aggregate investment have relatively little to say about working capital, at least so far as the United Kingdom is concerned (Feinstein, 1981; Crafts, 1985), and so it may be some time before a thorough investigation of this subject can be carried out.

10.3. Memory

Information is a durable good in the sense that it can be memorized. This means that the same information can be used over and over again. The average cost of information per decision diminishes as the number of times it is re-used increases.

The durability of information depends upon the form in which it is stored, and the kind of arrangements that can be made for its retrieval. Historically, the impact of writing has had a major impact on the durability of information. Oral transmision between successive generations is a good deal more costly, and probably less reliable, than the conservation of written records. In so far as oral memory is confined to a small number of key bits of information, however, it is easier to retrieve than information in a larger written archive—unless, of course, the filing and cataloguing of the archive is of a high standard.

One of the key economic advantages of modern information technology is the speed and accuracy with which individual items of information can be retrieved from a large library (see Chapter 6). Advances in the storage and retrieval of information have reduced the average cost of information by facilitating its re-use. This means that much more information is worth collecting than before. There are many items of information whose collection could not be justified if they were to be used only once, but whose collection is justified if they can be used many times over instead. As already indicated, the main obstacle to proliferating the storage of written information (apart from the sheer bulk of documentation) is the difficulty of selective retrieval. Now that this obstacle has been significantly reduced by computerized record search, a major increase in the volume of stored information is predictably underway.

Information, though durable, can obsolesce as a result of changes in the environment. From a decision-making point of view there is little point in memorizing information that is out of date. The more volatile the environment, the greater the problem of obsolescence becomes. To maintain the accuracy of information about a volatile environment it is necessary to observe the environment at frequent intervals, incurring a fixed cost of observation each time this is done. Indeed, when information costs are very high a volatile environment may not be worth keeping under observation at all because the information that is collected can be used for decision-making only once.

As volatility diminishes, the environment needs to be re-investigated less frequently, and so it becomes more worthwhile to investigate it and to memorize the results. At any one time, therefore, the information stored in memory tends to relate to the most stable aspects of the environment. Information on the more volatile aspects is either not collected at all, or is collected but not stored because it will be out of date when retrieved for subsequent use.

As the costs of storing and retrieving information fall it becomes more economic to store obsolescing information, on the chance that it may be needed several times in quick succession. The information that is stored becomes more ephemeral as a result. This in turn means that memory is updated more frequently than ever before. As memory costs fall, the net addition to information storage is concentrated on the latest information about the more volatile aspects of the environment. More information about more stable aspects of the environment (such as the scientific laws which govern the natural environment) is also accumulated, but the increase in it is not so great.

There is, indeed, a further complication that for reasons of space will not be considered here: namely that greater use of information may itself increase the volatility of the environment. By reducing the number of aspects of the environment which remain unchanged, it increases the need to update records regularly. Conversely, the increased ability to update records means that administrative obstacles to coping with such changes are reduced. Thus while falling communication costs may be the active instigators of increased volatility, improvements in the storage and retrieval of information are certainly important permissive factors in it.

10.4. Information costs and transaction costs

While it is clear that mainstream economics should have paid more attention than it has to information costs, New Institutional Economists (Williamson, 1985) are likely to claim that they are not at fault in this respect. Their concept of transaction costs, they may well assert, encompasses information costs as well.

There is, however, an ambiguity here. It is certainly true that most components of transaction costs can be attributed to the cost of handling one kind of information or another. It can therefore be said, loosely speaking, that most transaction costs are information costs. But the converse does not apply. There are important information costs which are not transaction costs. The costs of investigating a project to reduce its risks are a case in point. So too are the costs of developing a new technology through R & D. Thus information costs and transactions costs, though related, are certainly not the same thing.

Transaction costs are of two main kinds—namely the *ex ante* cost of setting up the contract and the *ex post* cost of ensuring that the contract, once set up, is properly fulfilled (see Chapter 4). The thrust of the New Institutional Economics lies with the second kind of transaction cost rather than the first. This kind of cost is incurred mainly in *validating* the information that was exchanged at the first stage when the contract was being set up. In particular it is concerned with the possibility that one or both of the parties to the transaction may deliberately mislead the other; they appropriate the other's property by the simple expedient of defaulting on their own side of the contract.

Costs of validating information manifest themselves in two main ways. The first is the cost of monitoring the other party's fulfilment of their obligations. The second is the cost of checking out the other party before the contract is agreed to see whether they are likely to be honest or not. These two approaches are to some extent substitutes for one another. The more confidence that is placed in the other party's integrity as a result of the preliminary screening, the less worthwhile it is to incur the costs of monitoring them afterwards.

Thus if the costs of preliminary screening are low—because, for example, reputation mechanisms are efficient, or business ethics are known to be strong—then monitoring may be unnecessary. It is sufficient to leave the other party to fulfil their own part of the contract in their own way, subject only to the normal sanctions for default afforded by the law. But if the costs of screening are high—either because reputation mechanisms are inefficient, or business ethics are weak—then it becomes important to supervise the fulfilment of the contract carefully.

In a society where screening costs are generally low it is therefore possible to transact at arm's length with other people without much attempt at monitoring or supervision. On the other hand, when screening costs are high this becomes more difficult. What tends to happen is that those of the greatest reputation, and the greatest skill in organizing monitoring, recruit those of lesser reputation and lesser skill in monitoring to work under their supervision. Those of lesser reputation trust those of greater reputation to honour their contractual obligations without supervision (to pay them for their work, for example), but those of greater reputation only trust those of lesser reputation because they can supervise them. This is, of course, the arrangement that prevails in most contracts of employment (see Chapter 3).

This suggests, therefore, that contracts of employment emerge when monitoring costs are low and screening costs are high. The emergence of employment contracts can therefore be explained by a fall in monitoring costs relative to screening costs. Indeed, of all the types of information cost, screening costs are, perhaps, the ones most likely to have increased. This is because greater population mobility, coupled with the ethic of individualism, make it increasingly difficult for people to obtain reliable information on the moral integrity of the people with whom they deal.

If screening costs do rise then the proportion of the population with reputation falls. As monitoring costs fall, those who possess reputation enjoy an increased opportunity to supervise those who do not. This encourages the population to divide into two groups, or economic classes—a small group of employers and a larger group of employees, linked by a relation based upon supervision.

Such changes could have been significant in the rise of the Factory System. There may be a link, for example, between advances in monitoring technique developed in the late eighteenth century (partly as a consequence of attempts at prison reform), the loss of individual reputations associated with the decline of traditional agricultural communities (following enclosure and technical progress in agriculture) and the growth of factory supervision. Large open-plan factories maximized the economies of scale involved in monitoring, and thereby helped to overcome the reputation problems created by the transient and relatively anonymous workforce that had migrated from the land to the towns. The factory system was applied mainly to unskilled manual work, which is the easiest to monitor, and much less to craft work, which involves intellectual input that is difficult to monitor in a reliable way.

The origins and rationale of the factory system have been much debated (Marglin, 1974; Landes, 1986; Williamson, 1980). It is contrary to the methodology of this book to favour one mono-causal explanation over another.

Both the technology of energy production and transmission, and the technology of monitoring, seem to have influenced the growth of the factory system. The suggestion is simply that this composite approach can be further developed by introducing screening costs into the picture as well. The point is simply that the concentration of industrial enterprise away from the agricultural communities made community-based knowledge and community-based sanctions difficult for employers to use, and that this may have been an additional factor encouraging a high intensity of supervision within the factory system.

10.5. From local monopoly to global competition

The information that needs to be validated by screening or monitoring relates to the terms of the contract. These terms are the outcome of a process of negotiation which is very information-intensive. Furthermore, negotiation can take place only once the parties have made contact and specified the nature of their requirements. Contact-making can be an information-intensive process too.

The general proposition that information costs are falling implies that the ease with which contact can be made has increased. This means not only that fewer opportunities for trade are passed up but also that people find it worthwhile to contact more potential partners for each transaction. In this way they can improve their bargaining power in negotiations by playing off different potential partners against each other. The advantage of doing this is greatest when all of the partners are equally attractive, for when each partner knows that his rivals are close substitutes for himself he is most likely to concede his best possible terms.

The idea that information costs are falling needs to be treated with some care when the costs of negotiation are being discussed, however. It is certainly true that the costs of communicating offers and counter offers have fallen with respect to distance, in the sense that it is now far easier to negotiate with someone far away than it used to be. This is particularly true when the quality of communication—in particular its speed—is taken into account. However the opportunity cost of the time spent by an individual in deciding what his offer or counter offer should be has risen—at least in the wealthier countries. This discourages lengthy iterations in negotiation and favours the use of once-and-for-all offers instead.

The combination of falling distance costs and rising time costs has created a situation where 'negotiation' increasingly means the dissemination of non-negotiable price quotations over a wide market area. Since each trader can afford to collect several quotations for comparison, this encourages people offering quotations to converge on the same set of terms. As distance costs fall, therefore, markets become more tightly integrated and more competitive too. If competition is equally intense on both sides of the market then a uniform price will emerge that corresponds to the equilibrium price predicted by the conventional analysis of demand and supply.

Competition is a mechanism for getting people to reveal their opportunity costs and benefits in a truthful way. As such, it is a substitute for other mechanisms, such as moral manipulation, which are also used to persuade people to tell the truth. Moral manipulation works best in small and compact groups. For a variety of reasons, it is difficult to implement on a global basis. The fact that the globalization of markets promotes competition by opening up alternative sources of supply and demand is quite fortuitous, therefore, in the sense that it naturally provides its own alternative to moral manipulation for getting people to tell the truth. This may explain the strength of contemporary sentiment amongst business managers that the world economy is an intensely competitive place.

10.6. From custom to contract

Falling information costs have changed the way in which products are traded. Some goods and services are intrinsically more difficult to trade than others. Differentiation, heterogeneity, specificity are all terms which capture those factors which make transactions information-intensive. They impinge on some goods far more than others. The characteristics of a product that make it information-intensive, and therefore difficult to trade, are summarized in Table 10.1.

When information costs are high some types of good may be impossible to trade at all. One reason why the rate of innovation is low in economies where information costs are high may simply be that novel products are difficult to market effectively because of the high information costs involved. This discourages investment in innovation, and traps the economy at a low level of economic development. From this perspective technological breakthroughs in mass communication are very significant, because by reducing the costs of marketing innovative products they stimulate other forms of technological innovation connected with mass production which it would otherwise be uneconomic to make.

Other goods may be traded through custom rather than contract. As Hicks (1969) has emphasized, custom economizes on information costs in a variety of ways. When information is costly to acquire it is uneconomic to update knowledge of the environment frequently. Unless information is updated there is little reason to adjust the price. Hence high information costs encourage the kind of rigidity associated with a customary price. When communication is costly, competition is restricted, as earlier remarks made clear. When the area of the market is very small, traders may get

TABLE 10.1. *Factors increasing the information-intensity of transactions*

Factor	Specific to
Mainly affecting promotional activity:	
1. *Dimensions of quality:* The number of relevant product characteristics, reflecting the multiplicity of performance characteristics which concern the customer.	Product, Customer
2. *Customization potential:* the premium that customers attach to a product that exactly meets their idiosyncratic needs, and the feasibility of achieving this without significant loss of economies of scale.	Product, Customer
3. *Novelty* of the product, and its complexity of use.	Product
4. *Product hazard:* The danger of imperfections in the product, and the extent of natural quality variability; the problem is compounded if samples of the product are difficult to display and if delivered supplies are difficult to check by inspection.	Product
5. *Security of property rights:* The complexity of property rights (as in house purchase) and the importance of assessing how early they can be enforced (as with patents).	Society
6. *Sophistication of the customer.*	Customer
7. *Reputation* of the middleman, and the general degree of trust in the society.	Society
Mainly affecting the management of transactions:	
Payment methods.	
8. *Difficulty of effecting spot payment,* owing to the use of common carriers for delivery or a significant component of 'after-sales' service.	Location
9. *Need for currency conversion,* when exporting to certain countries (or importing from them).	Location
10. *Need for customer finance,* owing to the large value of the purchase relative to the customer's wealth.	Customer
Pricing arrangements.	
11. *Price discrimination:* importance of price-inelastic demand and scale of economies in production, together with the feasibility of preventing resale.	Product
12. *Reliance on negotiation* rather than firm quoted prices	Product
Planning of supplies.	
13. *Provision for advance orders, reservations,* etc, owing to the need to guarantee access to a good or service at a particular time.	Product, Customer
14. *Secondary market* available for trading transferable claims (orders, reservations, etc.) prior to their maturity.	Product, Society
15. *Sophisticated queuing and rationing rules* used when orders are fulfilled spot at quoted prices: particularly important for perishable products for which inventory cannot be held (e.g. services).	Product, Society

TABLE 10.1. *Continued*

Factor	Specific to
Mainly affecting distribution of the product:	
16. *Pre-arranged delivery to customer's premises*; the administrative problem of timed consignment to a specified address is compounded by the large number of addresses associated with a diverse customer base, and is particularly common in consumer goods industries.	Product, Customer
17. *The product is a collection of components which needs to be separately delivered* and cannot be pre-packaged by the middleman.	Product
18. *The product is a claim to a sequence of timed deliveries, which may also be contingent on particular events*; this is particularly common with financial assets and insurance policies.	Product

Source: Casson (1994*b*), Table 7.1.

locked into a bilateral monopoly situation. When technology is primitive, products may also prove difficult to store, which exacerbates the potential indeterminacy in the bilateral monopoly price. Such indeterminacy may well be resolved by a price which is justified on moral rather than economic grounds. This does not matter provided that the morally justified price is within the bounds set by the opportunity benefits and costs of the parties involved. It does mean, however, that because the price is set by appeal to the kind of permanent information embodied in a moral system (see Chapter 6), it may prove difficult to change later on. As information costs begin to fall and communication becomes easier, it is more feasible to adjust prices regularly and to rely on competition rather than morality to set the appropriate level. Custom is therefore gradually undermined, and the formal impersonal market system of the kind that is familiar today begins to take over.

10.7. Information on property rights

Social consensus on who owns what is crucial to any market economy. It is only possible to go so far with the principle that people own what they have physically in their possession. It is no accident, therefore, that many of the earliest written records concern claims to ownership. Cheap information makes it easier to specify claims to ownership in greater detail. Thus as information costs fall it becomes economic to distinguish ownership by a family from ownership by a clan, and then to distinguish ownership by an individual from ownership by the family to which the individual belongs.

Thus cheaper information encourages property ownership to be assigned in more individualistic terms (Casson, 1997).

It also makes it feasible to record different items in an estate and to bequeath different items of the estate to different people. It permits the differentiation of the various uses to which assets such as land can be put, and the assignment of different specific user rights to different people, as in the contract between a landowner and a tenant farmer. In other words, when falling information costs are applied to the specification and allocation of property rights, they provide one possible explanation of the origins of economic individualism (for a wider view see Macfarlane, 1978).

Information about property rights becomes particularly significant when property is entrusted to other people. This is of special relevance in the field of banking, accounting, and finance. It is well-known that the information costs incurred in setting up a trade are considerably reduced by the use of money as a medium of exchange (see Chapter 2). The very factors that make money useful as a medium of exchange, however—its portability, homogeneity, divisibility, etc.—make the theft of money attractive too. Hence people entrust their money to banks for security. This means that their credits with the bank must be recorded. It is also well-known that when two people who use the same bank trade with each other they can clear payments by cheque (i.e. by an instruction to the bank to adjust their credits) rather than by a physical transfer of funds. This principle can be extended to allow for inter-bank clearing of cheques based on adjustments to the banks' own credits with a banker's bank (i.e. a central bank). All of this activity turns banking into a very information-intensive industry.

Falling information costs associated initially with the development of the postal system and, subsequently, with electronic data transfer has, as theory indicates, led to a considerable expansion of banking activity. Very recently, cheaper information flow, coupled with increased concern over petty crime has encouraged many people (particularly vulnerable groups such as tourists) to substitute cheque and credit card transactions for cash ones. Such substitution would be quite uneconomic unless information costs were low.

Banks are not the only institutions to act as stewards of other people's property, of course. Corporations of many kinds act as stewards of resources—another relevant example being the private company. An important feature of the private company is the shareholding principle, which requires the division of the profits according to the size of the equity stake. This requires both an income and expenditure account to calculate the profit and a rudimentary concept of a balance sheet too. The balance sheet is particularly important in valuing the shares on the death or retirement of a partner.

Historically, the development of a market in shares, allowing partners to quit a company at any time, has promoted the liquidity of shares and thereby encouraged wider share ownership. The growing opportunity for company promoters to advertise speculative opportunities, and the legal provision of limited liability to prevent innocent investors from being 'fleeced' too heavily as a result, has also encouraged share ownership. This in turn has led to an enormous expansion of accounting activity within firms, as well as to substantial information flows within equity markets themselves. Without a reduction in information costs, the bureaucratic burden associated with this activity would almost certainly have slowed down the growth of the joint stock enterprise system (Hoppit, 1986; Hunt, 1936).

10.8. The emergence of bureaucracy as a hierarchy of competence

The concept of stewardship applies not only between the individual and the institution he entrusts resources too—whether bank or firm—but also within the institution itself. This is because institutions in turn employ people to protect, and indeed enhance the value of, the resources that have been entrusted to them. Information is therefore required to check up on the performance of employees, as noted above. One of the earliest organizations to recognize this was the medieval state. An auditor was appointed to hear the accounts of the stewards who had been collecting taxes for the exchequer. Although the concept of public accountability was then in its infancy—few medieval monarchs would have felt the necessity to justify their expenditures to their citizens in any detailed way—the concept of private accountability to the monarch was taken very seriously.

The idea that everyone needs to be checked up on leads naturally to the concept of a hierarchy of supervision within an organization, in which those who do the checking are in turn checked up on by other people. The number of levels of this hierarchy depends upon the span of control. The fewer people any one person can supervise—i.e. the smaller the span of control—the taller the hierarchy tends to be. One of the major consequences of advances in the techniques of management accounting is that the effective span of control has become larger. The average costs of monitoring other people have fallen, and this has permitted firms to reduce their overheads by flattening the hierarchy of supervision.

Hierarchies do more than organize the supervision of people, however. They also structure the flow of information used to diagnose and treat a variety of problems. In this context an opposite tendency can be detected which promotes taller hierarchies rather than flatter ones.

The activities that are managed by organizations are becoming more complex and sophisticated, and so too is the way that these activities are configured for productive purposes. This means that the various component parts of an organization can now fail for many different reasons. It is reasonable for the employer to expect the ordinary employees to have some competence in diagnosing simple faults and correcting them. More precisely, it is sensible to train low-level employees to handle the most commonly occurring kinds of problem. But for more unusual problems it is probably better to involve a specialist. Because this specialist is called upon only intermittently, he will provide support for a number of ordinary employees.

The question then arises as to what happens when a very unusual kind of problem presents itself which even this specialist cannot cope with. The answer is that the problem may be referred to yet another specialist—a second-level specialist who supports several first-level specialists in order to keep himself fully occupied. A hierarchy therefore emerges amongst the specialists. The principle governing the hierarchical design is that of a sequential diagnostic procedure which begins by testing for the most probable cause of failure and finishes with testing for the most unusual one. This hierarchy of professional specialization is quite unlike the hierarchy of supervision in that the factor governing the 'span of control' has nothing to do with the monitoring of those at lower levels, but is concerned with the relative frequency with which different causes of failure arise (see Chapter 1).

As systems become more sophisticated, the number of reasons for failure is likely to increase, and this suggests that the number of different specialists required to support the system will increase as well. When these different specialists are ordered in hierarchical fashion, then the height of the hierarchy will increase.

Historically, many of the most sophisticated diagnostic systems have been dedicated to the provision of professional services—medicine, legal advice, etc.—rather than to the handling of material product flow. It is, therefore, in the field of office work rather than the factory that the hierarchy of diagnostic expertise is most likely to emerge. Hierarchies of this kind are notable in the public sector as well as the private sector, because of the nature of the services involved. The provision of government services, and the organization of tax collection, are notable areas of hierarchical organization in the public sector.

The recent computerization of office work has not necessarily changed this, because many computer systems still mimic previous manual procedures. Moreover the computer systems themselves often manifest forms of complexity which raise similar problems of diagnosis. This suggests that information processing in the office—whether computer-aided or not—is likely to continue to be organized on hierarchical lines. As the complexity of the problems with which the office deals increases, the hierarchy may even get taller as a result.

10.9. Managerial hierarchies

The previous argument appears to contradict current conventional wisdom in management circles, which asserts that hierarchies should be getting flatter rather than taller (Kanter, 1989). It is important to appreciate, however, that the conventional view applies mainly to *managerial* hierarchies rather than to hierarchies in general. Managerial hierarchies are hierarchies where successive levels are linked by authority relations. The primary purpose of these authority relations is to structure the taking of decisions. Information on the environment of the organization which is collected at lower levels is fed upwards to the top where it is summarized and synthesized with other information to generate a strategic decision. This decision is then transmitted downwards, where detailed information that has been trapped at particular levels on its way up is invoked to determine the tactics by which the strategy is to be implemented.

Managerial hierarchies usually coexist alongside hierarchies of supervision. The managerial hierarchy described above is concerned with collecting and processing information about the organization's environment, while the supervisory hierarchy described earlier is concerned with collecting information about the firm's own employees. In particular it is concerned with assessing whether the information they collect is accurate and is honestly reported, and whether they are impartial in using their information to take tactical decisions. Most people in an organization are involved in both kinds of hierarchies: they collect information on the environment themselves and supervise the collection of information by their subordinates too (Casson, 1994d).

A managerial hierarchy and a supervisory hierarchy may co-exist alongside a hierarchy of professional expertise within the same organization. In some cases all three may coincide, in the sense that both managerial authority and responsibility for supervision may be vested in those people who also have the expertise to handle the most unusual types of problem. This seems to apply, for example, in insurance companies, where routine insurance policies are dealt with by subordinates, but idiosyncratic policies which raise difficult issues are referred to higher levels. In other cases the hierarchy of expertise is confined to support staff based, for example, in the legal department or the personnel department, with information gathering and supervision being effected by the general management team.

The concept of information costs is absolutely critical in explaining why the managerial form of hierarchy exists. If information were costless then there would be no reason why strategic decisions should be separated from tactical ones. Indeed, some risk of misjudgement is likely to be incurred whenever a strategic decision is taken before the tactical means of implementing the strategy have been determined. Unless the best possible tactic for each possible strategy is determined in advance, it is impossible to make a proper comparison of alternative strategies, except where one strategy clearly dominates the others, whatever tactics are used. It is, therefore, a calculated risk to separate strategic and tactical decisions, and one that can be justified only because of the savings in information cost that are involved.

These savings arise principally because much of the key information about the environment is normally generated at the tactical level. It is obtained as a byproduct of implementing the previous period's strategy. Retaining this information at the tactical level rather than passing it up to a higher level economizes on communication costs. Another secondary source of savings is that the information obtained by people at the strategic level is often difficult to explain to other people, and so it is easier for them to encode it in the explicit form of the strategic decision itself than to explain it to the tacticians and leave it to them to decide both the tactics and the strategy for themselves.

It is in this context that the tendency of falling information costs to induce flatter organizational structures is best understood. Falling information costs reduce the savings that are available from separating strategic and tactical decisions. They encourage those responsible for strategy formulation to consult with the tacticians by asking them what they have learnt as a result of their experience in implementing the previous strategy. A wide-ranging synthesis of information is thereby effected, allowing the different tactics associated with each possible strategy to be fully investigated. The result is a more consultative style of decision-making, with a better quality of decision as a result.

This switch to greater consultation does not impact so much on the number of levels in the hierarchy as on the nature of the authority relation from which the hierarchy is built up. It means that those who implement decisions at the lower levels of the hierarchy are more likely to have been consulted about the decisions concerned. The top of the hierarchy is therefore less autocratic—it 'empowers' the people lower down to 'participate' in the decision-making. It is this change, rather than flatness *per se* which seems to be characteristic of recent organizational changes in large firms.

10.10. Hierarchies in the market system

While much has been written about hierarchical structures within the firm, relatively little has been said by economists about hierarchical structures in the market system. It is rather paradoxical that while trade ostensibly accords equal status to those who participate in it, the flow of information connected with trade nevertheless takes a hierarchical form. Hierarchy appears to be a general feature of information processing systems in whatever context they occur.

Hierarchy in trade manifests itself in two main ways. First, networks of trade are often coordinated by intermediators who are usually more powerful than the people with whom they deal. Secondly, these intermediators tend to agglomerate in entrepôt centres, some of which are subordinate to larger regional or global centres within a geographical hierarchy. These two aspects of 'market hierarchy' will be considered in turn.

The role of intermediators is explained by the need for synthesis (see Chapter 1). It is fairly unusual that a single item of information from a single source is sufficient to effect coordination. A synthesis of information from different sources is usually required. Thus in organizing a trade it is necessary to put together information on demand with information on supply, and normally to add in information on transport costs and legal regulations too.

Successful synthesis requires scarce abilities and therefore benefits from specialization. Specialized synthesis of trading information is effected by intermediators who buy and re-sell the product. In some cases the activity of the intermediator is internalized by one of the parties—for example in the marketing department of a major producer. In other cases the intermediator is independent of either side of the market—as in wholesaling, retailing, and commodity trading, for example.

The twentieth century has seen a growing tendency for the role of intermediator in consumer goods markets to be divided up between just two major economic actors—the marketing department of a branded good producer, and the supermarket chain. The key factor in the growing influence of the former is the dramatic rise of media influence—in particular, television—while in the growth of the latter increased car ownership has obviously played an important role as well.

Ever since the development of mass circulation newspapers in the eighteenth century, the media have provided the public with advice on many issues through their editorial writing and special features. One of the effects of this has been to encourage a growing belief amongst the public that they are experts in many fields—including consumer choice.

The development of brand names by manufacturers and the promotion of these names through celebrity endorsements has allowed private enterprise to exploit the authority of the media for their own purposes. Advertisements interspersed amongst newspaper articles and television programmes help to convince consumers that they can choose intelligently between alternative brands. They feel that they already know what they want when they go shopping and that they do not need to buy what the local retailer recommends.

This explains why the counter-service store has been replaced by the self-service supermarket. Since the customer no longer needs local advice, it is the logistics of distribution, and in particular the economies afforded by large-scale storage and one-stop shopping, that now dominate the distribution of consumer goods. These economies are most fully exploited by the supermarket. The demise of the counter-service store has in turn reduced the scale of independent wholesaling, leaving the wholesale stage of distribution (where it still exists) mainly in the hands of the producers and the supermarket chains.

10.11. Geographical hierarchies in trade

When information costs are high it is often advantageous to physically bring products to market to trade them, as in many 'primitive' economies. This avoids providing lengthy written specifications: the products can be inspected at first hand at the same time that negotiations are conducted face-to-face. Inspection also facilitates quality assurance: 'what you see is what you get'.

When only small quantities of goods are involved the cost of transporting the goods to market and then despatching them from the market to the buyer's address is not much greater than the cost of delivering them direct from seller to buyer. One trip to and from the market is normally sufficient for each trader. Because the fixed cost of this single trip can be spread over all the goods involved, the average cost of transport to and from the market is relatively low. But where larger quantities are involved it is more economic that deliveries are made direct.

The purpose of the market then becomes to negotiate contracts between the traders in the absence of the goods themselves, using only samples, or perhaps even just written descriptions of the goods, as indicated above. The advantage to the buyer and seller of the market as a 'central place' then resides purely in the potential for face-to-face communication with the intermediator, and the ease of shopping around the different intermediators to get competitive quotes.

When goods are physically brought to market, a geographical hierarchy of markets emerges because transport costs are reduced if demand and supply are balanced out on a local basis wherever possible. Only net surpluses are exported to other areas, and only net deficits are met by imports. These surpluses and deficits are then cleared at regional markets higher up the scale—markets where the average quantity traded per participant is higher and which consequently operate on a wholesale rather than a retail basis.

In the case where goods are no longer brought to market the hierarchical structure still remains because the balancing of demand and supply at local and regional levels still constitute distinct activities carried out by different groups of people. So long as buyers and sellers need to meet face-to-face, the local buyers and sellers will meet with local intermediators, who then attend the regional market where, together with local intermediators from other places, they meet regional intermediators face-to-face. This arrangement economizes both on the time spent and on the travel facilities used by the traders and the intermediators involved.

The advantage of face-to-face communication compared with remote communication lies in the wider variety of signals that can be exchanged between people. This reduces the risk of misunderstanding and helps people to appraise one another's integrity. Face-to-face interaction also provides an opportunity for building emotional bonds which reduce the incentive to cheat and, by facilitating gossip, it strengthens reputation mechanisms too.

Where products are relatively homogeneous (so that misunderstandings about their specification are rare) and opportunities for cheating are limited, face-to-face communication may not be worth the cost, however, and so remote communication may be used instead. This considerably reduces the advantage of the hierarchical structuring of markets, although it does not eliminate it altogether. There is still likely to be some advantage in exploring local opportunities for trade before inter-regional ones, even in a fully computerized trading system. The case for spatial hierarchy is, however, now reduced to the advantage of a particular sequential search strategy in matching supply and demand—a sequence which begins by examining only local options on which local information is required and progresses to other options on which other information is required only if difficulties are encountered in finding a satisfactory local solution.

The cost differential between this approach and a single-step approach in which all potential ways of matching up traders' needs are investigated at the outset may be a relatively modest one, however. If the single-step approach were to be followed in its entirety then all traders would communicate directly with a single computerized global market which would organize trade on everyone's behalf.

So far a mixed system has evolved in most markets, in which intermediators employ remote communication when dealing with each other but individual traders consult their local intermediators face-to-face. This is because the intermediators, being specialists, can afford to invest their time in learning how the system of remote communication works. Because they tend to deal regularly with each other, reputation mechanisms are still strong even though communication is mainly remote. The ordinary traders, lacking the intermediators' reputation and expertise, choose to access the network using their local intermediators as the 'gatekeepers' of the system.

This means that while a local hierarchy involving local traders and local intermediators is likely to persist, the other layers of hierarchy involving wholesale intermediators are somewhat unstable and are liable to collapse into a single global wholesale market if the relative costs of remote communication decrease even more.

10.12. The technological dynamics of falling information costs

While the primary focus of this chapter is on the response of institutional structures to exogenous changes in information costs, it must be recognized that changes in information costs may themselves be induced by the institutional progress that they make possible. For example, when technological advance widens markets by improving freight transportation and facilitating mass production, new demands arise for long distance communication between producers, intermediators, and retailers. Firms provide an institutional mechanism through which the increased profits afforded by wider markets can be appropriated. These prospective profits stimulate a derived demand for improved communications. Technological advances in communications are the natural supply response. Inventors and innovators are encouraged to switch their attention to communications, as this becomes one of the most profitable fields of research. As a result, the initial advances and transport and production technology induce the advances in communications that are required to exploit them fully. The connection can work the other way round, too, of course. A chance discovery which leads to improved communications may induce advances in transport and production technologies which take advantage of the potentially wider market.

Improvements in communications technology may not translate immediately into lower information costs because of the element of natural monopoly that is characteristic of the communications industry. Roads, railways, telephone, and telegraph lines all constitute infrastructure that is inefficient to replicate because of economies of scale. These economies derive both from spreading the fixed costs of customized construction over a wider number of users, and from the increased number of connections that can be made per user as the number of people using the same infrastructure expands. Even where earth-moving is not involved, economies of scale in construction may still be significant, as with satellites and television broadcasting. The initial impact of improved communication is often greater speed rather than lower cost, as the innovator seeks to recover his sunk costs by creaming off the most profitable part of the market where speed, confidentiality, and accuracy are at a premium. It is only later, as market growth facilitates additional entry, or regulation imposes price cuts, that the full impact of lower information costs is felt.

Innovations in different aspects of information technology have different consequences. This is because changes in different components of information cost have different strategic implications. Where the integration and globalization of markets is concerned, it is innovations that reduce communication costs which have been of paramount importance. The distance-related costs of communication have fallen most of all: it is the shrinkage of the 'information space' that has promoted the geographical expansion of market areas (Boisot, 1995). A study of academic scholarship suggests a rather different emphasis, however—on the lower costs of storing information brought about by libraries of printed books. Focusing on a specific field of scholarship—namely scientific research—suggests a different emphasis yet again. In this case the falling costs of making experimental observations has been a major driving force. This has been brought about by advances in precision engineering which are, in part, a byproduct of the Industrial Revolution.

At any one time, it may be suggested, there are particular 'bottlenecks' in the field of information processing which demand alleviation. The emergence of a bottleneck creates profit opportunities which attract researchers to the field, and this increases the probability of a technical advance that will alleviate it. The solution of this bottleneck facilitates an expansion of information flow and this in turn creates another bottleneck elsewhere. The dynamics of technological innovation in communications is therefore driven by the sequence in which bottlenecks appear.

It is a characteristic of many countries which are currently at an early stage of development that bottlenecks exist in the number of telephone lines available, and in the quality of the switchgear used. In the more advanced countries of today one of the more noticeable bottlenecks is the relatively high cost of random access memory in desk-top computers. This bottleneck is partly explained by the rapid increase in the speed with which computers can operate, stemming from technological advances in microprocessor development. These have temporarily run ahead of advances in memory production techniques.

When random access memory eventually becomes cheaper a new bottleneck may emerge in software development, as larger and more sophisticated programs become easier to run. This will in turn feed back on organizational design. As business decision-making becomes more computerized, only the most urgent, complex, and ambiguous decisions will be left to ordinary people. Apart from the entrepreneurial elite who take these decisions, managers will be increasingly diverted into supporting the computer systems that take the decisions that they used to be allowed to take for themselves. In this sequential process it is never entirely certain what the next stage will be, because if it were obvious people could plan ahead successfully and not be continually overtaken by events. While the general trend is clear, therefore, the speed at which the trend progresses, and the specific direction it takes, must remain a matter for speculation.

10.13. Cultural constraints on the response to falling information costs

Falling information costs call for an entrepreneurial response from individual firms, since they alter the relative profitability of different procedures and hence require a change of organizational form. Some firms may be slower than others to notice that information costs are falling, however. It was noted in Chapter 3 that changes in the firm's environment often manifest themselves through symptoms, and that to respond appropriately managers need some kind of theory of what particular symptoms mean. It was also noted that changes in procedures can prove controversial to long-serving employees who joined under certain assumptions about how the firm would be run—assumptions which may now cease to be valid.

Many of the most basic values and beliefs in a country concern what is the 'natural' or 'legitimate' way of organizing things. Changes in organizational structure which upset the traditional balance of power between constituent groups, or alter the relative status of individuals, are liable to meet with considerable resistance. For example, individuals who are used to taking decisions autocratically may find that they are expected to consult with people they regard as their inferiors. The perceived reduction in their relative status may undermine their loyalty to the institution.

Shared values and beliefs form part of the 'collective memory' of a society in the sense that they are often learnt from the previous generation. These values may well have been functionally relevant to an earlier regime in which information costs were relatively high. Some of them may be of little relevance now that information costs are lower, however. Other values will still be relevant; a successful society is one that can discriminate by retaining those values of permanent relevance whilst discarding those that have become out of date.

The principal values discussed in this book have centred on honesty and loyalty. These values are of the permanent rather than the transitory kind, in contrast to, say, unconditional respect for authority, which is appropriate only in autocratic organizations of the kind that tend to be undermined by falling information costs. It is quite remarkable that in a period when falling information costs have placed the quality of information at a premium, values that underpin the quality of information, such as integrity, have been allowed to fall into decay. This is particularly true of the Anglo-Saxon countries, where attacks on the legitimacy of unrestrained authority have spilled over to a questioning of all sources of traditional moral authority as well. (One explanation of this may be the 'value shocks' stemming from scientific progress, as described in Chapter 6.)

If societies adjust to falling information costs in an inappropriate way then international competition will punish them severely. The relative stagnation of Anglo-Saxon economies—particularly in relation to their major Asian rivals—may be one manifestation of this. The forces of competition are selecting for survival and growth those societies that are best equipped to process large amounts of information accurately. Those Asian societies that have preserved core values of honesty and loyalty whilst switching to more flexible and consultative organizational forms are currently doing well, whilst those countries that have weakened these core values in the course of making other necessary changes are doing badly. The perspective of this book suggests that until the losers rediscover their traditional values they will continue to be punished by the international competitive system.

10.14. Summary and conclusions

Information costs have wide ranging implications for economic organization, and it has only been possible to touch on some of the issues in this book. There are many aspects of the historical evolution of economic institutions which would benefit from being studied from an information cost point of view. The impact of modern telecommunications on the organization of the firm—on which much of the recent literature has tended to focus—is only one of these aspects, and perhaps not the most important one. The origins of government bureaucracy, the emergence of the factory system, the development of global markets and the restructuring of the distributive trades all reflect in one way or another the impact of information costs.

In some cases the most important 'stylized facts' of history can be explained in terms of a simple hypothesis of falling information costs. In other cases, though, the facts can only be explained by distinguishing different components of information cost and identifying relative changes in them. It appears, for example, that monitoring costs have tended to fall more rapidly than screening costs, and that this could explain the emergence of supervisory hierarchies and the development of the Factory System. Another differential change, which has only been hinted at above, is that storage and retrieval costs have recently fallen much faster than observation costs, so that stocks of information are actually increasing faster than is the flow of new information. Another differential that requires investigation is the cost of broadcasting messages to everyone as compared to the cost of addressing messages to particular people. This differential almost certainly has an important bearing on the growing influence of the mass media in society.

A major theme of this book has been that much information flow is structured in a hierarchical fashion. This applies quite generally to flows of information within firms and markets, and within government too. The common feature is that information which is initially dispersed around the lower levels of the hierarchy is channelled up in order to concentrate it at key points at the higher levels. It is at these points that the information is synthesized for decision-making purposes. The primary difference between the firm and the market is that the firm uses an authority relation to encode the resulting decisions in the form of instructions passed down to lower levels of the hierarchy, whereas the market does not. The market, by contrast, consults the lower levels by inviting them to respond to price quotations provided by the higher levels before any final decisions are made.

A secondary difference is that to check the quality of the information that each individual supplies to other people, the firm relies heavily on monitoring, whilst the market relies more on screening instead. Firms do most of their monitoring themselves whilst markets rely more on the police and the legal system to do it for them. There are other differences between firms and markets which also have implications for hierarchical structure—such as the allocation of risks between the parties—but there has been insufficient space to go into these in this book.

The study of the economy from an information cost perspective also highlights the social embeddedness of economic activity. It indicates that the shared values and beliefs of a society—its culture, in other words—affects the way that information is construed. Different societies interpret similar symptoms in different ways. They also respond to challenges to traditional sources of authority in different ways. While a society's culture can be a great economic asset, an unsuitable culture can be a serious liability. An unsuitable culture reduces a society's ability to take advantage of the economic opportunities afforded by the historical trend of falling information costs. Cultural differences explain why different societies have responded so differently at various times to the challenges of particular innovations that have reduced information costs. The Anglo-Saxon countries that have so far failed to make an appropriate cultural response to the latest technological stimulus to lower information costs are threatened by the forces of international competition. Their political and business leaders may find it useful to take note of some of the information encoded in this book. If an appropriate response, that reinforces functional moral values, is not forthcoming soon, then it may be too late to make an effective response at all.

Bibliography

Aoki, M. (1986), 'Horizontal vs. Vertical Information Structure of the Firm', *American Economic Review*, 76: 971–83.

——and Williamson, O. E. (eds.) (1991), *The Firm as a Nexus of Treaties*, Beverly Hills, California: Sage.

Arrow, K. J. (1962), 'The Economic Implications of Learning by Doing', *Review of Economic Studies*, 29: 155–73.

Babbage, C. (1832), *On the Economy of Machinery and Manufactures*, London: Charles Knight.

Baker, M. J. (1991), *Marketing: An Introductory Text*, 5th edn, London: Macmillan.

Banerjee, A. V. (1992), 'A Simple Model of Herd Behaviour', *Quarterly Journal of Economics*, 107: 797–811.

Becattini, G. (1990), 'The Marshallian industrial district as a socio-economic notion', in F. Pyke, G. Becattini and W. Sengenberger (eds.), *Industrial Districts and Inter-firm Cooperation in Italy*, Geneva: International Institute for Labour Studies, 37–51.

Bellandi, M., and Romagnoli, M. (1993), 'Prato e l'industria tessile', in R. Leonardi and R. Y. Nanetti, (eds.), *Lo sviluppo regionale dell'economia europea integrata. Il caso toscano*, Venezia: Marsilio, 183–211.

——and Trigilia, C. (1991), 'Come cambia un distretto industriale: strategie di riaggiustamento e tecnologie informatiche nell'industria tessile pratese', *Economia e Politica Industriale*, No. 70, XVII: 121–52.

Bergman, E., Maier, G., and Todtling, F. (eds.) (1991), *Regions Reconsidered: Economic Networks, Innovations, and Local Development in Industrial Countries*, London: Mansell.

Bernhardt, I. (1977), 'Vertical Integration and Demand Variability', *Journal of Industrial Economics*, 25: 213–29.

Best, M. H. (1990), *The New Competition: Institutions of Industrial Restructuring*, Cambridge: Polity Press.

Bikhchandani, S., Hirshleifer, D., and Welch, J. (1992), 'A Theory of Fads, Fashion, Custom and Cultural Change as Informational Cascades', *Journal of Political Economy*, 100: 992–1026.

Blois, K. J. (1972), 'Vertical Quasi-Integration', *Journal of Industrial Economics*, 20: 253–72.

Boisot, M. H. (1995), *Information Space: A Framework for Learning in Organizations, Institutions and Culture*, London: Routledge.

Boyce, G. H. (1995), *Information, Mediation and Institutional Development: The Rise of Large-scale Enterprise in British Shipping, 1870–1919*, Manchester: Manchester University Press.

Brown, J., and Rose, M. B. (1992), 'Introduction', in J. Brown and M. B. Rose (eds.), *Entrepreneurship and the Growth of the Firm*, Manchester: Manchester University Press, 1–8.

Brown, R. (1995), *Chinese Business Enterprise in Asia*, London: Routledge.

Brusco, S. (1982), 'The Emilian Model: Productive Decentralisation and Social Integration', *Cambridge Journal of Economics*, 6: 167–84.

——and Sabel, C. (1981), 'Artisan production and economic growth', in F. Wilkinson (ed.), *The Dynamics of Labour Market Segmentation*, London: Academic Press.

Buckley, P. J., and Casson, M. C. (1976), *The Future of the Multinational Enterprise*, London: Macmillan.

—————— (1988), 'A Theory of Cooperation in International Business', in F. J. Contractor and P. Lorange (eds.), *Cooperative Strategies in International Business*, Lexington, Mass: Lexington Books, 31–53.

—————— (1992), 'Organizing for Innovation: The Multinational Enterprise in the Twenty-first Century', in P. J. Buckley and M. C. Casson (eds.), *Multinational Enterprises in the World Economy: Essays in Honour of John Dunning*, Aldershot: Edward Elgar, 212–32.

Bull, A. (1992), *From Peasants to Entrepreneurs*, London: Chapman and Hall.

Cain, P. J., and Hopkins, A. G. (1993), *British Imperialism: Innovation and Expansion, 1688–1914*, London: Longman.

Cantwell, J. A. (1995), 'Multinational Corporations and Innovatory Activities: Towards a New Evolutionary Approach', in J. Molero (ed.), *Technological Innovation, Multinational Corporations and New International Competitiveness*, Chur: Harwood Academic Publishers, 21–57.

Caplin, A., and Leahy, J. (1994), 'Business as Usual, Market Crashes and Wisdom after the Fact', *American Economic Review*, 84: 548–65.

Carlos, A. M., and Kruse, J. B. (1995), 'The Decline of the Royal Africa Company: Fringe Firms and the Role of the Charter', *Economic History Review*, forthcoming.

Carlos, A., and Nicholas, S. J. (1988), 'Grants of an Earlier Capitalism: The Chartered Trading Companies as Modern Multinationals', *Business History Review*, 62: 399–419.

—————— (1990), 'Agency Problems in Early Chartered Companies: The Case of the Hudson's Bay Company', *Journal of Economic History*, 50 (4).

Carlton, D. W. (1979), 'Vertical Integration in Competitive markets under Uncertainty', *Journal of Industrial Economics*, 28: 189–209.

Carter, H., and Wheatley, S. (1982), *Merthyr Tydfil in 1851: Study of the Spatial Structure of a Welsh Industrial Town*, Cardiff: University of Wales Press.

Carter, M. J. (1995), 'Information and the Division of Labour: Implications for the Firm's Choice of Organisation', *Economic Journal*, 105: 385–97.

Casson, M. C. (1979), *Alternatives to the Multinational Enterprise*, London: Macmillan.

——(1982), *The Entrepreneur: An Economic Theory*, Oxford: Martin Robertson, reprinted Aldershot: Gregg Revivals, 1991.

——(1987), *The Firm and the Market: Studies in Multinational Enterprise and the Scope of the Firm*, Cambridge, Mass: MIT Press.

——(1990), *Enterprise and Competitiveness: A Systems View of International Business*, Oxford: Clarendon Press.

——(1991a), *Economics of Business Culture: Game Theory, Transaction Costs and Economic Performance*, Oxford: Clarendon Press.

——(1991b), 'Internalisation Theory and Beyond', in P. J. Buckley (ed.), *New*

Horizons in International Business: Research Priorities for the 1990s, Aldershot: Edward Elgar, 4–27.

——(1993), 'Cultural Determinants of Economic Performance', *Journal of Comparative Economics*, 17: 418–42.

——(1994a), 'Cultural Factors in Innovation: An Economic Analysis', in Y. Shionoya and M. Perlman (eds.), *Innovation in Technology, Industries and Institutions: Studies in Schumpeterian Perspectives*, Ann Arbor, Michigan: University of Michigan Press, 271–96.

——(1994b), 'Economic Perspectives on Business Information', in L. Bud-Frierman (ed.), *Information Acumen: the Understanding and Use of Knowledge in Modern Business*, London: Routledge, 136–67.

——(1994c), 'Institutional Diversity in Overseas Enterprise: Explaining the Free-standing Company', *Business History*, 36 (4): 95–108.

——(1994d), 'Why are Firms Hierarchical?' *International Journal of the Economics of Business*, 1: 47–76.

——(1995a), *Entrepreneurship and Business Culture*, Aldershot: Edward Elgar.

——(1995b), *The Organization of International Business*, Aldershot: Edward Elgar.

——(1996), 'Comparative Organisation of Large and Small Firms: An Information Cost Approach', *Small Business Economics*, 8: 1–17.

——(1997), 'Economics and Anthropology: Reluctant Partners', *Human Relations*, forthcoming.

——Loveridge, R., and Singh, S. (1996), 'The Ethical Significance of Corporate culture in Large Multinational Enterprises', in F. N. Brady (ed.), *Ethical Universals in International Business*, Berlin: Springer.

Chandler, A. D. Jr. (1977), *The Visible Hand: The Managerial Revolution in American Business*, Cambridge, Mass: Belknap Press of Harvard University Press.

——(1990), *Scale and Scope: The Dynamics of Industrial Capitalism*, Cambridge, Mass: Belknap Press of Harvard University Press.

Chapman, S. D. (1992), *Merchant Enterprise in Britain: From the Industrial Revolution to World War I*, Cambridge: Cambridge University Press.

Chari, V. V., and Jagannathan, R. (1988), 'Banking Panics, Information and Rational Expectations Equilibrium', *Journal of Finance*, 43: 749–63.

Chaudhuri, K. N. (1965), *The English East India Company: The Study of an Early Joint Stock Company, 1600–1640*, London: Frank Cass.

——(1978), *The Trading World of Asia and the English East India Company, 1660–1760*, Cambridge: Cambridge University Press.

Chesnais, F. (1988), 'Technical Cooperation Agreements between Firms', *STI Review*, No. 4, Paris: OECD, 51–119.

Coase, R. H. (1937), 'The Nature of the Firm', *Economica* (New series), 4: 386–405.

——(1960), 'The Problem of Social Cost', *Journal of Law and Economics*, 3: 1–44.

Commons, J. R. (1934), *The Legal Foundations of Capitalism*, New York: Macmillan.

Conlisk, J. (1980), 'Costly Optimisers versus Cheap Imitators', *Journal of Economic Behaviour and Organisation*, 1: 275–93.

Corley, T. A. B. (1993), 'Firms and Markets: Towards a Theory of Business History', *Business and Economic History*, 22: 54–66.

——(1994a), Foreign Direct Investment and British Economic Deceleration 1870–1914, in H. Pohl (ed.), *Transnational Investment from the 19th Century to the Present*, Zeitschrift fur Unternehmensgeschichte, Occasional Papers, 81: 153–172.

——(1996), 'The Free-standing Company, in Theory and Practice', in M. Wilkins and M. Schröter (eds.), *Free-standing Companies in the World Economy, 1830–1995*, Oxford: Oxford University Press.

Crafts, N. F. R. (1985), *British Economic Growth During the Industrial Revolution*, Oxford: Clarendon Press.

David, P. A. (1985), 'Clio and the Economics of QWERTY', *American Economic Review*, 75 (2): 332–7.

Davies, D. J. (1933), *The Economic History of South Wales prior to 1800*, Cardiff: University of Wales Press.

D'Cruz, J. R., and Rugman, A. M. (1994), 'Business Network Theory and the Canadian Telecommunications Industry', *International Business Review*, 3 (3): 275–88.

Debreu, G. (1959), *The Theory of Value*, New Haven, Conn.: Yale University Press.

Dei Ottati (1993), 'Metamorfosi di un distretto localizzato: la nascita del distretto industriale pratese', in R. Leonardi and R. Y. Nanetti (eds.), *Lo sviluppo regionale dell'economia europea integrata: Il caso toscano*, Venezia: Marsilio, 151–81.

Dosi, G., and Metcalfe, J. S. (1991), 'On Some Notions of Irreversibility in Economics', in P. Saviotti and J. S. Metcalfe (eds.), *Evolutionary Theories of Economic and Technological Change: Present Status and Future Prospects*, Chur: Harwood Academic Publishers, 133–59.

Dunning, J. H. (1977), 'Trade, Location of Economic Activity and the Multinational Enterprise: A Search for an Eclectic Approach', in B. Ohlin, P. O. Hesselbom and P. M. Wijkman (eds.), *The International Allocation of Economic Activity*, London: Macmillan, 395–418.

Easton, G. (1992), 'Industrial networks: a review', in B. Axelsson and G. Easton (eds.), *Industrial Networks: A New View of Reality*, London: Routledge, 1–27.

Etzioni, A. (1988), *The Moral Dimension: Towards a New Economics*, New York: Free Press.

Evans, C. (1993), *The Labyrinth of Flames: Work and Social Conflict in Early Industrial Merthyr Tydfil*, Cardiff: University of Wales Press.

Evans, N. (1989), 'Two paths to economic development: Wales and the north-east of England', in P. Hudson (ed.), *Regions and Industries: A Perspective on the Industrial Revolution in Britain*, Cambridge: Cambridge University Press, 201–27.

Feinstein, C. H. (1981), 'Capital Accumulation and the Industrial Revolution', in R. C. Floud and D. N. McCloskey (eds.), *The Economic History of Britain since 1700*, Vol. I, Cambridge: Cambridge University Press, 128–42.

Flinn, M. W. (1984), *The History of the British Coal Industry, Volume 2: 1700–1830 The Industrial Revolution*, Oxford: Clarendon Press.

Foss, N. J., Knudsen, C., and Montgomery, C. A. (1995), 'An Exploration of Common Ground: Integrating Evolutionary and Resource-based Views of the Firm', in C. A. Montgomery (ed.), *Resources in an Evolutionary Perspective: A Synthesis of Evolutionary and Resource-based Approaches to Strategy*, Dordrecht: Kluwer.

Fransman, M. J. (1995), *Visions of the Firm and Japan*, Oxford: Oxford University Press.

Furber, H. (1976), *Rival Empires of Trade in the Orient, 1600–1800*, Minneapolis: University of Minnesota Press.

Galbraith, J. K. (1958), *The Affluent Society*, London: Hamish Hamilton.

Gandolfo, V. (1990), 'Relazionalità e cooperazione nelle aree sistema', *Economia e Politica Industriale*, No. 65, XVI: 95–117.

Geanakopoulos, J., and Milgrom, P. (1991), 'A Theory of Hierarchies Based upon Limited Managerial Attention', *Journal of Japanese and International Economics*, 5 (3): 205–25.

Gille, B. (1965), *Histoire de la Maison Rothschild*, Geneva: Droz.

Goodhart, C. E. (1975), *Money, Information and Uncertainty*, London: Macmillan.

Goodman, E., and Bamford, J. (eds.) (1989), *Small Firms and Industrial Districts in Italy*, London: Routledge.

Granovetter, M. (1985), 'Economic Action and Social Structure: The Problem of Embeddedness', *American Journal of Sociology*, 91 (3): 481–510.

Grossman, S. J., and Hart, O. (1980), 'Take-over Bids, the Free-rider Problem and the Theory of the Corporation', *Bell Journal of Economics*, 11: 42–64.

——— (1986), 'The Costs and Benefits of Ownership: A Theory of Vertical and Lateral Integration', *Journal of Political Economy*, 94: 691–719.

Hagerstrand, T. (1969), *Innovation Diffusion as a Spatial Process*, Chicago: University of Chicago Press.

Harper, D. A. (1995), *Entrepreneurship and the Market Process*, London: Routledge.

Hayek, F. A. von (1937), 'Economics and Knowledge', *Economia* (New Series), 4: 33–54, reprinted in F. A. von Hayek (1959), *Individualism and Economic Order*, London: Routledge and Kegan Paul, 33–56.

Henderson, J. V. (1988), *Urban Development: Theory, Fact and Illusion*, New York: Oxford University Press.

Hennart, J-F. (1994*a*), 'International Capital Transfers: A Transaction Cost Framework', *Business History*, 36: 51–70.

——— (1994*b*), 'Free-standing Firms and the Internalisation of Markets for Financial Capital: A Response to Casson', *Business History*, 36 (4): 118–31.

——— (1996), 'Transaction Cost Theory and the Free-standing Firm', in M. Wilkins and H. Schröter (eds.), *Free-standing Companies in the World Economy, 1830–1995*, Oxford: Oxford University Press.

Hicks, J. R. (1969), *A Theory of Economic History*, Oxford: Clarendon Press.

Hirschman, A. O. (1958), *Exit, Voice and Loyalty*, Princeton, NJ: Princeton University Press.

Hodgson, G. (1988), *Economics and Institutions*, Oxford: Blackwell.

Hoppit, J. (1986), 'The Use and Abuse of Credit in Eighteenth Century England', in N. McKendrick and R. B. Outhwaite (eds.), *Business Life and Public Policy: Essays in Honour of D. C. Coleman*, Cambridge: Cambridge University Press.

Hudson, P. (1986), *The Genesis of Industrial Capital: A Study of the West Riding Wool Textile Industry c. 1750–1850*, Cambridge: Cambridge University Press.

Huenemann, R. W. (1984), *The Dragon and the Iron Horse: The Economics of Railroads in China, 1876–1937*, Cambridge, Mass: Council on East Asian Studies, Harvard University.

Hunt, B. C. (1936), *The Development of the Business Corporation in England, 1800–1867*, Cambridge, Mass: Harvard University Press.

Hymer, S. H. (1960), *The International Operations of National Firms: A Study of Direct Investment*, Ph.D. thesis, MIT, published 1976, Cambridge, Mass: MIT Press.

Johanson, J., and Mattsson, L. G. (1987), 'Interoganizational Relations in Industrial Systems—A Network Approach Compared with the Transactions Cost Approach', *International Journal of Management and Organisation*, 17 (1): 34–48.

John A. H. (1950), *The Industrial Development of South Wales, 1750–1850: An Essay*, Cardiff: University of Wales Press.

Jones, G. (1992), *British Multinational Banking, 1830–1990*, Oxford: Oxford University Press.

——(1995), 'Organisation and Strategy in British-based International Business Before and After 1914', *mimeo*, University of Reading.

Kaldor, N. (1939), 'Welfare Propositions in Economics', *Economic Journal*, 49: 549–52.

Kanter, R. M. (1989), *When Giants Learn to Dance*, New York: Simon and Schuster.

Kay, N. M. (1993), 'Markets, False Hierarchies and the Role of Asset Specificity', in C. Pitelis (ed.), *Transaction Costs, Markets and Hierarchies*, Oxford: Blackwell, 242–61.

Keynes, J. M. (1936), *The General Theory of Employment Interest and Money*, London: Macmillan.

Kirby, M. W. (1984), *Men of Business and Politics: The Rise and Fall of the Quaker Pease Dynasty of North-east England*, London: Allen and Unwin.

Kirzner, I. M. (1973), *Competition and Entrepreneurship*, Chicago: University of Chicago Press.

Klein, B. (1973), *Dynamic Economics*, Cambridge, MA: Harvard University Press.

——Crawford, R. G., and Alchian, A. A. (1978), 'Vertical Integration, Appropriable Rents and the Competitive Contracting Process', *Journal of Law and Economics*, 21: 297–326.

Knight, F. H. (1921), *Risk Uncertainty and Profit*, Boston: Houghton Mifflin.

Kogut, B., and Zander, U. (1992), 'Knowledge of the Firm, Combinative Capabilities and the Replication of Technology', *Organization Science*, 3: 383–97.

Kotter, J. P., and Heskett. J. L. (1992), *Corporate Culture and Performance*, New York: Free Press.

Krugman, P. (1991), *Geography and Trade*, Cambridge, Mass: MIT Press.

Lamberton, D. M. (1988), 'Theoretical Aspects of the Measurement of the Information Sector', in M. Jussawalla, D. M. Lamberton and N. D. Karunaratne (eds.), *The Cost of Thinking: Information Economics of Ten Pacific Countries*, Norwood, NJ: Ablex, 47–59.

Landes, D. S. (1986), 'What do Bosses Really Do?' *Journal of Economic History*, 46 (3).

Langlois, R. N. (1984), 'Internal Organisation in a Dynamic Context: Some Theoretical Considerations', in M. Jussawalla and H. Ebenfield (eds.), *Communication and Information Economics: New Perspectives*, Amsterdam: North-Holland, 23–49.

Lawson, P. (1993), *The East India Company: A History*, London: Longman.

Leff, N. H. (1978), 'Industrial Organisation and Entrepreneurship in the Developing Countries: the Economic Groups', *Economic Development and Cultural Change*, 26: 661–75.

Leibenstein, H. (1950), 'Bandwagon, Snob and Veblen Effects on the Theory of Consumer Demand', *Quarterly Journal of Economics*, 64: 183–207.

——(1978), *General X-efficiency Theory and Economic Development*, New York: Oxford University Press.

Lippman, S. A., and McCall, J. J. (1976), 'The Economics of Job Search: A Survey', *Economic Inquiry*, 14: 155–89 and 347–68.

Little, I. M. D. (1957), *A Critique of Welfare Economics*, 2nd edn, Oxford: Clarendon Press.

Loasby, B. J. (1976), *Choice, Complexity and Ignorance*, Cambridge: Cambridge University Press.

Lundvall, B.-A. (1992), 'Introduction', in B.-A. Lundvall (ed.), *National Systems of Innovation*, London: Pinter.

Macfarlane, A. (1978), *The Origins of English Individualism*, Oxford: Blackwell.

McGregor, D. (1960), *The Human Side of Enterprise*, New York: McGraw-Hill.

Machlup, F. (1962), *The Production and Distribution of Knowledge in the United States*, Princeton, NJ: Princeton University Press.

Mansfield, E., Schwartz, M., and Wagner, S. (1981), 'Imitation Costs and Patents: An Empirical Study', *Economic Journal*, 91: 907–18.

Marglin, S. A. (1974), 'What do Bosses Do?: Part I', *Review of Radical Political Economy*, 6: 60–112.

Marris, R. L. (1964), *Economic Theory of Managerial Capitalism*, London: Macmillan.

Marceau, J. (1989), *A Family Business The Making of an International Business Elite*, Cambridge: Cambridge University Press.

Marschak, J. (1974), *Economic Information, Decision and Prediction*, Dordrecht: D. Reidel.

——and Radner, R. (1972), *The Economic Theory of Teams*, New Haven, Conn.: Yale University Press.

Marshall, A. (1919), *Industry and Trade*, London: Macmillan.

Menger, C. (1871), *Principles of Economics* (trans. J. Dingwall and B.F. Hoselitz) Glencoe and New York: Free Press, 1950.

Milgrom, P. R., and Roberts, J. (1992), *Economics of Organisation and Management*, Englewood Cliffs, NJ: Prentice Hall.

Miller, G. J. (1992), *Managerial Dilemmas: The Political Economy of Hierarchy*, Cambridge: Cambridge University Press.

Mommsen, W. J. (1981), *Theories of Imperialism*, London: Weidenfeld and Nicolson.

Namier, L. D. (1929), 'Anthony Bacon, MP: An Eighteenth Century Merchant', *Journal of Economic and Business History*, 2: 20–70.

Nef, J. U. (1932), *The Rise of the British Coal Industry*, London: Routledge.

Nelson, R. (1993), *National Innovation Systems—A Comparative Analysis*, Oxford: Oxford University Press.

——and Winter, S. J. (1982), *An Evolutionary Theory of Economic Change*, Cambridge, Mass: Harvard University Press.

Nicholaidis, C. S. (1992), 'Cultural Determinants of Corporate Excellence in an Integrated World Economy: The Impact of National Cultures on Organisational Performance', in M. C. Casson (ed.), *International Business and Global Integration*, London: Macmillan, 205–25.

North, D. C. (1981), *Structure and Change in Economic History*, New York: W.W. Norton.

O'Brien, R. Cruise, and Helleiner, G. K. (1983), 'The Political Economy of Information in a Changing International Economic Order', in R. Cruise O'Brien (ed.), *Information, Economics and Power: The North-South Dimension*, London: Hodder and Stoughton, 1–27.

Olson, M. (1982), *The Rise and Decline of Nations*, New Haven, Conn: Yale University Press.

Origo, I. (1957), *The Merchant of Prato*, London: Jonathan Cape.

Ouchi, W. (1981), *Theory Z: How American Business can meet the Japanese Challenge*, Reading, Mass: Addison-Wesley.

Parkin, M., and King, D. (1995), *Economics*, 2nd edn, London: Addison-Wesley.

Penrose, E. T. (1959), *The Theory of the Growth of the Firm*, Oxford: Basil Blackwell.

Phipatseritham, K., and Yoshihara, K. (1983), *Business Groups in Thailand*, Singapore: Institute of South East Asian Studies.

Pigou, A. C. (1927), *Industrial Fluctuations*, London: Macmillan.

Piore, M. J., and Sabel, C. F. (1984), *The Second Industrial Divide: Possibilities for Prosperity*, New York: Basic Books.

Polanyi, M. (1964), *Science, Faith and Society*, Chicago: University of Chicago Press.

Pollard, S. (1981), *Peaceful Conquest: The Industrialization of Europe 1760–1970*, Oxford: Oxford University Press.

Pollard, S. J., and Robertson, P. (1979), *British Shipbuilding Industry, 1870–1914*, Cambridge, Mass: Harvard University Press.

Porter, M. E. (1980), *Competitive Strategy*, New York: Free Press.

Putnam, R. D. (1993), *Making Democracy Work: Civic Traditions in Modern Italy*, Princeton, NJ: Princeton University Press.

Rich, E. E. (1958), *Hudson's Bay Company, 1660–1760*, London: Hudson's Bay Record Society.

Richardson, G. B. (1960), *Information and Investment*, Oxford: Oxford University Press.

——(1972), 'The Organization of Industry', *Economic Journal*, 82: 883–96.

Ring, P. Smith, and Van der Ven, A. H. (1994), 'Developmental Processes of Cooperative Interorganizational Relationships', *Academy of Management Review*, 19: 90–118.

Robertson, D. H. (1923), *The Control of Industry*, London: Nisbet.

Rogers, E. M. (1983), *Diffusion of Innovations*, 3rd edn. New York: Free Press.

Sah, R. K., and Stiglitz, J. E. (1986), 'The Architecture of Economic Systems: Hierarchies and Polyarchies', *American Economic Review*, 76: 716–27.

Scharfstein, D., and Stein, J. (1990), 'Herd Behaviour and Investment', *American Economic Review*, 80: 465–79.

Schlicht, E. (1993), 'On Custom', *Journal of Institutional and Theoretical Economics*, 149 (1): 178–203.

Schumpeter, J. A. (1934), *The Theory of Economic Development* (trans. R. Opie) Cambridge, Mass: Harvard University Press.

——(1939), *Business Cycles: A Theoretical, Historical and Statistical Analysis of the Capitalist Process*, New York: McGraw-Hill.

Scott, W. R. (1912), *The Constitution and Finance of English, Scottish and Irish Joint-Stock Companies to 1720, Volume I: The General Development of the Joint-Stock System to 1720*, Cambridge: Cambridge University Press.

Scully, G. W. (1992), *Constitutional Environments and Economic Growth*, Princeton, NJ: Princeton University Press.

Shackle, G. L. S. (1979), *Imagination and the Nature of Choice*, Edinburgh: Edinburgh University Press.

Simon, H. A. (1947), *Administrative Behaviour*, New York: Macmillan.

——(1957), 'A Formal Theory of the Employment Relation', in H. A. Simon, *Models of Man: Social and Rational*, New York: John Wiley & Sons.

Sinclair, P. J. N. (1990), 'The Economics of Imitation', *Scottish Journal of Political Economy*, 37 (2): 113–44.

Smith, A. (1776), *An Inquiry into the Nature and Causes of the Wealth of Nations* (Glasgow edition, 1976), Oxford: Oxford University Press.

Spence, A. M. (1973), 'Job Market Signalling', *Quarterly Journal of Economics*, 87: 355–74.

Symons, M. W. (1979), *Coal Mining in the Llanelli Area: Volume One: 16th Century to 1820*, Llanelli: Llanelli Borough Council.

Tamburini, L. (ed.) (1945) *L'industria di Prato alla prova della guerra*, Prato: Unione Industriale Pratese.

Teece, D. J., Rumelt, R., Dosi, G., and Winter, S. (1994), 'Understanding Corporate Coherence: Theory and Evidence', *Journal of Economic Behaviour and Organization*, 23: 1–30.

Thomas, B. (1973), *Migration and Economic Growth: A Study of Great Britain and the Atlantic Economy*, 2nd edn, Cambridge: Cambridge University Press.

Tomlinson, B. R. (1989), 'British Business in India, 1860–1970', in R. P. T. Davenport-Hines and G. Jones (eds.), *British Business in Asia since 1860*, Cambridge: Cambridge University Press, 92–116.

Trigilia, C. (1989), *Il distretto industriale di Prato* in M. Regini and C. Sabel (eds.), *Strategie di riaggiustamento industriale*, Bologna: Il Mulino, 283–333.

Vernon, R. (1966), 'International Investment and International Trade in the Product Cycle', *Quarterly Journal of Economics*, 80: 190–207.

Ville, S. (1987), *English Shipowning during the Industrial Revolution: Michael Henley and Son, London Shipowners, 1770–1830*, Manchester: Manchester University Press.

Von Hippel, E. (1988), *The Sources of Innovation*, Oxford: Oxford University Press.

Waterson, M. (1982), 'Vertical Integration, Variable Proportions and Oligopoly', *Economic Journal*, 92: 129–44.

Welch, I. (1992), 'Sequential Sales, Learning and Cascades', *Journal of Finance*, 47: 695–732.

Werin, L. (1990), 'Rights and Costs in a Model of the Economic System', in H. Carlsson and B. Larson (eds.), *Problems of the Mixed Economy: Cooperation, Efficiency and Stability*, Amsterdam: North-Holland, 65–87.

Whiteley, C. H., and Whiteley, W. M. (1964), *The Permissive Morality*, London: Methuen.

Wilkins, M. (1988), 'The Free-standing Company, 1870–1914: An Important Type of British Foreign Direct Investment', *Economic History Review*, 2nd series, 41 (2): 259–82.

——(1996), 'Introduction', in M. Wilkins and H. Schröter (eds.), *Free-standing Companies in the World Economy, 1830–1995*, Oxford: Oxford University Press.

Wilkinson, R. (1964), *The Prefects: British Leadership and the Public School Tradition: A Comparative Study in the Making of Rulers*, London: Oxford University Press.

Willan, R. S. (1956), *The Early History of the Russia Company, 1553–1603*, Manchester: Manchester University Press.

Williams, G. A. (1978), *The Merthyr Rising*, London: Croom Helm.

Williamson, O. E. (1975), *Markets and Hierarchies: Analysis and Anti-trust Implications*, New York: Free Press.

——(1980), 'The Organisation of Work', *Journal of Economic Behaviour and Organisation*, 1: 5–38.

——(1985), *The Economic Institutions of Capitalism*, New York: Free Press

Winter, S. G. (1988), 'On Coase, Competence and the Corporation', *Journal of Law, Economics and Organisation*, 4: 163–80.

Wolfe, A. (1989), *Whose Keeper? Social Science and Moral Obligation*, Berkeley: California: University of California Press.

Index

Printed in the United Kingdom
by Lightning Source UK Ltd.
111046UKS00001B/56